Dispute Avoidance and European Contract Law

Europa Law Publishing, Groningen 2008

Dispute Avoidance and European Contract Law

Dealing with Divergence

Martin J. Doris

Europa Law Publishing is a publishing company specializing in European Union law, international trade law, public international law, environmental law and comparative national law.
For further information please contact Europa Law Publishing via email: info@europalawpublishing.com or visit our website at: www.europalawpublishing.com.

Typeset in Scala and Scala Sans, Graphic design by G2K Designers, Groningen/Amsterdam

NUR 822; ISBN 978-90-76871-90-5

British Library Cataloguing-in-Publication Data
A catalogue record for this book is available from the British Library

Para Sandra

Preface

The effects of European integration on private law are complex and precarious. One may define 'private law' through its 'traditional core areas' such as 'contracts, torts, property, inheritance or family law', which on the continent are covered by the relevant codes. The difficulty with such loose definitions is that they do not capture the historical, poltical and social embeddedness of private law. Like all other fields of law, private law has been affected by the development from a (more or less liberal) *Rechtsstaat* of the 19th century to the (more or less social) constitutional democracies forming the modern European Union. These changes have affected the social functions of private law and the notions of justice to which it is committed quite substantially. They are plainly visible in so many statutory interventions. Less visible but even more important is the impact of the regulalory environment which affects the conditions under which private relations operate. All of these developments have by no means been uniform. This is why the private law systems of the Member States of the European Union differ not just in terms of 'national' cultures but in terms of their social and political heritage. Can we hope therefore to create a more or less harmonised European private law? Due to the institutional and social embeddedness of private law, European legislative acts have always had disintegrative effects within national legal systems. Is it at all conceivable that a new comprehensive legal instrument could accomplish a more suitably integrated and normatively coherent European order of private law? Would the judicial system of the Union be able to cope with such an enormous challenge?

It is in my view the greatest merit of this book that it provides us with both constructive and original perspectives on the integration *problématique* which do not depend on answers to irresolvable issues. In part the challenge of integration is reduced, simplified significantly – there is life outside of absolute legal uniformity. We can live with diversity is the resounding message. We can further continue to trust the ingenuity of legal practice to find sensible outcomes to practical problems and cease pestering legislatures. We need not cede further control of private law to academic entrepreneurs. These messages are but rough abbreviations of truly subtle scholarly argument. The starting point for the study is a helpful critique of the European Commission's current initiatives in the field, in particular the strive for a 'Common Frame of Reference' which has stimulated broad academic activities and continues, the low profile of the notion notwithstanding, to inspire academic research aimed at delivery of a European code. The arguments militating against these efforts, which the author patiently and thoroughly, sometimes with a good sense of humour and never polemically develops are impressive. His argumentation is certainly to a significant degree reflecting common law traditions, but he is by no means solely relying on these experiences. His knowledge and understanding of the philosophical roots of contract law, and his deep comparative understanding, enables him to document the painful *Geschichtsvergessenheit* of the present initiatives, their insensitivity towards the historical, theoretical and political background of Europe's legal traditions in both general and consumer contract law visions in particular.

Whereas Jacques Delors in his famous response to the critics of the Commission's regulatory activities could simply point to the quests for regulation from the Member States and/or societal actors, the Europeanization process in private law is a supply policy, not responding to societal and political demands. The dichotomy of integration versus non-integration rather than an effort to understand practical difficulties and relevant impasses seems to provide the conceptual framework for the Commission's strategies. It is indeed striking to observe the Commission invoking the values of legal certainty and coherence which, as contract scholarship knows ever since legal sociologists back in the 1920s, and even earlier, started and then in the course of the law and society movement – most famously Macaulay's article of 1956 – intensified their enquiries into the realities of contractual acting, cannot be ensured through legislative formalism, and which the Commission through its legislative activism risks to erode further. Warnings that the Commission's projects are overly ambitious, that they are largely superfluous in the field of commercial contracting and will produce disintegrating effects have been articulated again and again in various facets for decades, but I have not as yet seen them developed so persuasively. And the alternative approach suggested by the author is truly original: that Europe's diversity in the field of contract law be re-conceptualised, he argues, as a problem of *interoperability* requiring not a Civil code but rather a viable methodology of dispute avoidance. The response to difficulties in cross-border contracting he suggests should be sought in a reflexive move, of contract law itself, in particular in the search for coherent practical approaches to preliminary agreements and precontractual reliance, in the continued resort to arbitration and ADR, in alternative strategies aimed at minimising the effects of divergence generally. Each and every step of this complex argument merits our attention.

Whereas the first chapter analyses primarily pragmatic and practical difficulties of the European Commission's initiatives in the field of contract law, the second provides a correction of their *Geschichtsvergessenheit*. It documents the author's deep understanding of European legal traditions in the field of contract law, their philosophical underpinnings and historical background. Not even in the classical era of economic liberalism and legal formalism had contract law in Europe arrived at uniformity. Nowhere, however, does one get the impression that the author's inquiries are just *l'art pour l'art*. They are practically important because they explain why it is inconceivable that we could arrive at a common contract law by adopting some uniform text. The plea for more modesty seems to me fully convincing, as does his quest for a revised understanding of the core problem of Europeanization: *"Rather than attempting to 'square the circle' through a pursuit of coherence common and civil lawyers would be better to engage with EC contract law's messiness and seek to provide workable solutions to established problematic divergences".*

This is the task which the author sets himself in the remainder of the book. On the basis of comparative analyses of the treatment of preliminary agreements and precontractual duties in English, US and Spanish contract law, he explores the tendencies which might indicate the emergence of doctrines helping to resolve the interoperability *problématique*. His hopes in that respect rest in part upon a new 'detrimental reliance doctrine' – as founded upon notions of fair dealing – in a future EC commercial contract law. I interpret this vision as a substantive general clause of supranational validity. In follow-up work the author may care to dedicate additional attention to the structural specifics of the EU multi-level system. On such a basis I could imagine an analytical and theoretical strengthening of this analysis. But this comment is not meant to change in any way my appreciation of his achievements. His sophisticated comparative analyses cover new ground. His methodological subtleness and care in this regard are moreover simply admirable. The current state of the academic debates on the future of European contract law and the strategies the European Commission pursues may not be favourable to Doris' pragmatic messages. Yet his scepticism as to any 'Europeanization from above' and the integrationalist logic of current Europeanisation policies may well turn out to be more realistic and hence also more constructive than many of today's mainstream suggestions. Be that as it may: this is a book of the highest quality which certainly deserves a wide audience.

Christian Joerges
Bremen, November 2007

Acknowledgements

'You'll never plough a field by turning it over in your head' says the timeless Irish proverb, and yet this book has been 'cultivated' slowly after much careful reflection. Consolidating and expanding on previously published research, this study is a largely revised version of my recent PhD thesis, prepared and defended at the European University Institute in Florence. It naturally bears the imprint of various scholars on both sides of the Atlantic, yet above all I remain greatly indebted to both Christian Joerges and Jacques Ziller, not least for their expert supervision during my time at the Villa Schifanoia. Christian has continued to offer me many alternative insights and reflections on aspects of my research. His own theories and seminars, particularly those devoted to the challenge of Europeanising private laws, have presented me with new horizons in this seemingly endless discipline, and it has been a true pleasure working with him. I am likewise indebted to Jacques. His expertise in comparative law methodology has been a constant source of inspiration and his openness and availability, even when operating to a hectic schedule as Head of the Law Department, remain greatly appreciated. I wish also to thank warmly Mark Van Hoecke, who visited Florence in 2002. His involvement with Jacques' seminars and his personal interest in my own research helped cement the methodological foundations of this book. I am of course equally grateful to both Horatia Muir Watt and Christoph Schmid who offered many insightful comments and suggestions during my thesis defence. Their views have certainly left a real impression on this book.

The generosity of the Department for Higher Education (DfES) in the UK in financing this project and the Spanish Ministry of Foreign Affairs in lending additional research funding deserves a special mention. As 'un mediterraneo del norte' it has been a great honour to be awarded a bursary that bears the name of Salvador de Madariaga. My research into Spanish private and commercial law would of course have been impossible without the help of so many institutions and professors. Moreover, whilst preparing this book, I have been fortunate to have been invited to participate in the research work of REDPEC. Mil gracias are especially owed to Miquel Martín-Casals and the entire private law faculty at the University of Girona for their many warm welcomes over the last few years. I am likewise grateful to Emilio Beltrán Sánchez at San Pablo-CEU in Madrid for discussing my work at an early stage, and owe a real debt of gratitude to José María León González at the University of Salamanca.

A certain *Brussels-isation* of this book has in practice been inevitable. Being in the employ of the Directorate General for Health and Consumer Protection at the European Commission in the spring monsoon season of 2004 has infused my research with helpful practical insights. It has been beneficial to gauge the degree of high-level political interest in the question of harmonising private laws and to witness at first hand the steady politicising of European contract law. Again I am grateful to the Law Department for affording me the opportunity to develop my research in Brussels and for the easy, relaxed nature of the local *bruxellois* who made my stay so pleasant. It would naturally be impossible to thank so many friendly faces at the Community institutions who have, in one way or another, left their imprint, but I would like to pay particular thanks to Klaus-Heine Lehne, MEP and to Robert Madelin, the Director General at DG SANCO, for his openness and approachability. In addition, I was priviledged to be involved in the research activities of the Commission's Inter-Services Working Group on EC contract law. The professionalism of the Commission library staff at Van Maerlant, like that of the library employees in Florence, also deserves a special mention. At the EUI, I would like to thank in particular Machteld Nijsten, Evelyn Flannigan and Aimee Glassel for their kindness and assistance.

Grateful thanks are similarly owed to my many friends and colleagues in the UK and Ireland. Everyone at the School of Law in Glasgow has been wonderfully supportive since my arrival in the summer of 2006. Prior to that David Johnston and Brian Childs, at the Queen's University in Belfast, provided wonderful support at critical moments. Special thanks are equally owed to Niall Hunt at the Bar Library in Belfast and to Michael Patchett-Joyce of Monkton Chambers in London. I greatly appreciate the level of interest they have shown in this study.

In the development of this book I have been fortunate enough to attend a number of highly professional conferences and symposia, from Montréal to Cape Town and back to Florence. At an early stage in my research I was invited to talk at a conference on the future of European contracting at the Centre for Business and Commercial Law at the University of Tromsø. The warmth of my many new Nordic friends has left a lasting impression. Whilst debating with Guiditta Cordero Moss, Ole Lando, Jan Ramberg and other founding 'fathers' of modern European contract law, I was treated to the most wonderful Norwegian hospitality. I would like to thank all the team at the Lex Mercatoria Monitor, and to especially thank Andreas Meidell at the University of Bergen for supporting me in this project. I wish him the very best success in his own investigations under the Commission's Common Frame of Reference programme.

Finally, it is a great honour to be included in this distinguished series and I would like to thank the series editors for taking the time to consider an earlier draft and Jacqueline Lensink at Europa Law Publishing for her friendly emails, her patience and a remarkable attention to detail. Of course it goes without saying that this book would never have been written but for the love and support of my fiancée, the great generousity and care of my family and the constant banter of so many friends.

Martin J. Doris
Glasgow, October 2007

Abbreviations

ABA	American Bar Association
AC	Appeal Cases, Law Reports
Act Civ	Actualidad Civil
ADC	Anuario de Derecho Civil
ALI	American Law Institute
All ER	All England Law Reports
Am Bus LJ	American Business Law Journal
Am J Comp L	American Journal of Comparative Law
Am J Int'l L	American Journal of International Law
AP	Audiencia Provincial (Appeal Court, Spain)
Ar Civ	Aranzadi Civil
Aus LJ	Australian Law Journal
Bell J of Econ	Bell Journal of Economics
Berk Tech LJ	Berkeley Technology and Law Journal
BGB	Bürgerliches Gesetzbuch (Civil Code, Germany)
Bus L Rev	Business Law Review
CA	Court of Appeal, England and Wales
Cal L Rev	California Law Review
Cambridge LJ	Cambridge Law Journal
Can Bus LJ	Canadian Business Law Journal
Cardozo L Rev	Cardozo Law Review
Case WR L Rev	Case Western Reserve Law Review
Cc	Código civil de España (Spanish Civil Code).
CFR	Common Frame of Reference
CISG	United Nations Convention on Contracts for the International Sale of Goods
CLP	Current Legal Problems
CML Rep	Common Market Law Reports
CML Rev	Common Market Law Review
Colum LJ	Columbia Law Journal
Colum L Rev	Columbia Law Review
Colum L WP	Columbia Law School Working Papers
Colum J Eur L	Columbia Journal of European Law
Colum J Trans L	Columbia Journal of Transnational Law
Cons LJ	Construction Law Journal
Cornell Int LJ	Cornell International Law Journal
Cornell L Rev	Cornell Law Review
Cornell L Q	Cornell Law Quarterly
CSGR	Centre for the Study of Globalisation and Regionalisation
DG Sanco	DG Health and Consumer Protection
Dickinson L Rev	Dickinson Law Review
Drake L Rev	Drake Law Review
Duke J Comp & Int'l L	Duke Journal of Comparative International Law
EBLR	European Business Law Review

ECJ	European Court of Justice
ECL	European Current Law
EJCL	Electronic Journal of Comparative Law
ERCL	European Review of Contract Law
ERPL	European Review of Private Law
EUI WP	European University Institute Working Papers
Eur Ct Reps	European Court Reports
Eur LJ	European Law Journal
Eur L Rep	European Law Reports
Eur L Rev	European Law Review
Eur J L Econ	European Journal of Law and Economics
EuZW	Europäische Zeitschrift für Wirstschaftsrecht
Fordham L Rev	Fordham Law Review
Geo Mason L Rev	George Mason Law Review
German LJ	German Law Journal
Glob J A	Global Jurist Advances
Glob J F	Global Jurist Frontiers
Glob J T	Global Jurist Topics
Hanse LR	Hanse Law Review
Harv Int'l LJ	Harvard International Law Journal
Harv J Law & Pub Pol	Harvard Journal of Law and Public Policy
Harv J Law & Tech	Harvard Journal of Law and Technology
Harv L Rev	Harvard Law Review
Harv Neg L Rev	Harvard Negotiation Law Review
Hastings Int'l Comp L Rev	Hastings International and Comparative Law Review
Hastings LJ	Hastings Law Journal
Hofstra L Rev	Hofstra Law Review
HL	House of Lords
IACCM	International Association of Commercial and Contract Managers
IBLJ	International Business Law Journal
ICC	International Chamber of Commerce
ICLQ	International and Comparative Law Quarterly
Int Arb L Rev	International Arbitration Law Review
Int'l J of Leg Info	International Journal of Legal Information
Int'l Rev L Econ	International Review of Law and Economics
JBE	Journal of Business Ethics
JBL	Journal of Business Law
JCL	Journal of Contract Law
JCP	Journal of Consumer Policy
JCMS	Journal of Common Market Studies
JLS	Journal of Legal Studies
J Econ & Soc	Journal of Economy and Society
J of Int'l L & Tech	Journal of Information, Law and Technology

J of Int'l Arb	Journal of International Arbitration
J of Int'l Econ Law	Journal of International Economic Law
J of Law & Com	Journal of Law and Commerce
J of Law & Econ	Journal of Law and Economics
J of Law & Soc	Journal of Law and Society
J of Leg Ed	Journal of Legal Education
J of Leg Stud	Journal of Legal Studies
J of Trans Law & Pol	Journal of Transnational Law and Policy
KB	Law Reports (King's Bench Division)
La Ley	La Ley (Revista española de doctrina y jurisprudencia)
La Semaine Jur	La Semaine Juridique
Law & Soc Rev	Law and Society Review
Lloyd's Rep	Lloyd's Law Reports
LMCLQ	Lloyd's Maritime & Commercial Law Quarterly
L Org	Ley Orgánica
Loyola LA L Rev	Loyola of Los Angeles Law Review
LQR	Law Quarterly Review
Maastricht J of E & Comp Law	Maastricht Journal of European and Comparative Law
MLR	Modern Law Review
MWP	Max Weber Programme (EUI) Working Papers
NBER	National Bureau of Economic Research (US)
NCCUSL	National Conference of Commissioners for Uniform State Laws (US)
NYU L Rev	New York University Law Review
Nw Uni L Rev	Northwestern University Law Review
OJ	Official Journal of the European Communities
Oxford J Legal S	Oxford Journal of Legal Studies
Ohio St LJ	Ohio State Law Journal
Pace Int L Rev	Pace International Law Review
PECL	Principles of European Contract Law (Lando Principles)
PICC	Principles of International Commercial Contracts (Unidroit principles)
QUB WP	Queen's University Working Papers Series
RCDP	Rivista Critica del Diritto Privato
RCE	Revista de Contratación Electrónica
RDP	Revista de Derecho Privado
RdP	Revista de Derecho Patrimonial
RdM	Revista de Derecho Mercantil
REDPEC	Red Española de Derecho Privado Europeo y Comparado
RGLJ	Revista General de Legislación y Jurisprudencia
RMCUE	Revue du Marché Comun et de l'Union Européene
RMUE	Revue du Marché Unique Européene
Rev int dr comp	Revue internationale de droit comparé

SECOLA	Society of European Contract Law
Stan L Rev	Stanford Law Review
STS	Sentencia del Tribunal Supremo (Spanish Supreme Court decision)
Temp L Rev	Temple Law Review
Tex L Rev	Texas Law Review
Tex Trans LQ	Texas Transnational Law Quarterly
Tex Wes L Rev	Texas Wesleyan Law Journal
Tilburg Foreign L Rev	Tilburg Foreign Law Review
Times Law Rep	Times Law Reports
TS	Tribunal Supremo (Spanish Supreme Court)
Tul L Rev	Tulane Law Review
UCC	Uniform Commercial Code (US)
UCTA	The Unfair Contract Terms Act 1977
U Chi L Rev	University of Chicago Law Review
U Cinn L Rev	University of Cincinnati Law Review
UCITA	Uniform Computer Information Transactions Act (United States)
UC Davis Bus LJ	University of California Davis Business Law Journal
UC Davis L Rev	University of California Davis Law Review
UETA	Uniform Electronic Transactions Act (US)
UNCITRAL	United Nations Commission on International Trade Law
UNIDROIT	International Institute for the Unification of Private Law
UTCCR	The Unfair Terms in Consumer Contracts Regulations 1999
Uniform L Rev	Uniform Law Review
U Penn L Rev	University of Pennsylvania Law Review
Vanderbilt J Int'l L	Vanderbilt Journal of International Law
Vanderbilt J Transnat L	Vanderbilt Journal of Transnational Law
Vanderbilt L Rev	Vanderbilt Law Review
Va J Int Law	Virginia Journal of International Law
Va L Rev	Virginia Law Review
Wash U LQ	Washington University Law Quarterly
Wayne L Rev	Wayne Law Review
Wisc L Rev	Wisconsin Law Review
Wm & Mary L Rev	William and Mary Law Review
WLR	Weekly Law Reports
Yale LJ	Yale Law Journal
Yale J of Int'l Law	Yale Journal of International Law
Yearbook of Eur L	Yearbook of European Law
ZEPR	Zeitschrift für Europäisches Privatrecht

Introduction

Precontractual obligations and information duties are an increasingly dominant feature of private law regulation, both at national Member State and European community level. A cursory overview of key Community directives, particularly secondary law aimed at enhancing consumer protection, reveals the increasing importance that the EC legislator attaches to the pre-formulation of contractual agreements as a means of ensuring the maximum degree of autonomy and protection for contracting parties. The theory underlying such instrumentalism is that the market requires not just the simplification and standardisation of contracts, but that contracts be agreed under optimal conditions. As Troiano observes, 'Where these [optimal] conditions lack, and where parties operate from a position of inequality – be it via an informative or economic imbalance – bargaining [becomes] inefficient ... requiring a rebalancing of market conditions'.[1] Contractual freedom and the need for adequate information-finding mechanisms are thus two complementary policy goals of an emerging body of contract-related Community law. Information asymmetries and other market failures with the potential to create structural inequality between economic actors have been addressed in diverse sectors, ranging from consumer credit contracts to package travel arrangements through to electronic contracts. This persistent restructuring of contractual agreements, and in particular the rules governing their formation, has come at a price however, producing lasting spill-over effects on the general apparatus of national private law systems, which have become imbued with novel legal concepts and alternative remedies.

In practice, the imposition of varying duties to inform allied to broad generalised clauses across a breadth of differing contracts, and without clear uniform rules and remedies, implies a danger to the overall coherence and resultant economic efficiency of European contract rules. Indeed, a general concern that divergences between Member States' national contract rules may in practice serve to impede the proper functioning of the internal market has prompted the Community institutions to undertake a series of consultation exercises with

---

1 S. Troiano, 'Formation of Contracts under EC Directives' in H. Schulte-Nölke & R. Schulze (eds), *Europäisches Vertragsrecht in Gemeinschaftsrechtp* (ERA Publication, 2002) at 97-112; See also R. Schulze, M. Ebers & H.C. Grigoleit, *Informationspflichten und Vertragsshluss im Acquis communautaire* (Siebeck, 2003). The rise of an information driven contract law and the effect on bargaining freedom has been assessed from an inter-disciplinary perspective in S. Grundmann, W. Kerber & S. Weatherill (eds), *Party Autonomy and the Role of Information in the Internal Market* (de Gruyter, 2001). The internet, in particular, is providing a new medium that facilitates the distribution of information, products and services that were traditionally distributed through physical means. Recent Community interventionism aimed at 'balancing' the formation of electronic contracts stage has, moreover, on occasion served to blur the line between precontract and contract formation. For a sound analysis of these developments in EC legislation, see R. Pinochet Olave, *Contratos Electronicos y Defensa de la Consumidor* (Marcial Pons, 2001) and A. González Gozalo, *La formación del contrato tras la Ley de servicios de la sociedad de la información y de comercio electrónico* (Comares, 2004). This study will instead consider the spill-over effects of consumer-orientated precontractual duties on the wider culture of European commercial contracting.

stakeholders,[2] and to promote a number of possible solutions aimed at removing identified inconsistencies and improving a general state of incoherence in the Community contract law *acquis*. It is widely accepted that, as a direct result of targeted, sector-specific interventionism at Community level, Member States' private law systems are currently gravely fragmented. The by-now stereotyped argument provides that the coherence of national private law systems is under threat from such sporadic and piecemeal legislation, typically undertaken without due regard to its potentially negative impact across Member States' contract law systems. Alarm at this progressive Community reorganisation and restructuring of national private laws has been felt most acutely in those civil law systems that have traditionally rationalised private law through the prism of a formal, closed and self-referential legal instrument, namely a civil code.[3]

As Community secondary law arises through a complex process of bartering and negotiation – including within the various Directorates General of the European Commission, and through lobbying from diverse social, economic and consumer interest groups – the resultant typically poorly conceived, periodic and a-systematic legislation tends to grate with the code methodology. Common law jurisdictions have generally encountered much less difficulty in assimilating this form of secondary legislation into their national structures given the characteristic flexibility and fluidity of their private laws. Indeed, this flexibility in the common law of contract, or what has been termed 'legal pragmatism', has meant a generally less hostile reception of Community directives in comparison

2 In July 2001 the Commission of the European Communities (the Commission) initiated a comprehensive consultation process with stakeholders in government, business and industry, legal practice and academia, with consumer associations and other interested parties on the potentially negative impact on the internal market of divergences in Member States' contract laws. See Communication from the Commission to the Council and the European Parliament on European Contract Law, COM (2001) 398 final, 11.07.2001. (Hereinafter cited as the 2001 Communication). Stakeholder feedback prompted a subsequent 'Action Plan' in February 2003 (hereinafter cited as the 2003 Action Plan) and a Follow-Up Communication in 2004 (hereinafter cited as the 2004 Follow Up Communication). See respectively, Communication from the Commission to the Council and the European Parliament, 'A More Coherent European Contract Law, An Action Plan', COM (2003) 68 Final, 12.02.2003 and Communication from the Commission to the European Parliament and the Council on 'European contract law and the revision of the acquis: the way forward', COM (2004) 651 final, 11.10.2004. These three primary Commission discussion documents on general European contract law ought further to be read in light of the Green Paper on European Union Consumer Protection, COM (2001) 531 final, 02.10.2001. The relevant documentation and additional background material may be currently accessed via the 'European Contract Law' website of the Directorate General for Health and Consumer Protection at: http://ec.europa.eu/comm/consumers/cons_int/safe_shop/fair_bus_pract/cont_law/index_en.htm.

3 For a fuller account of this contrasting approach see L. Niglia, *The Transformation of Contract in Europe* (Aspen/Kluwer, 2003) and by the same author, 'The Non-Europeanisation of Private Law' [2001] 9 ERPL 575. Niglia highlights a failure to secure consensus between the primary European political organs and national judiciaries and academia, particularly in civil law jurisdictions, as a primary factor in the rejection of Community inspired private law, particularly Directive 93/13/EEC, 5 April 1993.

with civil law jurisdictions. Resistance would undoubtedly increase however in the event of heightened Community regulation of commercial contracts.[4] Whilst the EU currently enjoys no competence to legislate in the field of general contract law,[5] a re-invigorated Community interest in the merits of a common European private law and the potentially negative impact of divergence on the internal market have served to resuscitate the hitherto largely sterile academic debate on the assumed need for a comprehensive European Civil Code.[6] Debate

4 It has been noted that the UK commercial and maritime legal services attract business to the value of £800 million in invisible earnings (see Gap Gemini/Ernst & Young, *Commercial Court Feasibility Study*, a report prepared on behalf of the Department of the Lord Chancellor 2001). Submissions from the Commercial Bar in London and the Law Societies of England and Wales to the European Commission (see Commission website, *supra* fn. 3) contend that the 'privileged position' of English contract law in international commerce may be threatened by the development of a uniform European contract law. Sound judicial decision-making, enforceable judgments and the location of London itself are just some factors cited in support of English commercial contract law and dispute resolution procedures, see M. Patchett-Joyce, *Why London is and will continue to be a Centre for the Resolution of International Commercial Law Disputes*, article accessible via the website of Monkton Chambers, London. These arguments are of key significance for the present study.

5 See *inter alia*, B. De Witte, *The European Union's System of Competence and Private Law Harmonisation*, paper delivered at conference on the theme of 'Codes and Constitutions – Processes and Cross-influences in the European Union and its Member States', European University Institute, Florence, October 8-9, 2004. The European institutions do presently enjoy competence to act in promoting the welfare of consumers yet no such competence exists vis-à-vis general contract law. The primary legal base for harmonising initiatives thus far has been Article 95 EC Treaty, though the constitutional ramifications of further Community interventionism, in adopting new harmonisation measures, has been dramatically highlighted by the decision of the European Court of Justice in the 'Tobacco Advertising' case of *Germany v. Council and Parliament*, C-376/98, October 5, 2000. The issue of competence has further been critically examined by C.U. Schmid, 'Legitimacy Conditions for a European Civil Code' (2001) EUI WP 14. Whilst the waters of European private law have evidently been deeply muddied by the ubiquitous presence of consumer law directives, commercial contracts have remained largely unregulated. To further complicate matters, as De la Rosa notes, "consumer law *per se* does not constitute an autonomous branch of the legal order but rather remains as an inter-disciplinary subset which affects different fields or legal sectors to varying degrees" in *La protección de los consumidores en el mercado interior europeo* (Comares, 2003). Importantly, he asserts that the process of harmonising consumer contract law has not fostered, nor is it likely to foster complete substantive uniformity within Member States private law systems, at 153.

6 An immense literature, both generally supportive and blatantly opposed to the codification project, is now widely available. See *inter alia*, A. Hartkamp et al, *Towards a European Civil Code* (Kluwer, 3rd edn, 2004) hereinafter *Towards 2004*. Among the most sceptical voices, see P. Legrand, 'A Diabolical Idea' in *Towards 2004*, at 245 et seq; 'European Legal Systems are not Converging' (1996) 45 ICLQ 52; 'Sens et Non-Sens d'un Code Civil Européen' (1996) 4 Rev int dr comp 779; 'Against a European Civil Code' (1997) 60 MLR 44; G. Teubner, 'Legal Irritants: Good Faith in British Law or How Unifying Law Ends Up in New Divergences' (1998) 61 MLR 11. Teubner has argued that transplanting the concept of good faith into English contract law has largely failed due to a clash with the commercial framework in wider

has intensified with regard to the legitimacy, viability and intrinsic value of a common European code of private law since the promotion of such an instrument by a series of resolutions of the European Parliament,[7] and subsequently in a number of highly influential academic publications. It had previously been suggested that European law was entering a period of 'decodificazione',[8] yet as Chamboredon observes:

> [T]aking into account the fragmentation of legal sources and the development of new forms of adjudication of private law disputes, the idea of codification, as an undertaking of legal rationalisation and democratisation, still appears to be topical.[9]

The codification project has further been reinforced by the degree of institutional credibility that the European institutions have afforded those leading academic study groups involved in the drafting of framework codes.[10] Yet, besides fundamental differences in legal culture and civil procedure enduring between the common and civil law legal communities, allied to 'the deep-seated fears of common lawyers about codification',[11] the weighted argument in favour of an agreed Code appears all the more unsettling when examined in the light of modern international business practice. In this book, the author adopts a sceptical approach to the potential academic misadventure currently being promoted under the European Commission's 'Common Frame of Reference'

British society. See also Wijffels, who though provocative in suggesting that proponents of codification may be 'demented', makes the valid point that, 'the whole matrix of values, social and economic interests, and logical principles has changed to such a degree as to affect the very foundations of our legal systems', A. Wijffels, 'European Private Law: A New Software Package for an Outdated Operating System' in M. Van Hoecke & F. Ost (eds), *The Harmonisation of European Private Law* (Hart Law, 2000) at 103.

[7] See Resolution on Action to Bring into Line the Private Law of the Member States, [1989] OJ C 158/400, 26.06.1989; & Resolution on the Harmonisation of Certain Sectors of Private Law in the Member States, [1994] OJ C 205/518, 25.07.1994. & Resolution on the Annual Legislative Programme of the Commission for 2000, [2000] OJ C 377/323, 16.03.2000 B5-0228, 0229-0230 Final, p. 326, pt.28, in which the European parliament states its view that 'greater harmonisation of civil law has become essential in the internal market'. In its reaction to the Commission's Green Paper, the European Parliament set forth a preliminary action plan and timetable aimed at 'paving legislation' for the introduction of a corpus of European contract rules, see Resolution on the Approximation of Civil and Commercial Law of the Member States, C5-0471, 15.11.2001.

[8] N. Irti, *L'Età della Decodificazione* (Guiffrè, 1989).

[9] A. Chamboredon, 'The Debate on a European Civil Code: For an Open Texture' in *The Harmonisation of EuropeanPrivate Law, supra* fn. 6, at 82.

[10] Discussed further in Chapter 1.

[11] M. Clarke, 'Doubts from the Dark Side – The Case Against Codes' (2001) JBL 605; see also P.Malaurie, 'Le Code Civil Europêen des Obligations – Une Question Toujours Ouverte' (2002) 6 La Semaine Jur 281.

(CFR) research strategy and questions the sustainability of an 'off-the-shelf' contract law for the differentiated EU multi-level system.[12] It is argued that current legal strategies aimed at systematising and ultimately codifying pan-European contract law principles for the internal market appear deeply flawed from an economic and legal perspective, and require urgent reassessment in the light of previous US experience in uniform private lawmaking. In the belief that the multi-level structure of the European Union is simply irreconcilable with the traditional idea of a unitary codified system, in this study the potential negative side effects of such a one-dimensional template for contract law will be critically explored. Weaknesses in the methodology to be employed under the CFR research programme will similarly be exposed. Alarmingly, the Commission's 'coherence' strategy appears to be operating from the potentially misguided premise that the mere supply of a new EC contract law will ensure demand for such a product. The integrationist strategy of 'simplifying' private law underway at the Community level is further fraught with risk due to the complexity of modern contracting processes, which are not easily reduced to abstractions and general principles.[13] Even more worryingly, the policy has thus far largely overlooked the importance of commercial contracting behaviour and the increased specialisation of business agreements. The role of contract drafting and the ability of parties to choose the most suitable forum and law applicable to their contract have similarly been downplayed.

By contrast, the lack of coordination between Member States' laws on parties' behaviour during negotiations and conflicting rules on precontractual liability do imply prima facie an obstacle for intra-Community trade[14] and the development of a more coherent, if perhaps merely *academic* European contract

---

[12] According to the Commission's current thinking '... the Common Frame of Reference will be used as a toolbox, where appropriate, when presenting proposals to improve the quality and coherence of the existing *acquis* and future legal instruments in the area of contract law. The CFR will provide clear definitions of legal terms, fundamental principles as well as coherent model rules of contract law, drawing on the EC *acquis* and on best solutions found in Member States' legal orders', See Non-paper of the Commission's Services, presented at Joint Conference of the European Parliament and European Commission, Brussels, 28 April 2004, and reaffirmed in the 2004 Follow-Up Communication. The process of formulating the format, scope and likely use of the Common Frame will be analysed in chapters 1 and 2.

[13] See M.J. Doris, *Beyond a stillborn European civil code? The European Commission's Action Plan for a More Coherent European Contract Law*, paper delivered at conference on 'European Contracting' organised by the Centre for the Study of Business Law and the Lex Mercatoria Monitor, University of Tromsø, March 2003.

[14] Precontractual duties and information disclosure requirements have been expressly recognised by the Commission as a specific area of concern in the 2004 Follow-Up Communication. Earlier drafts of the Communication (on file with author) and discussion within the European Commission's Inter-Services Working Group on European Contract revealed strong consensus on the need to tackle divergence in this field.

law.[15] A lack of cross-jurisdictional consistency on the treatment of precontractual duties is readily detectable. A notable difference in emphasis with regard to the importance of contract negotiations and drafting across national private law systems is similarly apparent. This has obvious negative implications on two levels: the applicability of sector-specific information disclosure obligations in diverse industries implies increased transaction costs for business-consumer (b2c) and specific business-business (b2b) contracts, whilst a lack of familiarity with foreign rules on disclosure, the 'appropriate' conduct during contract negotiations, and the potentially binding nature of certain statements, representations and/or precontractual drafting techniques suggests added complications for commercial parties operating in the internal market outside of their individual jurisdiction.

Cross-border contract litigation is infrequent and atypical, and difficulties arising at the precontractual stage are rarely litigated yet, left unchecked, the current state of incoherence could potentially result in a growth in complex, costly and time-consuming cross-border legal disputes. As Scott and Swartz observe, 'litigation explosions occur in transaction fields, such as contracts, when the law is obscure'.[16] Divergence, both doctrinal and in practice, does prima facie serve to obscure the law in Europe and reduce the attractiveness of cross-border contracting. Whilst a number of civil law jurisdictions have a clear tradition of finding and upholding precontractual duties, the English common law of contracts has typically considered their imposition a real risk to legal certainty and a potential cause of increased negotiation and/or litigation costs in a commercial context. The English courts seemingly resolute reluctance to impose obligations on negotiating parties has been largely overlooked by those most vociferous in promoting harmonisation, and particularly the codification of European private law.[17] To date there has been no such 'litigation explosion' in pre-contractual reliance claims before European courts, yet disputes have arisen

[15] This terminology is used by the primary European institutions and is now 'de moda' in academic literature – see *inter alia* H. Kötz & A. Flessner, *European Contract Law – Volume I* (Oxford Clarendon Press, 1998), C. Quigley, *European Community Contract Law – Parts I & II* (Kluwer, 1997), M.J. Bonell, 'The Need and Possibilities of a Codified European Contract Law' (1987) 5 ERPL 505. It is important to remind ourselves that at present, however, European contract law, as a coherent system, remains very much a 'work in progress'. That said, as Grundmann stresses, the emerging body of European Contract Law increasingly impacts upon the formation, the content and the termination of contracts, in S. Grundmann, 'The Structure of European Contract Law' (2001) 4 ERPL 505.

[16] R. Scott & A. Schwartz, 'The Law and Economics of Preliminary Agreements' (2005) Colum L WP, at 46.

[17] Evidence of a potential sea-change in attitude to divergence in the area of precontractual duties is the recent work of Sjef van Erp in 'The Precontractual Stage' in *Towards, 2004* at 363 et seq, who clearly appreciates the degree of common law resistance to a duty of good faith in negotiations. Van Erp equally acknowledges the need to explore wider social, economic, political and technological differences that exacerbate divergence in private law and suggests that a civil code is not the vehicle for removing those divergences

even where the parties share a similar legal background. In *Fonderie Officine Meccaniche Tacconi SpA v. Heinrich Wagner Sinto Maschinenfabrik GmbH*,[18] for instance, the European Court of Justice was required to consider a dispute regarding Article 1337 of the Italian Civil Code, which expressly upholds the notion that parties negotiating a contract must act in 'good faith'. The consequence of the obligation of good faith is that if negotiations are broken off, a claim for damages may arise even though a contract has not been formed. The Italian claimant in the Tacconi case was found to be entitled to commence court proceedings in Italy in relation to a claim for breach of 'good faith' in precontractual obligations, despite the German defendant's assertion that the Italian courts lacked jurisdiction because of an arbitration clause in the contractual document. Like the Italian civil law, German contract law has a strong tradition of finding and enforcing precontractual duties. Without doubt the differing emphasis placed on such duties across civil systems is as problematic for the harmonisation effort as the distinctly divergent, opposing position of English contract law.

A glance at the United States presents an equally cluttered legal picture across State lines. Perhaps surprisingly, it has been argued – though not always convincingly – that US contract law does recognise an obligation to negotiate a contract in good faith and it is possible to identify in the literature several possible grounds for imposing precontractual liability in the event of failed negotiations.[19] Whether or not such a good faith obligation exists at the start of negotiations, it is commonly argued that it carries substantial weight at the advanced stages of a deal. Doctrinally at least, in a typical case where parties reach partial

[18] C-334/00 [2002] ECR I-7357, discussed more fully in Chapter 1. As in Italian civil law, German contract law has a long tradition of upholding precontractual obligations. It is further notable that, under Dutch law a party who breaks off advanced negotiations is liable for expenses incurred by the other party, see W. Wils, 'Who Should Bear the Costs of Failed Negotiations? A Functional Inquiry into Precontractual Liability' (1992) 4 Journal des Economistes et des Etudes Humaines 93. See also E. Hondius, *Precontractual liability* (Kluwer, 1991). See also L.A. Di Matteo, 'The CISG and the Presumption of Enforceability: Unintended Contractual Liability in International Business Dealings' (1997) 22 Yale J of Int'l Law 111. Di Matteo notes the fact that uncertainty as to 'potential liability is compounded in the area of international contracts because of variations in contractual formalities among different legal systems", at 137.

[19] See E.A. Farnsworth, 'Precontractual Liability and Preliminary Agreements: Fair Dealing and Failed Negotiations' (1987) 87 Colum L Rev 217 (Hereinafter *Preliminary Agreements*, 1987). This influential article has had a significant impact on US judicial decision-making and the late Professor Farnsworth's analysis will be considered more fully in chapters 2, 3 and 4 of this study. In the US, a party may be liable for the other party's reliance costs on three possible grounds: Misrepresentation – see Restatement (Second) of Torts, §§525,530 and *Markov v. ABC Transfer & Storage Co.* 457 P.2d 535 (Wash.1969); if it benefited from the reliance (under the doctrine of unjust enrichment, see *Pancratz Co. v. Kloefkorn-Ballard Construction and Development*, 720 P.2d 906 (Wyo.1986); or, as has been widely argued in the literature, if a specific promise was made during the negotiations, see *Hoffman v. Red Owl Stores*, 133 N.W. 2d 265, (Wisc. 1965).

understanding over terms and agree to continue to negotiate any remaining outstanding issues, it has been argued that the parties are obliged to conclude pre-closing negotiations in good faith. According to this model the freedom to make and reject proposals would be no longer absolute. Importantly, whilst parties cannot be forced to conclude negotiations with a deal, and bad faith may not necessarily give rise to a remedy, negotiations themselves do imply a sunk cost for contracting parties, and it has been suggested that the threat of reliance damages may spur an otherwise unwilling contracting partner to enter into a less than satisfactory agreement.[20]

Such thoughts are generally seen as unconscionable for the English common law courts, which have explicitly rejected the notion of interfering in the precontractual stage as recently as 1998 in the landmark case of *Investors Compensation Scheme v. West Bromwich Building Society*.[21] This reluctance on the part of the judiciary to entertain a greater legal assessment of the precontractual phase of negotiations has not dissuaded academic contributors in common law systems from discussing the potential for reform. Giliker has raised the possibility of a greater role for tort and a closer approximation of common and civil law approaches,[22] whilst Bigwood has discussed the imposition of a general duty of transactional care.[23] Europeanisation and Internationalisation processes

---

[20] See L. Arye Bebchuk & O. Ben-Shahar, *Precontractual reliance* (2001) NBER WP. There is clearly substantial uncertainty as to whether a duty to negotiate in good faith applies in the US, and if so, what limits attach to any such duty. Gordley, for example, disputes its existence and argues that the US courts do not recognise such a duty, see J. Gordley, 'The Future of European Contract Law on the Basis of Europe's Heritage' (2005) 2 ERCL 163, at 172.

[21] *Investors Compensation Scheme Ltd v. West Bromwich Building Society* [1998] 1 WLR 896. The facts of the case and its wider implications will be analysed more fully in Part 3 in an assessment of the current legal approach in England and Wales to the admission of evidence related to commercial negotiations and the wider issue of precontractual liability.

[22] P. Giliker, 'A Role for Tort in Precontractual Negotiations? An Analysis of English, French and Canadian Law' (2003) 52 ICLQ 969. The case for an expansion of tort law into preliminary dealings in US contract law was explored previously by Grant Gilmore in 'Reconstructing Breach of the Implied Covenant of Good Faith & Fair Dealing as a Tort' [1985] 73 Cal. L. Rev. 1291, at 1316-18. In his highly influential *The Death of Contract* (Ohio State University Press, 1974) Gilmore identified the demise of classical contract law approaches and the number of instances in which courts had imposed 'what might be called a precontractual duty to bargain in good faith'. He further suggested that 'bad faith conduct' in negotiations should be classified as a tort. Wary of the limitations of a tortious vision of precontractual liability and the 'compelling policy grounds' presented by Iacobucci and Major JJ in the Canadian Supreme Court decision in *Martel Building Ltd v. Canada* (2001) 193 DLR (4th) 1 SCC for not finding a tortious duty of care in negotiations (at 18-20 and discussed further in Part 3), this thesis will explore the value of estoppel-based approaches and the doctrine of fair dealing as alternative legal avenues toward 'imposing' greater transactional care in negotiations.

[23] R. Bigwood, *Exploitative Contracts* (Oxford University Press, 2003). Ewan McKendrick, a leading common law authority on contract, has suggested that English courts will progressively entertain a greater policing of precontractual bargaining processes between commercial parties. See Opening

in contract law therefore constitute a challenge to the robustly commercial orientation of English contract law, particularly its traditional emphasis upon a distinctly literal approach to interpretation. As we will discuss presently, legal opinion in Australia, New Zealand and other common law systems has generally been more receptive towards concepts such as good faith and fair dealing in precontractual negotiations, aswell as subsequent reliance-based claims.

Arguably, the key challenge for the harmonisation strategy in both European and transnational contract law rests not with overcoming divergence between common and civil law systems *per se*, but rather requires a change of focus that concentrates on reconciling contrasting visions of contract law as founded upon distinct ideologies. Whereas civil law systems display a tendency to conceptualise contracts as premised upon party loyalty or solidarity, typically reinforcing fairness and similar policy considerations, common law systems have traditionally adopted an equally principled stance founded upon contract drafting and the importance of technical exactitude.[24] The growing emphasis upon contractual consociationalism or solidarity *inter partes* in EC directives has been presented by Lurger, and the resultant impact upon an agreed ethic for European contract law has been debated from a comparative perspective by Beale.[25] Collins has

---

Address and follow-up comments at conference on 'The Harmonisation of European Contract Law: Implications for European Private Laws, Business and Legal Practice', Keble College, Oxford, March 18-19, 2005. Lord Nicholls has further called extra-judicially for greater admissibility of precontractual evidence in commercial trials, in 'My Kingdom for a Horse, The Meaning of Words' (2005) 121 LQR 577.

24 For a thorough analysis of competing ideologies in English contract law see J. Adams & R. Brownsword, *Understanding Contract Law* (Sweet & Maxwell, 2nd edn, 1996), at 179 *et seq*. Similar ideological analyses of contract law are not as prevalent in civil law jurisdictions, though lawyers across Europe, particularly in Nordic jurisdictions, are increasingly discussing contrasting contract drafting styles. See *inter alia*, O. Lando, *The Battle of the Forms*, position paper presented at conference on 'European Contracting', *supra* fn. 13, and G. Cordero Moss, *Lectures on Comparative Law of Contracts* (Publications Series of the Institute of Private Law, Oslo 2004).

25 B. Lurger, 'The Social Side of Contract Law and the New Principle of Regard and Fairness', in *Towards 2004*. The article suffers however from an inadequate examination of existing penalties for breach of such broad EC 'fairness duties'. See also H. Beale, 'Codification & the English common law – A Model not to be Followed?' in G. Barrett & L. Bernardeau, *ERA-forum Special issue on Towards a European Civil Code*, 2002 (hereinafter ERA Special Issue, 2002). Importantly, Niglia correctly perceives a measured shift in English contract law away from rigid literal interpretation towards greater substantive reasoning (see L. Niglia, 'The Fall of Formalism in English Contract Law' (2004) 20(3) JCL 193 (hereinafter *The Fall, 2004*). However, as Niglia himself acknowledges this shift away from formalism is chiefly observed in one 'fragment' (at 193) of English contract law – business to consumer (b2c) standard form contracting. This author remains sceptical of the extent of any similar shift in commercial contracting and supports the view of Whincup that: *Insofar as English law finds nothing objectionable in contracting to give very little in order to obtain a great deal, on principle it is not concerned with the fairness or otherwise of bargains. Its basic attitude is still that of nineteenth century laissez-faire philosophy. It is a law for merchants and businessmen, supposedly bargaining on equal terms, each free to get the better of the other if he can. Once made, the bargain is binding, for better or worse. The law will not rewrite people's contracts for them in the*

been one of the lone voices considering the protection of reasonable commercial expectation via harmonised European commercial contract laws.[26] Despite this discrepancy in the literature, Lord Mansfield's oft-quoted assertion of yesteryear that the law is much better certain than fair remains acutely relevant in considering the potential for harmonisation.[27]

Whilst the hypothetical structuring and framing of future EC private law rules has dominated recent academic discourse, a more studied analysis of commercial deal-making, the primacy of contract drafting and the targetting of identifed practical difficulties faced by contracting parties operating cross border ought rather to be guiding the ongoing harmonisation effort. Equally critical is the need to rationalise the ever-greater specificity and sophistication of commercial agreements, a phenomenon that has not only resulted in an atomisation of legal rules and categories but has further prompted a simultaneous growth in arbitration and specialised courts. The development of uniform contract rules at EC level therefore implies the dedication of equal attention and

---

interests of abstract ideals of fairness or justice. English law is thus unique in having no general rule against unconscionable contracts, or in refusing to imply obligations of good faith between contracting parties in M.H. Whincup, *Contract Law and Practice* (1992), at 56-57.

26 See H. Collins, 'Formalism and Efficiency: Designing European Commercial Contract Law' (2000) 8(1) EPRL 211 and more fully H. Collins, *Regulating Contracts* (Oxford University Press, 1999), who suggests that future discussion on harmonised EC rules should consider how best to protect reasonable commercial expectation. We will discuss Collins thesis on the need to protect reasonable commercial expectation in chapter 4, however, a reasonable expectation approach has been attacked for its circularity, a circularity that fails to offer a truly solid theoretical basis for the coherent development of the law. As Kuklin notes 'reasonable expectation' [operates] as a 'mutual feedback mechanism' as the law "informs reasonable expectations and reasonable expectations inform the law. Each one affects the other in a dynamic relationship that leads to harmony and stability when they both align, but dissonance and instability when they are out of synch as, for example, when social mores undergo rapid change. In this latter circumstance, social pressure on the law pushes it to catch up with expectations, while, at the same time, the existing law puts the breaks on evolving expectations. Tension and social dissatisfaction persist until there is an accommodation between the law and expectations' in B.H. Kuklin, 'The Justification for Protecting Reasonable Expectations' (2001) 29 Hofstra L. Rev. 863, at 865.

27 "[I]n all mercantile transactions the great object should be certainty: and therefore, it is of more consequence that a rule should be certain ..." in *Vallejo v. Wheeler*, 1 Cowp 143 (1774). See also S. Whittaker & R. Zimmermann, 'Good Faith in European contract law: surveying the legal landscape' in *Good Faith in European Contract Law* (Cambridge University Press, 2000) at 39-48 (discussing the absence of duty of good faith in English contract law but noting where good faith principles have been assimilated in specific areas). Bradgate has also warned that, following implementation of the Unfair Terms in Consumer Contract Directive 93/13/EEC into domestic English contract law, innovation in the use of the good faith doctrine has been overstated. See R. Bradgate, *The Integration of Directive 93/13 into the National Legal Systems: Experience in the United Kingdom*, paper presented at conference on 'The Directive on Unfair Terms: 5 Years On – Evaluation and Future Perspectives, Brussel, 1-3 July 1999.

resources to the procedural implementation of any such agreed rules.[28] Dispute avoidance, as opposed to systematisation and codification, arguably presents itself as a more coherent and cost effective method and justification for tackling existing divergence. For instance, incompleteness in contract has become a major cause for judicial and academic uncertainty not just across Europe, but in the US and internationally. A growth in national court decisions examining the validity of preliminary agreements and the spectre of precontractual reliance exposes a complex puzzle for the ongoing harmonisation debate. When, if at all, can parties reach 'an agreement' sufficient to impose a duty to negotiate in good faith? And what behaviour would constitute a breach of such a duty? Under new European contract rules should parties be entirely free to negotiate? And perhaps more importantly, should such freedom extend to walking away from even advanced negotiations without threat of liability? Such controversies will not be easily answered by a modern codification effort but will be critically explored in this study.[29]

Methodology and structure

The core aim of this study is to confront conflicting law and policy approaches to preliminary agreements and precontractual reliance from a comparative perspective, and to critically examine the general debate on the feasibility and suitability of further harmonising and/or codifying initiatives at the European level. In the belief that the harmonisation effort has wrongly taken on a distinctly Eurocentric and consumer-oriented character, this analysis will concentrate upon commercial caselaw and doctrinal opinion in the English,

---

28 Regrettably such an analysis would far exceed the scope of the present study. Evidence of this thinking is apparent, however, in the emerging work of A. Schwartz, 'Enforcement of Private Law: The Missing Link in the Process of European Harmonization' (200) 8 EPRL 1 and K.D. Kerameus, 'Procedural Implications of Civil Law Unification' in *Towards, 2004*, at 145 *et seq.*

29 As Scott observed in 2006 the academic debate surrounding 'the law of preliminary [contractual] agreements in the US is 'only just beginning', and the question of precontractual reliance further implies major questions of taxonomy for common lawyers' in R.E. Scott, *Hoffman v. Red Owl Stores and the Myth of Precontractual Reliance* (2006) Colum L WP series, and reprinted in (2007) 68 Ohio St LJ (hereinafter *Hoffman and the Myth, 2007*) See also H. Beale, W.D. Bishop & M.P. Furmston, *Contract – Cases & Materials* (4th edn, Oxford University Press, 2005), at 274 *et seq.* The issue is intimately connected to the legitimacy question of when courts should fill gaps in incomplete contracts. For Kostritsky, however, finding a workable methodology for judicial intervention in the field of incomplete contracts is today 'the holy grail of contract scholarship'. Moreover, the question cannot be divorced from the wider role of general clauses such as the duty of good faith and fair dealing, which is considered more fully in chapter 4 of this study. See P. Kostritsky, 'Taxonomy for Justifying Legal Intervention in an Imperfect World : What to do when parties have not achieved bargains or have drafted incomplete contracts' (2004) Wisc L Rev 323 (hereinafter *Taxonomy for Justifying, 2004*). See also H. Kötz, 'Precontractual Duties of Disclosure: A Comparative and Economic Perspective' (2000) 9(5) Eur J L Econ 19 (noting that in resolving questions of disclosure, '... European legal systems merely offer vague formulas with little or no operational power', at 19).

Spanish and US legal systems in an attempt to ascertain the potential for greater uniformity and coherence. Unconvinced by the case made thus far by proponents of regional European harmonisation, this study draws heavily upon US case law and doctrinal opinion and evaluates the role and adoption of US legal methods in the design of transnational private laws. Importantly, the steady infilitration of US contract drafting techniques into Spanish legal practice has been highlighted by Beltrán Sánchez, who sees no need to discourage such a free flow. This position contrasts significantly with the views of the US lawyer Martin Shapiro and the Italian comparatist Ugo Mattei, who have both warned against US drafting methods that occasionally serve to weaken or openly flout national rules in the interest of corporations.[30] The three domains of interest for this research are therefore:

1. *Competing Strategies for the Europeanisation of contract law.* There is evidently a real logic to the argument that a single European market requires a common, centralised private law system, yet is the process of harmonisation at the regional European level either achievable or desirable? Have not the purported economic advantages of standardisation and codification of national contract rules been grossly miscalculated by an overly-enthusiastic internationalist legal elite? In examining the question whether the internal market requires a common contract law infrastructure, we firstly assess the assumed economic/legal need for uniformity and the validity of competing harmonising strategies. We consider whether the goal of codifying European contract laws risks producing little more than a stillborn legal product given the complexity and sector-specific emphasis of modern private law regulation.

2. *The impact of divergent legal approaches to preliminary agreements and precontractual negotiation duties. Is it not the case that national private law systems commonly arrive at largely comparable solutions albeit by differing methods?* One counter-argument to comprehensive harmonisation initiatives favours inaction on the grounds that national legal systems typically arrive at common solutions albeit by differing methods.[31] We aim to test this functional equivalence

30 See respectively E. Beltrán Sánchez & U. Nieto Carol, *Contratación Mercantil* (Cuadernos de Derecho y Comercio, Madrid 1998), M. Shapiro, The Common Core of European Private Laws – Some Outside Comments' in M. Bussani & U. Mattei (eds), *Making European Private Law: Essays on the Common Core Project* (Trento, 2000) and U. Mattei, 'Hard Code Now!" (2002) 2(1) Glob J F.

31 In relation to divergent legal approaches to precontractual liability, this functional equivalence theory is neatly summarised by Goderre as follows: 'Whether a country chooses to impose liability based upon an implied or explicit duty to act in good faith, or whether liability is imposed based solely upon specific contract theories such as restitution, misrepresentation or promissory estoppel, most systems nevertheless tend to reach the same end result – liability is imposed if a party has acted to the detriment of the other party, even if a contract has not been consummated' in D. Goderre, 'International Negotiations Gone Sour: Precontractual Liability under the United Nations Sales Convention' (1997) 66 U Cinn L Rev 258, at 266. However, Dagan in *The Law and Ethics of Restitution* (Cambridge University Press,

hypothesis via an exploration of legal approaches to precontractual duties in the English, US and Spanish legal systems. An examination of English and Spanish contract law is particularly instructive as both legal systems have a diminished interest, legal and political, in a proposed harmonisation of European private law and legal practice has remained distinctly dispassionate towards the harmonisation debate in comparison with other jurisdictions.[32] Exploring US caselaw and doctrinal opinion is equally important given the extent to which the harmonisation of private law in Europe has been modelled to date on previous US experience.

3. *The sustainability of contract codification and the treatment of precontractual reliance in new, emerging EC contract rules.* The logic of codification merits deeper reflection. A body of European academics are currently in something of a thrall to the challenge of codifying European private laws. The apparent shift in favour of codification in leading academic circles and among elements of the Community institutions is assessed in light of recent experience in the US with harmonisation and code-making techniques. It is argued, in particular, that key lessons ought to be drawn from the development and sustainability of the US Uniform Commercial Code (UCC). In contrast to a comprehensive codification initiative, we outline the framework of a novel 'interoperability' approach to identified problems arising through divergence in Member States' contract laws. It is suggested that such difficulties may in large part be viewed and confronted as mere infrequent 'interoperability' problems. This prompts reflection on the merits of such a 'solution' in the treatment of problems arising in the precontractual formation of commercial contracts.

Chapter 1 is divided into three main parts. The negative impact of sector-specific Community interventionism and the assumed need for enhanced coherence is firstly discussed. Thereafter, a preliminary assessment is made of the economics of harmonisation and the merits of continued inter-jurisdictional competition. Building upon these preliminary observations, the potential for a continued plurality of European contract laws and reinvigorated inter-jurisdictional competition is subsequently examined. The Commission has underscored contractual freedom, or party autonomy, as the guiding principle for its coher-

---

2004) correctly suggests the need for consistency of approach nonetheless, and for scholars to debate which system's model rules best promote efficiency and a reduction in transaction costs.

32 As Ewoud Hondius notes, '... hithero the bulk of academic discussion on the creation of a European Civil Code in recent years has taken place in Germany, Italy and the Netherlands', in *The Private Law Systems in the EU: Discrimination on Grounds of Nationality and the Need for a European Civil Code* (2000) Working Paper Series of the Legal Affairs Committee of the European Parliament, JURI-103 EN, at 138. Interestingly, the late Professor Birks recently opined that, given the lack of sound systematisation of the common law of contract, if left unreformed it would progressively 'dissolve into incoherence' in P. Birks (ed.), *English Private Law – Volume I* (Oxford University Press, 2004), at p.li. Leading UK based judges, practitioners and academics are further steadily challenging the traditional view that the English law of contract can remain largely insulated from wider developments at Community level.

ence strategy,[33] and chapter 2 seeks to explore the power of the drafting pen as a tool to circumvent current 'interoperability' difficulties in cross border contracting. A number of recent decisions of the European Court of Justice that serve to weaken both party autonomy and legal certainty are discussed and criticised. Chapter 2 further exposes the latent difficulties that arise in seeking to enhance or inspire greater legal certainty in modern European (pre-) contract laws. Given the market-inspired tendency towards divergence, allied to the complex material and substantive elements of the contract law *acquis*, it is doubtful whether the stated Community goal of improved coherence in European contracting can ever be adequately achieved. Chapter 3 thereafter examines the degree of functional equivalence in the treatment of preliminary agreements and precontractual liability in English, US and Spanish case law and doctrinal opinion. We focus on a specific cluster of recent cases in each jurisdiction that have examined incomplete agreements in a commercial context. We assess the law in relation to letters of intent, agreements to agree, comfort letters, and agreements to negotiate in good faith.[34] Such preliminary drafting techniques have not been

[33] The European Commission has consistently underscored contractual freedom as the guiding principle for its 'coherence' strategy. See, *inter alia*, opening comments of D. Byrne, *European Contract Law – Towards a Common Frame of Reference* at Joint Conference of the European Parliament and European Commission, *supra* fn. 12 and D. Staudenmayer, 'The Way Forward in European Contract Law' [2005] 2 ERPL 95.

[34] The rise in standard form contracts in modern business has by no means eliminated negotiation and drafting. Reliance on letters of intent, comfort letters and other preliminary documents that bear many of the attributes of a contract are in many instances the first meaningful communication between the parties and their legal effects are commonly the cause of problematic domestic litigation. Spanish legal theory recognises a range of precontractual models that are gradually giving rise to an increased caseload, see A. Viguri Perea, *Los Tratos Preliminaries: las cartas de intenciones y otros documentos legales precontractuales* (PPU Barcelona, 1994). In 2004, the Provincial Court of Madrid observed that: "In the process of concluding a contract it may occur that the parties agree certain aspects and draft a document to detail this agreement. This document does not result in a contract, as no agreement is reached in relation to all the necessary aspects, rather there is a non-binding 'letter of intent' (*carta de intención*) or (*minuta no vinculante*). The court did recognise, however, the legal effects of a 'preparatory contract', a 'preliminary contract' and an 'option contract'. The 'preparatory contract' is a contract whereby the parties agree the terms and conditions of a possible future contract but are under no obligation to ultimately bind themselves to an agreement. The 'preliminary contract' determines the content of a future binding contract either between the parties or with a third party. Option contracts afford one party the exclusive right to enter into a future contract – a right that he is entirely free to exercise or relinquish. It is notable that, in arriving at its decision, the court gave detailed consideration of the treatment of preliminary agreements under French, German and Italian civil law theory. See SAP de Madrid decision, JUR 2004\89221. Such judicial parallelism, or what Joerges terms 'interactive adjudication', is arguably the surest method to a more uniform EC contract law and will be discussed in the latter part of this thesis. See C. Joerges, 'Interactive Adjudication in the Europeanisation Process? A Demanding Perspective and a Modest Example' (2000) 1 ERPL 1. For a similar argument see S. Camara Lapuente, 'Un Derecho Privado o un Código Civil para Europa' in *Derecho Privado Europeo* (Colex, 2003).

subjected to any real, sustained comparative analysis in mainstream European contract law literature, despite their increased penetration into US caselaw from the 1970s onwards.[35] Chapter 4 thereafter considers the need for a sound methodology for judicial interference in commercial bargaining and the protection of reasonable expectation, and examines the possibility of forging greater European and transnational uniformity.

35 In the 1970 US case of *Garner v. Boyd*, 330 F. Supp 22 (N.D. Tex 1970) the court stressed that '[a] letter of intent is commonly employed to reduce to writing a preliminary understanding of the parties' but warned of the risk of being accidentally bound by such agreements. The work of Furmston, Norisada and Poole on *Contract Formation and Letters of Intent* (Wiley, 1998) remains the most comprehensive, if largely descriptive comparative analysis of the international role of letters of intent.

CHAPTER I

The Primacy of Certainty

1 System building, the triumph of two formalisms and the design of a 'Common Frame of Reference'

The twin aims of this chapter are firstly to survey the competing academic strategies for eradicating divergences between Member States' contract laws and to critically examine the original tripartite approach of the European Commission – as distilled initially in the 2003 Action Plan and reaffirmed in part in the 2004 Follow-Up Communication. This strategy originally proposed (a) the improvement of the contract law *acquis* through the elaboration of what is termed a 'Common Frame of Reference' containing common rules and terminology (b) the promotion of EU-wide standard terms and conditions, and (c) further reflection on the need and value of a horizontal Optional Instrument. Particular close attention is paid to the first and third proposals, which still remain somewhat oblique and poorly defined. Thereafter, we highlight the lack of importance afforded to divergent approaches to the negotiation and drafting of cross border commercial contracts and the negative impact of a steady growth in sector-specific information and precontractual duties on the coherence of private law systems. Contrary to the majority academic view, it is suggested that the Commission strategy is directed more towards itself – and a necessary improvement of the law-making techniques of the Community institutions – than economic actors on the market and is strongly in keeping with both the Governance White Paper[1] and the Better Regulation Action Plan.[2] The general orientation of the Action Plan, and the encouragement of 'best practices', point towards increased and improved co-regulation in private law. It is submitted that the need for a Common Frame of Reference was conceded reluctantly as a possible method of ensuring greater legitimacy and support for future Community interventionism in matters of private law, and as an important means of appeasing influential academic opinion, particularly in civil law countries. We explore key weaknesses in the CFR strategy and question the ability of the Common Frame to foster and sustain greater legal certainty in the field of precontractual duties.

We begin our analysis by considering the following scenario sketched out in a PLC study[3] in the early 1990s: *In a conference room somewhere in Europe, after days of negotiations, offers and counter-offers, you have just persuaded your opposite number to sign a letter outlining terms on which a seller will sell its business to your company. The letter states that only the final paragraph is legally binding; this paragraph prevents the seller from negotiating with any other party for the sale of the business for one month. One week later, after teams of lawyers, accountants and other*

1 White Paper on Governance, COM (2001) 428 final. The primary aim of the White Paper is the simplification of EU law and the five guiding principles underpinning the strategy are openness, participation, accountability, effectiveness and coherence.

2 Communication from the Commission – Action Plan Simplifying and Improving the Regulatory Environment, COM (2002) 278 final.

3 See 'Lock-out Agreements – Can the UK learn from Europe?' (Practical Law for Companies, 1991)

investigators have been working around the clock carrying out due diligence investigations on the business, the seller contacts you and says that a third party has offered more money for the business, and the seller instructs you to stop investigations and refuses to attend further negotiating meetings. Can you do anything to prevent this, or to recover any of the money you have spent on investigations?

The answer to this preliminary question will very much depend on which European jurisdiction has control of the contract and the acceptable degree of judicial 'interference' that a particular national legal order envisages for the 'proper' monitoring of the precontractual stage of contract negotiations. The study suggested that in twelve of the then Member States, eleven different legal solutions – of varying degree- would have been possible. Yet, is such divergence necessarily problematic and does it constitute a practical impediment to cross-border commerce? Is it likely to dissuade commercial operators from operating outside of their domestic market or impede the proper functioning of the internal market? In other words, is the solution to identified divergences in national contracts a move towards a single legal template founded upon a comprehensive body of uniform rules, and/or the eradication of legal diversity in private law, or can Europe's multi-level system of governance countenance a differentiated, plurality of competing private laws and theoretical approaches?[4]

Certainly it could be strongly argued that spontaneous private law harmonisation, via Watsonian legal transplants, has better served the uniformity goal not just in Europe but internationally, and that the trend towards harmonisation is irreversible regardless of the CFR. Indeed, dynamic theories of European integration suggest that in developing a supranational constitutional legal order, the combined effect of market forces, lobbying within the European institutions, a growth in litigation with jurisdiction before the European courts, allied to the integrative role of Community judicial decision-making will ultimately succeed in supplanting national legal orders.[5] This 'joint market and polity-building

4 The primary legal texts currently dealing with transnational contracts are the Brussels 1 Regulation, Council Regulation (EC) Number 44/2001 of 22 December 2000 on jurisdiction and the recognition and enforcement of judgments in civil and commercial matters, OJ L12 of 16.01.2001 and the Rome Convention on the law applicable to contractual obligations of 19 June 1980. OJ C 27 (26.01.98) Both enactments share a common model. The Brussels 1 Regulation establishes the rules governing party autonomy at the jurisdictional level. It answers the question of whether and under what circumstances a 'forum selection clause' will be valid and effective. The Rome Convention establishes the rule governing party autonomy at the law applicable level. It answers the question of whether and under what circumstances a 'law-governing' clause will be valid and effective. Both are uniform rules which prevail over national laws and which aim to strike a balance between what has been termed the 'logic of facilitation', or freedom of contract, and the 'logic of protection', per F. Garcimartín Alférez, *Party Autonomy and its Limits in Cross Border Commercial Contracts*, AALS/ELFA conference on Transatlantic Business Transactions: Choice of Law, Jurisdictions and Judgements, Barcelona, June 2003.

5 A. Stone Sweet, 'Integration and the Europeanisation of Law' [2002] 2 QUB WP. It is suggested that the interaction between litigants, national judges, and the European Court of Justice produces 'spill-over effects' and that the 'self-reinforcing' nature of the EC system will ultimately force the success of inte-

project' clearly impacts upon the harmonising potential in European contract law yet the question of uniformity must be firmly posited in the context of wider globalising market pressures, and is answerable not solely to the internal logic of integration. Whilst the project of market building has entailed a consistent program of social and economic regulation of contractual practices at European level, and a steady infiltration of novel secondary rules into national private law systems, general private law and particularly commercial contracts have, thus far, largely evaded 'direct' Community regulation.[6] 'Direct' in so far as commercial contracts form part of the overall 'system of private law' in all European jurisdictions and are thus indirectly affected by reforms in specific sectors given the traditional commitment of private law to generality and universality. This generality has a tendency to impede differentiation as the sector specific regulation of consumer contracts, for example, puts pressure further up the 'system' provoking calls for similar rules to be applied to commercial contracts.[7] Niglia has referred to a possible contagion of 'substantiveness' that could potentially tighten the regulatory grip of Community-inspired rules. Those same rules and standards may gradually seep directly from consumer contracts into purely commercial settings as the Community institutions become ever more deeply involved in standard form contracting. The danger exists that such regula-

gration. Pollack notes that 'supranational agents are typically fuelled by a common desire for evergreater competence' and that these organisations further represent their preferences consistently vis-à-vis other actors despite the presence of internal conflicts within each organisation. The Community institutions seek such competence both for the liberalisation of the internal market and the re-imposition of social regulations from the European level, see M.A. Pollack, *The Engines of European Integration – Delegation, Agency and Agenda Setting in the EU* (Oxford University Press, 2003).

6 An exception being the Commercial Agents Directive, 86/653/EEC of December 18, 1986 on the Coordination of the Laws relating to Self Employed Commercial Agents, 1986 OJ (L382) 17. As Basedow observes, 'contract law, in the eyes of the Community, does not exist as a body of law per se, but as an instrument to attain specific goals of the EC Treaty' in J. Basedow, *The Case for a European Contract Act*, SECOLA Leuven conference on the Communication from the Commission on European Contract Law, 30 November-1 December, 2001 (Hereinafter *SECOLA, 2001*).

7 See *EU consumer law: Vehicle or Obstacle for a European Civil Code?* proceedings of the EIPA Antenna conference, Luxembourg, 15-16 July, 2002. A notable example of this form of indirect pressuring is the recent move by the Law Commission of England and Wales and the Scottish Law Commission to consider a uniform system on unfair terms, applicable both to busines to consumer (b2c) and commercial (b2b) contracts. See *Unfair Terms in Contracts*, A Joint Consultation Paper of the Law Commission (Discussion Paper Number 166) and Scottish Law Commission (No199). Both Law Commissions have ultimately proposed the retention of two distinct regimes but suggested a number of potential reforms aimed at improving legal certainty. In calling for the establishment of a European Private Law Association, the author has consistently argued that this type of collaborative research between European Law Societies may serve as a more effective and legitimate means of ensuring greater coherence and uniformity of approach across Member States. See M.J. Doris, 'The Continued Resonance and Challenge of the Ius Commune for Modern European Contract Law' (2006) 34(2) Int'l J of Leg Info 391, and discussed further below.

tory 'interference' could ultimately 'decouple' contract law from its 'traditional formalist imprint'.[8]

To date, whilst the Community has limited itself to business-to-consumer contracts, the specificity of Community legislation has required national private law adjustments. As Collins observes, these new EC rules must be 'domesticated', or transformed into adequate concrete rules for the regulatory traditions and private law systems of each Member State. The failure to adequately implement European regulation at national level typically requires domestic courts to strive to achieve harmonisation through the manipulation of all sources of national law, including private law. As a consequence 'private law reasoning has to be adjusted as far as is possible to achieve harmonisation with European regulatory goals'. Collins terms this phenomenon the 'productive disintegration of private law'. The disintegrative effects of Community legislation are thus a primary motivation behind the drafting of model rules and framework codes yet, somewhat perversely, as Ladeur observes, these very soft law initiatives aimed at inspiring greater system and coherence in national laws become part of a legal practice – alongside private standard-setting in professional networks – that merely serve to further undermine the original homogeneity of national legal systems.[9] The importation of US styled 'Restatement' techniques and a growth in international soft law, far from a panacea, further weakens the authority of national laws which are forced to compete in an ever wider market for international dispute resolution.[10] As such, tradition-based national contract

[8] L. Niglia, *The Fall, 2004*, at 209.

[9] K. Ladeur, K., 'Methodology and European Law' in *The Harmonisation of European Private Law, supra* Introduction fn. 6, at 95, who identifies an 'explosion des savoirs particuliers' citing Guéhenno, J. (L'avenir de la liberté, 1990). Van Gerven refers to the 'bright side' (convergence between Member States laws in certain limited areas) and the 'dark side' (disruption, within each Member State, of areas of the law which were previously united) of Community intervention. Yet, despite consistent reference to 'legal islands' created by Community law we must not overstate the assumed calculability of national systems, which equally display inherent inconsistencies that arise independently of 'external' influence. As Joerges puts it, "a multiplicity of state and non-state actors are required to operate at differing levels of the 'legal system', according to divergent norms, processes and legal (sub) cultures". See C. Joerges, 'Who Would be the Author of a Common European Private Law?' in C. Schmid & M.J. Doris, *European Tenancy Law and Procedure*, Electronic Publications of the European University Institute, Florence, 2005.

[10] Faith in the practical value of soft law, and in particular the promotion of US-styled Restatements, is largely premised upon the achievements made hitherto by the International Institute for the Unification of Private Law (Unidroit) in Rome which has presented *The Principles of International Commercial Contracts* [PICC] 1994 and the European Commission on Contract Law or Lando Commission. The Lando Commission was established in 1980 under the chairmanship of Professor Ole Lando and to date has published Parts I-III of *The Principles of European Contract Law*. Additional details regarding the work of this non-governmental body of academics and contract law specialists and a bibliography of relevant material is currently accessible at: http://www.cbs.dk/departments/law/staff/ol/commission_on_ecl/ It has been argued that with the successful elaboration and publication of the PECL, the Lando

rules and doctrinal approaches are being increasingly challenged by an emerging body of Community rules in search of tradition.

Whilst preparation of the Common Frame of Reference has recently stymied debate on the supposed need for a comprehensive codification of European private laws – a debate that regrettably lies merely dormant, the previous clamour for codification during the Commission's consultation process has had a detrimental impact upon the Commission's ongoing coherence strategy. As noted the ideal form (codified, Restatement-ed, Convention based, etc), scope (applicable to all EU contracts, solely applicable to cross border contracts, applicable to b2c contracts only) and content (mandatory rules, default rules) of European contract rules have inspired a wealth of commentary. This dominant trend in the academic debate has largely served to deflect attention away from the need for robust empirical evidence of actual problems caused in the internal market by existing private law diversity. The quest for common principles has further downplayed the ability of sound contract drafting to circumvent many of the arguably 'academic' or theoretical problems caused by divergence in practice.

Intriguingly, as opposed to empirical enquiry and/or law and economics research, comparative law has emerged as the method of choice for the development of the CFR. Indeed, a primary advocate of the lex mercatoria, Klaus Peter Berger has previously suggested that comparative law provides the most suitable means for legitimately advancing the harmonisation effort.[11] This

Commission has largely concluded "a private codification [of the law of contract] without too much difficulty. See Castronovo, C., *Contract & The Idea of Codification in The Principles of European Contract Law*, in Festskrift til Ole Lando (Copenhagen, 1997) 109-124, at 109. For a detailed overview of the role of the PICC, see M.J. Bonell, *An International Restatement of Contract Law* (Kluwer Law International, 1997). For Hartkamp, "... the achievements of the groups are highly remarkable. For the first time it has proved possible for scholars originating from civil and common law systems and – in the case of the Unidroit Principles – from the different economic and political systems of the world, to reach consensus on a broad range of issues in general contract law. New uniform rules have been worked out on topics which traditionally have divided legal systems, such as the principle of good faith and fair dealing, etc. The outcome suggests that an international unification of Principles of contract law is not as unrealistic a project as many have considered it to be until now. At least it is clear now that if the undertaking were left to legal scholars (as opposed to politicians), such a unification would be possible", in A. Hartkamp, *Perspectives forthe Development of a European Civil Law*. The article is currently accessible via the official homepage of the Lando Commission. Crucially, however, as we will discuss presently, this ringing endorsement of private-law making initiatives in European academic circles can be sharply contrasted with heavy criticism in the US of the 'Restatement' technique and a move away from Federal law-making towards state and local government – a debate that has thus far largely failed to register in European academic comment. See also M.J. Doris, *Academic Misadventure or Model for Future European Governance – The Commission's CFR for a More Coherent EC Contract Law*, paper delivered at the Annual Society of Legal Scholars conference, Keele University, September 4-6, 2008.

11 K.P. Berger, 'Harmonisation of European Contract Law: The Influence of Comparative Law' (2001) 50 ICLQ 877. For Schulze, 'the doctrine of private law is today faced with the question of whether the reduced regulatory power of the legislature in the pluralism of fragmented and pluralistic private law

view is shared by the primary study groups involved in the preparation of the Common Frame. The Study Group on a European Civil Code and its precursor the Lando Commission, for instance, have consistently argued that only 'dispassionate comparative law research'[12] has the potential to reveal key points of divergence and convergence across national legal systems. Such noble claims for comparative law have however been somewhat overshadowed by those very research groups pioneering the harmonisation effort and leading the Commission's research strategy. The presumption that detached, neutral rules based on 'best solutions' can be unearthed, documented and transplanted uniformly into national legal systems does reveal a certain *naïveté* in relation to the resistance of prevailing national legal and business cultures, enduring procedural law differences, and of course the previous failure of legal transplants. If not a betrayal of comparative law, the *modus operandi* of the primary systematisers involved in drafting uniform rules and framework codes does bend and distort the traditional role of comparative law. Above all, by emphasising rule-comparison the CFR strategy similarly lacks sensitivity to broader social, economic and cultural influences that provoke divergence. In examining and comparing legal rules, these pioneers of abstraction or 'better solution comparatists'[13] have tended to reinforce and promote 'common' rules operated by the majority of legal systems, whilst isolating legal differences that fail to conform to an emerging uniform, harmonised picture.[14] It has previously been suggested that uniform conventions are:

> inevitably and confessedly drafted as multi-cultural compromises between different schemes of law. Consequently, they will normally have less merit than most of

can partly be compensated by extra-legislative legal elaboration and harmonisation' in *A Century of the Bürgerliches gesetzbuch: German Legal Uniformity and European Private Law* (1999) Colum J Eur L 461. Yet, no individual Member State is considered to be in a position to present its legal system as a basic template on which to found a European contract law. Such an approach, it is suggested, would neglect to make full use of existing European expertise in legal scholarship and would 'offend against the principle that [private law rules] should be formulated from a genuinely European perspective rather than from a national and therefore partial standpoint'. See O. Lando and C. von Bar, 'Communication on Contract Law: Joint Response of the Commission on European Contract Law and the Study Group on a European Civil Code, dated 25 October 2001 and reprinted in Schulte-Nölke, R. Schulze & L. Bernardeau, *European Community Contract Law* (Schriftenreihe der Europäischen Rechtsakademie, 2002) at Chapter X, (Hereinafter *Joint Response*) at paragraphs 62-63, and Chapter X, Summary of Conclusions and Recommendations, No. 14.

12 It is therefore something of a surprise that Von Bar, the founder of the SGECC, has recently argued that comparative law techniques are unnecessary for the development of European private law and can be left to 'the notes'. See Von Bar, 'Comparative Law of Obligations: Methodology and Epistemology' in Van Hoecke, M., *Epistemology and Methodology of Comparative Law* (Hart Law, 2004).

13 J. Hill, Comparative Law, Law Reform and Legal Theory (1999) 9 Oxford J Legal S 101.

14 The absence of the common law doctrine of consideration in previous framework codes and principles is one such example.

> the individual legal systems from which they have been derived ... they lack coherence and consistency and create problems regarding their scope. They introduce uncertainty where no uncertainty existed before. They probably deprive the law of those features which enable it to be an effective tool for the use of international commerce.[15]

The fear must remain that the CFR will display many of the same characteristics. Indeed, the uniformity goal in EC contract law has typically required the Lando Commission to distinguish or jettison awkward or uncompromising national rules, without adequate examination of either the validity of maintaining a private international law approach, the specific national function of the rule and/or the wider economic advantages of continued divergence. In turn, those areas of private law that display particularly distinctive socio-political characteristics across jurisdictions have consequently been ignored or avoided by modern systematisers.[16] In addition, a significant problem for the drafters of the CFR relates to scope of the project itself. Whilst the primary academic contributors were correct to highlight the interaction of contract law with tort and property law, the Commission ultimately opted, on the grounds of cost and feasibility, to limit the CFR to matters of contract law.[17] It will be interesting to assess how this rather artificial approach to European private law has been addressed during the preparation of the CFR. Importantly, Constantinesco affirms that each legal system displays core legal components, or *partículas jurídicas elementales*, comprising general rules, principles, concepts, etc but that a legal system is much more than the sum of its parts and comparatists regularly err in not ascertaining the positioning of specific elements within the overall legal system.[18] De la Sierra further highlights the difficulty, not only in unearthing the common core elements of national legal systems, but in judging what weight to attach to such features.[19] Rule-fixation evidently neglects these wider political and socio-economic dimensions in private law. Market building through harmonisation implies only the need for common rules and makes no assumption as to the quality of the common rule nor its resultant impact upon the general apparatus of national private law systems. However, in practice, as Kennedy has routinely highlighted, political choices regarding required stan-

---

15 J. Hobhouse, 'International Conventions and Commercial Law: In pursuit of Uniformity' (1990) 106 LQR 530. Similar reservations are expressed in H. MacQueen & R. Zimmermann (eds), European Contract Law – Scots and South African Perspectives (Edinburgh University Press, 2006) (Reviewed by M.J. Doris (2007) 32 Eur L Rev 606).

16 For example, despite their real significance for European citizens, the heavy politicisation of tenancy contracts and their strong socio-economic dimensions has forced their exclusion from the remit of the CFR strategy.

17 This study has since been published, see C. von Bar & U. Drobnig (eds), *The Interaction of Contract Law and Tort and Property in Europe* (Sellier, 2004).

18 J.L. Constantinesco, Traité de droit comparé (Economica, 1972), at 213.

19 S. de la Sierra, *Una Metodología para el Derecho comparado europeo* (Cuadernos civitas, 2004).

dards of consumer protection, for example, have a significant impact across the entire system of private law.[20] As we must await the content of the finalised Common Frame let us turn then to consider more concretely the background to calls for greater uniformity in EC contract law and the Commission's initial tripartite strategy and its recent modification.[21]

2 The privatisation of private law and the expansion of transnational dispute resolution – What need for a common European contract law?

As noted at the outset, adherents to the cause of a common European contract law have consistently reinforced the need to cement the internal market with a body of uniform rules. Assumed prohibitive transaction costs arising out of existing legal diversities can, it is argued, only be effectively eradicated by a coherent corpus of agreed general principles. Such an initiative would, it is suggested, secure tremendous positive advantages for Community trade and competitiveness by promoting greater legal certainty for contracting parties operating between Member States, by significantly reducing costly and time-consuming legal disputes and, in particular, by eradicating problems arising through reliance on private international law rules.[22] Such an initiative may

---

[20] See, *inter alia*, D. Kennedy, 'The Political Stakes in Merely Technical Issues of Contract Law (2001) 1 ERPL 7.

[21] The Commission's first 'Annual Progress Report' on the CFR and Acquis Review (2005) COM 456 final, reveals that an eclectic mix of legal categories, concepts and fields have been considered by the CFR drafters to date; including the functions of contracts generally, the notion of the 'consumer' and the 'professional', in addition to specific franchise, agency and distribution contracts, services contracts, personal security rights, benevolent intervention and unjust enrichment, see para. 2.2.2. The Progress Report also highlights the extent to which an 'appropriate differentiation' between B2B and B2C contracts is considered 'paramount'. Again, rather cryptically, the Commission has 'invited the researchers to consider [this differentiation] when preparing future of revised drafts', see para.2.6.

[22] The economic rational underpinning the cause of a common European contract law has been consistently developed and repeated by those leading academic research groups involved in the design of the Common Frame of Reference. Members of the Study Group on a European Civil Code have been among the most vociferous. The Study Group was established in 1999, having evolved from the Lando Commission. This body of 'systematisers' favours utilising the Lando Principles, and other model rules, as a point of departure for a European Civil Code. The European Commission has entrusted this group, among other study groups, with developing the academic backbone of the Common Frame of Reference. More details regarding the ongoing work of the Study Group are available at: http://www.sgeec.net The *Joint Response* to the Commission's 2003 Action Plan provides a non-exhaustive examination of the primary obstacles to the full exploitation of the internal market resulting from a continued divergence in the contract laws of EU Member States: see Chapter II, paragraphs 11-28. See also O. Lando, 'Some Features of the Law of Contract in the Third Millenium' (2000) 40 Scandinavian Studies in Law 343.

it is argued further, ultimately, pave the way for the advancement of a coherent, transnational global code.[23]

Divergent national contract laws, in contrast, it is argued, give rise, 'in all sectors of business activity' to a need to determine foreign substantive and procedural law rules, which merely serves to increase costs for the economy, for business and for consumers. It is noted that often a business is unable to exploit the Community market to the full because it cannot pursue a uniform strategy for its sales or services, and that less economically dominant Member States and SMEs are those most adversely affected by the current legal landscape. The primary proponents of harmonised contract laws have consistently argued that business encounters 'significant obstacles to the effective exploitation of the internal market in all phases of trade, whether planning economic activities, negotiating and concluding contracts, performing obligations, or ... seeking legal redress' and that these elevated transaction costs 'can only be effectively eliminated by a harmonisation of the systems of private law in Europe, even if such harmonisation involves costs of its own'.[24]

This formalist argument has triumphed within the Community institutions, particularly the Commission. Whilst studies in behavioural law and economics, allied to a more nuanced analysis of commercial and consumer activity in the internal market, reveals strong support for a combined strategy of targeted 'top-down' and 'bottom-up' harmonisation approaches, the Community has opted for an academic-backed strategy that arguably overlaps best with the technical design of future Community law-making.[25] The Commission, moreover, appears

23 See the work of M.J. Bonell, 'Do we need a global commercial code?' (2001) 106(1) Dickinson Law Review 87 and O. Lando, 'The European Principles in an Integrated World' (2005) 1(1) European Review of Contract Law 3 (suggesting that the PECL can form the backbone of a future global code for business transactions). In its response to the 2001 Communication, the Department of Policy and Business Practices of the International Chamber of Commerce in Paris similarly endorsed comprehensive harmonisation and considers the PECL an excellent starting point for such an initiative. Somewhat surprisingly the *Report of the Committee of Legal Affairs and the Internal Market of the European Parliament* further suggested that the existence of a body of uniform contract rules applicable throughout the EU would provide the Community with a competitive advantage vis-à-vis the United States, see 'Explanatory Statement', No.4., Final A5-0384/2001, 06.11.2001.

24 See *Joint Response*, 'Obstacles to the exploitation of the Internal market created by diversity in contract law in the Member States, at 11-28.

25 See, for instance, H. Kerkmeester, 'Uniformity of European Contract Law – An Economic Study Between Logic and Fact' in J. Smits (ed.) *The Need for a European Contract Law – Empirical and Legal Perspectives* (Europa Law Publishing, 2005). Code-making and the isolation of common rules and principles has a natural appeal to legislatures and bureaucratic institutions which typically display a diminished interest in traditionally *academic* peculiarities. Much to the chagrin of many in the Trento based Common Core group, for example, the Commission has largely overlooked their insistence upon the need for 'legal cartography' research aimed at pinpointing points of divergence and convergence without any underlining political agenda. Yet, as Nottage noted in 2001, the most rational strategy must involve parallel research on both common rules and 'underlying context'. See L. Nottage, 'Convergence,

to be operating from the potentially misguided premise that the supply of a new EC contract law will provide the demand for this product from European business, commercial arbitrators, national judges, the Community institutions and other users. Indeed, occasional references by the Commission to the possible role of the CFR in arbitration is further revealing as the contract law *acquis* is overwhelmingly consumer law and, according to Dezalay and Garth, for decades the Commission has looked askance at those primary sites of arbitration involved in the resolution of international business disputes.[26] The references do imply a pursuit for greater competence and influence both in terms of shaping and/or ultimately regulating arbitration and/or business contracts.

Importantly, an evaluation of modern commercial contract claims reveals that business parties typically aim to avoid the traditional court infrastructure in favour of primary sites of international commercial arbitration. National courts inability to adequately protect reasonable business expectation, costs and delays in attaining judicial redress, allied to what Collins terms a 'virus of formalism' – a phenomenon that arguably afflicts both common and civil law systems – have added to the attractiveness of alternative forms of dispute resolution. It is widely perceived that commercial arbitrators have better facilitated commercial actors operating across jurisdictions by providing a greater degree of predictability and legal certainty and estimates suggest approximately 85 percent of all European commercial contracts are submitted to arbitration. Such findings are clearly of direct relevance to the harmonisation debate as they weaken the argument of other leading contributors who have discussed the need for a specialised division of the European Court of Justice to be created in order to handle a growth in private law litigation.[27] There is surely a certain contradiction in promoting, on the one hand, the cause of uniform rules in the interests of reducing complexity and the likelihood of litigation and simultaneously advocating a restructuring of the European court structure to handle a potential growth in caselaw. Yet the case for specialised divisions is further embarrassed by the timidity of the European Court in the recent case of *Freiburger Kommunalbauten*.[28] The judgment can be seen as a missed opportunity to develop the law of contract autonomously

Divergence and the Middle Way in Unifying or Harmonising Private Law' (2001) EUI WP 01, and X. Blanc-Jouvan, 'Reflections on the Common Core of European Private Law Project' (2001) (1)2 Global J F.

26 See Y. Dezalay & B.G. Garth, *Dealing with Virtue – International Commercial Arbitration and the Construction of a Transnational Legal Order* (University of Chicago Press, 1996). Importantly, both authors note that, '... international commercial arbitration can be transformed or even replaced because it forms part of a larger international *market* for commercial or business dispute resolution, a market which is inevitably unstable', at 298.

27 See, in particular, O. Lando, 'The Future Development of the Principles of European Contract Law and a European Civil Code' in ERA-Forum Special Issue, 2002.

28 *Freiburger Kommunalbauten gmbh Baugessellschaft & Co. KG v. Hofstetter* [2004] ECR I-3403. The Court stressed that it could not provide an autonomous meaning of 'unfairness' under the Unfair Terms Directive 93/13/EEC, delegating the question to national courts. Whilst the ruling may be supported on the grounds of subsidiarity, this non-interventionist ECJ approach significantly weakens Lando's case

at Community level, since the ECJ determined that its role was merely to make 'general interpretative decisions' with the aim of defining the concept of unfair terms. Decisively, it was argued, 'only the national court could carry out the required level of investigation into a particular term'. This ambiguous approach to its own interpretative power is far from inspiring and the effective abdication of responsibility by the Court for the development of a uniform interpretation of unfairness under the Unfair Terms Directive would appear to be based on pure policy grounds – in particular a desire to limit the caseload appearing before the court itself. Van Gerven has rightly questioned the ability of the European Court of Justice to successfully develop generalised EC contract or consumer contract laws through consistent precedent. For Gerven that would mean, that the Court when asked to interpret a specific directive provision, would be prepared to situate its ruling in a broader perspective of consumer contract law as a whole'. Gerven cites the ruling in *Océano Group*[29] where the court similarly failed to provide adequate clarification on when national courts could declare unfair terms in consumer contracts non-binding.[30]

Of course, the view that an increased privatisation of contract law, and the building up of alternative a-centric governance arrangements weakens the case for a uniform EC law in the interest of business actors is not supported by a recent Clifford Chance/Grace Church Consulting survey of 175 European firms across a spread of industries.[31] Divergence was largely perceived to be a "cost problem" and 83.4% (88.2% SMEs) were 'favourably' or 'very favourably' disposed to the concept of a harmonised European contract law. Whilst in domestic markets, business actors appear more inclined to rely on agreed trade practices and social norms generated within a specific industry, as opposed to the generalised principles of national private law systems or international instruments, the lack of homogeneous business practice and standards across Europe, allied to psychological obstacles, such as cultural and linguistic differences, reveals strong business support for uniform contract laws.[32] The study

---

for building ip the central European court infrastructure in order to handle an increased contract law-related caseload.

29 Joined cases C-240/98 to C-244/98 *Océano Grupo Editorial SA v. Rocío Murciano et al* [2000] ECR I-4941. That said, as was reinforced in *Faccini Dori*, the European courts are Treaty-bound to respect the 'latitude' granted to Member States in respect of levels of consumer protection, and the *Océano* decision is arguably best understood as a reinforcement of that position. See Case C-91/92 *Paolo Faccini Dori v. Recreb Srl* [1994] ECR I-3325, at 17.

30 W. van Gerven, 'The ECJ Case-law as a Means of Unification of Private Law' in *Towards, 2004*, at 122-3.

31 2005 Clifford Chance/Grace Church Consulting Survey on European Contract Law, presented by S. Popham at Oxford conference, *supra*, March 18, 2005. The study, now published in S. Vogenauer & S. Weatherill, Harmonisation of European Contract Law (Hart, 2006) is revealing of business support for harmonised EC contract laws. Regrettably for the purposes of this study, though the overall response was high, Spanish business accounted for a mere 7% of overall participants.

32 Fernando Mantilla-Serrano counsels that, 'parties who chose international arbitration as a means of dispute resolution generally did so because they perceived the process to be more informal, more

further reveals that 65.1% (67.6%) of SMEs encounter obstacles "to some extent or to a large extent" when operating cross border. Variations in legal systems were considered to be the second most significant obstacle to trade after divergent tax regimes.

Crucially, however, the study suggests that divergence in contract laws would be unlikely to act as a deal-breaker.[33] This finding is perhaps unsurprising. Certainly business operates in the shadow of the law, but rarely do commercial actors insist on their full legal entitlements or apply a legal mind to business questions. Indeed, Galanter uses the neologism *litigotiation* in reference to the fact that the majority of contract disputes do not result in full-blown trial and adjudication but rather subsequent 'negotiation and manoeuvre in the strategic pursuit of settlement through a mobilisation of the court process. Full-blown adjudication might be thought of as an infrequent alternative. Settlement is the typical outcome, as roughly half of contracts cases settle'.[34]

---

confidential, more expeditious and less expensive than litigation. This is no longer the case', in *Towards a Transnational Procedural Public Policy* [2004] 20 JIA 4, at 353. Carbonnier, the author of a leading commentary on arbitration, has highlighted a '[g]rowing dissatisfaction with arbitral adjudication in both specialised and non-specialised fields' due to a rise in cost and increasingly protracted proceedings that are disrupting litigant's business relationship. See T.E. Carbonnier, 'Arbitral Justice: The Demise of Due Process in American Law' (1996) Tul L Rev 1945. Discussion of the merits of arbitration and ADR vis-à-vis litigation in the resolution of business disputes will doubtless continue to rage. See D. Jiang-Schuerger, Perfect Arbitration = Arbitration + Litigation (1999) 4 Harv Neg L Rev 231 and M. Petsche, 'The Growing Autonomy of International Commercial Arbitration, PhD thesis of the European University Institute, 2004. Curiously, thus far, few commentators have sought to explore the various Communications on contract law against the Commission's Green Paper on alternative dispute resolution in civil and commercial law. See Green Paper of the European Commission (Justice and Home Affairs Directorate-General), COM (2002) 196 Final, 19.04.2002.

33 A series of individual comments highlighted a perceived formalism and dogmatism inherent in civil law systems: *"The common law is such a minority partner in Europe. We in the common law world would be at risk that this much more prescriptive, inflexible civil law would dominate to our detriment"*. Business expectation and speculation was further revealed: *"In fringe areas it might make a difference between whether a deal is viable or not, but it wouldn't get in the way of a lucrative deal"* and the importance of securing a good business arrangement: *"If there was a business opportunity to be had in a particular Member State, then we would pursue it in almost every case, but EU directives and legislation of a Member State is something that would need to be factored into the equation, but almost certainly it would never be a deal breaker"*, study at p. 5.

34 M. Galanter, 'Worlds of Deals: Using Negotiation to Teach about Legal Process' (1984) 34 J of Leg Ed 268. Empirical research conducted in the United States reveals contract litigation to be 'low visibility, even to legal professionals', though highly dependent on input from lawyers. See M. Galanter, *Symposium on Contracts: Contract in Court; or Almost Everything You May or May Not Want to Know About Contract Litigation* (2001) Wisc Law Rev 577, at 622. Litigation is 'overwhelmingly business' driven with a knock-on effect on the design of contract laws. Decisively, businesses are four times more likely to litigate than individuals and a small subset of enterprises – in particular large corporations – frequently resort to litigation. In total, cases involving firms and organisations accounted for 'roughly seventy six

The Clifford Chance study was commissioned independently and had no direct impact upon the decision to prepare the Commission's CFR. Indeed, it remains significant that the Commission failed to undertake any similar impact assessments nor feasibility studies prior to commencing the Common Frame research programme and has been little motivated by empirical enquiry. Of course, such surveys are not without their own wrinkles. In the US, Katz and Macaulay have repeatedly highlighted the limitations of such empirical enquiry. Macaulay in particular notes that 'business people and lawyers are busy, and they will not devote much, if any, time to answering questionnaires ... Whatever methods are used, we always will be dependent on the skill, bias, implicit theories and bias of the researcher ... Social science results ... are always suggestive at best'.[35]

3 Exploring the Community's original tripartite vision for enhanced coherence

That European private laws have until relatively recently remained in splendid isolation from the wider process of Community integration is perhaps unsurprising when one considers that the constitutional significance of private law discourse is seldom appreciated by public law communities. In turn, European private law scholars rarely forage deep into areas of public law. The absence of such an interdisciplinary dialogue is doubtless one of the primary reasons why private law specialists, in discussing the regulatory framework required for contractual relations to flourish in the new Europe, have tended to promote codification as a definitive solution. The potential negative side-effects of such a one-dimensional template for economic governance will be explored presently, yet what is detectable from the recent engagement of the Community institutions in the field of contract law is support for a new public/private sector partnership, and the potential utility of a new hybrid mix of hard and soft law legal instruments. In part the consultation process initiated by the original 2001 Green Paper and endorsed via the subsequent Communications has encouraged this newly textured argumentation.[36]

per cent of all contract cases' analysed. A similar or higher percentage is probable in an examination of English caseload. See, for example, C. Staughton, How do the Courts Interpret Commercial Contracts (1999) 58(2) CLJ 303 who notes that, 'commercial contracts are virtually the only contracts which in these days anyone can afford to litigate', at 303. It is regrettable that similar empirical inquiries were not undertaken in advance of the CFR research strategy.

35 S. Macaulay, 'Almost Everything I Did Want to Know About Contract Litigation: A Comment on Galanter' (2001) Wis L Rev 629, 634. See also A. Katz, 'On the Use of Practitioner Surveys in Commercial Law Research' (2000) 98 Mich L Rev 2760.

36 The various Communications and Action Plan are the product of deliberations between the Commission's *Inter-Services Working Group on European Contract*. The group comprises members of the Directorate General for Health and Consumer Protection (the lead DG), DG Internal Market, the Directorate

Such glimmers of a new horizon for European private law are not, however, so readily apparent from the bare text of the Action Plan nor the notably stremlined 2004 Follow-Up Communication, which instead adopts a narrowly restricted and largely value-free approach to contract law based on the need to address 'concrete and practical problems' impeding the proper functioning of the internal market.[37] The removal of technical and legal impediments to cross border trade and the improvement of existing and future legislation therefore form the frontispiece of the Commission strategy and, as a consequence, debate on wider fairness and distributive justice concerns in private law,[38] and the political and symbolic significance of unified civil legislation are largely

---

General for Justice and Home Affairs, DG Enterprise, and the Legal Service. Sensitivities across the various DG's has prompted the Commission to concentrate on the CFR. Reflection on the feasibility and suitability of a future horizontal measure is seen as dependent upon initial reform of the *acquis* and the elaboration of the CFR. This 'Russian doll' approach of arriving at an Optional Instrument via the CFR appears logical, yet in this regard the Commission is much less direct than the European Parliament, which has long advocated 'a body of comprehensive rules ... applicable to any given contract', *A More Coherent European contract law*, viewpoint of Klaus-Heiner Lehne, chair of the European Parliament's Committee on Legal Affairs and the Internal Market, The Law Societies monthly Brussels Agenda, 01.04.2004. The most notable aspect of the Action Plan is, nonetheless, a furtive attempt to do justice to such a goal and shift from sector specific interventionism to a more uniform, generalised approach to contract.

[37] 2003 Action Plan, *Identified Problem Areas*, point 3.14. Preparatory discussion and drafts of the 2004 Follow-Up Communication revealed strong disagreement within the Inter-Services Working Group on the parameters of the CFR. DG Internal Market expressed its deep reservations as to the utility of a comprehensive research strategy and the drafting of general principles and model rules. It stressed the principle of contractual freedom and argued the case for targetted regulation to overcome specific, identified problems as opposed to an holistic, generalised approach. This problem-solving strategy was countered by DG Health and Consumer Protection which vigorously promoted the case for the CFR as constituted. This difference of opinion within the Commission – which mirrors academic discourse – allied to purely practical problems, such as translation, resulted in long delay in the release of the 2004 Communication.

[38] It barely merits repeating that soft law instruments, code-making and the building up of the *lex mercatoria* has become synonymous with business inspired and business-driven private law. Indeed, it is commonly overlooked that in initial discussions in the 1970's it was towards a European commercial code that Professor Ole Lando and members of the DG Internal Market were aiming and this idea continues to find expression in the writings of leading 'codifiers'. For many of this persuasion, as Zumbansen neatly puts it: "political problems of exclusion and freedom have allegedly been resolved by the universal spread of private autonomy" per P. Zumbansen, 'Piercing the Legal Veil: Commercial Arbitration and Transnational Law' [2002] 8(3) ELJ 400. The emergence of a transnational private law society or "privatrechtsgesellschaft" has thus far come at the expense of consumer interests and behind *softened* globalised private laws, Mattei perceives a narrow conservative political agenda subservient to business self-interest. Somewhat perversely his solution to combat 'corporate rapacity' through a surrender of the law is a 'hard' European civil code that imposes binding legal rules. For equally strong academic criticism of the technocratic agenda promoted via the CFR, see 'A Social Justice Manifesto

circumscribed.[39] In line with this reduced vision, current difficulties in European contracting may arguably be considered and confronted as mere 'interoperability' problems. Whilst national contract law systems function more or less efficiently internally, it is their punctual 'non-compatibility' with other Member States legal orders and/or EC secondary legislation that provokes a partial malfunctioning of the market and requires partial readjustment of national private law.

The 2003 Action Plan identified a range of 'interoperability' problems between national contract rules and defects in the *acquis*. Divergent national rules on the formation of contracts have been pinpointed as primary obstacles, as have differences in the interpretation of abstract legal terms, which result in higher transaction costs for economic operators, required to sound out local legal knowledge on the validity of certain contract terms. Business, it is argued, is further hampered in the widespread use of standard forms and impeded from adopting comprehensive EU wide sales and marketing techniques. One concrete example is the impossibility of offering a single EU wide insurance contract.[40] Requirements of form further diverge significantly across private law systems and grave disparities exist as to when certain contracts must be in writing, notarised and/or authenticated. In the field of consumer protection, the primary complaint both from business and academia relates to diversity in national regimes as a result of the minimum harmonisation strategy pursued to date at Community level. The Commission argues that such divergences and resultant legal complexity constitute practical obstacles or disincentives to cross-border transactions, which are liable to "... prohibit, impede or otherwise render less advantageous such transactions".[41] Intrinsic inconsistencies within the EC legislation in the fields of contract law have further been pinpointed and problems that result from the use of abstract legal terms in directives, with terms either not defined or too broadly defined.[42]

The Action Plan built upon the scaffold provided by the earlier 2001 Communication, which included a non-exhaustive list of four possible solutions,

---

for European Contract Law' (2004) 10(6) ELJ 653, and E.S. Cohen, 'Allocating Power and Wealth in the Global Economy: The Role of Private Law and Legal Agents' (2002) CSGR Working Paper, 101/02.

39 The decision to ratify a European civil code evidently has strong political dimensions – see M.W. Hesselink, 'The Politics of European Contract Law' (2002) 2(1) Global J F; see also T. Wilhelmsson, The Legal, the Cultural and the Political – Conclusions from Different Perspectives on Harmonisation of European Contract Law (2002) EBLR 541. In order to quell opposition to the idea of codification, Schmid suggests that the Commission has adopted the euphemistic term 'Optional Instrument' see C. Schmid & M.J. Doris, *European Tenancy Law and Procedure, supra* fn. 9.

40 2003 Action Plan, p. 14, pt. 48. This author recognises the important work of the Project Group on European Insurance Contract Law and has previously highlighted the important role of the Group in influencing the potential reform of UK insurance rules, see M.J. Doris, 'A European Insurance Market and EC Contract Law – Is There Life For One Without The Other?' (2007) ECL 1.

41 2003 Action Plan, § 3.2.26

42 2003 Action Plan, § 3.1, para. 16, 17 in fine.

including: 1. a market solution to divergence; 2. the promotion of non-binding common contract law principles, which would be useful in promoting an increased convergence of national laws; 3. the re-examination, simplification and improvement of existing EC legislation; and/or 4. the adoption of entirely new measures at the EC level.[43] A market solution has been ruled out on the grounds that it cannot eradicate problematic inconsistencies in national law. Moreover, an analysis of the myriad responses to the Commission's original 2001 Communication revealed an overwhelming endorsement for improvements to be made to the *acquis* and for continued work on common principles. As the preferred immediate solution to problems resulting from continued divergences in national contract laws this thinking was transplanted directly into the 2003 Action Plan and Options II and III became the central pillars of the Commission's coherence strategy.[44]

Faced with such a broad range of conflicting opinion and an internal competence conundrum, the Commission adopted a deliberately cautious approach, stressing the need to continue on the basis of a mix of 'regulatory and non-regulatory initiatives', whilst allowing for improvements to the existing *acquis.*[45] This conservative approach to European private law is well entrenched and can be viewed as "the legal expression of fundamental tensions in the Community's wider economic and political evolution" yet the changing nature of EU governance and, in particular, a marked shift away from the goal of facilitating economic expansion through trade liberalisation, with its concomitant ideal of a uniform legal regime, to the securing of additional competences to advance the

---

[43] *Ibid.* Though the documents'' emphasis rests on persuasion and encouragement, the original options articulated by the Commission were rejected as non-options by Reich, who condemned the 'methodological naïveté' of the Commission in proposing as options what in reality are EU obligations and/or initiatives that are beyond competence of the Community, see N. Reich, *Some Critical Comments,* position paper presented at SECOLA conference, 2001, pp. 1-7. For further criticism of the Communication's stipulated options and original premise, see H. Collins, 'Transaction Costs and Subsidiarity in European Contract Law' in S. Grundmann & J. Stuykk, *Academic Green Paper on European Contract Law* (Aspen, 2002).

[44] The critical need to re-structure and simplify the *acquis* and remove problematic inconsistencies has been accepted in full by the Commission, however, Auke Haagsma at DG Internal Market has been one of the few internal voices who has consistently warned that the creation of new rules at Community level should not become a mere *academic* project. He has regularly emphasised divergent legal and economic cultures across Member States and has been critical of inflexible, formalistic law-making initiatives in Community contract law. Citing the landmark study by Geert Hofstede in the 1960's which examined national cultures and their effects on organisations – *Culture's Consequences : International Differences in Work-related Values* (Sage Publications, 1980), which was further developed in Hofstede's *Cultures and organizations : Intercultural Cooperation and its Importance for survival – Software of the mind* (McGraw-Hill, 1991) – he questions the logic of blanket, uniform rules and suggests that the Treaties provide for the adoption of flexible solutions and a range of regulatory techniques, see A. Haagsma, 'The EU Citizen between Market and State [2003] 5 Web JCLI.

[45] 2003 Action Plan, § 4, p. 14 *et seq.*

social welfare of European citizens has created a 'fundamental indeterminacy' in the programme of economic integration, further complicating the quest for coherence.[46]

3.1 The Institutionalisation of a self-styled private law network industry

In the opinion of the Commission, coherence in EC private law and the groundwork for a possible horizontal instrument will require sustained comparative law research on common rules and agreed terminology. The decision to finance research on the content of the CFR under the Sixth Framework Programme for Research and Technological Development did meet a degree of resistance from the Directorate General for the Internal Market within the Inter-Services working group, particularly in relation to the methodology to be employed and scope of the CFR itself.[47] Whilst it is now envisaged that the Common Frame of Reference will ultimately serve as a 'toolkit' for Community and national legislators when drafting legislation, initial discussions within the Commission's Inter-Services Working Group became protracted and difficult due to the concerns of DG Internal market that stakeholder participation would falter, and that as such the CFR would become a grossly academic venture. The slimlining of the 2004 Follow Up in part reflects the lack of consensus reached within the Working Group itself and the extent to which DG Internal market in particular sought to reduce the parameters of both the CFR and the European Contract Law initiative itself. Returning to the text of the 2004 Communication, it is suggested that the CFR will inform Community lawmakers in the preparation of future sectoral measures and may potentially aid arbitrators and private parties in negotiating agreements and settling disputes. Community courts will further be assisted by the CFR when interpreting and gap-filling legislative texts. The CFR may similarly be used ultimately in contracts involving the Community institutions. The working hypothesis of the Commission is that such a Common Frame of Reference should represent a body of general principles that

[46] See M. Dougan, 'Minimum Harmonisation and the Internal Market' (2000) 37 CML Rev 853, at 856-859. As Dougan stresses, 'It is clear that the Community no longer dances to the tune of the internal market alone ... the shifting policy goals of the Community have required a willingness to accept a greater degree of legal diversity'. See also C. Joerges, 'The Impact of European Integration on Private Law: Reductionist Perceptions, True Conflicts and a New Constitutional Perspective' (1997) 3(4) ELJ 378.

[47] The primary *pioneers of abstraction* spearheading the academic dimension of the CFR are drawn from within the self-styled CoPECL-Network of Excellence. This network, now termed the CFR-Net, includes in particular the Study Group on a European Civil Code and the Acquis group. See the Commission's website, *supra* Introduction fn. 2, for a full list of participants. The Acquis Group is equally dedicated to a 'principled' approach to European Private Law, yet takes as its primary point of departure the existing Community private law *acquis*. For further details of the group and its working methods see the Group's homepage at: www.acquis-group.org.

underpin modern contracts, such as the principle of freedom of contract and the right of withdrawal. It should further provide a lexicon covering abstract legal terms, such as 'damage' and 'force majeure', which given their open texture can mean very different things in the various EU jurisdictions. It may further cover specific model rules on the formation, performance and conclusion of contracts. The development of the CFR is seen as dependent upon input from contract law specialists from across the EU. Though it is evidently vital to ensure that any agreed rules and definitions represent best solutions and that no one jurisdiction or legal tradition is able to monopolise the content of the CFR, this Eurocentric focus is unsustainable, particularly given recent US experience in uniform private law-making.[48]

Equally critical to the shaping of the CFR are the Community institutions, the Member States, and judicial opinion. The broad target of addressees that may potentially be affected only serves to highlight the critical importance of stakeholder involvement. In order to gain much needed legitimacy for the CFR it is considered essential that such a far-reaching document is structured with input from relevant parties who must ensure the practical utility of the Common Frame and guard against it becoming little more than an academic misadventure. The promotion of the CFR ought to be viewed in conjunction with the Commission's Consumer Policy Strategy 2002-2006, which emphasises the need for greater convergence in EU consumer law. Two stages are foreseen as necessary for the approval of the CFR, firstly a definitive report will be prepared and presented by the contracted consortium of researchers, which will encompass the progressive input of stakeholders. It is estimated that the research groups should complete the principles and subsequent comments and annotations by late 2008/early 2009. This work will thereafter be 'road tested' and, on the basis of a feasibility study, the Commission plans to draft a final non-binding evaluative text on the merits of the CFR. The Action Plan had implied that a future 'common frame of reference' would assume a binding role upon national Member States and prevail over existing contract rules as the declared goal of the CFR is to facilitate the convergence of national laws behind common rules. The Commission has since reinforced that the intention for the CFR is that it will be a non-binding, soft law instrument.[49] This policy should, however, be viewed in conjunction with the Commission's Consumer Policy Strategy 2002-

[48] M.J. Doris, 'Bargaining and Reliance in New European Contract Law' (2007) 3 InDret 1. Currently accessibile at http://www.indret.com/pdf/460_en.pdf. This article examines in a shortened form many of the primary controversies explored in detail in this study.

[49] 'Non-paper of the Commission's Inter-Services', *supra* Introduction fn. 12. The 2004 Follow Up to the Action Plan outlines that the CFR 'could be used by national legislators when transposing EU directives in the area of contract law into national legislation and when enacting legislation on areas of contract law which are not regulated at Community level. The European Parliament suggests that the CFR could be used in arbitration. And that 'arbitrators entrusted with the interpretation of contracts or the decision on legal problems not foreseen in existing contracts would have the possibility to refer to the CFR to find unbiased and balanced solutions to resolve conflicts arising between contractual parties'.

2006,[50] which emphasised the need for greater convergence in EU consumer law and articulated a willingness to shift from minimum to maximum harmonisation. Indeed, differences between national laws of implementation as a result of minimum harmonisation in consumer protection will continue to be assessed in order to better understand and ultimately eliminate internal market barriers and distortions of competition for business and consumers alike.[51] The suitability and appropriateness of current precontractual information requirements are similarly being addressed.[52]

3.2 Private law production and the drafting of a 'Common Frame of Reference'

How will the process of compiling the common frame of reference develop? What form will this proposed new instrument take? It has been suggested that the CFR will emerge as a set of definitions and/or a compendium of black-letter rules with commentaries similar to existing soft law principles. The Commission's CFR strategy has commenced despite the absence of any significant feasibility studies and surprisingly little comment has been passed upon the legitimacy of the working methods of those "private legislatures" or research think tanks currently engaged in its drafting. Whilst academia has

50 For a critical appraisal of the Consumer Policy Strategy 2002-2006, see J. Dickie, 'The European Commission's Consumer Policy Strategy 2002-2006: A Critique' (2003) Web Journal of Current Legal Issues, who suggests that the Commission over-reaches itself in pressing for maximum harmonisation and passes over other areas of concern in need of more urgent attention. The case for maximum harmonisation is viewed as 'inherently weak' and 'entirely unworkable at least until existing problems with Community consumer law are resolved, particularly in the current context of geographic expansion'. This article is currently accessible at: http://webjcli.ncl.ac.uk/2003/issue3/dickie3.html

51 The eight directives first scrutinised under the acquis review were: Directive 85/577/EEC of 20.12.1985 to protect the consumer in respect of contracts negotiated away from business premises (OJ L 372 of 31.12.1985; Directive 90/314/EEC of 13.06.1990 on package travel, package holidays and package tours (OJ L 158 of 23.06.1990; Directive 93/13/EEC of 05.04.1993 on unfair terms in consumer contracts (OJ L 95 of 21.04.1993; Directive 94/47/EC of 26.10.1994 on the protection of purchasers in respect of certain aspects of contracts relating to the purchase of the right to use immovable properties on a time-share basis (OJ L 280 of 29.10.1994; Directive 97/7/EC of 20.05.97 on the protection of consumers in respect of distance contracts (JO L 144 of 04.06.1997; Directive 98/6/EC of 16.02.1998 on consumer protection in the indication of the prices of products offered to consumers (OJ L 80 of 18.03.1998; Directive 98/27/EC of 19.05.1998 on injunctions for the protection of consumer's interests (OJ L 166 of 11.06.1998); Directive 1999/44/EC of 25 May 1999 on certain aspects of the sale of consumer goods and associated guarantees (OJ L 171 of 07.07.1999). The directives on misleading and comparative advertising, consumer credit and distance marketing of financial services were not included, as these were either newly introduced or were being amended. For a recent analysis of the 2004 Review see C. Poncibò, 'The Challenges of EC Consumer Law' (2007) MWP 24, who suggests that the Commission's activity is leading in the direction of a 'horizontal instrument' of Principles of EC consumer law, at p. 9.

52 See 'Annex 1 – Possible Structure of the CFR', 2004 Follow Up Communication.

been heavily critical of the Community legislator's role in private law, virtually no empirical studies exist to examine the choices made by private law-making groups, such as the Lando Commission or Unidroit in the framing of European contract law. In a previous assessment of the working methods of the American Law Institute (ALI) and the National Conference of Commissioners on Uniform State Laws (NCCUSL),[53] Alan Schwartz and Robert Scott[54] have argued that such private law-making institutions reveal:

a) a strong bias towards preserving the status quo and rejecting significant reforms;
b) frequently produce highly abstract rules that delegate substantial discretion to courts; and
c) produce clear, bright line rules that confine judicial discretion commonly when and because dominant interest groups influence the process. These bright line rules ordinarily advance the particular agenda of these interest groups.

In Scott's eyes, the experiment with uniform codification of contract law has performed poorly in terms of the substantive objectives of a uniform law? The state's primary role in uniformly enforcing commercial contracts is to regulate

[53] Established in 1923, the ALI is a private lawmaking body comprised of high-profile lawyers and judges involved in the harmonisation of US commercial laws. Both ALI and NCCSL members are typically prestigious and successful professors or practitioners. In the view of Schwartz, both bodies are 'status quo orientated' and find it difficult, if not impossible to adequately evaluate the need for law reform. Their experience in the fields of law under examination in various harmonising projects is normally limited from the outset and they subsequently have limited means of recovering adequate data in order to make informed decisions. They cannot hold public hearings and cannot demand parties involvement. Whilst they may consider themselves to be law reformers, they adopt a consistently conservative stance and seek to avoid courting controversy. The NCCUSL is a similar private lawmaking organisation. It is comprised of 'commissioners' appointed by each state governor. These commissioners are typically eminent lawyers and judges. The Study Committee proposes a uniform law to the conference, and thereafter it becomes a lobbying body for the proposed reforms. During the course of the 1990's almost every article of the UCC was revised, although the status of the revisions within NCCUSL and with state legislatures differs according to the article. For additional information regarding the NCCUSL revision projects see NCCUSL, Introductions & Adoptions of Uniform Acts, at http://www.nccusl.org/uniformacts.asp. Importantly, Schwartz and Scott stress that Restatements increasingly resort to 'reasonableness' and 'good faith' which merely delegates hard questions to the courts and offers little by way of legal certainty. "The UCC has very few bright line rules but rather relies heavily on 'standards' such as reasonableness and good faith ... This appearance of solving problems shifts the burden onto the courts".

[54] A. Schwartz & R.E. Scott, 'The Political Economy of Private Legislatures' (1995) 143 Uni Penn L Rev 595. Importantly, Schwartz and Scott stress that Restatements increasingly resort to 'reasonableness' and 'good faith' which merely delegates hard questions to the courts and offers little by way of legal certainty. "The UCC has very few bright line rules but rather relies heavily on 'standards' such as reasonableness and good faith ... This appearance of solving problems shifts the burden onto the courts".

incomplete contracts and Scott observes that the UCC has failed to provide for predictable interpretation. What is required from a set of contract rules is clarity, flexibility and sensible defaults. These have to cover those areas where the law permits the parties to agree on issues but where they tend not to in practice. Codes are impliedly comprehensive instruments. As organic laws that contain the principles for their own interpretation, they are required to be able to provide legal solutions from within their four corners. Yet, for Scott:

> The decision "to construct the Code in the tradition of continental codifications required the development of a *super-eminent safety valve*. The net effect of this institutional design is a highly contextualised interpretative methodology, one that seeks to embed the explicit terms of a contract within the larger jurisprudential context of the Code as well as within the specific commercial context being regulated ... The result in terms of maximising the benefits of substantive uniformity could hardly have been worse ... over time, the uniformity value of predictable interpretation has been eroded. Thus, the Code quite self-consciously has squandered whatever efficiency gains are achievable through uniform, objective methods of contract interpretation.[55]

It is widely felt that the common law approach of regular judicial decision-making and precedent provides much greater consistency and legal certainty for commercial actors. Instead, as Scott observes,

> the code methodology tends to produce a stasis that impedes the evolution and promulgation of novel default rules and contract terms ... The process of Code interpretation inevitably resists the dynamic process inherent in standardisation ... In short, the UCC has failed to produce substantive uniformity.[56]

The European legal community's inattention to the 'hermetic regulatory framework' presented by traditional code-design therefore remains unjustified. Though it would evidently be premature to prejudge their findings, we ought to remain sceptical of the academic approaches and methodologies to be employed by the competing research think tanks currently engaged in the harmonisation effort. The fear must remain that much of the doubtless high

---

[55] The *Llewelynian* project has been criticised, in particular, for encouraging the elimination of the merchant jury whilst 'retaining the pervasive notion of commercial reasonableness'. The consequence, in Scott's view was 'a drafting disaster', delegating ultimate discretion to expert bodies, not judges and lay jurors. See R.E. Scott, 'The Uniformity Norm in Commercial Law: A Comparative Analysis of Common Law and Code Methodologies' in P. Benson, *The Theory of Contract Law – New Essays* (Cambridge University Press, 2001). Slawson has been equally critical of the code methodology for weakening legal predictability and lauds the role of the common law judge in successfully reforming the law more effectively than codemaking. See W.D. Slawson, *Binding Promises – The Late 20th Century Reformation of Contract Law*, (Princeton University Press, 1996).

[56] Scott, *supra* at 166.

quality, detailed legal scholarship to be undertaken risks becoming little more than an exercise in 'legal taxidermy' if those primary research groups engaged in the search for common European principles fail to radically re-assess the nature of the uniformity project in the light of recent US experience in uniform private lawmaking.[57] As Schwartz and Scott affirm, 'the form and substance of a law are significantly endogenous to the law-creating institution. Put more simply, a legislature's output is a function both of the preferences of the legislators, whether selfish or altruistic, and of the institutional structure in which the legislators perform. As such, [the] outputs [of private lawmaking agencies] also should be endogenous to their organisational forms'.[58] These findings have important ramifications for the Commission's coherence strategy, particularly given the Community's interventionism in matters relevant to the European consumer. Above all, it is the procedures and mechanisms for drafting common contract law principles that require added assessment.

A timely warning bell for the leading *pioneers of abstraction* encouraging the drafting of general principles is further provided by recent US experience with the Uniform Computer Information Transactions Act, the product of a private

---

57 Per M. Shapiro, *supra* Introduction fn. 30.

58 *Supra* fn. 58, at 598. See also A. Schwartz, *The History of US Codification*, paper presented at the European University Institute, Florence, Spring 2003. As Gordley notes, 'Modern civil codes have two characteristics. First, they are attempts to state the basic rules of private law comprehensively and systematically. Second, they are legislative acts with an authority that is either ultimate or second only to constitutions". Because they have these two characteristics, I will argue, modern codes interfere with the work of legal scholars ... In that respect modern codes differ from pre-modern 'codes' such as the Corpus iuris civilis of Justinian or the medieval Corpus iuris canonici [containing] general maxims and a host of specifics ... In contrast, in a modern code, the authoritative starting point is a comprehensive set of rules. It looks less like raw material and more like a final product. That is the reason, I believe, why modern codes can only get in a jurist's way', J. Gordley, 'Codification and Legal Scholarship', Symposium Issue on Codification in the Twenty-First Century (1998) 31 UC Davis L Rev 735, at 735-8. For sustained critiques, from a consumer law perspective, of the NCCUSL revisions of Articles 3 and 4 UCC, see K. Patchel, 'Interest Group Politics, Federalism, and the Uniform Laws Process: Some Lessons from the Uniform Commercial Code (1993) 78 Minn L Rev 83 (discussing the manner in which uniform laws process can be affected by interest groups, and applying this thesis to UCC revisions); E.L. Rubin, 'Thinking Like a Lawyer, Acting Like a Lobbyist: Some Notes on the Process of Revising Articles 3 and 4' (1993) 26 Loy LA L Rev 743, which provides an account of the political biases of participants in the drafting process. For more general discussions of consumer issues raised in the Code revision project, see J. Braucher, 'Consumer Protection and the Uniform Commercial Code' (1997) 75 Wash U LQ 1; K. Macintosh, 'Liberty, Trade, and the Uniform Commercial Code: When Should Default Rules Be Based on Business Practices?' (1997) 38 Wm & Mary L Rev 1465 who develops a framework for determining the extent of UCC involvement in consumer issues; F. Miller, 'Realism Not Idealism in Uniform Laws—Observations from the Revision of the UCC' (1998) 39 South Texas Law Review 707 (discussing various previous revision efforts) and A. Brooke Overby, 'Modeling UCC Drafting' (1996) 29 Loy LA L Rev 645, 650-68 who provides an analysis of the relationship between consumer protection and Code revision processes.

lawmaking initiative gone wrong. Whilst the UCITA has been formally adopted in Maryland, California – though only after key modifications in favour of the consumer – and Virginia, it has prompted bomb-shelter legislation in several states and galvanised opponents in both industry and consumer associations.. Indeed, there are currently more individual States with bomb-shelter legislation blocking the Act than States that have ratified it (Iowa, North Carolina, West Virginia and Vermont, with the State of Massachussets considering following suit). A number of other US states have similarly contemplated anti-UCITA laws to stipulate that any term in a computer information agreement providing for the interpretation of the agreement in accordance with the UCITA is voidable.[59] The model State law was the product of a major lobbying drive by the Business Software Alliance (led by Microsoft) that aimed to ensure that all EULA, or End User License Agreements, would become strictly enforceable as though free negotiated between the parties (this despite the often heavily one-sided terms and conditions). Opponents of the Act rallied under the banner AFFECT (Americans for Fair Electronic Commerce) and were highly successful in defeating the UCITA, which was bitterly criticised on the grounds that it was poorly drafted, biased in favour of the software industry, that it would increase the cost of software contracting generally, and that the primary rationale for the UCITA (that it would attract high-tech business to those States introducing the Act) was flawed.[60] The counter-lobbying against the Act effectively rendered the UCITA a dead letter from the moment it was first passed. In like manner, the spectre of Member States or individual contracting parties seeking to avoid the effects of a future CFR should not be overlooked. A number of businesses have revealed that they typically seek to avoid the application of the Vienna Sales Convention, the UNIDROIT Principles and other non-binding rules in favour of national laws

59 Notable events in the revision process included the refusal of the NCCUSL and ALI to approve the draft revisions of Article 2 (Sales) presented at the July 1999 meeting, allegedly due to business pressures, which resulted in the resignation of the Reporters to the project. See generally W. Woodward, 'Private Legislation in the United States—How the Uniform Commercial Code Becomes Law' (1999) 72 Temp L Rev 451 (describing the breakdown of negotiations in 1999 relating to Article 2 revisions. A new drafting committee was formed shortly thereafter). Press Release, NCCUSL, ALI and NCCUSL Announce New Drafting Committee for UCC Articles 2 and 2A (Aug. 18, 1999), available at http://www.nccusl.org/pressrel/pr-18-99.asp. After objections to proposed Article 2B governing intangibles were raised, the ALI and NCCUSL ultimately abandoned the effort to include the Article in the UCC and the NCCUSL alone sponsored what is now the Uniform Computer Information Transactions Act (UCITA) as a separate uniform act. See B. Kobayashi & L.E. Ribstein, 'Uniformity, Choice of Law and Software Sales (2000) 8 Geo Mason L Rev 261 (particularly at 265-66 detailing the history of the UCITA). In the case of the 1990 revisions to Articles 3 and 4, consumer rights advocates were able to secure non-uniform amendments and, in some cases, delay enactment of revised Articles 3 and 4 after concerted political lobbying against the revisions.

60 For further background information, see http://www.UCITA.com

which provide the advantage of a complete law of contract, encompassed within an over-arching legal system.[61]

3.3 Promoting the use of industry-wide Standard Terms and Conditions

An alternative and potentially less controversial strategy for enhancing the coherence of European contract law, in preference to the introduction of sector-specific directives and the development of general principles, could still rest with the development of European wide standard terms and conditions, despite the criticisms levied at this proposal by the author. Indeed, much of the groundwork for regulating standard form contracts is concretised with the implementation of the Unfair Terms Directive 1993 and Section 4.2 of the Action Plan did discuss the need for work on future Community-wide STCs. Yet, it remains difficult to envisage a role for the Commission in this field beyond that of a mere facilitator. Whilst the private sector and various trade associations have a long established tradition of drafting model contracts and standard form tailored to specific industries, the Commission is neither resourced nor empowered to undertake such an endeavour. At best the role of the Commission would therefore be limited to publicising national mandatory provisions and EC competition rules that may impact upon the widespread use of STCs.

In early 2004 the Commission services, under the initiative of the DG Internal Market, convened a workshop on the practical utility of standard terms and conditions in business-to-business (B2B) and business-to-government (B2G) contracts.[62] Arising out of this workshop a proposal was made for the establishment of Commission sounding boards and an interactive website for the exchange of information. The non-policy of developing an interactive website on standard terms and conditions suggested a lack of clear focus on the part of the Commission. Previously this author queried the legal and practical validity

[61] See comments of delegates at ERA conference on European contract law, Trier 2003. The Vienna Convention for the International Sale of Goods (CISG) was enacted in 1980. Ziegel is convinced that ratification of the Vienna Convention by the UK government has been resisted out of fear that it 'may jeopardise London's pre-eminent role as an international arbitration and litigation centre' in 'The Future of the International Sales Convention from a Common Law Perspective' (2000) 6 New Zealand Business Law Quarterly 336, 347. Yet, the refusal to implement the CISG into English law may have as much to do with wider concerns regarding the breadth of Art. 7 of the Convention, in addition to acceptance in practice of the legal consistency provided by domestic Sale of Goods legislation.

[62] A summary of the debate and conclusions of the STC workshop are still available via the website of DG Internal market at http://ec.europa.eu/internal_market/contractlaw/2004workshop_summary_en.htm. Grundmann and Cafaggi have similarly considered the design of commercial contract laws and the likely impact of codification. Cafaggi has raised the potential for both sunset legislation and an increased use of default rules. See F. Cafaggi, *Una governance per il diritto europeo de contratti* and S. Grundmann, *The Role of Drafting and Discussion in the Process Leading to a Common Frame of Reference and European Contract Code*, European University Institute, Florence, October 24-25, 2003.

of such a website and the Commission's policy generally,[63] and many of these ideas appear to have been 'lifted' and transplanted directly into the First Annual Progress Report on the CFR and Acquis Review.[64] The author's concerns appear to have registered fully with the Commission's Inter-Services group and it is notable that the idea has since been largely axed. The 2005 First Progress report appears to have supplanted this thinking directly. It accepts that 'the circle of economic actors' who would use agreed STCs appears reduced, as they are typically drafted for a specific sector, that the 'increasing speed of legislative change requires STCs to be constantly updated and that STCs posted on a Commission website would therefore quickly 'outlive their usefulness'. Though feasible to create, such a platform would be ultimately dependent upon the concrete engagement of stakeholders in industry, yet for leading law firms and legal departments in major enterprises STCs constitute a very precious know-how and it is most unlikely that any leading economic operator would freely distribute such a 'product' to their competitors. An additional concern of this author was that a website would need to be consistently updated in order to avoid its petrification.[65] The Commission now accepts that the 'complexity and need for constant review' of STCs remains a key weakness, and that European business actors will be loathe to divulge their drafting techniques nor, as the Commission puts it, 'be eager to share the final result at no cost with competitors'. (see para. 4.1). Intriguingly, however, implicit in the Progress Report's admission that the 'increasing speed of legislative change requires STCs to be constantly updated' is an acknowledgement that not only STCs, but the law generally cannot be adeqately 'captured', and that the wider coherence project itself develops under the constant threat of legal petrification.

Moreover, Niglia's previous analysis of the implementation of the Unfair Terms Directive into English, French, Italian and German national law suggests that the difficulty rests not with commercial actors exchanging information on STC's but rather with the implementation of the Directive by national courts. Though he does not use the phrase himself, Niglia suggests that, in particular, the open texture of the good faith principle has provoked the courts to effectively resort to largely unreflective smell tests, or in his words:

> ... the manner in which the Unfair Terms Directive is being applied by national courts is *not* to fill gaps in a system of rules considered to be insufficient to protect consumers; rather it is a matter of unbounded discretion ... 'a particular claim may be successful in one case but not in another. The issue will turn on how the courts balance the interests of the parties' interests in the light of one or more market factors. It is impossible to crystallise the courts' decisions into rules for the simple reason that the courts are no longer operating through the

63 M.J. Doris, 'Cross Border Contracting in the EU – Interoperability Problems and the Impact of a Community Wide Optional Instrument' (2004) 12(1) Tilburg Foreign L Rev 36.

64 See http://ec.europa.eu/consumers/cons_int/safe_shop/fair_bus_pract/cont_law/progress05_en.pdf

65 *Supra* fn. 65.

> rules. In each case the courts balance the parties' interests, that is, they consider the consumer interests at stake, as endangered by pre-formulated rules shifting contractual risks upon them, and balance them against the entrepreneurs' interest in the light of a host of market-facilitative factors. Unfairness becomes dependent upon an unending, case-by-case balancing of consumer and firm interests. In short, contract law is no longer a system of rules that protect or not consumers depending upon the term under scrutiny, but a set of *ad hoc* decisions.[66]

Undoubtedly, this fundamental shift in contract interpretation away from the largely mechanical application of bright line rules to a more open-textured and case-by-case analysis weakens the case for additional restatements and common abstract rules. Wilhelmsson has questioned whether 'ethical uncertainty' itself in postmodern Europe has created a modern 'need' for ever greater legal contextualism, yet curiously as noted above in the US the 'new formalists' have succeeded at least partially in capturing much of recent contract law scholarship and in transforming the legal climate. What appears most significant in the harmonisation debebate is, to borrow a phrase, this clash of legal cultures. Whereas the US, and by extension the common law of Europe, has grown comfortable with legal indeterminancy, the demand for legal certainty (or coherence) remains a core feature of civil law debates; a demand that as Komesar observes is becoming ever more difficult to satisfy.[67] To further complicate matters, the term 'legal certainty' itself has been used and abused, particularly

[66] L. Niglia [2002] *supra* Introduction fn. 3, at 204. He identifies a fundamental break from a 'rule-based' contract law to a 'market-orientated', contextualised law of contract that is ever dependent upon judicial interpretation. A similar analysis is offered by Krawiec and Zeiler who suggest that cases concerning disclosure in US contract law will rest on a 'knife-edge' see Krawiec, K.D. & Zeiler, K., *Common law duties and sins of omission*, available at nber.org. In similar vein the breadth of judicial discretion in determining the effect of preliminary agreements is highlighted by H. Temkin, 'When Does The Fat Lady Sing? An Analysis of Agreements in Principle in Corporate Acquisitions' (1986) 55 Fordam L Rev 125.

[67] See N. Komesar, *Law's Limits – The Rule of Law and the Supply and Demand of Rights* (Cambridge University Press, 2001), at 156 *et seq.* Indeed, delegates at a recent conference on the theme of 'Legal Certainty' highlighted the difficulty of reaching any satisfactory meaning of the term. Most US delegates suggested that lawyers in the States have by now grown comfortable with Feinman's 'legal indeterminancy' and suggested that even the New Formalist movement in the US had grudgingly accepted that contextualism would continue to play a role in the resolution of commercial contract disputes. Maxeiner, whilst highlighting the advantages of syllogistic application of rules and applauding the clarity, accessibility and coherence of German law, noted that in the US an attitude of resignation has developed with regard to legal uncertainty. So much so that the very notion of achieving legal certainty would today be dismissed as 'childish thinking'. See E. Maxeiner, *Legal Certainty through Legal Methods: Why Germany has legal certainty and the US has legal indeterminancy*, GGLS conference on Legal Certainty, Glasgow, September, 2006. In addition, see Bucholtz's view of the remarkable 'vibrancy and vulnerability' of the common law of contracts. For her, whilst the vibrancy of the law 'continues to be illuminated by its responsiveness to societal changes'; its vulnerability continues to reflect the flip-side of that responsive-

in the harmonisation debate. Wagner correctly differentiates between subjective uncertainty (uncertainty as to the content of the law) and objective uncertainty (denoting an absence of law; the inexistence of law or a legal rule, and/or an inability to enforce certain rights, etc). We can further point to 'sleeping' legal uncertainty, which suggests a risk that the law applicable *ex ante* when parties entered into contract may subsequently be changed *ex post*. In this sense, every commercial transaction contains a degree of 'sleeping uncertainty' which the parties must assume in entering into contracts.[68] Ott and Schäfer perceive legal uncertainty as a pure cost issue and define transaction costs as outlay in obtaining information regarding an alternative legal system. Yet Ribstein and Kobayashi distinguish in much greater detail the specific transaction costs that may be reduced by legal uniformity.[69] Both authors prioritise tackling inconsistency costs – i.e. those that arise through inconsistent State laws, information costs (the cost of determining what law applies in each State), potential litigation and instability costs, and other externalities, such as divergence inspired or sustained by purely national interest. Certainly, no amount of cultural sentiment alone in favour of a European contract law is likely to persuade Member States to abandon their own national rules and procedures. Moreover, identifying the degree of legal uncertainty in one national system is a highly complex issue, thus endeavouring to assess incoherence in a multi-lingual, legally pluralistic market of twenty seven Member States may ultimately prove to be a challenge 'which [simply] exceeds our learning capabilities and creativity'.[70]

3.4 Interoperability problems and an Optional Instrument for cross border contracting

On a more micro-level, however, the case of *Comyn Ching Ltd. et al v. Radius PLC* (unreported, 17 March 1999) reveals that transactions are commonly entered into for the supply of systems and services of enormous value and complexity without the parties having drafted a formal written contract. In the event of litigation the courts are commonly required to elect the most suitable law. The proposal for an Optional Instrument for cross border contracts consti-

ness: an inherent indeterminancy', see 'Rules, Principles or Just Words: The Interpretative Project and the Problem of Legitimacy' (2005) 11(2) Tex. Wes. L. 377, 378.

68 See I. Macneil, *The Persistence and Significance of Uncertainty in Commercial Law*, GGLS conference, *ibid.*

69 See B.H. Kobayashi & L.E. Ribstein, 'Contract & Jurisdictional Freedom, Choosing Law by Contract' in F.H. Buckley, *The Fall and Rise of Freedom of Contract* (Duke University Press, 1999).

70 Per C. Joerges, *supra* fn 11. As Smits observes: '[i]n order to build up a new European private law, one cannot just draft solutions in the form of principles by looking at the positivistic rules of European legal systems. These rules are just formalistic shadows of the policy considerations that underlie them ... it is with these policy considerations, together with an economic analysis of law and the insights of legal history, legal theory and empirical evidence that a new European private law has to be built up', in J. Smits, *The Europeanisation of national legal systems: some consequences for legal thinking in civil law countries*, at http://edata.ub.unimaas.nl/wwww-edocs/loader/file.asp?id=944

tutes an innovative solution for this type of problem. In order to be effective in cases where parties fail to choose an applicable law to govern their contract, the Optional Instrument would have to be applied on an 'opt-out' basis, i.e. binding on all parties contracting cross border in the internal market unless the parties have expressly chosen to 'opt-out' of such an Instrument. Such a proposal would to a certain extent limit the contractual freedom of parties. The Commission's consistent affirmation of the principle of freedom of contract suggests that such a horizontal measure would ultimately apply on an 'opt-in' basis, thus requiring contracting parties to choose the Optional Instrument as the law to govern their contract. It is foreseen that the modernised Rome Convention on the Law Applicable to Contractual Obligations, 1980, will allow parties to choose a future EU horizontal measure. To date the Commission has failed to state how such an Optional Instrument would function and interact in relation to other international instruments such as the CISG convention. Critical to the success of the proposed initiative is the need to identify practical problems that can only be overcome by employing such a regulatory tool. Yet, legal practice is replete with situations where choice of law clauses have operated negatively for contracting parties, even where they share a common language. The case of *Ansys Incorporated v. Lim Thuan Khee and Another* [71] is a suitable case in point: Without seeking legal advice in the UK or the US, the parties agreed that their contract should be governed and construed in accordance with the law of Pennsylvania. The litigation was complicated immeasurably as a result. Distinguished lawyers from the United States were called to testify as expert witnesses, which added to the cost and delay in resolving the dispute even though the judge ultimately concluded that the law of Pennsylvania was probably operationally identical to English contract law on all essential issues. Judge Park accepted that an American software house would typically favour the legal system with which it is most familiar, but suggested that:

> ... in future it should bear in mind that foreign licences subsist under foreign copyright laws, that foreign insolvency laws may well apply on termination and that any agreement with a foreign distributor must be enforced abroad.

The disagreeable consequences of similar litigation in Europe could perhaps be reduced via an agreed EU regulatory instrument however if, as suggested, it remains non-binding parties will continue to exercise party autonomy in choosing applicable law and no notable improvement in terms of legal certainty is likely to be achieved. US authors have previously suggested that federal intervention in areas of State competence is warranted only when a uniform laws process does not satisfactorily advance stated policy goals.[72] Where interstate commerce

[71] Unreported, 19 May 1999.

[72] E.L. Rubin, *Types of Contracts, Interventions of Law* (2000) 45 Wayne L Rev 1903, at 1925, who promotes federal action only when state law fails to attain an efficient result. See also A. Ogus, 'Competition Between National Legal Systems. A Contribution of Economic Analysis to Comparative Law' (1999)

is threatened by a substantial lack of legal uniformity the likelihood of federal intervention increases, as does the likelihood of new harmonised law proposals emerging from within private law study groups, etc. Crucially, however, even with the academic backbone of the CFR nearing completion surprisingly little empirical data exists in support of this European convergence thesis, or perhaps it would be more fitting to refer to a 'convergence consensus', given the level of broad academic and political support for a closer approximation of private law. Nevertheless, in the absence of concrete economic facts and supporting empirical data, it has been counter-argued that the administrative costs of harmonising Member States' contract laws, allied to the costs of subsequent adaptation, could prove such a step to be economically unsound.[73] This argument has largely failed to register in the mainstream debate, however, is certainly deserving of deeper analysis.

4 The economics of standardisation and a lack of empirical evidence. Inter-jurisdictional competition as an adequate response to legal diversity in the internal market?

When applied to the internal market, the alternative argument advanced by Kobiyashi and Ribstein in a U.S. context[74] would suggest prima facie that the continued existence of a variety of competing contractual regimes may in effect be the most appropriate method of ensuring the introduction of consistently efficient laws. Proponents of such a view highlight the efficiency gains to be harnessed from competition between legal orders and contend that by allowing contracting parties the maximum freedom to 'forum-shop' (in choosing the laws applicable to their individual contracts and specifying a par-

ICLQ 495. See, in contrast, P.B. Stephan, 'The Futility of Unification and Harmonization in International Commercial Law (1999) 39 Va J Int'l Law 743.

73 *Supra* fn. 71. See also position paper of *The Law Reform Committee of the General Bar Council of England and Wales*, which is bitterly opposed to the mandatory codification of European contract laws on the grounds that this would adversely affect a significant sector of the European economy. In this context, the detailed proposal adopted by Grundmann and Kerber, who advocate the retention of all fifteen national regimes of contract allied to the emergence of a new European system of contract laws, merits more detailed study. Such a dual system of European contract laws has undoubtedly much to offer, particularly in that it preserves the functioning national systems and sidesteps the problem of latent hostility to codification. The downside is that it potentially risks adding yet another layer of non-binding, complex and untested contract law. See S. Grundmann & W. Kerber, W., *A European System of Contract Law: A Map for Combining the Advantages of Centralised and De-Centralised Rule-Making*, SECOLA Leuven Conference, *supra* Introduction fn. 8.

74 B.H. Kobayashi & L.E. Ribstein, 'Contract & Jurisdictional Freedom, Choosing Law by Contract' in F.H. Buckley, *The Fall and Rise of Freedom of Contract*, *supra*. See also R. van den Bergh, *Forced Harmonisation of Contract Law in Europe – Not to be continued*, position paper presented at SECOLA Leuven conference 2001.

ticular state whose courts would have jurisdiction) we maximise party autonomy.[75] Advocates of freedom of contract view a choice of applicable law, indeed even the very language used in the negotiating, drafting and concluding of a contract, to be matters for the contracting parties. The existence of a standardised regime of European contract law would arguably serve to weaken this state of affairs and reduce the possibilities for exercising individual preference. As opposed to comprehensive harmonisation and codification initiatives, regulatory competition theoretically serves the development of increasingly efficient rules in a plurality of legal systems whilst affording contracting parties the maximum degree of freedom to choose the law most suited to their particular contract. Again, it is important to be sensitive to the inadequacies of a pure 'competition for the better rule' approach and one such limitation would appear to arise in relation to divergent European approaches to precontractual reliance duties (considered more fully below). It is not at all clear why such notions of inter-jurisdictional competition in private law have so spectacularly failed to impact on the Community institutions, and why they have been so heavily sidelined whilst the CFR develops. Perhaps the European Commission and Parliament were simply unpersuaded by the carefully advanced argument of Wagner and other law and economics scholars.

Writing in 2002, Wagner set out the primary difficulties in ascertaining a sound economic case either for or against harmonisation and determined that the case remained 'at best inconclusive'.[76] Applying directly the 'logic' of economic arguments employed in the US to the European market, he warned that whilst the economics of federalism strongly council against a harmonisation of European contract law – as such an effort would destroy competition

---

[75] In particular, Beale stresses the primary benefits of a plurality of contractual regimes in *Continuing contract law harmonisation under the White Paper of 1985 – partly with modifications*, SECOLA Leuven conference 2001. For Beale, 'diversity encourages experimentation and experimentation encourages legal development', at p. 3. Lord Goff suggests that Europe ought to be 'profoundly grateful' for its diversity of legal cultures as 'far more [can be learnt] from these diverse systems than could ever be derived from a single monolithic regime' in B.S. Markesinis (ed), 'The Coming Together of the Common and the Civil Law' (Hart Law, 2000), at 239. It is largely self evident that from a theoretical perspective the existence of a plurality of legal orders or *legal laboratories* – per Justice Brandeis in *New State Ice Corporation* v. *Liebmann*, 285 U.S. 262, 311 (1932) – serves to promote competition between systems, but in the EU's multi-lingual context inspiring competition for more 'efficient legal rules' is far from straightforward, particularly in areas of the law where the ECJ has a diminished role. Joerges cites the *Centros* case as a suitable example of the ECJ effectively requiring the Danish authorities to justify their legal rule on corporate law vis-à-vis the English position, but it is difficult to see how competition between pure contract law rules can be promoted on a European level. See also S. Deakin, 'Two Types of Regulatory Competition: Competitive Versus Reflexive Harmonisation. A Law and Economics Perspective on *Centros*', 2 Cambridge Yearbook of European Legal Studies (1999).

[76] G. Wagner, *supra*. See also J. Wool, *Economic Analysis and Harmonised Modernisation of Private Law*, paper delivered at the 75th Anniversary UNIDROIT Congress examining the theme of 'Worldwide Harmonisation of Private Law and Regional Economic Integration, Rome, 27-28 September 2002.

for the best legal rule, remove the beneficial constraints generated by competition among local lawmakers and in turn greatly increase the political impact of interest groups, a more studied analysis of economic realities in Europe revealed that many of the economic assumptions applied in the US do not find a similar expression within the Union's internal market. In particular, affording contracting parties the maximum freedom to forum-shop undoubtedly enhances the bargaining autonomy of contracting parties, yet the limitations of private international rules in a European setting are considerable and 'a widespread choice of law within a multilingual system would in practice lead to a situation in which the law is applied by a more or less incompetent judge in the majority of cases'.[77] The decision of the European Court of Justice in the case of *Ingmar GB Ltd v. Eaton Leonard Technologies*[78] highlights an added danger for contracting parties relying on a choice-of-law clause as in this case the court determined that the individual parties choice of Californian law, as the law applicable to their contract, would in effect be trumped by mandatory Community law rules. The case provides an insight into the manner in which the ECJ approaches the relationship between the principle of party autonomy and the binding force of mandatory EC rules. The ruling has met a mixed, yet strangely largely muted reaction, despite setting an arguably dangerous precedent in weakening the power of contract drafting to side-step legal diversity.[79]

Whilst his preliminary observations similarly suffer from a lack of empirical data, importantly, Wagner argued that the greatest benefits of harmonisation would undoubtedly accrue to small to medium sized enterprises for whom the relatively high transaction costs associated with legal diversity operate as effective impediments to entry into foreign markets. He suggested that this 'resulting brake on competition within the European Union should be taken seriously, given the fact that the European economies are dominated by SMEs, and not by multinational corporations, who are largely undeterred by divergences in national contract laws'.[80] As such Wagner concluded by arguing the case for a restricted, targeted process of harmonisation in order to eliminate a consider-

77 Wagner argues that the average European consumer displays a strong tendency to shop locally. He provides the example of a study of the Swiss canton of Zürich where the average consumer travels a mere 6.8 km to satisfy his needs, Statische Berichte des Kantons Zürich, Heft 1/1996, verkehrsverhalten im Kanton Zürick, p. 19f, 1994.

78 [2000] ECR I-9305.

79 The reasoning of the ECJ has been bitterly criticised by Verhagen for limiting the contractual freedom of individual contracting parties. See H. Verhagen, 'The Tension between Party Autonomy and European Union Law: Some Observations on Ingmar GB Ltd v. Eaton Leonard Technologies Inc' [2000] 51 ICLQ 1, 135-154. As EC contract law-by-directives continues, traditional PIL rules applicable within the multi-level system do appear to be at risk of being progressively trumped, see J. Fawcett (ed), *Reform and Development of Private International Law ~ Essays in Honour of Sir Peter North* (Oxford University Press, 2002). Cf. the earlier decision in *Ålsthom Atlantique v. Sulzer*, C-339/89, [1991] ECR I-107.

80 Indeed recent studies suggest that in the UK alone, SMEs generate almost 50% of Gross Domestic Product (See website of the National Statistics Online, http://www.statistics.gov.uk.

able part of the transaction costs incurred by Community SME's. Such a tightly focused and restricted process based on avoiding legal disputes would arguably have received much greater support, and arguably proved much less costly. Importantly, however, Wagner's view of the potential impact of legal divergence on SME's was not shared by national professional associations representing the majority of SME's operating throughout the Community. The European Association of Craft, Small and Medium Sized Enterprises (UEAPME) was firmly convinced that differences between the private contract laws of Member States did not constitute a significant problem for cross border transactions. SMEs it would seem typically target a concrete foreign market and try to adapt to it, without aiming to adapt an EU wide sales and marketing strategy. The majority view within the UEAPME stressed that whilst this information has a cost, that cost should not be 'overestimated'.[81]

In strict commercial settings, the weakness of the uniformity goal appears even more pronounced than in the case of SMEs. A feature of modern business practice involves gaining competitive advantage by exploiting gaps and divergences in national legal systems for client advantage. Indeed, a significant number of contracts can only be fully understood once they are viewed as artificial legal constructs formed through a trading and negotiating of legal concepts and ideas. The somewhat paradoxical attitude of business to harmonised law is confirmed by McBarnet who stresses that "although there is a standard rhetoric among businesses complaining about variations between legal regimes, and calling for harmonisation, in practice variation between regimes is routinely exploited for client advantage".[82]

4.1 Precontractual reliance and the 'Common Frame of Reference' research strategy

As noted in the introductory comment, divergences between national private law systems in the area of precontractual duties has been included as an area of research interest in the Commission's coherence strategy. The CFR will seek to address, *inter alia*, the nature of precontractual obligations, i.e. whether voluntary or binding through mandatory law; the specific contractual situations when information must be provided prior to the formation of a contract, i.e. information to be given regarding the main characteristics of goods or services, price and additional costs, information related to the rights of the consumer, and specific information related to electronic contracts; where and when parties enjoy a right to precontractually agree to have any later dispute submitted to arbitration is another area identified in the Annex of the 2004 Follow-Up Communication. Yet, it would appear that the broader commercially

[81] At http://ec.europa.eu/consumers/cons_int/safe_shop/fair_bus_pract/cont_law/stakeholders/2-24.pdf

[82] D. McBarnet, 'Transnational Transactions: Legal Work, Cross Border Commerce and Global Regulation' in M. Likosky (ed) *Transnational Legal Processes – Globalisation and Power Disparities* (Lexis-Nexis, 2002).

sensitive question of whether parties should be required to negotiate in good faith in 'arms length' negotiations will fall outside the scope of the CFR. Moreover, commercial parties do not appear unduly concerned about the passivity of Community law in this area. In addition, it is commonly argued that whether one jurisdiction chooses to impose liability based upon an implied or explicit duty to negotiate in good faith, or whether liability is imposed with reference to specific theories such as restitution, misrepresentation, or promissory estoppel, most systems nevertheless tend to reach the same end result – liability is imposed if a party has acted to the detriment of the other party, even if a contract has not been consummated. This is a thesis clearly worth testing.

4.2 The (non) applicability of inter-jurisdictional competition theory to the question of precontractual reliance

Few economic studies have been undertaken in Europe to test the validity of differing approaches to incomplete contracts and precontractual liability across jurisdictions. Of the small number that have addressed the optimal level of interference in the contract bargaining process, the majority have been US based. The subject of precontractual reliance has recently been the focus of extensive scholarly debate and the comparative analysis of Ayre Bebchuk and Omri Ben-Shahar is significant.[83] Both commentators suggest that the potential for precontractual liability does not necessarily have an adverse effect on parties' willingness to enter into contractual obligations – a view reinforced by the anecdotal evidence gathered within the Clifford Chance/Grace Consulting survey – but that the two polar regimes, either a strict or a non-liability approach, are suboptimal. In the absence of any precontractual liability, parties may be inclined to engage in opportunistic behaviour during negotiations and potentially abuse potential contracting partners, whereas in an overly rigid system parties freedom to negotiate and barter may be adversely restrained. Crucially, however, whereas parties may be free to contract into a particular system of rules to govern a signed contract via a choice of law clause, inter-jurisdictional competition on precontractual liability means little or nothing to a party facing a claim for breach of good faith in negotiations following a failed deal. There is also the sunk cost of the negotiations themselves, which will likely be further increased in a European context due to language difficulties.

---

83 See A. Bebchuk and O. Ben-Shahar, 'Precontractual Reliance' (2001) 3 J Leg Stud 423, who notes that 'during contractual negotiations, parties often make expenditures that would increase the surplus should a contract be made. [...] Investments in reliance will be socially suboptimal in the absence of any precontractual liability – and will be socially excessive under strict liability for all reliance expenditures', at 423-4. See also R. Craswell, 'Precontractual Investigation as an Optimal Precaution Problem' (1988) 18 J Leg Stud. 401 who addresses the impact that various awards of contract damages may have on parties' incentives to protect themselves, be it through greater information gathering, prior to formally committing to a deal.

At present, inter-jurisdictional competition in relation to rules on precontractual liability seems a somewhat hollow notion in practice but does offer a theoretical template for an analysis of the most efficient legal regime. Clearly, where a legal system fails to adequately protect precontractual reliance investments it falls to the individual parties to safeguard their own self-interest through the mechanism of contract – irrevocable offers, termination fees and option contracts have been the primary tools of choice – or through trust in their business partner's reputation. It is notable that recent US law and economics analysis of contract law has consistently promoted optimal investment in precontractual reliance. Whilst the traditional method of determining contract formation via the classical notions of offer and acceptance do present a wholly fictitious account of modern business contracting, recent suggestions of US scholars reveal the extent to which precontractual reliance is seen as a major issue of real practical substance. The imposition of precontractual liability more readily by the courts and the imposition of contractual liability even in the absence of consent have been just two of the more controversial suggestions raised Stateside within the last decade.[84] There can be little doubt that such theories will gradually impact upon European contract law systems and as such this study is preempting that future debate. In particular US scholars have been insistent on the need for a workable judicial methodology for handling incomplete agreements.[85] We will turn to this question of a methodology for legal interference in bargaining in chapter 4.

5 Beyond rule fixation – Dispute avoidance, comparative case law and functional equivalence

Comparative law has emerged as the method of choice for the development of the CFR. The Commission and Parliament appear convinced that such an approach is the most legitimate for advancing the harmonisa-

[84] O. Ben-Shahar, 'Contracts Without Consent: Exploring a New Basis For Contractual Liability' (2004) 152 U Penn L Rev 1829. See also, R. Craswell, 'Offer, Acceptance, and Efficient Reliance' (1996) 48 Stan L Rev 481 and J.S. Johnston, 'Communication and Courtship: Cheap Talk Economics and the Law of Contract Formation' (1999) 85 Va L Rev 385.

[85] J.P. Kostritsky, 'When Should Contract Law Supply a Liability Rule or Term?: Framing a Principle of Unification for Contracts (2000) 32 Arizona State Law Journal 1283. For Kostritsky, the doctrine of promissory estoppel accounts for 'the moral hazard problem endemic to precontractual negotiation, and the central problem of opportunism posed by the promisee's reliance on sunk costs." Kostritsky's analysis, in particular, is of much merit and will be analysed more fully in chapter 4; A. Katz, 'When Should an Offer Stick? The Economics of Promissory Estoppel in Preliminary Negotiations' (1996) 105 Yale LJ 1249; J.P. Kostritsky, 'Bargaining with Uncertainty, Moral Hazard, and Sunk Costs: A Default Rule for Precontractual Negotiations' (1993) 44 Hastings LJ 621; R.G. Shell, 'Opportunism and Trust in the Negotiation of Commercial Contracts: Toward a New Cause of Action (1991) 44 Vand. L. Rev. 221, etc.

tion effort. Both the Lando Commission and the Study Group on a European Civil Code have consistently argued that only 'dispassionate comparative law research'[86] has the potential to reveal key points of divergence and convergence across national legal systems. Such noble claims for comparative law have however been somewhat overshadowed by those very research groups pioneering the harmonisation effort and leading the Commission's research strategy. In examining and comparing legal rules, these pioneers of abstraction or 'better solution comparatists'[87] have tended to reinforce and promote 'common' rules operated by the majority of legal systems whilst isolating legal divergences that fail to conform to an emerging uniform, harmonised picture. Indeed, what has become ever more apparent in a period of dominant interlegality, characterised in part by the flexibility, fluidity and travelling of legal norms, is the abject failure of traditional legal science to adequately address or rationalise this phenomenon with existing legal instruments. Comparative law strategies, the supposed transnational problem-solving role of private international law and Community law itself have in turn failed satisfactorily to address the complexities of the Europeanisation process. The heritage of traditional legal scholarship is further deeply challenged by the dynamic and promise of technological innovation. Beyond this 'contest of legal disciplines', Joerges observes future private law regulation becoming ever more dependent upon heightened 'deliberative supranationalism, or improved communication between competent legal and non-legal actors, given the current state of interdependence in the EU's polycentric multi-level system of governance'.[88] Awareness of this reality has led to suggestions that European academia ought to focus less on harmonising substantive private law rules and concentrate more on the varying institutions and processes of governance that continue to shape modern European contract and consumer protection laws. As Marciano and Josselin stress, 'one of the major effects of the continual process of European integration is the growing importance of transnational institutions and the accompanying legal harmonisation'[89] and that, as a consequence, it is only through a proper understanding of the interplay between these various institutions that we begin to fully grasp the scope of 'transnational responses to transnational problem constellations'.[90] This in turn prompts reflection upon the reality that academic private lawyers are increasingly being displaced as the primary carriers of private law. Despite the plea of Gralf-Cal-

86 *Joint Response, supra.*

87 J. Hill, *supra.*

88 C. Joerges, 'Who could be an author of European Private Law?' in Schmid, C. & Doris, M., *supra* (2005). See also C. Joerges, 'The Challenges of Europeanization in the Realm of Private Law: A Plea for a New Legal Discipline' (2004) 14 Duke J of Comp & Int'l L 149 and B. Fauvarque-Cosson, *Comparative Law and Conflict of Laws: Allies or Enemies? New Perspectives on an Old Couple, Position paper presented at conference on The Europeanisation of Contract,* The European University Institute, Florence, October 24-25, 2003.

89 A. Marciano & J.M. Josselin (ed), *The Economics of Harmonizing European Law* (Edward Elgar, 2002).

90 C. Joerges, *supra* fn. 92.

liess, in calling for a five-year moratorium on EC Directives whilst the CFR is compiled, it is self evidently unrealistic to expect the process of Community lawmaking and reform in matters of private law to grind to a halt in expectation of a future agreed blueprint on European contract law. Yet in itself such a plea to the Community legislator instead betrays a deeper unease as to who ought to have control of private law production for European markets.[91]

Evidently, comparative law research alone is unable to provide the comprehensive solutions necessary for the harmonisation endeavour in European private law. Instead, comparative law must assist the ongoing rationalisation and simplication of law process by identifying points of convergence and functional equivalence, particularly through case-law analysis. Assessing the level of correspondence and uniformity in legal solutions is preferable to the pro-active comparative methods of the leading academic study groups promoting the end goal of systematisation and codification. Crucially, as Örücü warns, "comparative law cannot, be regarded solely as an instrument of integration or an instrument of construction and statutory interpretation, though the knowledge gained through comparative legal studies may be put to such uses. It is essentially an instrument of legal understanding and communication".[92] Van Hoecke further observes that 'deep level' comparative research requires a more fluid, inter-disciplinary focus that transcends mere rule comparison and relies upon observations from legal history, sociological studies, political science and other relevant fields.[93] He outlines five areas[94] of potential divergence that require added sensitivity when undertaking comparative assessment:

---

[91] P. Gralf-Calliess, 'European Contract Law – Substantive and International (2003) 4(4) German LJ

[92] E. Örücü, 'Critical Comparative Law: Considering Paradoxes for Legal Systems in Tradition' (2000) 4 EJCL 1. See also J. Kozyris, 'Comparative Law for the 21st Century: New Horizons and New Technologies' (1994) 69 Tul L Rev 165 (discussing 'the many futures of comparative legal science'). Holding firm to the importance of comparative research as a language of communication between legal systems, if not the sole tool for promoting uniformity, this study will benefit from a detailed comparative analysis of caselaw and its background 'context' (including national court procedures, contract drafting styles, cost of litigation, etc).

[93] *Supra* fn. 14, at 165. In turn Brooke Overby emphasises the need for an institutional analysis of consumer law, for '[b]y moving away from modern views of law based on formal rationality and static universal norms into a post-modern regime for evaluating law and legal acts based on particulars and concepts of fit, an institutional legal perspective brings with it two consequences. With respect to law reform proposals, it demands that political and legal organisations and structures receive consideration along with the traditional legal emphasis on social policy goals or ethical norms. As a by-product of this stance, in evaluating products of legal organisations, institutional theory de-emphasises formal evaluative criteria in favour of a much more open-ended and flexible inquiry into the relations and fit among institutions, organizations, and values. This approach to evaluation of legal systems and their products presents a more completely post-modern theory of law, with an "emphasis on the particular and [a] . . . corresponding distrust of generalisations', in A. Brooke Overby, 'An Institutional Analysis of Consumer Law' (2001) 34 Vand J Transnat L 1219.

[94] *Supra* at 192

a) Legal concepts, that play an important role in one legal system and are absent in the other (e.g. consideration, *cause*);
b) The structure of the field or its environment (e.g. a different borderline between contracts and torts);
c) Procedural elements (kinds of actions available, etc);
d) Different dominating views and conceptions; and
e) Different rules.

To Van Hoecke's legal concepts, we ought to add legal practice, as certain contract drafting techniques that are widely employed in one jurisdiction are commonly seen as either superfluous or unconscionable in another. Moreover, a number of jurisdictions, the US in particular, are particularly generous procedurally when it comes to pleadings. In a highly litigious system, the dominant view appears to be that parties should be afforded the opportunity to have their case aired. This produces an inflated number of annual claims but with the overwhelming majority of weak claims being routinely dismissed via summary judgment procedure. The 'structure of the field' also has a critical bearing in a comparative assessment of preliminary agreements and precontractual duties due the blurring of the line between contract and tort in particular. Legal categorisation, and the types of action available to litigants, further has a decisive bearing on the manner in which disputes are pleaded and fought. For example, under English law, claims involving contract negotiations are typically litigated on the grounds of a lack of consideration, mistake, fraud, misrepresentation, or negligent mistatement under the rule in *Hedley Byrne*,[95] etc as opposed to breach of a precontractual duty which the courts will disavow.[96]

---

95 *Hedley Byrne v. Heller and Partners* [1964] AC 465. Importantly, reliance plays a key role in a claim for negligent misstatement under the *Hedley Byrne* liability as a statement must play 'a real and substantial part, though not by itself a decisive part, in inducing a plaintiff to act' (per Judge Stephenson in *JEB Fasteners Ltd v. Marks Bloom & Co. (a firm)* [1983] 1 All ER 583, at p. 589). However, unlike Giliker who sees much scope for developing tort law in line with delict in French law, this author shares the view of Brown that 'whereas tort provides a broad base from which particularised duties could develop in precontractual bargaining ... the vagaries of the tortious duty of care are inappropriate as instruments with which to dissect the intricacies of commercial negotiations' in I. Brown, 'The Contract to Negotiate: A Thing Writ in Water' (1992) JBL 353, at 357.

96 Unlike in the US, the English courts have consistently adopted a conservative reluctance towards promissory estoppel. The position is arguably more confused than principled. As Giliker notes, a key difficulty in developing the law in this area rests with the fact that promissory estoppel is available to a claimant only if the parties have an existing contractual relationship. A close negotiating relationship will not suffice. This limitation serves to maintain the boundaries of the law of contract, ensuring that the doctrine will be confined to a temporary modification of an existing agreement and will not create any new obligations without the required consideration. By contrast, it would seem that estoppel by representation requires no pre-existing contractual relationship. See P. Giliker, *Pre-contractual liability in English and French Law* (Kluwer, 2002) at 234. Indeed, even Lord Denning a stout defender of estoppel based remedies warned against 'stretching [the law in the area] too far, lest it should be endangered',

This procedural framing of disputes undoubtedly has an impact upon the issue of harmonisation. In the *Tacconi v. Heinrich Wagner* case, the European Court of Justice considered liability for the breach of the duty to act in good faith in negotiations (culpa in contrahendo) as tortious, whereas in leading commentaries in German law it is treated as contractual.[97] The *Tacconi* position was partly followed by the Court in *Shearson*, when considering a preliminary ruling from the German Bundesgerichtshof on the scope of Article 13 of the Rome Convention.[98] The Court was asked to consider whether the expression "concerning a contract" would also cover claims based on an infringement of the advisory duty in precontractual negotiations and whether such claims should be afforded the same treatment as claims based on the main contractual obligation. The case concerned a failure to provide information concerning the risks connected with speculative transactions. It was argued that such a claim should be framed on grounds of unjust enrichment as the aim was to recover payments made without a solid contractual basis.

The Court further stressed that during the precontractual phase of negotiations parties are under a reciprocal duty to act with care and diligence. A claim for liability arising out of a failure to fulfil that obligation cannot itself be regarded as contractual,[99] however "once it is combined with a claim based on contractual liability under a contract to which the precontractual negotiations themselves succeeded in giving rise, it appears that a claim for precontractual liability becomes inseparable from the contract". The situation is clearly unsatisfactory and appears to be caught between the contract vision of precontractual liability presented under German law and the alternative tortious vision of inappropriate behaviour in negotiations.[100] As is apparent, the Commission's

and the idea that estoppel should create 'new causes of action where none existed before' was categorically rejected by Denning in *Combe v. Combe* [1951] 2 KB 215, at 219.

97 See, for example, O, Palandt, *Buergerliches Gesetzbuch* (Munich 2003) regarding Article 40 EGBGB at 2605.

98 *Shearson Lehman Hutton v. TVB Trenhandgesellscahft für Vermögensverwaltung und Beteiligungen mbH*, Case C-89/91 (see, in particular, the rather confused picture offered at paragraphs 96 and 97).

99 The absence of a contractual nexus between the parties is critical, however the rationale for the ECJ approach was based on common sense grounds aimed at limiting claims for liability which 'could be regarded as contractual even if, in the end, the contract had not been concluded', at p. 96. See Opinion of the Advocate General Darmon delivered 27 October 1992.

100 German doctrine holds the blameworthy party liable to the innocent party who suffered damages due to the other party's "fault in negotiation" and his reliance on the contract. Departing from a notably similar starting point, modern Spanish doctrinal opinion appears deeply confused as to where to 'site' precontractual liability, referring at times to the notion as a claim in contract, tort or quasi-contract. Reglero Campos sees the distinction between contract and extracontractual liability as entirely artificial and dogmatic. He argues that the adverse effects of this split are particularly noticeable when lawyers seek to bring a claim procedurally as the caselaw is by no means settled. For a helpful discussion of this difficulty, see F. Reglero Campos, *Lecciones de Responsabilidad Civil* (Aranzadi, 2002) at paras. 5.3 *et seq.* He further notes that once a party frames a claim on the basis of contract he must disavow an extrac

sole focus to date on problems arising through divergences in contract law and its decision to exclude tort law and other potential clashes with property and securities law, etc, from the primary remit of the CFR risks leaving a number of equally problematic legal lacunae or non-Europeanised 'legal islands' which will persist in the aftermath of the coherence research strategy.[101]

Importantly, Schwintowski suggests that the test that the European Community should meet prior to passing any future directives in the field of private law is whether the transaction costs incurred from harmonisation are lower than those if no intervention takes place, or lower than those achieved through regulating from mutual recognition, or competition between systems.[102] In opposition to the 'ineffective' plethora of information and precontractual duties that the Community has developed in the mass of consumer contract law directives, Schwintowski argues that it would instead suffice to accord mutual recognition to each Member States' individualised approach to such duties. As Schwintowski points out, in commercial transactions the content of contractual agreements will largely be determined by a) the level of search and information costs involved; b) the degree of ignorance and information deficits; c) the prevention of *ex ante* and *ex post* opportunism; and d) the possibility to make subsequent amendments (contractual modifications). It is further suggested by Schwintowski that the current trend of imposing precontractual duties is flawed as a result, as almost all information and other (loyalty) duties are ineffective 'because they are disproportionate'.[103] As such he is of the view that the European Community should be under an obligation to enforce a principle of mutual recognition and cheapest cost. This he believes would result in a new type of law-making that would contain no compulsory legal rules but rather catalogues of possible terms and enumerated risk scenarios. As for the thrust towards

---

ontractual claim, and vice versa, leading to calls for a uniform approach. See also Y. Tolsada, *Sistema de Responsabilidad civil contractual y extracontractual* (Dykinson, 2001). Certainly, Spanish legislation has introduced an entirely extracontractual basis of recovery for damage caused by defective products and reform in the area of precontractual liability could follow the contractual lead of the Principles of European Contract Law (discussed below in chapter 2).

101 As noted previously, the Commission's DG Health and Consumer Protection initially commissioned a study on the impact of clashes arising between contract, tort and property, yet opted to proceed with the CFR centred virtually exclusively on contract law. This decision has been sharply criticised by Mattei. Bussani and Palmer similarly observe that it is at 'the frontier between contractual and tortious liability' that divergences across systems prove most cumbersome and obscure, in *Towards*, 2004.

102 H.P. Schwintowski, 'Contractual Rules Concerning the Marketing of Goods and Services – Requirements of Form and Content Versus Private Autonomy' in Grundmann, Werber & Weatherill, *supra* Introduction fn. 1. See also 'Regulatory Competition or Harmonization of Laws? Guidelines for the European regulator' in A. Marciano & J.M. Josselin, *supra* (2002).

103 'Via Article 5 EC both the principle of mutual recognition of laws and the cheapest cost principles are basic, valid European law – a fact that has not dawned on the authorities in Brussels and the European Court of Justice', *supra* fn. 106, at 344.

codification at Community level, Joerges neatly summarises the weakness of code-making as an instrument for legal certainty:

> And what about a codification of Europe's private law? This is an idea for books about European private law, not for the law in Europe. Europe will remain heterarchical and plural; it will legitimate anybody to do away, either top-down or bottom-up, with its rich legal cultures; it will have to live with its complex mixture of 'primary law' which grants basic freedoms and rights; transnational governance arrangements which organise regulatory activities; legislative and judicial interventions which irritate. This mixture is the 'state of the (European) Union'...[104]

6 Concluding remarks

A new faith in codification in Europe mirrors a declining belief in the utility of this form of law-making in the United States. With increasing regularity commentators are questioning the value of the UCC in providing adequate solutions to commercial problems. The bulk of recent European comparative law scholarship has entailed a largely unthinking application of neo-classical economic assumptions to contract law and has typically proposed solutions based on the worst types of formalism from both disciplines. Macaulay and Teubner suggest that this mechanical approach to contract law has further erred in its failure to adequately understand the complexities of legal and business culture.[105] Academic insistence on the need for enhance coherence in private law further appears to have been further grossly inflated. As Lord Steyn once stressed in the House of Lords case of *Williams v. Natural Life Health Foods Ltd*, 'coherence must sometimes yield to practical justice'.[106] If a European system of

[104] C. Joerges (2005) *supra*. Or as Smits puts it: '...[i]n order to build up a new European private law, one cannot just draft solutions in the form of principles by looking at the positivistic rules of European legal systems. These rules are just formalistic shadows of the policy considerations that underlie them ... it is with these policy considerations, together with an economic analysis of law and the insights of legal history, legal theory and empirical evidence that a new European private law has to be built up', in J. Smits, *The Europeanisation of national legal systems: some consequences for legal thinking in civil law countries, supra*. Chapter 2 of this study will provide some key insights from legal history regarding future methodology and the need for a guiding ethic for European private law.

[105] S. Macaulay, 'The Real and the Paper Deal: Empirical Pictures of Relationships, Complexity and the Urge for Transparent Principles' (2003) 66 MLR 44. See G. Tuebner, 'In the Blind Spot: The Hybridization of Contracting' (2007) 8(1) Theoretical Enquiries in Law 4. On the dominance of classic economics in law, see C. Goodhart, 'Economics and the Law: Too Much One Way Traffic?' (1997) 60 MLR 1. See also J. Alfaro Águila-Real, 'Imperialismo Económico y Dogmática Jurídica', Revista de Derecho Mercantil, Julio-Septiembre, Número 233, 1999.

[106] [1998] 1 WLR 830, HL (at 837). The House of Lords equally sceptical view of absolute certainty in law in the case of *Re Spectrum Plus Ltd (in Liquidation)* [2004] EWCA Civ 670 is equally of significance. Yet, in relation to the CFR, perhaps the views of Corbin almost 50 years ago are most appropriate: 'certainty in

contract laws is to emerge at some future point it will require a radical change of focus that concentrates primarily on resolving practical problems. Equally, a consensus must emerge among practitioners, judges and other users that such a uniform law is in the common interest. Importantly, whilst US contract law has evolved under the influence of precedent, economics and common history, etc it has been primarily a thirst for a shared legal education and, above all, the desire among lawyers to be part of a common legal culture that has promoted greater substantive and procedural uniformity. Yet, beyond the harmonisation of legal rules, US lawyers are evidently presented with much less hindrance in practising across State lines than European lawyers who aim or elect to practice in an alternative Member State. Providers of legal practice courses, for example, are notoriously conservative and users cite excessive cost, delay and confusion for qualified lawyers who aim to have their national qualifications afforded equal weight and standing in other EU jurisdictions.[107] These practical disincentives arguably exacerbate a sense of legal isolationism within each Member State. Though a similar proposal has been overlooked in the framing of the Action Plan and 2004 Follow Up Communication, a co-ordinating 'European Private Law Association' (EPLA) should be reconsidered upon completion of the CFR research.[108]

A formally established, public organisation could play a critical role in continued Member State surveillance, in disseminating information on enduring diversity in national private laws and in undertaking cross-jurisdictional

the law is largely an illusion at best, and altogether too high a price may be paid in the effort to attain it' in A.L. Corbin, *Corbin on Contracts: A Comprehensive Treatise on the Rules of Contract* (West Publishing, 1960) at 689.

107 For an example of this problematic ingrained conservatism see Chapter 4, Preliminary Report of the Irish Competition Authority on Competition in Legal Services in Ireland, 2005. The European University Institute and similar academic institutions are pioneering change in this regard by offering degrees that are fully recognised across all Member States.

108 This proposal for a European Private Law Association was first made in 2003 (see M.J. Doris, 'Seizing the Constitutional Moment? Governance, Interlegality and a Law of Lawmaking for the Europeanisation of Contract' in F. Astengo & N. Neuwahl (eds), *A Constitution for Europe? Governance and Policy Making in the European Union* (Montréal University Press, 2004). Van Gerven has similarly made the case for a 'European Law Institute' and a 'Curriculum Commission' which would seek to 'educate practitioners in the use of any emerging codified law and to determine law curricula for universities thus promoting a common European legal culture', in W. van Gerven, 'Codifying European Private Law? Yes, if ...!' (2002) ELR 156. See also, C.U. Schmid, 'The Emergence of a Transnational Legal Science in European Private Law' (1999) 19 Oxford J Legal S 673. Hesselink similarly detects the emergence of a new European legal culture, characterised by a rejection of the formalism of the past and the promotion of a 'more substance-oreintated and pragmatic approach' in M.W. Hesselink, *The New European Legal Culture* (Dewenter/Kluwer, 2001) but Smits *supra* is more enlightening in observing the manner in which the implementation of selective private law is effectively giving rise to a dual methodology in private law, forcing greater convergence where EC directives are applicable and a continuation of national approaches where greater Member State autonomy is conceded, at p. 5.

research similar to that currently provided by the Scottish Law Society and the Law Society of England and Wales. Indeed the working methodology employed by both bodies in carrying forward joint proposals for reform could form the basis of a useful future enquiry for the wider development of EC private law. An EPLA could equally assist in road-testing the initial Common Frame and any subsequent Optional Instrument(s) by triggering trial and error processes with the help of any newly emerging rules, and in devising means to negative the 'irritating' effects of any new legal constructs.[109] Perhaps the most crucial role would be that of widely publicising work in progress. This would encourage an open learning process as to the advantages and drawbacks of the initial Common Frame and may help to better embed the CFR progressively. An EPLA could further assist the Commission in deciding on the suitability and ultimate role of the Common Frame itself. In addition, there is an ongoing need to better document 'best practice' in European contracting generally, in part in order to instil indirect peer pressure on those national legal systems that fail to comply with accepted EU norms and standards.

[109] Per G. Teubner, 'Legal Irritants: Good Faith in British Law or How Unifying Law Ends Up in New Divergences' (1998) 61 MLR 1. This author sympathises with Teubner's analysis that the English law's assimilation of the doctrine of good faith is unlikely to succeed as a 'direct transplant' but will instead provoke a uniquely English doctrinal reshuffling. Regrettably of course, though influential, Teubner's theory remains just that, it has yet to be tested. On the basis of his theory, Teubner wisely advocates a differentiated system of EC contract law as opposed to comprehensive harmonisation (at p. 31-32).The doctrine of good faith, on the other hand, has provoked little difficulty in practice through its implementation via the Unfair Terms in Consumer Contracts Regulations 1999.

CHAPTER 2

The Quest for Coherence Tormented

No jurisdiction has a monopoly of excellence in contract law, including the European Union.[1]

1 Information rights, party autonomy and the social justice dimensions of modern European contract law

In chapter 1 we discussed a number of variables impacting upon the Europeanisation process in general commercial and consumer contract law and relying upon evidence gained primarily from recent US experience in harmonising commercial contract laws we summarily concluded gloomily as to the outcome of the process of convergence via the Commission's 'Common Frame of Reference' research strategy. In particular, we questioned the logic of undertaking comprehensive unifying efforts at a regional, EU level given the declining role of national private law systems in the adjudication of consumer and commercial disputes and the growth in alternative, transnational forms of dispute resolution, which typically provide their own tailor-made solutions to contractual conflicts. We further drew attention to heightened judicial discretion at Member State level in the resolution of contract disputes, which has thus far served to weaken predictability and legal certainty. In chapter 2 we explore the functions of modern EC contract rules in order to further illustrate the difficulties in seeking to benchmark 'coherence' and consider in particular the generalised treatment of precontractual duties under modern framework codes, international treaties and soft law 'Principles'.

For Samuel the harmonisation debate should act as "[t]he catalyst for rethinking legal theory, since the theories that are presently underpinning legal analysis are, arguably, incapable of handling the epistemological complexities presented by unification".[2] This view is reinforced by Benson who observes that:

> at the close of the twentieth century, the situation of contract law presents the following contrast. On the one hand, in both the common law and civil law the definitions of and mutual connections between the various principles of contract law are for the most part well-settled and no longer subject to controversy. Indeed, despite differences in formulation, the main elements of the law of contract are strikingly similar in both legal systems, and these systems, whether directly or by derivation, prevail throughout most of the contemporary world. The authoritative public articulation of the law of contract has achieved a certain apparent completeness and acceptability. The same cannot be said, however, of efforts to understand the law at a reflective level ... Unless we are able to make explicit the conception of contract that underlies these doctrines and principles, we do not

---

1 Per H. Verhagen, 'The Tension between Party Autonomy and European Union Law: Some Observations on Ingmar GB Ltd v. Eaton Leonard Technologies Inc' (2002) 51 ICLQ 135.

2 G. Samuel, 'English Private Law in the Context of the Codes' in *The Harmonisation of European Private Law, supra* Introduction fn. 6, at 47-58.

> fully understand them and whatever understanding we may have of them must of necessity be partial and deficient. At a time when the public authoritative articulation of the main elements of contract is relatively settled and complete, this failure is particularly unsatisfactory.[3]

It has further been suggested that the current perceived frailty of modern European contract doctrine, in both civil and common law jurisdictions, derives from the fact that the philosophical foundations of contract were lost as the theological and philosophical certainties of early and middle age legal theory met the free-thinking rationalism of the late eighteenth and nineteenth centuries. This analysis provides that the iconoclasm of the Enlightenment thinkers allied to the exigencies of the early development of *laissez faire* liberalism in effect produced something of a legal mutation and bequeathed a more practical but theoretically impoverished doctrine to the European contract lawyers who succeeded them. Whilst we may not wish to clone these earlier more philosophically rooted species, we may presume, prima facie, that, in seeking to rationalise the modern phenomenon of contract, existing theoretical disorder owes something to the severing of the umbilical cord of its philosophical life-support.[4] This alternative historical analysis further reveals important lessons with regard to the partial success and failure of legal transplants[5] and the emergence of dominant legal positions/theories in legal mainstream thought due to their wide distribution and accessibility. Evidence of a partial legal fusion of the common and civil law worlds and the emergence of a novel system also lends much greater support to Vivienne Grosswald Curran's convincing argument that the new emerging body of European laws will display fragments of both systems.[6]

3 P. Benson, 'The Unity of Contract Law' in P. Benson (ed.) *The Theory of Contract Law – New Essays* (Cambridge University Press, 2001) at 118.

4 See J. Gordley, *The Philosophical Origins of Modern Contract Doctrine* (Oxford University Press, Oxford, 1991) at 73. Hereinafter cited as *Origins, 1991*. Gordley makes the startling claim that modern theories of contract law cannot function logically without much of the Aristotelian and Thomistic concepts that were purged from the law during the Enlightenment era. For this reason, '[t]wo hundred years later, when we theorise about contract law, we still find ourselves at the same crossroads' in J. Gordley, 'Contract Law in the Aristotelian Tradition' in P. Benson, *ibid.* See also, D.J. Ibettson, *A Historical Introduction to the Law of Obligations* (Oxford, 1999) and R. Zimmermann, *Roman Law, Contemporary Law, European Law: The Civilian Tradition Today* (Oxford University Press, 2001).

5 A. Watson, *Legal Transplants* (Harvard University Press, 1987) at 12. For a contrary opinion of legal transplant theory, see Legrand's work on divergent legal 'mentalité' or 'moralité', which act to prevent the harmonisation of common and civil law legal systems. Legrand contends that a synchronisation between common and civil law systems is impossible due to their being founded upon a distinct 'volksgeist' or 'moralité', see P. Legrand, 'The Impossibility of Legal Transplants' (1997) 4 Maastricht J of Eur & Comp Law 111.

6 V. Grosswald Curran, 'Romantic Common Law, Enlightened Civil Law: Legal Uniformity and the Homogenization of the European Union' (2001) 7 Colum J Eur L 63. See also V. Grosswald Curran, 'Comparative Law and Language' in R. Zimmermann & M. Reimann (eds), *Oxford Handbook of*

Indeed an analysis of the *ius commune* evokes contract law's rich historical tapestry and the various classical, materialised and procedural visions that continue to shape modern doctrinal debate. It further calls to mind the quest for a satisfactory supporting ethic for modern practice. Fleeting references to the age of classical contract law, to codification and to modern Europe being divided between *Thibauts* and *Savignys*[7] currently rhyme with a general concurrence among contemporary common lawyers that the early formation of the English law of contract owed much to the 'creative plagiarism' of earlier civil law jurists.[8] This knowledge may add little to the current harmonisation debate but retains a certain modern charm since it may be argued that Restatements are likewise the product of similar acts of 'creative plagiarism', seeking to extract, rationalise and synthesise the 'common core' of European and transnational contract law from existing national legal systems.[9]

1.1 The enduring remnants of classical contract and their impact upon modern conceptions of European contract law in *'statu nascendi'*

Despite the deep inroads made by the Community legislator into national contract laws, the continued resonance of freedom and autonomy persists in the modern harmonisation/codification debate.[10] Reich observes that the:

Comparative Law (Oxford University Press, 2006) (highlighting the important role of language in the Europeanisation of law debate and signalling the 'ascendancy, if not dominance' of English). There can be little doubt that English has become the lingua franca in the debate surrounding the harmonisation of contract law.

7 Lando considers the 'codifiers' to be modern-day *Thibauts*, after Professor Anton Friedrich Justus Thibaut who, in 1814, advocated the enactment of a civil code in Germany and the 'cultivators' as *Savignys*, after Friedrich Carl von Savigny, who in the same year published a manifesto opposing such a project, see O. Lando, *Why does Europe need a Civil Code?*, SECOLA 2001.

8 J. Adams & R. Brownsword, *Understanding Contract Law* (Sweet & Maxwell, 2nd Edition, 1996) at 32., and P. Grossi, 'Historical Models and Present Plans in the Formation of a Future European Law' in A. Gambaro & A.M. Rabello (eds) *Towards a New European Ius Commune* (UP Jerusalem, 1999).

9 An argument previously developed in M.J. Doris, 'The Continued Resonance and Resonance of the Ius Commune for Modern European Contract Law', 34(2) Int'l J of Leg Info 391.

10 During the last two decades contractual fairness or solidarity has been the recurring theme of most European contributions. By contrast, the US has recently been gripped by a 'new' formalist trend, in part motivated by discontent with the UCC and its reform processes. Particularly illustrative of this trend are the recent works of Schwartz and Scott. See *inter alia*, R.E. Scott, 'The Uniformity Norm in Commercial Law – A Comparative Analysis of Common Law & Code Methodologies' in J. Kraus & S. Walt, *The Jurisprudential Foundations of Corporate and Commercial Law* (Cambridge University Press, 2000). See further B.K. Bucholtz, 'Rules, Principles or Just Words? The Interpretative Project and the Problem of Legitimacy' (2005) 11(2) Texas Wes 377.

> European Community law does not expressly recognise freedom of contract but presupposes its existence. No border crossing transaction concerning goods, services, capital, employment and establishment would be possible without a broad guarantee of contractual freedom. The European economic constitution based on a system of "an open market economy with free competition" (Art. 4 EC) could not function without contractual freedom ....

Orthodox common and civil law opinion provides that the doctrines underpinning classical contract theory, were creations of the late eighteenth and nineteenth centuries and it has been widely suggested and repeated that the concept of freedom of contract was "the inevitable counterpart of a free enterprise system".[11] Common law opinion, in particular, has almost universally accepted that the emergence of the doctrine of freedom of contract in English law owed much to the dominance of classical liberalism and *laissez faire* economics in the late eighteenth and nineteenth centuries. The leading proponent of this analysis is Atiyah,[12] who argues that, "the fact is that freedom of contract was at the very heart of classical economics, and there is ground for thinking that the common lawyers may have taken over the concept from the economists in the early part of the nineteenth century". Indeed, in the majority of European jurisdictions, a similar analysis prevails. It would appear that contract theorists have universally accepted that the pillars of classical contract theory were, "the masterpiece of the philosophy of law that dominated the nineteenth century: that of legal individualism".[13] Or as Williston suggests, "freedom of contract and the will theories arose because [a] *gospel of freedom* was preached by both metaphysical and political philosophers in the latter half of the eighteenth century.... It was a corollary of the philosophy of freedom and individualism that the law ought to extend the sphere and enforce the obligation of contract. The law did so by requiring a meeting of the minds for the formation of a contract and by allowing the parties to contract on whatever terms they might choose".[14]

This view of contract as an emblematic institution encompassing the various economic and liberal philosophies of the nineteenth century evidently

---

[11] R. Pound, 'Liberty of Contract' (1909) 18 Yale LJ 454.

[12] P.S. Atiyah, *The Rise and Fall of Freedom of Contract* (Oxford Clarendon Press, 1979) at 294 *et seq.* Atiyah's analysis of the historical development of the doctrine of freedom of contract and the 'will theory' is predicated upon this observation which forms the basis of his work. Undoubtedly, the author has had a seminal influence on the majority of modern commentators.

[13] See, *inter alia*, J. Ossorio Morales, 'Crisis en la Dogmática del Contrato' (1952) 1 ADC 1175, 1176; V. Ranouil, *L'autonomie de la volonté: naissance et evolutión d'un concept* (P.U.F. Paris, 1980).

[14] S. Williston, 'Freedom of Contract' (1921) 6 Cornell LQ 365, 366-9. Traditional European legal historians and contract theorists commonly view the French theorists Jean Domat, the great initiator, to whom we owe the concept of 'natural equity' and Robert Pothier, whose analysis of contract formed the basis of the French Code civil of 1804, as the founders of the 'will theory'. Where discussion exists of the French theorists' legal ancestry, those most commonly cited as being influential upon their thinking are the German natural lawyers Grotius and Pufendorf.

still appeals to many modern theorists.[15]. Nevertheless a novel historiography of the genealogy of European contract law, as articulated in part by Wieacker, Watkin and Ibbetsson, and most notably by Gordley, provides that reverence for Romano-Canon contract doctrine and in particular the principle *pacta sunt servanda* endured throughout continental Europe and enjoyed a renaissance in the sixteenth and seventeenth centuries, under the influence of the 'School of Salamanca' or 'Spanish Late Scholastics'.[16]

Influenced by the moral teachings of Aristotle and St. Thomas Aquinas[17], and imitating the progress made in other European law faculties or legal *scuola* which were flourishing throughout Europe, a corpus of scholastic humanists, led primarily by Luis de Molina (1535-1600), Domingo de Soto (1494-1560) and the Belgian Leonard Lessius (1554-1623) sought to further moralise private law and additional legal concepts with Christian principles. The late scholastics meticulously analysed the phenomenon of contracting in its entirety, including the binding force of promises, consent and its vitiation, the requirement of 'una justa causa' or 'just cause' for the enforceability of agreements, the theory of offer and acceptance, the content of contracts and the concept of equality in exchange, ultimately outlining a complex and intricate contractual system with detailed, specific rules[18] to govern particular sale, hire, barter and loan contracts[19] which found its justification not solely with recourse to the will of the parties – though this was evidently an important factor – but rather on the basis of virtues such as promise-keeping, liberality and substantive justice[20]. Despite a

---

15 See, *inter alia*, M. Lete del Rio, *Derecho de Obligaciones* (Tecnos, 1995), F.J. Orduña Moreno, *Contratación y consumo* (Tirant lo Blanch, 1998), at 261-265.

16 "La Escuela Escolástica Salmantina" per F. de Castro y Bravo, *Derecho civil de España* (Civitas, 1949); and the works of Gordley to whom we owe the term 'the late scholastics'. See also A.E. Perez Luño, *La Polémica sobre el Nuevo Mundo, Aproximación al Iusnaturalismo Clásico Español* (Ed. Trotta, 1992) at 32-33. Other prominent Spanish humanists of the era included Diego de Covarrubias y Leyva, 'the Spanish Bartolo' (1512 – 1571), Francisco de Vitoria (1480-), Francisco Suárez (1489 – 1546), and to a lesser extent Melchor Cano, Martín de Azpilcueta, Juan de la Peña, Domingo Bañez, etc. See respectively, F. Weiacker, *A History of Private Law in Europe – With Particular Reference to Germany* (Oxford Clarendon Press, 1996). T. Glyn-Watkin, *An Historical Introduction to Modern Civil Law* (Dartmouth, 1999). D.J. Ibbetson, *An Historical Introduction to the Law of Obligations* (Oxford University Press, 1999).

17 'Los grandes humanistas españoles fueron influidos por la doctrina de Aristotolés y *la Summa Theologica* de Santo Tomás', see De Castro y Bravo, *ibid* at 155.

18 A 'just' contract required that both parties were familiar with all relevant terms and conditions, that the parties established a fair price, which created a warranty on the quality of the object of the contract.

19 Grundmann has highlighted the teleological approach of the European legislator over the last decade in introducing contract law rules which focus upon a specific type of transaction and adopt a particular regulatory approach. EC contract law concentrates upon transactions which typically concern large volumes and that are not purely domestic. It is primarily obstacles to these transactions and resultant risks which are eliminated, see S. Grundmann, 'The Structure of European Contract Law', *supra*.

20 The late scholastics similarly adopted a teleological vision of contract arguing that an agreed transaction ought to be upheld, not because it was the expressed will of the parties – though this was evidently

certain collective amnesia in the literature regarding the role of the late scholastics, suggests that the scholastics were the founders of reliance-based theory extrapolated from the virtue of promise keeping.

The theories developed[21] by these pioneering European law and economics scholars were further analysed by leading advocates of natural law in northern Europe, such as Grotius and Pufendorf,[22] who continued the late scholastic tradition but simplified much of the early humanist concepts. In particular, Schermaier notes how the northern natural lawyers simplified and refined the doctrines of mistake, primitive conceptions of modern information duties and above all the earliest notions of precontractual reliance. It was determined that only if the recipient of a declaration could rely on an intention inferred therefrom did the giver of that information remain bound to his declaration. However, if the recipient knew of the diverging intention of the giver or if he should have known of it can he rely on his *iusta expectatio*, i.e. his reliance on the declaration.[23]

---

an equally important factor – but because of the validity, legal and moral, of the ultimate goal or object of the parties in entering into contractual relations, see J. Gordley, *Origins 1991*, at 240-1. See also, in particular, *Part I: Some Perennial Problems* in J. Gordley (ed.), *The Enforceability of Promises in European Contract Law* (Cambridge University Press, 2001).

21 Though not completely 'de novo'. The late scholastic thinkers were evidently building upon the scaffold erected by the Romano-canon lawyers of the fourteenth and fifteenth centuries. The Spanish civilian jurists of the preceding generations had advanced highly innovative and progressive contractual theories. In particular, they had expressly advocated the principle of freedom of contract in *Título XVI* of the Ordinance of Álcala, of 1345. Whilst the canonists had concluded in principle that contracts were binding because of the consent of the contracting parties, the late scholastics reached the same conclusion by arguing from the standpoint of neo-Thomist and Aristotelian philosophy.

22 A. Watson, *The Making of the Civil Law* (Harvard University Press, 1981), 83 *et seq.* Both humanists were undoubtedly familiar with the writings of the Spanish humanists, and Gordley suggests that Grotius in particular was a 'late scholastic at heart'. Wieacker adds that, Grotius '... frequently invokes Vitoria, Covarruvias, Ayala and Fernando Vázquez: their influence was all the greater because despite the War of Independence the cultural links between Spain and the Netherlands were still strong', *ibid*, at p. 229. For an alternative analysis see H. Welzel, *Introducción a la Filosofía del Derecho* (Aguilar, 1971) at 128-129, who posits the theories of Grotius in the earlier philosophies of stoicism. See also A. Marín López, *La Doctrina del Derecho Natural en H. Grocio* (2 Anales de la Cátedra Francisco Suárez, Universidad de Granada, 1962) at 205-211.

23 Schermaier traces a direct line between this earliest conception of reliance and the later anchoring of reliance in statute in the ABGB's law on mistake in 1811. Section 876 of the 1811 Code (the Code was later re-enacted in 1916) stated that: if the promisor himself and alone is at fault with regard to his mistakes of whatever kind, the contract remains valid; unless the circumstances were such that the promisee must have recognised the prevailing mistake. See M.J. Schermaier, 'Mistake, Misrepresentation and Precontractual Duties to Inform: the Civil Law Tradition' in R. Sefton Green (ed), *Mistake, Fraud and Duties to Inform in European Contract Law* (Cambridge University Press, 2005), at 57 *et seq.* He adds that the 'common core of modern reliance theories originate from this late natural law discussion. It was Raymond Saleilles who in 1907 advanced the view that after parties have entered into negotia-

In simplifying the earlier scholastic doctrines, Grotius and Pufendorf succeeded in popularising the legal concepts but in the process, according to Gordley, much of the detail and theoretical precision was lost.[24] Gordley and Weiacker suggest that Pufendorf and Barbeyrac were greatly influenced by contemporary scientific and mathematic thought, particularly that of Descartes and as such "allowed philosophical principles and legal doctrine to drift apart"[25] and with Christian Wolff, who developed contract theory scientifically and deductively on a pragmatic basis,[26] the late scholastic debate finally dropped out of sight, as he failed to comprehend the Aristotelian tradition that he was attempting to modernise and revive.[27] It is important, however, to stress what most commentators fail to recognise: the existence of two very different though not distinct 'Schools' of Salamanca, which in the gloss of history have largely been fused as one. As Brett observes, the terms 'school of Salamanca' and 'second scholastic' usually apply to the entire period of sixteenth-century Spanish scholasticism, from Vitoria to Suárez.[28] They therefore span both the early

---

tions, both must act in accordance with good faith and neither can break off negotiations 'arbitrarily' without compensating the other for reliance damages. Reliance theory received a further 'shot-in-the-arm' from Raymond Saleilles. In *De la responsibilité précontractuelle* written in 1907 he advanced the view that after parties have entered into negotiations, both must act in accordance with good faith and neither can break off negotiations 'arbitrarily' without compensating the other for reliance damages. R. Saleilles, 'De la responsibilité précontractuelle' (1907) 6 Rev. Trim. Dr. Civ. 697, at 718-719. In the US it would not be until the mid-1930's and the publication of Fuller and Perdue's seminal work on the reliance interest (L. Fuller & W.R. Perdue, 'The Reliance Interest in Contract Damages, Parts 1 and 2' (1936-7) 46 Yale LJ 52 before reliance liability would enter the contract mainstream. There is a certain irony that today reliance notions are re-entering the European debate via a re-examination of US Restatements, caselaw and doctrine. Though not without dissenters on both sides of the Atlantic. See D. Friedmann, 'A Comment on Fuller and Perdue, the Reliance Interest in Contract Damages' (2001) 3 Issues in Legal Scholarship, available via bepress.com. and discussed further in chapter 4.

24 Whether through an inability to completely comprehend the 'late scholastic' doctrines or indeed as a consequence of their rejection by the German natural lawyers, the end result was the loss of philosophical and moral justifications underpinning contract law.

25 See J. Gordley, *Origins 1991*, at 133 *et seq.* See also R.C. Van Caenegem, *An Historical Introduction to Private Law* (Cambridge University Press, 1994) at 116.

26 *Ibid* at 119.

27 '... los humanistas ... liquidaron en el plano histórico-crítico la pretensión de identificar a Aristóteles con la Verdad', por E. Garin, *La Revolución cultural del Renacimiento* (2nd edn, Crítica Barcelona, 1984) at 256. A point reinforced by Gordley in *Origins 1991*, at 133.

28 Francisco de Vitoria, (1480-1546). Thomas Glyn Watkin views Vitoria as the modern founding father of the European law of obligations. See Watkin, *supra* fn 16, at 114. Francisco Suárez (1548-1670), has been singled out by one historian of legal interpretation as one of the most vigorous and sophisticated thinker on issues of legal textual interpretation and meaning of his time, see C. Lefebvre, *Les Pouvoirs du Juge en Droit Canonique* (Paris, 1938). Lefebvre's study points to the qualities of Suárez's work in comparison with that of his contemporaries, even though it did not form part of the "common stock of ideas and theories in the first third of the seventeenth century, even if it necessarily falls within

Dominican period and the later, Jesuit-dominated stage, when the movement had ceased to be centred on the University of Salamanca. However, "the Jesuit continuation of work of the School is a study in its own right".

A decisive change occurred, however, in the intellectual climate of western Europe in the late seventeenth and early eighteenth centuries with the dawn of the Enlightenment; a philosophical movement which sought to liberate the individual from the medieval bondage of traditional authorities in religion, politics, law and culture, and to subject these powerful bastions to 'rational' criticism[29]. It was with the advent of 'natural reason' that the authority of Aristotelian and Thomistic philosophy collapsed, the dominance of the Roman Catholic church declined and the validity of the scholastic natural law theories of contract was finally rejected[30]. The historic precepts of the law of contracts predicated upon ancient doctrines emanating from a vague confluence of Roman legal thought and the moral authority of Aristotle and St. Thomas Aquinas were hollowed out and replaced by a new ideology, which stressed the sovereignty of the individual. The novel project of the natural lawyers was the intellectual enlightenment of society, thus legal doctrine and moral philosophy under the influence of the northern natural law school began to drift apart[31]. As Simmonds observes, "the shift away from Aristotelian jurisprudence had a number of consequences. It gave rise to a vision of political order spanning two contrasting traditions of

---

the conceptual paradigms of that time". Suárez's *Tractibus de Legibus ac deo legislatore* was published apparently for international consumption in Coimbra, 1612, Antwerp 1613, Lyons 1613 and Mainz in 1619. Importantly, Klein observes that Francisco Suarez 'worked to define more precisely the scope of the good faith obligation as applied to secular considerations' and that 'the continuing relevance of the Scholastic view of good faith is readily apparent in light of the decline of the caveat emptor doctrine ... Under the Thomistic view, contracts entered into under the influence of duress or fraud are 'not only evil, but also invalid', see J. Klein, 'Good Faith in International Transactions' (1993) 15 Liverpool Law Review 115, at 121. Yet, Watkin provides illuminating evidence as to why the theories of the scholastic thinkers failed to gain a dominant position within mainstream European legal thought: Suárez was published expensively in folio, whereas many monographs appeared in smaller, cheaper formats; and his work was not included under the rubric *libri juridici* in the book fair catalogues. Instead his volume, financed initially by the Bishop of Egitania and not, apparently, by a speculative publisher, was produced with the needs of Jesuit colleges in mind, and was addressed to canon, not civil, lawyers', *supra* fn. 16, at 114. This fact also resonates in the modern harmonisation debate since it has been argued that it is a small, vocal nomenklature – who are fluent in English but not necessarily the leading contract lawyers in their individual jurisdictions that our currently driving the codification project. Gordley has similarly highlighted a danger that the CFR project maybecome 'monopolised' by only one academic viewpoint. See Gordley, *supra* Introduction fn. 19.

29 W. Friedmann, *Legal Theory* (5th edn, Steven & Sons, 1967) at 114-115, and R.C. Van Caenegem, *supra* at 117. This analysis is not shared by Watson however, who discounts any hostility toward the established order on the part of the German natural lawyers, see A. Watson (1981), *supra*, at 88.

30 "It was at this point that the authority of Aristotle collapsed in the seventeenth and eighteenth centuries and the philosophical foundations of the law of contract were lost", see Gordley, *Origins 1991*, at 161.

31 *Ibid*, at 133.

juridical thought – exemplified by Grotius and Hobbes – that continue to exercise their influence".[32] The desire to achieve conceptual clarity and to present a general law of contractual obligations which could be defended with recourse to 'natural reason', prompted the later "pioneers of abstraction", the French theorists[33] to systematise the prevailing natural law theories, which were of late scholastic origin, into a rational and popular legal doctrine. Van der Walt completes the picture. He notes that, "many theorists wanted to ensure that choices among competing rights were constrained by clear and unambiguous principles, so that judicial judgment could be separated from the uncertainties of political rhetoric and metaphysical theory. The lawyers of the Enlightenment were, in a word, looking for a legal science in which certainty was guaranteed through method. Ever since the Enlightenment this implied that the legal story ... would have to be transformed from a religious fable into a scientific dissertation.[34]

The eighteenth century ferment of ideas was itself a reflection of the needs and tensions of a changing society based on the new scientific knowledge of the seventeenth century, which bred a new faith in reason and progress. The philosophers whose intellectual radicalism fuelled the Enlightenment rejected

---

32 The tradition of positivism was ultimately to yield a conception of legal scholarship quite different from that of Grotius and his successors, see N.E. Simmonds, 'Protestant Jurisprudence and Modern Doctrinal Scholarship' (2001) 60 CLJ 271, at 300. See also Brett's discussion of the impact of late scholastic thinking on both Grotius and Hobbes legal and political theories. She discusses the divisions among contemporary theorists as to whether the late scholastics sought a return to an authentic Thomist-Aristotelian theory, founded on such notions as pure natural law and of right as the object of justice (objective right), or whether, although on the surface these Spanish neo-Thomists appeared faithful to Aristotle and Thomas Aquinas, in reality they thought of right as a faculty or liberty of the individual (subjective right) and that as such their political theory, as premised upon such legal rights, ought to be viewed therefore as a forerunner to Hobbes legal philosophy. For an analysis of late scholastic doctrine in the development of European philosophy, see also Q. Skinner, *The Foundations of Modern Political Thought – Volume II* (Cambridge, 1978).

33 See, *inter alia*, E. Gómez Arboleya, *El Racionalismo Jurídico y los Códigos Europeos*, (Estudios de Teoría de la Sociedad y del Estado, Centro de Estudios Constitucionales, Madrid, 1962) at 476-7. The German systematisers, Wolff and Savigny, were undoubtedly influential, yet in the ambit of contract law, it was the French legal theorists Domat y Pothier, who were instrumental in the birth of a generalised, abstract theory of contract, premised upon the principles of autonomy and freedom, which were justified with recourse to 'natural reason'. Domat's general law of contract is often reduced to the basic principle that, 'all contracts, whether they have a particular name or not, always have their effect, and oblige the parties to do what is agreed on' (J. Domat, *Les loix civiles dans leur ordre naturel.*) See J. Remy, *Les Oeuvres Complets de Jean Domat* (1830). This subjective 'internalisation' of contractual obligations – the meeting of minds or concurrence of two or more independent wills – became the cornerstone of the French natural law theory of contract.

34 See A. Van der Walt, 'Marginal Notes on Powerful Legends: Critical Perspectives on Property Theory' (1995) 58 *THRHR* 402. Indeed, when analysing the role of the late scholastics in the formation of the law of contract in Europe one is minded of John Henry Newman's fable of 'The Man and the Lion', who noted that Lions would undoubtedly have fared better, had lions been the artists.

traditional authority and asserted the 'Rights of Man' expressed in Rousseau's statement that 'man is born free but is everywhere in chains'. The concepts of reason, freedom and tolerance were a dominant force in a society undergoing rapid industrialisation. The new economic wisdom was *laissez-faire* capitalism which combined with the philosophical drive of the Enlightenment theorists who proclaimed man to be a free, rational individual whose right it was to order his own affairs freed from the formulaic exigencies of the past. The new economic and political order that evolved from rapid industrialisation and the post Enlightenment democratic rationalism saw a swift expansion in the area of contractual litigation with the concomitant necessity to find an effective law of contract based on the new doctrines of reason and free market liberalism, freed from historical and moral anachronisms. To such a mind-set the ceding of any moral authority to the theologically inspired philosophers of the past would have appeared as a betrayal of the new age of realism. In addition, the philosophical discourse of the 'late scholastics' belonged to an age of scholastic theorising often freed from the practicalities of legal interpretation.[35] The new age theorists faced a different dynamic; to produce a practical blueprint for a society with a rapidly expanding need for a workable law of contract. As Zimmermann stresses, a desire to promote 'greater publicity of the law' was an equally 'admirable philosophical and educational idea espoused and energetically promoted by eighteenth century enlightened authoritarianism: the comprehensive and systematic re-organisation of law and society along the lines of natural reason and in the form of codification aimed at making the law accessible, at instructing all subjects'.[36]

However, perhaps more important in the evolution of classical contract theory than the writings of the legal theorists was the period of the Enlightenment itself; like any social revolution it was greater than any individual. Much more than any pure theory it was the general thrust of an era.[37] Northern natural law claimed that men had an inalienable right to own property and contract as they saw fit. To the principles of *laissez faire* and *laissez passer* was added *laissez contracter.* As such, whether as a result of legal practicalities and the prevailing economic and political realities of the age, or as a consequence of latent hostility to the earlier more theologically based philosophies, or perhaps even due to an

[35] It is important to note, however, that the doctrines of the Spanish natural lawyers, premised upon an ideal of justice that formed part of a universal law, failed to find legal expression in practice, either in the courts or in legislative enactments, and are thus largely consigned to history.

[36] R. Zimmermann, 'Codification: History and Present Significance of an Idea' (1995) 3 ERPL 95. Of course, rather than pure legal history, Zimmermann is unabashed in presenting an applicative and ideologically-driven approach to legal history that in many respects continues a distinctly internationalist Roman law tradition in German legal science since the post War era.

[37] It was a general thought and a particular perception of society, of morality, of order. The 'ethereal intellectual constructions' – per K. Zweigert & H. Kötz, *An Introduction to Comparative Law* (3rd edn, Oxford University Press, 1998) at 142 – of the advocates of the law of reason, provided an alternative approach to the analysis of conceptual problems.

inability to properly comprehend them, when the body of learning developed by the late scholastics was taken up by the northern natural law school the most important elements of promise keeping, virtue and substantive justice were lost. The moral arguments from which obligations emerged and on which they were premised were abandoned, and only the part of the theory concerned with the will of the parties, together with its structure of concepts based on offer and acceptance as the expression of the parties' agreement, was retained.[38]

The Assimilation of French Natural Law Theory and the Development of English Commercial Contract Law

The process of assimilation into English law of a generalised law of contract founded upon the classical theory of private contractual autonomy, which was dubbed 'the will theory', and the mantra of freedom of contract evolved during the late eighteenth[39] and early nineteenth century, beginning in earnest with the publication of Robert Pothier's, *Traité des Obligations* in 1806. The 'novel' theory that the mere consent or willingness of both parties to form contractual relations should prove sufficient for the legal system to afford legal protection to contractual agreements had a profound effect on the English treatise writers and judiciary. The French theorists' abstract analysis of contract as an *accords de volontés* or meeting of minds, premised upon a reciprocal offer and acceptance, provided a generalised system that fitted the spirit of the age and was readily welcomed into English law.[40]

It seems irrefutable that, before the writings of Blackstone, in England 'the science of law in all that relates to contracts was left almost without cultivation'.[41]

---

38 Gordley suggests that when the authority of Aristotle collapsed in northern Europe what remained of the 'late scholastics' theory to the untrained mind was the concept of the will of the parties. See J. Gordley, 'Myths of the French Civil Code' (1994) Am J of Comp L 459.

39 *Hawkes v. Saunders*, 1 Cowper 289, 98 Eng. Rep. 1091 (K.B. 1782). In the late eighteenth century Lord Mansfield suggested that in English law, as in the civil law, all promises seriously made should be considered as legally binding, subject to a broad theory of what may be called 'invalidating cause', which was remarkably similar to the civilian concept of the 'justa causa'; see also *Payne v. Cave*, 3 Term R. 148, 100 Eng. Rep. 502 (1789) and Cooke v. Oxley, 3 Term R. 653, 100 Eng. Rep. 785 (1790) in which distinctly civilian terminology was employed by the courts; yet, as Horwitz notes, "only in the nineteenth century did judges and jurists reject the belief that the justification [for enforcing] a contractual obligation is derived from the inherent justice or fairness of an exchange. In its place they asserted for the first time that the source of the obligation of contract is the convergence of the wills of the contracting parties", see M.J. Horwitz, 'The Historical Foundations of Modern Contract Law' (1974) 87 Harvard Law Review 917.

40 "The authority of Pothier ... is as high as can be had, next to the decision of a Court of Justice in this country", *per* Best J, *Cox v. Troy* (1822) B & Ald 474, at 480. Without doubt the generality and abstraction offered by Pothier's analysis was warmly received into an English legal system that had endured since the sixteenth century the uncompromising system of assumpsit.

41 A. Carey, 'A Course of Lectures on the Law of Contract: Lecture 1', The Law Times (1845) at 463. The main corpus of the general principles and theory of the modern English law of contract, including the

Similar to the proliferation of legal schools throughout continental Europe from the twelfth century onwards, the adoption of continental contract theories arose via the promotion in England of the legal treatise,[42] which heralded a new common law approach to the analysis of the law, provoking theorists and students to engage in debate and conceptualise legal problems in a traditionally civilian manner. [43] Identical motivations to those that drove the Enlightenment theorists in a previous age demanded that the general principles and legal theory behind many of the developments in the courts be enunciated. The attempts to systematise the law of contract, however, marked a significant break with common law tradition.[44] As Cornish and Clark affirm, the judges wanted rules and were searching for principle in a rapidly expanding area of their business, and their small number constrained their ability to make precedent.[45] The

concepts of offer and acceptance, the intention to create legal relations, the various forms of vitiation of consent etc, were developed and elaborated in the late eighteenth and early nineteenth century via treatise.

42 J.J. Powell's *Essay upon the Law of Contracts* of 1790 developed upon Blackstones' *Commentaries* (1765-69) which devoted a mere forty pages to 'contracts' and focused primarily upon contracts for land, however it was Pothier's *Traite des obligations* of 1761 which proved most influential both in the courts and among legal academics, prompting the works of the later treatise writers such as Chitty (1818), Pollock (1875), Anson (1879), etc. In this regard, it is important to highlight the important role of Ibbetson in unearthing Sir Jeffrey Gilbert's unprinted treatise on contract: *which has a good claim to be the first serious work on the subject in England* and which bears a strong imprint of the thinking of Thomas Hobbes social contract theories. Moreover, 'Pufendorf's influence is abundantly clear in the first published English work on contract with any pretension to treat the subject on an abstract basis, a *Treatise on Equity* published anonymously in 1737, but probably the work of Henry Ballow or Bellewe of Lincoln's Inn. For the most part his discussion of contract consists of brief paraphrases of or unattributed quotations from the English translation of Pufendorf's *De iure nature et gentium*, followed by illustrative material from English caselaw', see Ibettson, J., *ibid*, at p. 121. In similar fashion to the continental legal schools of the Middle Ages, the use of the legal treatise in England and later in the US, can be viewed as both the forum and the emerging vehicle for the debate and promotion of contract theories.

43 An importation of a civilian outlook into the common law was the logical result of an acceptance of civilian theories; see A.W.B. Simpson, 'The Rise and Fall of the Legal Treatise: Legal Principles and the Forms of Legal Literature' (1981) 48 Uni of Chi L Rev 632. This is of relevance today as a number of contemporary European private law study groups have opted to employ notably common law techniques when analysing general principles. The Spanish private law network, REDPEC, for example, has taken caselaw as its primary point of focus and is currently examining leading higher court judgments in Spain, rather than provisions of the Spanish civil code, in the light of the Principles of European Contract Law.

44 The common lawyers 'engaged upon an enterprise that was new to the common law ... but old to the civilian tradition; they were trying to do what the civilians, the canonists and the natural lawyers had been doing for centuries', A.W.B. Simpson, 'Innovation in Nineteenth Century Contract Law' (1975) 91 LQR 254.

45 See W.R. Cornish & G. Clark, *Law and Society in England 1750 –1950* (Professional Books, 1989), at 200 *et seq*. See also G.R. Rubin, *Law, Economy and Society, 1750 – 1914: Essays in the History of English Law*

English judiciary, similar to the Enlightenment theorists before them, were faced with a new legal challenge; their immediate priority was to produce a practical legal framework for an industrialised society with a rapidly expanding need for a coherent law of contract. Formal recognition of the adoption of natural law theories in the English courts was forthcoming as evidenced in the leading case of *Adams v. Lindsell*[46] and by the mid nineteenth century, 'will theory' had taken root in English law[47].

Indeed it has been suggested that the northern natural law theories were so popular among the legal fraternity that the caselaw ought to be viewed as a mere reinforcement of the doctrine or as 'fruits on the conceptual tree'.[48] The universality of this abstract construct was similarly attractive to academic and judicial opinion, which was endeavouring to discern the general basic principles of contract law.[49] The courts were evidently highly influenced by the treatise writers who had merely translated natural law theories into English.[50] In turn the natural lawyers had developed their contractual theories from the writings of the late scholastics, which were defended with recourse to the philosophy of Aristotle and Thomas Aquinas. And yet, "this philosophy was almost unintelligible to the nineteenth century jurists. Consequently, the treatise writers often borrowed superficially, repeating the phrases of the natural lawyers with little understanding of their original meaning. They often borrowed selectively, neglecting doctrines that seemed alien and repugnant. The nineteenth century jurists arrived at their will theories by starting with the doctrines of the natural lawyers and purging them of older Aristotelian concepts they did not understand. Will was the single most important concept that remained".[51] The expressed will of the parties thus became the impetus to the formation of contracts and constituted the justification for their enforcement; as such the intention of the contracting parties became the kernel of early nineteenth century contract law. With increasing regularity English judges were referring to Roman law concepts such as the requirement that the courts find a 'consen-

(London, 1984).

46 (1818) 1 B & Ald 681. This case is widely regarded in English contract law as constituting the birth of the concept of 'offer and acceptance'. Simpson *supra* suggests that the court relied heavily upon Pothier's *Treatise on the Contract of Sale* which provided that 'a contract is affirmed by the coincidence of the will of [the two contracting parties], where one promises something to the other, and the other accepts the promise that he was made'.

47 P.S. Atiyah, *supra* at 407. See also the wealth of caselaw; including: *Pole v. Leask* (1863) 33 L.J. Ch. 155; *Dickinson v. Dodds* (1876) 2 Ch.D 463, at 472; *Cundy v. Lindsay* (1878) 3 App. Cas. 459, at 465.

48 See R. Danzig, 'A Study in the Industrialisation of Law – Hadley v. Baxendale' (1975) 4 J of Leg Stud 249.

49 'When Pothier's works began to be read in England they must have appeared a revelation of clarity of exposition', per J.N. Adams & R. Brownsword, *supra*, at 32.

50 J. Gordley, *supra* at 161.

51 J. Gordley, *Origins 1991*, at 162.

sus ad idem'[52] between the parties who were at liberty to 'realise their wills' and to the late scholastic theory of the binding force of promises. Unless the two minds were *ad idem* there could be no contract. Dicta in *Cundy v. Lindsay*[53] further reveal that judicial support for the will theory was still enduring in the late nineteenth century and that contracts were consistently being interpreted as the product of a 'consensus of minds'.

However, having assimilated and promoted the subjective concept of autonomy, the English courts were further required to interpret the sense of the reciprocal declarations and determine whether, in fact, the parties had agreed to contract. In the event, the test imposed by the courts was evidently an objective test. Objectivity prevailed since the courts, having regard to the external manifestations of agreement, were obliged to rule on whether or not an agreement had in fact been made;[54] and ensure that commercial common sense was not adversely affected by the operation of a subjective 'will theory'. As noted previously, in the period prior to the assimilation of Continental legal theories English law had laboured under the cumbersome doctrine of assumpsit; as the legal remedy for situations in which one party was in breach of an undertaking made to another. In such cases it was necessary to examine the external acts of both parties. It was thus logical for the courts in considering whether there had in fact been an intention on the part of the contracting parties to create legal relations to apply an objective test as a means of rationalising the subjective will theory. The majority of Anglo-American legal academics have reasoned from the perspective that classical contract doctrine was elaborated in the courts and fitted into the spirit of the age. Yet only those such as Watkin, Ibbetsson and perhaps more emphatically, Gordley have begun to recognise that the traditional doctrine as introduced into Britain was incomplete, thus provoking the courts to 'bend and stretch the doctrines they had borrowed to do the work of those they had not'[55].

Importantly, O'Malley asks the all important question why the complex doctrines of the late scholastics were 'sloughed off' in favour of a 'stripped down will theory'. He suggests that most of the commentaries are 'strangely silent on the question, perhaps because a principal item on their agenda is the denial of propositions concerning the impact on common law of capitalistic economic

[52] *Haynes v. Haynes* (1861) 1 Dr & Sm 426, 433 – 'when both parties will the same thing, and each communicates his will to the other, with a mutual agreement to carry it into effect, then an engagement or contract between the two is constituted', *per* Kindersley VC.

[53] (1878) 3 App Cas 459, at 467. Agreement is necessarily the outcome of consenting minds.

[54] *Smith v. Hughes* (1871) LR 6 QB 597 – "If, whatever a man's real intention be, he so conducts himself that a reasonable man would believe that he is assenting to the terms proposed by the other party, and that other party upon that belief enters into the contract with him, the man thus conducting himself would be equally bound as if he had intended to agree to other party's terms", *per* Blackburn J. Similar observations were made in *Bardell v. Pickwick* and in the later US case of *Hotchkiss v. National City Bank*, 200F. 287, 293 (S.D.N.Y.) 1911.

[55] J. Gordley, *Origins* 1991, at 135.

interests and liberal political theory'. However, the influence of classical liberalism in the shaping of English classical contract theory, with its emphasis on the sovereignty of the individual, and the economic theories of those such as Adam Smith, has largely been accepted without engendering much controversy. In particular, Anglo-American analyses of the historical development of the pillars of classical contract theory have been presented by those such as Horwitz,[56] who suggests that the emergence of classical contract theory was due primarily to the demise of the 'moral obligation' doctrine in the law of consideration,[57] a formal recognition of the executory contract, the awarding of expectation damages; and in particular due to deliberate judicial activism in order to promote the capitalist system and commercial interests.

In support of the Horwitz thesis it is widely accepted that the role of equity in the area of contract law declined, as the 'moral obligation' doctrine in the law of consideration was expunged by the courts.[58] This radical and intentional doctrinal shift in contract theory in the early nineteenth century away from the old system of equity, which was viewed as being antagonistic to the interests of commerce, and the embracing of novel concepts to support the capitalist system was undoubtedly due to the influence of economic liberalism on the English judiciary. As Cornish & Clark observe, 'the generalisations evolved by the text-writers and judges undoubtedly buttressed freedom of dealing and sanctity of bargaining, the economic security of market place pricing over government regulation and the moral righteousness of self sufficiency and self improvement'. There was without doubt a common belief among those judges sympathetic to the *laissez faire* economics of the era that just as Adam Smith's 'hidden hand' analysis of the market would ensure the proper functioning of the economy, so the hidden subjective 'meeting of minds' would ensure the smooth operation of contract law. As Pollock affirms: The sort of men who became judges towards the middle of the century were imbued with the creed of the philosophical radicals for whom the authority of the orthodox economists came second only to Bentham's and whose patron saint was Ricardo.[59] The judge most commonly cited as reflective of the general attitude as George William Bramwell, a leading advocate of *laissez faire* economics and a persistent champion of 'real' consent.[60] The liberal judiciary prided itself on its rejection of moral paternalism. The prevailing view, consistent with liberal ideology, remained that individuals should be permitted the maximum liberty

56 Though his thesis has been rejected by Simpson as being 'oversimplified' in A.W.B. Simpson, 'The Horwitz Thesis and the History of Contracts' (1947) 46 U Chi L Rev 533, at 600.

57 See *Eastwood v. Kenyon* (1840) 11 A & E 438, 113 ER 482.

58 See P.S. Atiyah, *supra*, at 388 *et seq.*

59 39 LQR 163, at 165, *per* Frederick Pollock.

60 P.S. Atiyah, *supra*, at 375 et seq, and J. Tillotson, *Contract Law In Perspective* (2nd edn, Cavendish, 1995) at 42, who notes that 'enthusiasm for freedom of contract went hand in hand with support for the operation of a free market'.

to contract[61]. Moreover, the small number of practising judges[62] reveals that it would have been possible for the ideology of freedom of contract and *laissez-faire* to be promoted through the courts.[63]

For this reason it is possible to view the absolutist dogma of 'freedom of contract' as operated in classical English contract law as essentially a judicial construct and as a 'larger ideological orientation which accompanied the growth of industrial capitalism', though the philosophies used to support this novel theory were in reality something of a continental European pastiche.[64] Importantly, the adherence of the English common law judiciary to classical liberalism and the capitalist system meant that the inherent injustices of that system were merely transplanted into nineteenth century contract law since 'the contractarians ideology above all expressed a market conception of legal relations. As the only measure of justice was the parties' own agreement, all pre-existing legal duties were inevitably subordinated to the contract relation. The law had come simply to ratify those forms of inequality that the market system produced'.[65] The English common law judiciary adopted these novel civilian contractual theories and concepts, which were considered most suitable for an emerging industrialised society, and thereafter embarked upon a process of commercialisation of the law, characterised by a pragmatic attitude and a close tracking of commercial interests. Indeed, even those with the most rudimentary legal schooling in the historical development of contract law in European legal systems would have quickly grasped that the English law of contract, having borrowed so liberally from the civilian traditions, thereafter chose to bend and mould these new 'legal transplants' to best suit the will of the business elite. The moral dimension or concept of *good faith*, was largely viewed as an impediment to trade. It may be

---

61 H. Collins, *Legal Theory and Common Law* (Oxford University Press, 1996) at 144. As Atiyah stresses, the common belief was that 'people could be trusted to look after themselves, to see to their own interests, and this led to a rejection of paternalism' and the adoption of an abstentionist position by the courts. See P.S. Atiyah, 'Freedom of Contract and the New Right', in *Essays on Contract* (Oxford Clarendon Press, 1996) and G.R. Rubin, *Law, Economy and Society* (1980) at 12-13 and 70-71.

62 W.R. Cornish & G. Clark, *supra*, at 206.

63 In addition, the introduction of the Common Law Procedure Act 1852 further assisted the development of the concept of freedom of contract by abolishing the various procedural forms of action in the courts.

64 Cornish and Clark, *supra*, at 202. Moreover, as Gilmore notes, 'the classical theory of contract did not come as the natural result of case-law development ... it represented a sharp break with the past', G. Gilmore, *The Death of Contract* (Ohio State University Press, 1974) at 17-18. Importantly, the population of London more than doubled in the period between 1800 and 1850 and the social conditions in Britain during the age of classical contract are perhaps best illustrated by Blakes' poem 'London'.

65 G.R. Rubin, *supra*, 70. Curiously, Gordley rejects any grander ideological motives on the part of the common law judiciary. He suggests that in practice, 'we find little direct borrowing from philosophers, economists or political theorists. Only rarely do we find any sign of commitment to liberal values of freedom or individualism. We find almost the opposite: an insistence that the jurist can do his job without taking account of economics, philosophy, politics or values such as freedom ... They said almost nothing about any larger principles on which they were building', *Origins 1991* at 215-6.

argued that this skewed assimilation was due to a degree of legal naivety on the part of the English judiciary, prompted by a lack of familiarity with the fundamental structures of continental contract theory, which resulted in the erroneous interpretation of the principle of freedom of contract and contributed in part to its irrational interpretation.[66] The principle of freedom of contract, which had been advocated by the canonists in fourteenth century Spain and which was impliedly enshrined in the French Code civil was merely that; a principle. Yet the English courts elevated the principle of freedom of contract into a fixed rule or end in itself[67] and thus embarked on a somewhat illogical process of upholding contractual agreements even where parties were operating from an unequal bargaining position.[68] By the late nineteenth century, however, there was a general realisation that this absolutist dogma of freedom of contract, operating without regard to social, equitable or moral considerations, was at best a utopian ideal and at worst a pernicious concept open to corruption by the wealthiest and most powerful sections of society. In this I find myself agreeing with Atiyah and Friedman that the dogma of freedom of contract as it operated in England applied to an age of *laissez faire* liberalism and as a 'mere theoretical construct, which [had] little or nothing to do with the real world, would not – or could not- change as the real world changed'.[69] It emerged as an absolutist doctrine at odds with a rapidly changing political and economic climate, for as Gilmore attests, 'its natural habitat was the law schools, not the law courts. On the whole, however, the theory was in its origins, and continued to be during its

[66] M.A. León González, *La evolución histórica del concepto del contrato, Lecciones sobre las obligaciones y contratos*, Salamanca, May 12-14, 1998. This analysis of the development of freedom of contract in English law is a minority opinion which evidently questions much of the traditional thinking, though this author finds it highly persuasive.

[67] In the nineteenth century, freedom of contract was regarded by many philosophers, economists and judges as an end in itself, finding its philosophical justification in the 'will theory' of contract and its economic justification in *laissez-faire* liberalism. *Chitty on Contracts – Volume 1* (27th edn, Sweet & Maxwell, 1994), at 5 *et seq*. Caselaw in modern times reveals judicial recognition that the operation of an absolutist analysis of freedom of contract cannot be justified and that the doctrine has been reduced to a 'general principle', see for example *Suisse Atlantique Société d'Armement Maritime SA v. NV Rotterdamsche Kolen Centrale* [1967] 1 AC 361, 399 and *Photo Production Limited v. Securicor Transport* [1980] AC 827, 848.

[68] As Cornish and Clark note, the common law courts renounced their 'earlier willingness to rectify elements of unfairness in bargains and instead insisted upon enforcing whatever terms had been agreed'. The common law support for a severely individualistic conception of freedom of contract contrasted with the courts of equity, which constituted 'a protective jurisdiction of conscience', *supra* at 203. Evidently, as Horwitz notes, the role of the courts of equity had greatly diminished.

[69] Per Friedman in G. Gilmore, *supra* at 7. Cornish and Clark suggest that the decline of the classical vision of contract ought to be traced from the year 1876 onwards; as, following the Judicature Acts of 1873, in 1876, 'the liberal hegemony of the mid-Victorian years was threatened by a novel, democratic "collectivism" and in that year a directive was issued giving preference to the rules of equity over the common law rules', *supra* at 203.

life, an ivory tower of abstraction'.[70] Whilst the late scholastics had discussed not only the will of the parties, but the virtues of promise-keeping, liberality, and commutative justice, the final cause and essence of a contract, natural terms and equality in exchange, the jurists of the nineteenth-century rejected them[71]. In turn 'They were left with few other concepts than the will of the parties' as almost every important doctrine 'raised problems the will theorists tried in vain to resolve'.[72] Thus, whilst the will theory provided the law with the source, the content and the justification for the enforceability of contractual agreements, it failed to explain the reasons for the courts necessary intrusion into the realm of private agreements and provided no rational manner of resolving disputes raised by the operation of the theory in practice[73].

1.2 The rise of a market-orientated, sector-specific and information-driven EC contract law

Whilst party autonomy, or freedom of contract, remains the touchstone or basic guiding principle for Community contract law, in seeking to redirect the outcomes of market processes the Community legislator has consistently developed an ever more emboldened policy of interventionism in defence of the consumer as a perceived weaker market actor. The primary justifications for such legislative interventionism are the safeguarding of specific rights and interests and the promotion of a more equitable position between the parties.[74] Rather than being viewed as detrimental to the interests of the contracting parties, such interventionism has been promoted as a defence mechanism for the promotion of both private and public interests, and to ensure the proper development and functioning of the agreed contract. The progressive implantation of

70 G. Gilmore, *supra* at 18.

71 'All these specific, substantive, moral considerations were omitted when this civilian law of contract was received into common law. What was taken on board was only that part of the theory concerned with the parties will, and the categories based on offer and acceptance that were held to be the expression of their agreement'. This, as Gordley stresses, was to create problems for the later development of contract law. As a result of stripping away requirements for full understanding the common law had no way of dealing with the implied lack of consent. Contract law in the first half of the century was far from the logical and complete doctrine that is imagined in discourses on liberalism. It also exhibited major lacunae that would later need to be filled. See P. O'Malley, 'Uncertain Subjects: Risks, Liberalism and Contract' (2000) 29(4) J of Econ & Soc 460, at 483.

72 J. Gordley, *Origins 1991*, at 160-1, who suggests that having failed to retain these earlier concepts they were unable to make their 'will theory' work.

73 As Gilmore notes, classical contract was 'an ivory tower of abstraction' whose 'natural habitat was the law schools, not the law courts', *supra* at 18.

74 J.M. León González, *Lecciones sobre el Futuro de los Contratos en una sociedad transformada*, Salamanca, dated May 9th 1998. The primary role of the legislator and the courts is therefore to encounter and maintain a balance between state intervention and individual autonomy, see J. Ossorio Morales, 'Notas para una teoría general de contrato' (1965) RDP 1071.

social contract theory has provoked a significant ideological transformation.[75] The classical model of contract, which relied upon a utopian position of equality of bargaining power and symmetric information between the parties, has declined as a result of dramatic shifts in the technological, political and social organisation of society heralded by the unprecedented growth in the production of goods and services and the dominance of standardised business contracts throughout the twentieth century. Niglia has documented the manner in which market forces have dictated the simplification and standardisation of contracts and highlighted a marked shift from a 'rules based' contract law to a largely 'market-centred' economic law.[76] The primacy of the market has given rise to a new consumer policy premised upon the informed consumer. For Reich, the classical paradigm can now be transferred to the European scene "only by private, voluntary *restatements* that must prove their feasibility on the "market" for optimal legal solutions. The regulatory and information functions have, on the other hand, already been transferred to a great extent to the European arena with a diminishing tendency of autonomous Member state involvement and an increasing stake of "Europeanisation".[77]

However defined, paternalism and paternalistic aims, as opposed to efficiency gains, have characterised the majority of Community private law directives and this policy goal of favouring the European consumer has had a clear impact on the design of Community contract rules.[78] Cooling-off periods are now standard, and specific protection is consumer scenario-orientated (e.g. doorstep selling for instance), with remedies now overwhelmingly concerned with damages for the breach of broad, generalised duties to inform, to notify, etc.[79] Less well defined, however, are the remedies that will apply in the event of

75 See, *inter alia*, T. Wilhelmsson, R. Brownsword, G. Howells & T. Wilhelmsson (eds.), *Welfarism in Contract Law* (Dartmouth Publishing, 1994).

76 See in particular L. Niglia, 'Standard Form Contracts in Europe and America' in I. Ramsay (ed.), *Consumer Law in the Global Economy: National and International Dimensions* (Ashgate, 1997). See also W.D. Slawson, 'Standard Form Contracts and Democratic Control of Lawmaking Power' (1971) 84 Harvard Law Review 529 and L. Niglia, *The Transformation of European Contract Law* (Aspen/Kluwer Law Publishing, 2002).

77 N. Reich, 'The Tripartite Function of Modern Contract Law in Europe: Enablement, Regulation, Information' (on file with author)

78 Howells and Wilhelmsson see the correction of market failures as the main aim of EC consumer protection law in *EC Consumer Law* (1997). The view is supported by S. Grundmann, 'Information, Party Autonomy and Economic Agents in European Contract Law' (2002) 39 CMLR 269, at 273. D. Kennedy, 'Distributive and Paternalist Motives in Contract and Tort Law, With Special Reference to Compulsory Terms and Unequal Bargaining Power' (1982) 41 Maryland L Rev 563.

79 Under the Distance Selling Directive, for example, a consumer is entitled to a right of withdrawal of seven working days during which he may revoke the contract. That said, besides the infelicities of syntax in the Directive, significant lacunae mean that, in and of itself, it is incapable of providing comprehensive consumer protection for the online consumer. For this reason, the Spanish Parliament has felt it necessary to pass the 'Ley de Servicios de la Sociedad de la Información y Comercio Electrónico'

a breach of general precontractual obligations. even if previous categories such as contract mistake are less employed. In particular, the Directives"rather than with specific performance or avoidance of the contract, which will be employed rarely".[80] Yet, a more controversial tendency is the encouragement, both judicial and parliamentary, of contractual consociationalism, with a heavy emphasis on co-operation.[81] New European welfarists justify not only judicial interventionism in agreements and the policing of standard terms but, in addition, the notion that parties should similarly consider the needs and legitimate interests of their co-contracting partners.[82] Under the heading of good faith and fair dealing, new positive duties to inform as opposed to negative duties not to harm the other side (i.e. through deception, duress or misrepresentation, etc) have fundamentally changed the ideological orientation of European contract law. The patchwork of new information and precontractual duties identifiable from the mass of Community Directives are evidently lacking in sound systematisation, thus complicating their systematic analysis.[83] Indeed, no such analysis will be

---

(LSSICE) as a more coherent national line of defense for the online consumer. For an analysis of these developments, see A. González Gonzalo, 'La Formación del Contrato tras la Ley de Servicios de la Sociedad de la Información y de Comercio Electrónico', (Comares, 2004).

80 Reich notes how the modernisation of German contract law has met with violent resistance from among the majority of German civil law professors. He suggests that whilst the old distinctions and categories have not completely disappeared and cannot therefore be discarded, many categories of contract doctrine have been heavily Europeanised and internationalised. Reich places his hope in the German judiciary and suggests that when "fine tuning" the new law of obligations they ought to look more frequently than before into European and/or international law, including the European principles, *supra* Introduction fn. 15. Studies are slowly emerging examining the overlap between Community rules and and wider transnational rules. See, for instance, S. Grundmann, 'Consumer Law, Commercial Law, Private Law: How can the Sales Directive and the Sales Convention be so Similar' (2003) 14 EBLR 237.

81 Collins has highlighted the piecemeal approach of the English courts in promoting a gradually more co-operative model of contract (see H. Collins, *The Law of Contract* (Oxford University Press, 2003) at 329 et seq, and 'The Implied Duty to Give Information During Performance of Contracts' (1992) 31 MLR 561. See also R. Brownsword, 'From Co-operative Contracting to a Contract of Cooperation' in D. Campbell & P. Vincent Jones, *Contract and Economic Organisation* (Dartmouth, 1996).

82 Contractual solidarity is now well entrenched as a principle of Dutch, French and Spanish contract law. For instance, the Dutch Supreme Court decision in the case of Baris/Reizenkamp of 15 November 1957 was followed by the PECL which articulates a general duty to co-operate under Article 1:202. It is routinely suggested that this loyalty vision is at the heart of new EC consumer contract law. Much less clear is the extent to which this solidarity approach should permeate European commercial contracting.

83 Though see Ebers treatment of 'Information and Advising Requirements in the Financial Services Sector: Principles and Peculiarities in EC Law' (2004) 8(2) EJCL and more robustly K. Riesenhuber's *Europäisches Vertragsrecht* (de Gruyter, 2003). To take one example, a key element of the EC Distance Selling directive for instance, is a requirement of prior information. As the parties to the contract are not physically present to conclude the agreement in one another's presence, the consumer must be provided with comprehensive information before binding himself contractually. It is not possible to contract out of the provisions of the directive and any inconsistent term is automatically void.

attempted here as, for the purposes of this study, the wder ideological orientation is more relevant. Hartlief refers to a new contractual *altruism*[84] and is one of the few commentators to question this new direction.

Whilst Smits refers to two contract models – a self interest based, 'morality of the trade' model and a paternalistic, 'morality of the welfare state' model – for Hartlieff such a threat to the generality of contract law (as a body of principles apt for the resolution of any contractual dispute) could spell the end of European contract law as a system. Hartlieff objects fundamentally to the increased division of contract law, and the rise of a consumer specific legislation. He suggests that following the lead of Smits, 'a major part of contract law would be based on new foundations, greatly differing from those on which classical contract law is based'. Hartlieff's misgivings are understandable but the trend towards ever greater specificity is irreversible and will continue to resist generalisation and abstraction. Smits model does therefore correspond to the reality of EC contract law in practice. This increased schizophrenia – or as Hondius terms it, 'the serving of two masters' – in contemporary contract law policy has been under-evaluated. Little thought in particular has been given to the relevant place for continued market individualism. Rather than attempting to 'square the circle' through a pursuit for coherence, common and civil lawyers would be better to engage with EC contract law's messiness and seek to provide workable solutions to established problematic divergences.

Importantly, Corripio Gil-Delgado observes that parties conduct when entering into contracts cannot now be understood in a closed sense and must be determined against the broad 'factual matrix' – to borrow Lord Wilberforce's terminology – of the parties specific agreement, including the degree of 'trust' between the parties. She acknowledges that this opens the door for greater judicial 'creativity' but posits this development within broader 'socio-ethical developments in contract law'.[85] Gomez Calle goes further in arguing that 'every development in precontractual bargaining' must clearly serve to 'reinforce a model of conduct based on loyalty and cooperation'.[86] Indeed, it is only relatively recently that precontractual information duties have been examined autono-

84 T. Hartlieff, 'Freedom and Protection in Contemporary Contract Law', 27 JCP 253. For Hartlieff, freedom of contract should be put back on the European agenda and considers the limitations of consumer welfare policy.

85 M.R. Corripio Gil-Delgado, *Los Contratos Informáticos – El deber de Información Precontractual* (Comillas, 1999), at 146. See also, A. Manzanares, *La Responsabilidad precontractual en la hipótesis de ruptura injustificada de las negociaciones preliminares* (1984) 2 ADC 689 (examining the impact on both business-consumer and strictly commercial contracts of this new orientation).

86 The duty to disclose – or at the very least the duty not to remain silent – in order to prevent one's contracting partner from being wrongly induced into a contractual mistake *(error)* has been distilled and justified on the basis of the doctrine of good faith. See STS November 21 1988 RJ 7595, February 23 1988 RJ 1278, STS December 23 1991 RJ 9476 which reveal the Supreme Court's unwillingness to entertain situations where one party's passive attitude during negotiations may induce a mistake. For in the court's eyes there are situations 'when he who is silent ought to speak'.

mously in Spanish legal opinion – independently of vices in consent. Corripio Gil-Delgado suggests that the need to guarantee good faith in the negotiation of contracts is paramount and that new precontractual information duties have evolved naturally to address the subjective imbalance between parties engaged in modern contracting processes, given the often superior knowledge of one professional party.

Moreover, Llobet I Agado sees no difficulty applying notions of good faith to the factual circumstances *ex post* in order to determine whether the party in possession of such superior knowledge owed a duty to inform, and whether that duty was in effect breached.[87] As Corripio Gil-Delgado observes, Spanish contract law has continued to develop ever more robust standards in relation to the precontractual formation and negotiation of contracts particularly through the regulation of consumer contracts and by targetting misleading advertising. The social dimension of contract law has been reinforced by the legislator through the doctrine of good faith which has been the primary motor for developing enhanced loyalty duties. Importantly, however, as she acknowledges, this 'new autonomy' in the field of precontractual duties has failed to produce uniformity in analysis.

Fernando Martínez Sanz boldly asserts that the principle of good faith in effect exists all over Europe and can not be considered as alien to any of the Community's national legal systems. Strangely, for Martínez Sanz, the proof of this assertion rests with "the adoption" of the Principles of European contract law. The view is supported by Forbin who argues that international business practice has given rise to an 'autonomous' good faith principle which is of prime importance in precontractual relations.[88] Such statements require clarity as to the meaning and scope of the doctrine of good faith in the European setting, and of course its interaction with fair dealing. Writing in 2002, Auer argued that the notion of good faith in contract law typically has three dimensions:

1) a substantive dimension of justification of good faith duties in terms of, for instance, contractual ethics;
2) a formal dimension concerned with its structure as a vague standard; and
3) an institutional competence dimension raising the question of judicial freedom and constraint in adjudication based on open standards such as good faith.

---

[87] J. Llobet I Agado, *El deber de información en la formación de los contratos* (Madrid) at 37. The majority academic view provides that the doctrine of good faith and the terms of the contract may independently serve to establish a general information duty. Article 7.1 C.c. articulates the principle of good faith and Article 1.258 Cc provides a general catch-all provision regulating contracts, which when combined with Article 7.1 provides a flexible legal base. Above all, it has been to the elastic and expandable good faith principle that academics have turned in advancing the precontractual duty to inform.

[88] See F. Martínez Sanz, 'Buena Fe' in S. Camara Lapuente (ed), *Derecho Privado Europeo*, *supra* Introduction fn. 34, 481 *et seq*. She suggests that this 'autonomous good faith principle' in precontractual bargaining is further 'demonstrated notably by the obligation to inform [one's] co-contracter', 'Comment gérer les informations confidentielles en cour de pourparlers' (1998) 4(5) IBLJ.

Controversies between an individualist ethic of freedom of contract and the opposing altruist value of interpersonal responsibility, between the danger of judicial arbitrariness and the demand for equitable flexibility, and, finally, between the legitimacy of judicial law making and an insistence on judicial restraint all to an extent serve to clutter the harmonisation debate.[89] Each of these three dimensions gives only a partial view of the role of good faith in European contract law, a role which is rarely constant. Moreover, these three dimensions are not necessarily congruent; in fact, they often are not. Even if most applications of the principle of good faith can be seen as inspired rather by a communitarian than by an individualist ethic, others seem to protect individualist positions in order to promote certainty in contractual relationships, without imposing an altruist logic. Further, the fact that one party has to take into account the interests of the other party in a given respect often discharges the other party from a similar duty. Thus, many duties to inform imposed on one party discharge the other party from informing himself on the same point, and thus shift the burden of examination from one party to the other. This raises doubts about the possibility of ever giving the notion of good faith an adequate substantive meaning.[90]

Hartlieff suggests that enhanced consumer welfare and the *ex post* re-structuring of contracts may also have the effect of weakening the very notion of 'pact sunt servanda'. He draws attention to the cost of aggressive forms of consumer protection, that may result in the binding force of contracts being 'taken less seriously' by consumers, with a reduction in individual responsibility. As such he proposes that consumer lawyers should in future concentrate more on the regulation of information and the role of competition law, as opposed to contract law, in advancing consumer interests.[91] What is less understood is the extent

---

89 See M. Auer, 'Good Faith: A Semiotic Approach' (2002) 10 ERPL 279. See also M.E. Storme, 'Good Faith and the Content of Contracts in European Private Law' (2003) 7(1) EJCL.

90 See, *inter alia*, S. Wegner, 'Good Faith and the Need for a Uniform Standard' (1990) 73 Marquette Law Review 639. See also, M.W. Hesselink, 'The Concept of Good Faith' in *Towards*, 2004, at 471 *et seq.* (offering the sensible suggestion that, as opposed to good faith, the term 'equity' may be an 'acceptable compromise' in EC contract law given the recognition of the term in both common and civil law jurisdictions, at 498 and discussed later again in Chapter 4 of this study).

91 'The application of competition law and the regulation of information have a higher priority than mandatory substantive contract law', *supra*, at 265. This finding is supported by the ECJ's ruling in Case C-120/78 *Cassis v. Dijon* [1979] ECR 649 where the Court noted that information duties should take priority over substantive law (see judgment, at para. 13). See also the more recent decision in Case C-2/88 *GB-INNO-BM v. Confédération du commerce luxembourgeois* [1990] ECR I-667. Importantly, for Grundmann such information rules, even when mandatory, are essentially instruments 'for fostering party autonomy', *supra*, at 7. The battle between the classical and the social vision of contract law has now shifted to a European setting. Lurger (*Vertragliche Solidarität*, Nomos, 1998) and Votinius have picked sides (*Friends or Foes: A Philosophical Study of the Role and Importance of Human Relationships in the Sphere of Contract Law*, PhD thesis, Lund University, 2004) but the real challenge rests with squaring the circle between each of the two ideological approaches. Europe must follow Rosenfield in rethinking

to which this welfarist model is impacting in the field of commercial contracting. In this regard, studies in the US on co-operative commercial contracting have reached a greater level of sophistication than currently exists in European markets, by concentrating on sector-specific fields.[92]

1.3 From consumer to commercial contracts? The wider implications of the new information paradigm and a rise in precontractual duties in EC (consumer) contract law

One of the primary concerns for commercial lawyers is that the development of the information paradigm and a rise in mandatory precontractual obligations in consumer contexts will indirectly influence the courts to be more forceful in finding duties based on good faith and fair dealing in commercial settings. The spill-over effects of consumer contract law into general and commercial contract law are readily apparent in civil law systems, particularly in Germany and France. Reich and Giliker identify a heavy case load based on precontractual duties to inform, with references to the doctrine of "*culpa in contrahendo*". In addition, such duties have in Spain been regularly justified and regulated via the doctrine of good faith.[93] In part, recourse has been had to the notion of 'buena fe' due to the limited number of articles in the Civil code that actually refer to precontractual responsibilities (arguably only arts 1.460, 1.483 and 1,486.2). In terms of litigation the regulation of precontractual negotiations in Spain is most commonly encountered in franchise agreements and in computer software contracts, where one party is relying to a greater or lesser degree on the specialist knowledge on the other side.

In contracts for the creation and provision of software, recent decisions in the Spanish Provincial Courts (SAP de Barcelona of the 16 December 2001 and the SAP de Valencia of the 28 of October 2002) support the view that additional positive duties will arise for a seller, unless the consumer possesses sufficient knowledge or both parties agree responsibility for the final product.[94] Soler

that relationship, see M. Rosenfeld, 'Contract and Justice: The Relation Between Classical Contract Law and Social Contract Theory' (1985) 70 Iowa L. Rev. 769.

92 See for instance, L. Bernstein, 'Private Commercial Law in the Cotton Industry: Creating Cooperation through Rules, Norms and Institutions' (2001) Mich L Rev 1724. In particular, she identifies the specific interests of merchants in the cotton industry, who elevate for example performance over damages for breach of contract, at 1754-5.

93 Under arts 7.1, 1.258 of the Spanish civil code and article 57 of the commercial code. For long periods the law owed much to Ihering's original theories, yet as is revealed in chapter 3, modern notions of precontractual liability have reached a greater degree of sophistication and clarity via the interpretative role of the Supreme Court.

94 The increased specialisation and diversity of software products and services in practice entails that only those professionals engaged in their provision have sufficient knowledge as to their proper functioning. This information imbalance is further exacerbated when we consider the added complexity, specialisation and indeed on occasion uniqueness of particular bespoke products developed in the industry.

Matutes argues that enforcing a general duty to inform, as founded on the doctrine of good faith, is of critical importance for the future of the software industry. The need for cooperation and the provision of specific details is evident and parties must be encouraged by mandatory legal rules, if necessary, to fully inform one another of their needs and services. Such cooperation is seen as necessary on the grounds that 'the client seeking the provision of software is the sole party that can inform the supplier of his specific needs, whilst the developer of software has the technical know-how to make the project a reality'.[95]

It is notable that this view of Matutes and the approach advocated before the Spanish provincial courts has been mirrored in the English case of *Anglo Group Plc v. Winther Brown & Co. Ltd.*[96] At first instance the trial judge expounded a mutual duty of co-operation in the precontractual development of a 'systems supply' contract. Again the case concerned a typical dispute over a software package that failed to live up to the customer's expectations. It is important for two reasons. The trial judge firstly observed that it was well understood that the design and installation of a computer system requires the active co-operation of both customer and supplier, and in the courts opinion such a duty of co-operation extends to the customer accepting, where possible, reasonable solutions to address problems that may arise. Secondly, it was held that the following were implied terms of any computer supply contract:

a) the purchaser communicates clearly any special needs to the supplier;
b) the purchaser takes reasonable steps to ensure that the supplier understands those needs;
c) the supplier communicates to the purchaser whether or not those precise needs can be met and if so how they can be met. If they cannot be met precisely, the appropriate options should be set out by the supplier;
d) the supplier must take reasonable steps to ensure that the purchaser is trained in how to use the system;
e) the purchaser devotes reasonable time and patience to understanding how to operate the system;
f) the purchaser and supplier work together to resolve the problems which will almost certainly occur. This requires active co-operation from both parties. If such co-operation is not present it is likely that the purchaser will achieve the desired results from the system.

Anglo Brown reveals new judicial thinking on the informative imbalance, as opposed to pure economic weakness, that may in practice put both parties in a position of equality largely in much the same manner as the civil law courts would approach the issue. The decision is further illustrative of the ability of the English courts to provide sensible disclosure and fair dealing duties incremen-

95 P. Soler Matutes, *El Contrato para la Elaboración de Programas de Ordenador* (Aranzadi, 2004), at 237. See also 241 *et seq.* examining the rights and liabilities of each party in relation to information-disclosure.

96 [2000] TCC., unreported 8 March 2000.

tally despite the absence of a general duty of good faith and fair dealing.[97] It can, however, be contrasted with the decision of the Technology and Construction Court in *SAM Business Systems v. Hedley*, which suggests that notions of contractual solidarity and good faith in negotiations will remain merely skin deep in commercial settings. The court was dealing in a sense with a Y2K action. A specific software package was ordered near the end of 1999 by the defendants, who feared that their otherwise serviceable, if admittedly old-fashioned, DOS based transaction processing system would not function properly in the new millennium. The claimant was first approached in July 1999 and demonstrated the system to the defendants in September 1999. The judge's starting point was that the defendants needed a Y2K compliant system and that they could only acquire one on the claimant's terms. The facts further reveal the power of the drafter's pen under English law. The claimant was able to circumvent any potential liability for precontractual representations via an entire agreement clause (discussed further in chapter 3).[98] The clause provided that:

> this agreement constitutes the entire understanding between the parties relating to the subject matter of this agreement and, save as may be expressly either referenced to or referenced herein, supersedes all prior representations, writings, negotiations or understandings with respect hereto but nothing in this section ... shall exclude liability for any fraudulent misrepresentation.[99]

Importantly, it was found that other suppliers in the industry used similarly exclusion and limitation clauses and the court found such terms necessary to

97 A point reiterated judicially by Bingham L.J. in the oft-quoted case of *Interfoto Picture Library v. Stiletto Visual Programmes Ltd* [1989] QB 433, who observing the growth of good faith based doctrines, lauded the fact that English contract law had consistently arrived at much the same position by developing 'piecemeal solutions to demonstrated problems of unfairness' (at p. 496). The learned judge further emphasised the reality that: 'In many civil law systems, and perhaps in most legal systems outside the common law world, the law of obligations recognises an overriding principle that in making and carrying out contracts, parties should act in good faith ... it is in essence a principle of fair and open dealing'. (at p. 496). This analysis has been warmly received by civil lawyers yet, as is highlighted below in chapter 3, is a view that is not always shared by UK academics when it comes to the judicial treatment of incomplete agreements and the monitoring of precontractual bargaining.

98 Such clauses will effectively exclude any prior representations during negotiations. They are subject to a test of reasonableness under the Unfair Contract Terms Act (UCTA) 1977 and their drafting is not a straightforward matter due to the restrictive principles adopted and applied by the courts. That said, they do operate as a powerful arm against the threat of precontractual liability. It was suggested that in the claimant's brochure and and in subsequent correspondence, as well as during the precontractual phase, the supplier made various claims as to the suitability and reliability of the product. Claims that allegedly induced the defendants to purchase the software. Regardless of these alleged inducements the courts had little desire to look beyond the specific clause.

99 The breadth of the entire agreement clause, and the number of exclusion clauses employed, were not viewed as excessive or beyond existing standard business practice, at para [19]3 of the judgment.

enable suppliers to carry out their business. Critically, however, in this case the *Anglo v. Winter Group* vision of contract solidarity took a heavy dent. As the trial judge noted:

> Although it has not been said in so many terms, [the supplier's] attitude seems to be, "We did not have to take on this contract. Having taken it on our terms, why should the contract be re-written to expose us to a huge risk and possibly put us out of business?" That is a freedom of contract attitude that would have been entirely acceptable in the nineteenth and early twentieth centuries. Can it survive since Parliament intervened at the behest of the Law Commission in 1977?"

In His Honour's view it could. The parties were operating from a position of equal bargaining power in terms of their relative size and resources and the defendants were in a difficult position of their own making because of their lateness in tackling the problem of Y2K compliance. The evidence from the supplier supported the view that other companies similar to theirs made use of comparable exclusion clauses and the defendants did not even try to negotiate for terms more favourable to them. Judge Bowsher's assertion that the parties were operating from a position of equality of bargaining power may be defensible if examined from an economic standpoint but given the customers' lack of familiarity with computer software systems, should the asymmetries of information between the parties not have played a greater role in the deliberations of the trial judge?[100]

More importantly, if the English courts were to introduce a generalised duty to negotiate in good faith, would such a duty prevent the future use of entire agreement clauses under English law? Waddams, for example, has maintained that whilst a general rule of disclosure is not desirable, English law should seek instead to enlarge specific exceptions to ensure that, in particular contexts, parties should be more forthcoming with specific information, particularly where that information would be extremely costly or time-consuming for the other side to acquire.[101] European courts and legislators may increasingly be speaking the language of disclosure and reliance (justified on the basis of one party's special expertise, the costs of acquiring specific information; the ability of other party to provide information without harming his own self-interest, etc) yet the approach in *SAM Business Systems* is consistent with a continued prag-

[100] Besides revealing that litigation before the Technology and Construction Court in London is not the most cost-effective way of resolving computer supply disputes (at the end of a tremendously expensive process the claimant was awarded less than £10,000 in damages) this complex litigation reveals that it is still possible for suppliers to limit or even avoid liability for specific representations, which may well verge on the cusp of misrepresentation, during the precontractual stage in a computer supply contract by means of contract terms, notwithstanding the provisions of UCTA 1977, so long as the customer is allowed reasonable post-sale redress.

[101] See S. Waddams, 'Precontractual duties of disclosure' in P. Cane & J. Stapleton (eds.), *Essays for Patrick Atiyah* (Oxford Clarendon Press, 1991) at 254.

matic case-by-case analysis in English courts that emphasises pure contractual freedom sense and that severely questions the possibility of Smits 'commercial morality' vision taking hold.

Moreover, in *Watford v. Sanderson* the Court of Appeal identified strong factors against intervention in commercial contracts.[102] The parties were regarded as being of equal bargaining power (although there was no other package available on the market which appeared to meet Watford's needs and system supply contracts generally came with exemption clauses). As has been indicated, it was recognised that the provision of a computer system was one in which there was a 'significant risk' that the system would not perform to the customer's satisfaction, thereby losing the customer profits or efficiency savings. It was also recognised that the risks should have been contemplated by both parties when they made the contract, that the loss was likely to be capable of being covered by insurance (at a cost), and that both of them should have contemplated that the contract price would be affected by who was to bear the risk of that loss. In the instant case, there were seen to be strong indicators that justified allowing the losses to fall in accordance with the provisions of the exemption clause. As Chadwick LJ further observed, the parties "should ... be taken to be the best judge of the commercial fairness of the agreement which they have made; including the fairness of each of the terms in that agreement."[103]

---

[102] *Watford Electronics Ltd v. Sanderson CFL Ltd* [2001] 1 All ER (Comm) 696.

[103] Chadwick LJ articulated a distinctly classical vision: 'Where experienced businessmen representing substantial companies of equal bargaining power negotiate an agreement, they may be taken to have had regard to the matters known to them. They should, in my view be taken to be the best judge of the commercial fairness of the agreement which they have made; including the fairness of each of the terms in that agreement. They should be taken to be the best judge on the question whether the terms of the agreement are reasonable. The court should not assume that either is likely to commit his company to an agreement which he thinks is unfair, or which he thinks includes unreasonable terms. Unless satisfied that one party has, in effect, taken unfair advantage of the other – or that a term is so unreasonable that it cannot properly have been understood or considered – the court should not interfere'. (at 711). See also E. MacDonald, 'Watford v. Sanderson: The Requirement of Reasonableness in System Supply Contracts and More Generally' (2001) WJCLI. McDonald suggests that the decision may have a wider significance in general commercial contracting: "... it has been emphasised that each case on the requirement of reasonableness is dependent upon its own facts: 'It may be fair and reasonable to disclaim against X when it would not be fair and reasonable to disclaim against Y' (citing *Stevenson v. Nationwide Building Soc* [1984] EGD 934). That militates against the adoption of any general approach to the reasonableness test under the Unfair Contract Terms Act that takes a non-interventionist approach to commercial contracts generally. In addition, it must not be forgotten that the burden of proof lies upon the party seeking to rely upon the clause and, even if Chadwick LJ's dictum is widely cited and seen as an approach which should be carried into effect, each case will still be dependent upon its own particular facts even if there is a non-interventionist impetus". See also E. Macdonald, 'Y2K and Contractual Exemption Clauses' (1999) 2 Journal of Information, Law and Technology.

2 The weakness of a pure values-based approach to European contract law

Of course, potentially overriding these broader ideological questions is the extent to which national and supranational private law is as much a product of its institutional setting and other social and cultural factors, as it is strictly dependent upon 'values' and political orientation. Brooke Overby[104] and Hesselink[105] have highlighted the limitations of both rule analysis and underlying values or concept-based analysis in the absence of parallel consideration of institutional arrangements. Brooke Overby, for instance, points out the degree of divergence between EU and US consumer laws in four key fields – deceptive advertising, unfair contract terms, consumer credit issues, and dispute resolution – but suggests that such differences often do not emerge from serious differences over consumer values or ideology, but rather from institutional constraints, including political, social, and cultural constraints that are particular to the systems themselves.[106]

Importantly for the purposes of this study, in this regard the ostensibly differing treatment of precontractual reliance in the United States and across the European Union suggests another example of how an institutional dialogue in this area might develop. Taking Overby's institutional theory towards consumer law generally and applying it to the notion of commercial reliance we would presumably bring into the debate issues of state autonomy, institutional design and wider social, political and cultural considerations. In addition, the fact that certain consumer welfare concerns promoted in the EU are frequently rejected in the U.S. 'would not be regarded as inconsequential'.[107] As Overby herself observes, 'the English common law approach under the rubric of freedom of contract recognises the concerns of business by presumptively invalidating clauses that bind parties to the negotiation process ... whereas the United States broadly upholds a notion of good faith and fair dealing'.[108] She suggests that broad judicial support has been found for the notion of a duty to negotiate in good faith. Yet, whether these theoretical suppositions actually apply beyond the textbooks, to the modern law in action, is what we wish to test in chapter 3

104 A. Brooke Overby (2001), *supra*, at 1321.

105 M.W. Hesselink, 'The Politics of European Civil Code' (2004) 10(6) Eur LJ 675. See also, T. Wilhelmsson, 'The Legal, the Cultural and the Political – Conclusions from Different Perspectives on Harmonisation of European Contract Law' (2002) 1 EBLR 541.

106 *Supra* at 1323

107 *Supra* at 1324. For Overby an institutional framework for developing and critiquing consumer law holds greater promise for broader application than a values-based approach, thereby circumventing the 'parochialism' of the latter values based analysis as "fully developed, it holds the promise of being capable of guiding lawmakers on when uniformity is acceptable while remaining respectful of local culture ...". (at 1331) Brooke Overby bases much of her institutional analysis on the previous works of Komesar, particular, N. Komesar, *Imperfect Alternatives* (University of Chicago Press, 1994) and *Law's Limits, supra.*

108 *Supra* at 1325.

via an examination of the degree of divergence/functional equivalence in the judicial treatment of preliminary agreements and managing precontractual reliance.

3 Assessing the treatment of precontractual duties in global initiatives and framework codes

We will return to the broader ideological conundrum in chapter 4 but let us briefly explore the treatment of precontractual liability in previous global initiatives, International conventions and Framework codes.

3.1 Analysing precontractual liability under the CISG

One of the most controversial compromises during the drafting process of the Vienna Convention on the International Sale of Goods concerned the omission of a provision stipulating that parties must act in good faith during contract negotiations. Sufficient agreement was reached to allow for the inclusion of a generalised provision requiring merely that, in interpreting the provisions of the Convention, courts and arbiters must consider the need to promote the observance of good faith in international trade. Indeed, the use of the very term 'good faith' generated considerable controversy during the drafting of the Convention. Throughout the process of compiling the CISG, delegates disputed what type of good-faith provision, if any, should appear.[109] Supporters of a principle of good faith and fair dealing applicable to the formation of contracts faced opposition from those who argued that the 'subjective' and 'moral' dimension apparent within both concepts would defeat the harmonisation goal enshrined in Article.[110] An earlier draft of Article 5 of the proposed Convention had sought to provide that in the course of the formation of the contract parties would be required to observe the principle of fair dealing.[111] In the end, opponents of the draft principle would be only partial successful as the inevitable result was compromise.

Article 7(1) now requires parties and decision makers to interpret the Convention in light of its international nature, the necessity of promoting its uniform application, and the need for observance of good faith in international trade, but under the Convention parties are under no express obligation to act in good faith or fairly during negotiations and the CISG does not explicitly cover

---

109 See J. Klein & C. Bachechi, 'Precontractual Liability and the Duty of Good Faith Negotiation in International Transactions' (1994) 17 Houston Journal of International Law 1, at 19.

110 *Ibid.*

111 See Report of the Working Group on the International Sale of Goods, 9th session, para.70, UN Doc. A/CN.9/142 (1977). The draft provision read: "In the course of the formation of the contract the parties must observe the principles of fair dealing and act in good faith.". See J. Honnold, *Documentary History of the Uniform Law for International Sales* (Kluwer, 1989).

the issue of precontractual liability.[112] Though the proposed good faith in negotiations provision was not suggested until the eighth meeting of the UNCITRAL working group, and was conclusively rejected shortly thereafter, it is clear that the delegates remained bitterly divided. Only for the presence and recognition of the good faith doctrine elsewhere in Article 7 this may have prolonged and/or frustrated the deliberations. Indeed, despite the absence of such a duty in the Convention, Perillo suggests that an expansive interpretation of Article 7(1) woud allow the courts to consider the duty to negotiate in good faith and provide sufficient basis for imposing precontractual liability even in the absence of an express provision.[113] For this reason anyone relying on the CISG must be aware of the threat of a liability for 'culpa in contrahendo' in a foreign jurisdiction. Regrettably for the Convention framers, this may in part explain the continued reluctance of the UK to ratify the CISG and explain why European lawyers across the continent are increasingly recommending businesses to opt-out of the Convention when preparing model contracts.[114]

The Drafting History and Support of Good faith in Negotiations

The drafting history indicates that there were numerous arguments both supporting and opposing a provision that would place a duty on the parties to act in good faith during contract negotiations.[115] First, those delegates who supported the provision argued that good faith is a universally recognised principle because many national commercial codes carry similar good-faith

---

[112] See also CISG, *supra*, note 4, art. 7(1). Article 7(1) states in full: In the interpretation of this Convention, regard is to be had to its international character and to the need to promote uniformity in its application and the observance of good faith in international trade.

[113] J.M. Perillo, 'UNIDROIT Principles of International Commercial Contracts: The Black Letter Text and a Review' (1994) 63 Fordham LR 281. Moreover, even absent the underlying duty of good faith in negotiations, as happens in the US, precontractual liability may still be imposed under the Convention on the grounds of detrimental reliance or restitution. Article 8(3) empowers the court when deciding whether parties have created a contract to have reference to "all relevant circumstances of the case including the negotiations, any practices which the parties have established between themselves, usages and any subsequent conduct of the parties".

[114] See comments of delegates at ERA conference on European contract law, Trier 2003. Ziegel is convinced that ratification in the UK has been resisted out of fear that it 'may jeopardise London's pre-eminent role as an international arbitration and litigation centre' in 'The Future of the International Sales Convention from a Common Law Perspective' (2000) 6 New Zealand Business Law Quarterly 336. Yet, the refusal to implement the CISG into English law may have as much to do with wider concerns regarding the breadth of Art. 7 of the Convention, in addition to acceptance in practice of the legal consistency provided by domestic Sale of Goods legislation.

[115] Klein & Bachechi, *supra*, at 20. ('It was considered that the extension of this provision into an instrument regulating an aspect of international trade was a valuable extension of a widely recognised norm of conduct'.) Honnold, *supra* note 29, at 369.

obligations which have been instrumental in the development of trade rules.[116] In light of the number of countries represented, which generally adhere to and approve of an obligation of good faith in international transactions, the delegates argued that it would be inappropriate not to extend this duty of good faith to negotiations within the final text of the Convention.[117] Additionally, the delegates observed that public international law recognises the concept of good faith and the United Nations Charter makes specific reference to the doctrine. A number of delegates feared that should the provision be deleted, the drafters would receive rebuke from the wider business community for opposing good faith principles in international trade.[118] Yet, given the business community's lack of vocal concern about precontractual liability to date, such fears appear groundless. A group of delegates further contended that the provision would actually create uniformity in the long run because national courts would be able to rely upon the body of case law that would develop in dealing with questions concerning the interpretation and scope of the Convention. Supporters of the provision further asserted that individual parties and the courts would be reminded via the good faith provision that a high standard of behaviour is expected from the bargaining phase through to the performance of international transactions.

Resistance to the Duty of Good Faith in Negotiations and Proposed Alternatives

Other convention delegates who opposed the provision felt that the requirement to act in good faith was implicit in all laws regulating business activity and they, therefore, perceived the provision as largely superfluous.[119] The underlying theory appears to have emerged that provided the general duty was enshrined in the Convention it would permeate through to the regulation of contract negotiations. However, the failure of the Convention to specify sanctions for non-compliance with good faith notions concerned a number of delegates who foresaw the possibility of non-uniformity in application.[120] Remedies would fall to the national courts, inevitably resulting in inconsistent treatment.[121] Additionally, opponents argued that good faith provisions, along with the appropriate sanctions for non-compliance, belong in a convention on the validity of contracts

[116] See also M.J. Bonell, 'Formation of Contracts and Precontractual Liability Under the Vienna Convention on International Sale of Goods' in *Formation of Contracts and Precontractual Liability* (ICC Publishing, 1990). Bonell equally supports Perillo's view that Art.7 of the CISG provides a national court with sufficient authority to sanction bad faith and 'fault' in negotiations, at p. 167.

[117] See D. Goderre, *supra*.

[118] See J. Klein, *supra* (1993) at 115-141

[119] Klein & Bachechi, *supra*, at 20.

[120] See also R. Novoa, 'Culpa in Contrahendo: A Comparative Law Study: Chilean Law and the CISG' (2005) 22(3) Arizona Journal of International & Comparative Law 583. (noting the concerns that the 'moral and subjective' character of good faith would result in 'a multitude of interpretations'. As 'reliance by courts upon their own legal and social understanding of the terms would result in non-uniform interpretation of the provision') at 608.

[121] *Supra*.

and not in a convention on formation.[122] Much dissent existed concerning the incorporation of a provision to impose a duty of good faith upon the parties. Because the delegates to the Convention were so evenly divided on the issue, they believed that it would be unwise to either incorporate or entirely delete such a provision based upon such a slim majority. Considering that the goals of the Convention focused upon representing the interests of all countries involved and formulating a document that a majority of them would enact, the delegates sought to find a middle ground upon which a majority of the delegates could agree. It is interesting that non-legal sanctions aimed at remedying or curtailing bad faith conduct in negotiations was not even discussed by delegates. Nor was the possibility that the Convention could encouragement the use of specific drafting techniques between the parties to an International Sales contract.

In response, UNCITRAL established a second working group to prepare an alternative to the original good faith provision. Several compromise positions were suggested and, although none appeared to entail the same difficulties as the original provision in terms of sanctions, most were nevertheless deemed inadequate. One suggestion was to incorporate the provision as written into the preamble rather than to incorporate it as its own article. The delegates did not favour this proposal because placing the provision in the preamble would have been essentially equivalent to deleting it, as it would have no binding effect upon the parties. A second proposal was to incorporate the good faith requirement in the rules of interpretation of the statements and conduct of the parties. However, this approach too was rejected by the delegates. The provision was intended to direct the conduct of the parties by laying down a particular standard to which they must adhere, not to address the intentions of the parties. Therefore, delegates found this compromise inappropriate. Ultimately, the compromise upon which the delegates settled consisted of imposing a duty of good faith in the interpretation and application of the provisions of the Convention.[123] Some delegates objected to this proposal primarily because they believed it was inappropriate to place the duty upon the courts rather than upon the parties.[124] In spite of this discontent, delegates generally agreed that the new provision was a realistic compromise solution.[125]

Since Di Matteo wrote back in 1997 there appears to have been little shift in CISG jurisprudence – or rather a real absence of CISG jurisprudence dealing

[122] An approach that won favour among the members of the Commission on European Contract Law and that was subsequently adopted in the preparation of the *Principles of European Contract Law* (see below at 4.3).

[123] As Klein points out, an earlier Hungarian proposal encouraged support for a provision that read 'In the course of the formation of the contract the parties must observe the principles of fair dealing and act in good faith', see Klein, *supra* (1993), at p. 141. Klein notes that a Canadian proposal was also entered here would have prevented, as in the UCC, parties from opting-out of the good faith requirement of the Convention.

[124] See Honnold, *supra*.

[125] Klein & Bachechi, *supra*.

with incomplete agreements and/or precontractual liability. It had been argued that if courts found this area of law to be unsettled under the Convention, that they would base their decisions upon the general principles of the Convention or, in the absence of applicable general principles, apply local law[126] to supplement the existing Convention provisions.[127] However, the general principles of the Convention are not expressly stated in this area and as a result, several alternative positions may well be adopted. Di Matteo had anticipated *original interpretation* under the CISG playing a key role in determining the enforceability of comfort instruments, letters of intent and other inchoate agreements. In reality the opposite is true. The law on precontractual liability remains largely untested under the CISG, is certainly no more coherent today, and there has been a notable lack of jurisprudence that actually bothers with the issue. The potential for inconsistency in interpretation therefore abounds. Particularly in the context of precontractual liability in which Article 7 is subject to diverse interpretations and courts are influenced by their own understandings of the phrase 'good faith', a lack of uniformity is almost inevitable. It was envisaged that Article 8, which allows the courts to examine the 'circumstances of the case including the negotiations', would help foster greater legal certainty as to the boundaries of precontractual liability and the appropriate use of preliminary agreements but today CISG lawyers are left groping in the dark in the absence of judicial direction. Arguably, the notion of (detrimental) reliance could create a further possibility for imposing precontractual liability under the Convention, particularly in the US. Claims in restitution are not ruled out in the text of the Convention, and promissory estoppel claims have been played out in the context of 'firm offers' under Article 16(2)(b) which provides that an offer will become irrevocable "if it was reasonable for the offeree to rely on the offer as being irrevocable and the offeree had acted in reliance on the offer". In the US case of *Geneva Pharmaceuticals Technology Co. v. Barr Laboratories Inc.*[128] it was noted that promissory

[126] Which di Matteo (*supra*) perceives as a factor increasing the 'riskier' side of international trade under the CISG as an 'American businessperson' could in certain circumstances be fully liable in contract for 'culpa in contrahendo', at 30.

[127] Di Matteo et al see these key contract 'norms' under the CISG as 'the principle of good faith, fairness in exchange, compensation for justifiable reliance, and the belief that one should keep promises' (*supra*, at 35). All worthy goals of course but as will be illustrated further such norms are proving difficult to apply to incomplete preliminary agreements under the CISG and elsewhere. That said, the French case of *SARL Bri Production Bonaventure v. Societe Pan African Export* (1995) and more expressly the Australian court of appeals case in *Renard Construction (ME) Ltd. v. Minister for Public Works* are just two examples of the courts viewing good faith as a guiding norm underpinning the CISG. Moreover, In *Société Muroiterie Fraisse v. Micon et Autres*, applying the CISG, a French court found that Micon had been in breach of its obligation to act in good faith due to the 'conduct of [its] negotiating team'. The case does lend support to the view articulated by Bonell and Perillo that the courts will find an implicity duty to bargain in good faith from Article 7.

[128] 201 F. Supp. 2d 236 SDNY 2002.

estoppel claims could be entertained but that applying an American or other national approach could "stymie" the the uniformity goal.

Although good faith is a subjective term under the Convention, the drafters may have had a better chance of fostering uniformity had they actually imposed an express duty of good faith upon parties to negotiations under the Convention. If the drafters had adopted such an explicit duty, case law would doubtless have emerged to test the waters. How much caselaw is of course debatable. As LeTourneau notes in France, the number of cases on a national level dealing with bad faith or a breakdown in negotiations is miniscule.[129] He suggests that our understanding of negotiations is as a result more anecdotal and academic than practical. The point is reinforced by Buckley who notes in particular the neglect of the adversarial side of commercial bargaining. He identifies an over emphasis on ethics and cooperative strategies in the literature that misses an unavoidable, if occasinally 'distasteful' dimension to modern contracts – the fact that it is hard-bargaining that ultimately in most cases gets parties to 'yes' and a finalised agreement.[130]

That said, perhaps the absence of a rule has prevented the emergence of greater cross-jurisdictional uniformity. A CISG rule on precontractual behaviour, even an inefficient rule, would most likely have generated case law allowing other national courts to follow or distinguish past decisions thus providing a gateway for a more uniform body of law to slowly emerge. As it stands, because the Convention has not adequately addressed this issue, courts must look to the general principles upon which the Convention is based or to private international law. Let us therefore examine the UNIDROIT Principles which have laid down rules governing the negotiation process in commercial contracts.

3.2 Analysing precontractual liability under the UNIDROIT Principles

Article 1.7 of the UNIDROIT Principles of International Commercial Contracts promotes a typically civil-law approach to commercial deal-making. Parties are required to 'act in accordance with good faith and fair dealing in international trade' and unlike the CISG Convention, the US Uniform Commercial Code and the Restatement (Second) of Contracts, the Principles require that parties act in good faith not only in the performance of the contract, but also throughout the negotiation phase. As with the CISG convention, no definition of good faith is provided under the Principles but a party may be liable for entering into negotiations without a sincere intention to reach an agreement under Article 2.15(3) or for breaking off negotiations in bad faith under Article 2.15(2).

---

129 See F. Le Torneau, 'La Rupture des Négotiations' [1998] Revue trimestrialle de Droit Commercial 479, at 483.

130 R.P. Buckley, 'Adversarial Bargaining: The Neglected Aspect of Negotiation' (2001) 75 Australian Law Journal 181.

Article 2.15(3) specifically refers to the act of entering into or continuing negotiations without a true intention of reaching an agreement as an example of what constitutes bad faith.[131] It would certainly assist the harmonisation effort to know in domestic settings the average yearly quantity of cases where parties have entered into negotiations without a sincere desire to conclude a contract. The author's presumption is that the number of such cases is likely to be negligence. This reference to breaking off negotiations in bad faith, however, may have been intended as a concession to the common law, and indeed it has previously been suggested in the US that the doctrine of good faith is best understood and rationalised in reverse. Livitnoff suggests that: "Perhaps good faith emerges with more clarity out of a contrast with its opposite. Thus, if in general terms *bad faith* consists in the intention of obtaining an unfair advantage at another's expense, even if an advantage results for one who acts without that intention, the lack of such an intention constitutes good faith, even if an advantage results for one who acts without that intention ...".[132] For Van Houtte, one of the great innovations of the Unidroit principles is that they provide standards for conducting negotiations. Crucially, however, determining the meaning and content of those standards is by no means straightforward. The lack of significant caselaw or arbitral awards citing or relying on the Unidroit Principles is further revealing. In the last decade, only one arbitral award of the ICC Court of Arbitration in Paris has had a bearing on precontractual liability under the UNIDROIT Principles, and even then merely tendentially.[133]

The ICC Tribunal was asked to determine whether the parties, having agreed to 'meet promptly and negotiate in good faith' a number of international supply and service contracts, were duly obliged to negotiate in good faith. The parties failed to make an express or implied choice of law but the contract had a close connection to the laws of England (which was also the seat of the arbitration), Saudia Arabia, Georgia, New York and New Jersey. Much of the negotiation phase of the deal had taken place in the US, and the Defendant urged the

---

[131] The relevant section is entitled Bad Faith in Negotiations. Article 2.15(1) sets out a freedom of negotiation rule that is supplemented by subsection 2 (However, a party which negotiates or breaks off negotiations in bad faith is liable for the losses caused to the other party) and under subsection 3 (it is bad faith, in particular, for a party to enter into or continue negotiations when intending not to reach an agreement with the other party). The commentary further includes the idea of inducing a party into a mistake as to the content of the contract during negotiations as evidence of bad faith.

[132] Per Saul Livitnoff quoted in H. MacQueen & R. Zimmermann (eds) *European Contract Law: Scots and South African Perspectives* (Edinburgh University Press, 2006). A similar *bad faith* approach to the doctrine of good faith is identified by MacQueen in Israeli precontractual law which does not stipulate categories of positive conduct for parties to negotiations but rather censures evidence of legally unacceptable behaviour. Curiously, on the basis of wider international experience and in particular the Principles of European Contract Law, MacQueen sees scope for restructuring the doctrine of 'culpa in contrahendo' under Scots law but is less than forthcoming as to the form that such changes would take.

[133] Source – Unilex caselaw reserve of the CISG convention and the Unidroit Principles. A summary of the ICC award is accessible via http://www.unilex.info/case.

Tribunal to reject the application of English or Saudi law which are both decidely cool on good faith in negotiations. Instead the Defendant stressed that such a duty would be enforceable under the laws of Georgia, New York and New Jersey. In the alternative the Defendant invited the Tribunal to rely on the Unidroit Principles, by virtue of which – in the eyes of the Defendant – the 'express commitment' of the parties to 'negotiate in good faith is enforceable'.[134]

Relying on the fact that a previous non-disclosure agreement had been agreed between the parties and contained a specific choice of law clause in favour of 'the law of New York' the Tribunal had little difficulty in extending this express choice to the entire contract.[135] The ICC Tribunal further accepted on the evidence that the parties had indeed obligated themselves to meet promptly and negotiate in good faith and as such determined that 'the Parties could not have intended that the governing law of the contract would render this obligation unenforceable'. In seeking to do justice to the parties expressed 'wish', the Tribunal seized upon previous New York case law in order to the flesh out the enforceability of a duty to negotiate in good faith under both New York state law and 'general principles of law'.

The Tribunal received submissions from Farnsworth, and other 'learned American jurists' before outlining a highly contextualised vision of preliminary agreements. The binding nature of such agreements it was argued could only be determined via an examination of "the circumstances surrounding the negotiations of the agreement, the conduct of the parties, and, of course, the terms of the agreement, including the number and significance of open terms'. It is notable that the Tribunal felt it necessary to consider the treatment of preliminary agreements when determining the duty to negotiate in good faith, and the Tribunal adopted enthusiastically the position of Judge Leval in *Teachers Ins. and Annuity Ass'n v. Tribune Co.*[136] that:

---

[134] Evidence was presented that the choice of applicable law was discussed, if only briefly during negotiations in Georgia in 1993, but no firm decision either way was ultimately reached. The suggestion of New York or New Jersey law was countered by a proposal for Saudi law. It was therafter suggested that no applicable law should be expressly chosen by the parties.

[135] 'We do consider highly relevant, however, the fact that the Non-Disclosure Agreement, which was signed bt the parties ... contains a choice of law clause in favour of the law of New York, including the statement that "the parties are familiar with the principles of New York Commercial Law, and desire and agree that the law of New York shall apply in any dispute arising with respect to this Agreement.', at para. 5 of the Award. The Tribunal was similarly persuaded by the fact that one of the Parties appeared to be a corporation organised under the laws of the State of New York.

[136] 670 F. Supp. 491, 497 (S.D.N.Y, 1987). (the case being referred to by the panel as the 'Tribune case'). The Tribune case itself differentiated between two types of preliminary agreement. In the first type the parties are considered to have reached 'complete agreement (including agreement on the binding nature of their commitment) on all issues requiring negotiation. All that remains to be done is for the parties to carry that agreement forward into practice'. The second type of preliminary agreement is, according to Judge Leval, one that 'expresses mutual commitment to a contract on agreed major terms, while recognising the existence of open terms that remain to be negotiated. Although the existence of open

> Notwithstanding the importance of protecting negotiating parties from involuntary judicially imposed contracts, it is equally important that the courts enforce and preserve agreeements that were intended as binding, despite a need for further documentation or negotiation. It is of course the aim of contract law to gratify, not to defeat, the expectations that arise out of intended contractual agreement, despite informality or the need for further proceedings between the parties.

Like a lower District Court, The Tribunal moved further to endorse Judge Leval's position on the duty to negotiate in good faith, which 'arises (often implicitly)'. The arbitration panel accepted that the obligation does not guarantee that a final contract will necessarily materialise, as the parties may simply lose interest as circumstances change. Crucially, however, the panel endorsed the decision in *Tribune* that the obligation does 'bar a party from renouncing the deal, abandoning the negotiations, or insisting on conditions that do not conform to the preliminary agreement'. The ICC panel found such reasoning 'compelling and appropriate' and further endorsed Farnsworth's 'sound interpretation of the pertinent articles' of the UNIDROIT principles. Farnsworth carried forward an argument he has consistently advanced that:

Plainly, although the Principles impose a duty of good faith on negotiating parties quite apart from the agreement, it would be inconsistent with the Principles to hold an agreement to negotiate to be unenforceable.[137]

Yet, despite the endorsement of the UNIDROIT Principles and the view of the ICC arbitrators that 'international arbitrators are fully justified to turn to general principles of law', this case concerns not the role of the Principles as such, but rather the role of New York state law. Advocates of the UNIDROIT Principles will argue that the case reveals how the Principles accord with wider international practice but that view is open to an alternative interpretation. The high degree of uncertainty as to the applicable law – with four competing legal systems connected to the case – revealed a highly suitable occasion when retreat to 'general principles of international law' would have afforded the panel with an appropriate and less costly remedy. The case only serves to highlight the absence of meaningful caselaw applicable to preliminary agreements and precontractual

terms generally suggests that a binding agreement has not been reached, that is not necessarily so. For the parties can bind themselves to a concededly incomplete agreement in the sense that they accept a mutual commitment to negotiate in good faith and to reach final agreement within the scope that has been settled in the preliminary agreement'.

137 The Tribunal added that '... the undertaking to negotiate in good faith ... would thus be valid, binding and enforceable under general principles of law as reflected in the UNIDROIT Principles'. Farnsworth's orthodox view that if parties have agreed to negotiate in good faith, then pacta sunt servanda should apply is a typically Farnsworthian analysis (See also E.A. Farnsworth, *Preliminary Dealings*, "There is no adequate reason to refuse to give effect to the explicit intention of the parties to an agreement to negotiate"). The contractual argument is not altogether convincing, however, given the uncertainty attached to the limits of any such obligation. It is equally problematic under the UNIDROIT Principles as the Principles are silent as to what constitutes good faith generally, and more specifically during negotiations.

duties under the UNIDROIT Principles themselves. Unless New York State law (and similar caselaw decisions affirming broad duties to negotiate in good faith, etc) is to become a proxy surrogate for the Principles themselves, it is clear that the UNIDROIT Principles will continue to offer greater uncertainty than coherence in seeking to regulate international commercial negotiations and preliminary agreeements. Far from an independent source of ready-made commercial rules, the case reveals greater support for the view that the interpretation of the UNIDROIT Principles is ever dependent upon domestic court decisions.[138] As Schödermeier notes, 'All in all, the statutory construction according to the functional considerations of international practice is embedded in the values of the respective domestic legal system – there is trust in international practice, but it is controlled and verified according to our own fundamental legal values. Domestic laws can hardly be denied this influence'.[139]

Yet, Klaus Peter Berger, who acknowledges that the UNIDROIT Principles and other soft law initiatives are mere 'comparative snapshots' sees this domestic dependency as an opportunity rather than an obstacle for the development of generalised soft law principles and suggests that domestic judges and international arbitrator's should consistently strive toward the 'internationally useful' interpretation of contract in the light of 'transnational commercial law'.[140] The domestic judge or international arbitrator who applies a certain domestic law may therefore use this discretion to strive towards an internationally useful interpretation of that law. In transborder trade and commerce this will be a solution which is sensible under the economic circumstances of the case. If the parties have included a choice of law clause in their contract it can be assumed that they will accept a certain margin of possible decisions based on this law. Within this natural 'margin' the judge or arbitrator may decide to apply an

[138] This view is not supported by M. Suchankova, 'The Unidroit Principles of International Commercial Contracts and Precontractual Liability' (2000) 6 IBLJ 691 who argues that the Principles provide 'clear and accessible rules which assure predictability for those that refer to them'. That said, she acknowledges that 'judges and arbitrators have reasons to hesitate before applying them'. A fact borne out by the ICC Arbitral award above. See also J. Paulsson, 'La lex mercatoria dans l'arbitrage de la CCI (1990) 1 Revue de' lArbitrage 55, who argued at that time that the degree of divergence across national systems would prevent a satisfactory arrival at transnational norms governing precontractual behaviour, at 96.

[139] M. Schödermeier, *Sonderprivatrecht für internationale Wirtschaftsverträge* (1998) at 198.

[140] K.P. Berger, *The Concept of the 'Internationally Useful' Construction of Domestic Law*, accessible via the Center for Transnational Law database (TLDB). Berger argues that the primary advantages of the UNIDROIT Principles and other soft law codes rest in the fact that they provide a domestic judge or international arbitrator with discretion to strive towards an internationally useful interpretation of that law. 'In transborder trade and commerce this will be a solution which is sensible under the economic circumstances of the case. If the parties have included a choice of law clause in their contract it can be assumed that they will accept a certain margin of possible decisions based on this law. Within this natural 'margin' the judge or arbitrator may decide to apply an internationally useful method of construction which finds a solution that takes into account the particularities of international trade and the economic interests of the parties'.

internationally useful method of construction which finds a solution that takes into account the particularities of international trade and the economic interests of the parties.

There is a certain attraction underlying his would-be globalised law via domestic law (or *glocal* law) approach, but the thesis still fails to adequately square the circle. Where the UNIDROIT Principles are arguably at their strongest is in relation to precontractual liability in damages. The UPICC make clear that the damages will be assessed on the basis of 'loss caused', and aim to recompense parties' out-of-pocket expenses and any lost opportunity or loss of a chance to contract with a third party.[141] Evidently, the Principles have sought to find a mid-point between traditional common and civil law positions yet it is further notable that they remain silent about the contractual or tortious foundation of liability. The implication being that good faith alone will provide the procedural sticking plaster. Having considered the weaknesses of the UPICC, let us consider briefly the treatment of precontractual liability under the Principles of European Contract Law.

3.3 Analysing precontractual liability under the Principles of European Contract Law

It is widely argued that the Principles of European contract law have neglected the protective dimensions of consumer law, and it is noticeable that the 2004 Follow Up Communication in Annex 1, Section 2 highlights many of the areas already covered by the PECL as requiring continued comparative labour. Again, Berger notes that the primary difference between the UNIDROIT Principles and the Principles of European Contract Law is that PECL 'allow the user to make his own judgement as to the comparative persuasiveness of the rule, while the UPICC do not reveal the comparative depth and basis of [a]

[141] Article 2.16 UPICC also enshrines a broad duty of confidentiality. Any improper use or disclosure of confidential information may result in an award in damages. Berger has recently added that, 'Even in purely domestic cases, German doctrine looks at the approach of 'modern lawmakers' such as the Lando Commission and the UNIDROIT Working Group. It is an open question in German legal doctrine whether pre-contractual liability in case of breach of a duty of confidentiality involves a duty to pay compensation based on the benefit received by the party in breach'. He concurs with Canaris that, in order to resolve this question German doctrine should look at Art. 2.16 of the UPICC for guidance. Citing Canaris in J. Basedow (ed), *Europäische Vertragsrechtvereinheitlichung und deutsches Recht* (Archiv für die civilistische Praxis, 2000) he agrees that 'the step [to accept a duty to pay compensation based on the benefit received] would find strong support in Art. 2.16 (2) UPICC. This would increase substantially the weight of this argument and would tip the balance in favour of such an approach, given that German legal doctrine is undecided and open on this issue. This would apply in particular if Art. 2.16 (2) UPICC is grounded on a broad comparative basis and does not result from a more or less isolated idea of its drafters'.

rule to its user'.[142] Many of the same UNIDROIT based negotiation duties are expressly included in the PECL. Yet, the European Principles are more fulsome in their treatment of information duties. The Principles further draw a strong distinction between strictly commercial and business-to-consumer contracts in setting out stronger safeguards for weaker parties.[143] Building upon Article 1.202 PECL, which expressly advocates contractual solidarity, withholding information in the precontractual stage is treated by the PECL under the broad headings of mistake, fraud, threat or unfair advantage. The standard remedy for breach of these obligations is an award in damages. In the case of incorrect information, compensation for damage is granted 'even if the information does not give rise to a fundamental mistake under Art. 4:103, unless the party which gave the information had reason to believe that the information was correct'. Such a rule has been justified on the grounds that it acts as an incentive for both parties to work towards an agreement and in unison to prosper the contract.

The European Principles are similarly more coherent when it comes to remedies. Four possible remedies for information defects are presented. Compensation in damages and the recovery of a party's 'reliance interest' is the remedy for the breach of an information duty. The specific right to information is conceived of as an obligation for the other party to consider and in the event of non-performance, specific performance is perceived as the most appropriate remedy. A third remedy is the loss of certain rights for a failure to fulfil information duties, whilst a final remedy suggests that a party should be bound by any information willingly or mistakenly given that inspires the other party to act on this knowledge. Art. 4:106 provides that "a party which has concluded a contract relying on incorrect information given by the other party may recover damages

[142] *Ibid.* Berger hints at the superiority of the PECL over the UNIDROIT Principles, as the 'comparative persuasiveness' of the UPICC is entirely dependent on the 'composition, authority and reputation of the UNIDROIT working group, at para. 4. Information duties and precontractual obligations similarly receive strong treatment in the Pavia European Contract Code. Title II, Section 1, Article 7 imposes a broad general duty to inform one's co-contracting partner during the negotiation stage. Parties are required to bring to one another's attention 'all factual and legal circumstances' which may have a bearing on the validity of the contract. Setting such a high, arguably impossible standard of compliance, illustrates the weakness of capturing business practice with broad generalised fairness clauses. General statutory formulae in the continental civil codes provide little or no operational guidance in this area either. Similar to the position advanced in the Spanish Supreme Court, Art. 3:44 of the Dutch Civil Code, for instance, provides that there is deceit in negotiations if silence is intentionally maintained on matters 'which the silent party was under a duty to communicate'. Yet as Kötz observes, 'it does not say when such a duty exists. Indeed it could hardly do so, since it is a question to which, as the draftsmen of the German Civil Code realised, 'the legislator can provide no answer', in *Precontractual Duties of Disclosure, supra* Introduction at fn. 29, at 28.

[143] Article 6:101(2) does draw a distinction between information provided by a professional supplier and other party, however the duties to inform are largely identical. That said, the Principles do acknowledge that professional suppliers have typically greater access to information and enhanced bargaining power and on this basis, there is a justification for imposing greater precontractual (information) duties.

in accordance with Article 4:117(2) and (3). Article 4:117 further specifies that damages are to be "limited to the loss caused" by the provision of incorrect information.

A number of rules do, however, appear largely superfluous. For instance, the Principles differentiate between situations where essential information (necessary to carry forward the contract) is provided but is incomplete, and situations where the information is provided after a period of delay. In either case, however, the PECL foresees a remedy in damages.[144] Where incorrect information results in a mistake[145] the remedy presented by the Lando Commission is to entitle the injured party to avoid the contract or to have it performed as it was understood by the injured party with the agreement of the other party. The same remedy is foreseen where incorrect or erroneous information results in the other side committing a mistake under the contract.[146] It is notable, however, that a recent 2005 comparative analysis of contract remedies edited by Cohen and McKendrick provides ample consideration of the UNIDROIT Principles but comparatively little examination of the Principles of European Contract Law, particularly in the work of US scholars (on whom the PECL have thus far largely failed to register).[147] It would be unwise to suggest that this signals either that the PECL are not being used in practice, or are being treated as an analgous to the UNIDROIT Principles but it will doubtless alarm the drafters – and should equally register with the CFR-Net.

Clearly, the general rules of interpretation laid down in Art.5:101 will allow a court applying the Principles to consider 'the negotiation phase' (which includes both the parties conduct and words), yet the vagueness of the PECL is clearly unsatisfactory as no guidelines are offered as to what precontractual material should be admissible in evidence at trial. Admittedly, this is arguably a procedural issue, rather than a question of substantive law, yet the open-endedness of the Principles is likely to prevent their easy assimilation into practice, particularly in common law jurisdictions. Article 5-102 of the Principles states that: In interpreting a contract, regard shall be had, in particular, to:

a) the circumstances in which it was concluded, including the preliminary negotiations;
b) the conduct of the parties, even subsequent to the conclusion of the contract;
c) the nature and purpose of the contract;
d) the interpretation which has already been given to similar clauses by the parties and the practices they have established between themselves;

[144] Art. 1:301(4) states that non-performance denotes 'any failure to perform an obligation under the contract, whether excused or not, including delayed performance, defective performance and/or a failure to co-operate in order to give full effect to the contract'.

[145] Under Art. 4:103 (1)(a)(i).

[146] Under 4:104.

[147] N. Cohen & E. McKendrick, *Comparative Remedies for Breach of Contract* (Oxford University Press, 2005).

e) the meaning commonly given to terms and expressions in the branch of activity concerned and the interpretation similar clauses may already have received;
f) usages; and finally
g) good faith and fair dealing.

In relation to commercial contracts, paragraphs (a) and (b) go beyond what is permitted under the current judicial approach to interpretation in the courts of England and Wales, although McKendrick has previously argued that the law should develop along these general lines.[148] Paragraph (g) would seemingly present an insurmountable hurdle, at least for the purposes of pure b2b contracts in the light of *Walford v.* Miles (analysed further below in chapter 3), given the resistance to the doctrine of good faith and fair dealing.[149] However, with influential figures such as McKendrick criticising the approach to *Walford* and the 'suspect' English stance on the admissibility of evidence of precontractual negotiations, those keen to promote a greater opening up of their Lordship's stance in *Walford* (and indeed beyond *Walford*) will doubtless rely on Article 5-102 to promote a greater contextualist approach to interpretation.

There is a certain danger, however, in presenting the Principles of European Contract Law as a 'superior' default option for the development of European contract law generally, particularly given the lack of caselaw the PECL are currently generating. However, this danger is not troubling those such as Berger, who notes that Article 3:204 PECL provides that precontractual statements by an agent acting without authority will not bind the principal. He explains that the comparative reflections on Art. 2:302 reveals that under Italian, Portuguese, Dutch, English and Scottish law, damages for misuse of information include the defendant's profits, while under Austrian, Belgian, Danish, French and Luxembourg law, only the aggrieved party's loss is compensated.[150] Thus, 'the drafters of the PECL have made it clear that Art 2:302 (2) does not constitute the common core of the legal systems compared, but rather what the Working Group considered the 'best' solution from an interest-oriented perspective'. According to Berger, this approach cannot be criticised since the codification of the 'best' or 'most suitable' solution is 'a legitimate purpose of the functional comparative analysis'.[151] We will return to query the validity of this role for 'functional comparative law' in the concluding chapter.

---

148 See E. McKendrick, 'The Frontiers of Contract Law – Interpretation of Contracts and the Admissibility of Precontractual Negotiations' (2005) 17 Singapore Academy of Law 248.

149 [1992] AC 128.

150 *Supra.* Berger argues that Article 2.302(2) should above all be used to reach an 'internationally useful' interpretation and application of German law.

151 *Ibid.*

4 Concluding remarks

The notion that the Principles of European Contract Law and other existing International conventions and soft law instruments could provide anything other than a skeletal framework for advancing towards a workable common EC contract law has only gradually been conceded by many within the primary academic study groups pioneering the development of the CFR but is starkly apparent from the lack of meaningful caselaw in discrete areas such as those relating to precontractual liability. Moreover, seeking to benchmark a more coherent triple-pillared contract law lacks logic unless undertaken as a means of better streamlining the law. Reich suggests that it would certainly be useful under the CFR research programme to better structure and systematise the rather confusing and contradictory bulk of legislation related to information and precontractual duties and to elaborate uniform principles, rules, and remedies, always under the interpretative authority of the ECJ. Yet, as was highlighted above, the recent tendency of the European Court of Justice is away from such a broad interpretative role.[152] What is equally apparent is that Community directives on private law consistently resist generalisation, particularly precontractual duties which tend to be highly sector specific, making their generalising and wider application in other fields potentially hazardous. The remainder of this study is therefore devoted to a critical cross-jurisdictional analysis of preliminary agreements and the question of reliance.

[152] In notable contrast, it is possible to identify a clear trend away from centralisation towards greater decentralised enforcement in other areas of private law, such as EC competition law (with the 2004 Modernisation Package), see M.J. Doris & S. Marco Colino, *Swings and Roundabouts in European Private Law*, paper presented at PriME conference on the theme of 'Private Law and the Many Cultures of Europe', University of Helsinki, August 27-29, 2006. For more information on the Modernisation Package, see: J. Stuyck, 'EC competition law after modernisation: More than ever in the interest of consumers' (2005) 28(1) JCP 1.

CHAPTER 3

Dealing with Divergence

The law excludes from the admissible background the previous negotiations of the parties and their declarations of subjective intent. They are admissible only in an action for rectification. The law makes this distinction for reasons of practical policy and, in this respect only, legal interpretation differs from the way we would interpret utterances in ordinary life. The boundaries of this exception are in some respects unclear. But this is not the occasion on which to explore them.[1]

There is ... a very fine borderline between the admissible and the inadmissible. One may look at the facts and circumstances surrounding the negotiation and that about which the parties were negotiating, but not at what the parties said during negotiations or previous drafts. The rationale, at least in part, appears to be a wish on the part of the courts to encourage open negotiations and to discourage the creation of self-seeking documents or utterances.[2]

1 Preliminary agreements and the doctrine of reliance in comparative perspective

In chapter 3 we seek to explore the treatment of preliminary agreements and precontractual duties in modern English, US and Spanish contract law. In particular, the aim is to uncover the law in action. It has been

1 Per Lord Hoffman in *Investors Compensation Scheme, op cit.* Lord Hoffman's 'restatement' on the modern interpretation of contracts fails to offer any real light as to when negotiations may have consequences in contractual disputes. The failure to delve deeper into the question of precontractual duties, whilst upholding the exclusion of evidence of negotiations on the grounds of 'practical policy', is clearly unsatisfactory. What is clear is that the court may continue to have regard to precontractual negotiations for the purposes of rectification. Of course, rectification will only come into play once the meaning of the words used by the parties has been ascertained. A contract can be rectified if there has been a defect in the recording of the contract so that the written agreement does not reflect the agreement that the parties intended to make. In such a case it may be possible for a court to rectify the document so as to bring it into line with the poorly expressed intentions of the parties. One reason why rectification has always been treated differently in the context of interpretation of contracts is that the court can have regard to a much wider range of materials in a rectification case than it can in a case concerned solely with the interpretation of the contract.

2 Per MacDuff J in *Sykes v. Pannell Kerr Forster,* unreported QBD, 30 March 2001. This self-serving use of precontractual negotiations has equally been heavily frowned upon by the Spanish courts for complicating and prolonging litigation. In a recent commercial case involving an alleged verbal promise to contract, the Provincial court of Girona found that both parties made self-seeking statements – with one party arguing that there was a binding promise to contract, the other that there was a mere non-binding letter of intent, yet upon a 'simple reading of the document' the court determined that a specific promise to contract had indeed been agreed in accordance with the requirements of Article 1.261 of the Civil code. See AC 2004\1748 Sentencia del Audiencia Provincial Girona núm. 261/2004 (Sección 2ª), July 12, 2004.

suggested that the English courts are currently in a period of flux, shifting from a traditional, literal approach to the interpretation of contract, to a more open-textured, flexible method. But to what extent do the commercial courts of England and Wales arrive at functionally equivalent decisions when considering incomplete bargains? And is there sufficient scope to foster a more civilian approach to the question of precontractual reliance? In seeking to answer these questions the chapter is divided into two self-reinforcing sections. Firstly, the current resolute unwillingness of the courts in England and Wales to admit into evidence at trial material arising from the precontractual stage of negotiations is examined. This largely descriptive analysis prompts deeper reflection on the resultant impact on contract drafting of a distinctly commercially orientated interpretative and adjudicative style. Thereafter a specific cross-jurisdictional case cluster is identified and comparatively assessed.

Our point of departure is the courts of England and Wales, where the judiciary has had an enduring difficulty divorcing the content of precontractual negotiations and the phenomenon of bargaining from the doctrine of freedom of contract. A rugged individualist approach to both deal-making and drafting has dominated. Particularly in arms-length commercial relations, where parties are considered to be operating from a position of equality, the courts have reinforced notions of hard-ball tactics of winner-takes-all, thus encouraging contracting parties to act in their own self-interest.[3] It is perhaps unsurprising therefore that commercial contract law in England and Wales has failed to develop any broad reliance-based duties or an obligation to negotiate in good faith. In the majority view whilst the current position may appear to operate harshly it avoids the courts wasting time and resources policing parties' negotiations.[4] Thus, at present the preference for certainty and bright line rules appears to override any arguments in favour of a more civilian-styled approach. Added to an absence of any generalised duty to negotiate in good faith, contracting parties are moreover under no fixed, general duty to disclose:

> Where parties are contracting with one another, each may ... observe silence even in regard to facts which he believes would be operative upon the mind of the

3 By maximising the impact of their bargaining strength, access to superior resources, access to legal advice, etc.

4 See G.H. Treitel, *The Law of Contract* (11th edn, Sweet & Maxwell, 2003) at 390. In Australia and New Zealand the courts have shown much greater sympathy to a the notion of a broad duty to negotiate in good faith (see for instance the comment of Finn J in *Hughes Aircraft Systems International v. Air Services Australia* (1997) 146 ALR 1, discussed below in chapter 4) yet a key concern in the UK relates to the calculation of damages following breach of such a duty. Should the disappointed party get the full anticipated profit under the proposed contract, merely a proportion for the 'loss of a chance' (as in *Chaplin v. Hicks* [1911] 2 KB 786), an estimated sum for speculative missed opportunities lost in reliance on the failed agreement or merely wasted expenditure arising out of the failed negotiations. These questions have been considered as an aside in *Harmon CFEM Facades v. Corporate Officer of House of Commons* (2000) 72 Con LR 21 (p251).

> other, and it rests upon those who say that there was a duty to disclose, to show that the duty existed.[5]

Absent any representation(s) that may induce a false assumption, there is thus no obligation to provide one's contracting partner with information that may potentially influence his decision either way,[6] or to correct a false assumption on which the other party is relying.[7] Indeed, the notion that any broader moral dimension should infiltrate hard-edged commercial contracting was rather flippantly dismissed as far back as 1871 in *Smith v. Hughes*, and this classical approach appears to endure largely untroubled, despite the impact of Community directives and wider international impulses. In the commonly cited example, A buys oats from B but is mistaken as to the quality of those oats. He would not have purchased the specific oats had he known of their true quality. In the absence of any false representation by B as to the type of oats on offer or any contractual term to the effect, A cannot avoid the contract.[8] In the words of Lord Atkin:

> All these cases involve hardship on A and benefit B, as most people would say, unjustly. They can be supported on the ground that it is of paramount importance

5 *Davies v. London & Provincial Marine Insurance Co* (1878) 8 Ch D 469, 474 *per* Fry J. See also *Keates v. Cadogan* (1851) 10 CB 591; 138 E.R 234 (landlord not liable for failing to warn a prospective tenant of the ruinous condition of the premises), *Fletcher v. Krell* (1872) 42 L.J. Q.B. 551 and *Bradford Third Equitable Benefit Building Society v. Borders* [1941] 2 All E.R. 205, 211: 'mere silence, however morally wrong, will not support an action of deceit'. Halson argues that this is in reality 'no more than an application of the more general disinclination on the part of the common law to recognise a duty to negotiate in good faith' in R. Halson, *Contract Law* (Longman, 2001) at 31. See also *Banque Financiere v. Westgate Insurance Co* [1989] 2 All ER 952, at p. 1010 (... ordinarily in the absence of misrepresentation, our law leaves that other party entirely without a remedy).

6 See Lord Atkin in *Bell v. Lever Bros* [1932] A.C. 161 at 227: 'Ordinarily the failure to disclose a material fact which might affect the mind of a prudent contractor does not give the right to avoid the contract. The principle of *caveat emptor* applies'. Similar thinking has had a heavy bearing on US contract law but increasingly, as was noted previously, Spanish legal theorists have reinforced the practical and economic benefits of a strong disclosure duty.

7 (1871) LR 6 Q.B. 597 (at 607). The buyer, a racehorse trainer, wanted old oats for his horses and believed that the oats on offer were indeed old. The seller, a farmer, knew full well that his oats were new, and he also knew that the buyer wrongly believed them to be old, though he had done nothing to encourage the buyer's mistaken belief. Cockburn J. said, 'The question is whether, under such circumstances, the passive acquiescence of the seller in the self-deception of the buyer will entitle the latter to avoid the contract. I am of opinion that it will not' (at 603). It is notable that Dutch law has imposed a positive duty to correct a false assumption but does not stipulate exactly when such a duty of disclosure will arise. Indeed, Kötz is not surprised as when preparing the German civil code, the drafters realised that the 'legislator can provide no answer'. Cited in *Motïe zu dem Entwurfe eines Bürgerlichen Gesetzbuches.* 1896, I, p. 208.

8 And Lord Atkin in *Bell v. Lever Bros* [1932] A.C. 161, at 224.

> that contracts should be observed, and that if parties honestly comply with the essentials of the formation of contracts, *i.e.*, agree in the same terms on the same subject matter, they are bound, and must rely on the stipulations of the contract for protection from the effect of facts unknown to them.[9]

The question of interfering in precontractual negotiations in a commercial context is therefore overwhelmingly perceived as a bridge too far, and the idea of admitting evidence of negotiations has been firmly, if rather unhelpfully, ruled out on pure policy grounds.[10] The non-imposition of such duties can be strongly defended on the basis that it serves to foster greater legal certainty and

---

9 *Ibid.*

10 Importantly, post *Investors*, the Court of Appeal in *Scottish Power plc* v. *Britoil (Exploration) Ltd, The Times*, 2 December 1997 criticised the width of Lord Hoffman's restatement, in particular the phrase 'factual matrix' for risking legal certainty and raising the cost of litigation. Clearly, the restatement was not intended to be revolutionary. Rather, it sought to build on the principles established by Lord Wilberforce in *Prenn* v. *Simmonds* and raffirmed in *Reardon Smith Line Ltd* v. *Hansen-Tangen* [1976] 1 WLR 989. Yet, Staughton LJ has been particularly critical of the breadth of Lord Hoffmann's second principle and his use of the phrase 'factual matrix'. He noted that 'it is often difficult for a judge to restrain the enthusiasm of counsel for producing a great deal of evidence under the heading of matrix, which on examination is found to contribute little or nothing to the true understanding of the parties' contract. All, or almost all, judges are now concerned about the huge cost of litigation. I have to say that such a wide definition of surrounding circumstances, background or matrix seems likely to increase the cost, to no very obvious advantage'. In the Court of Appeal case of *National Bank of Sharjah* v. *Dellborg*, unreported, July 9, 1997, Saville LJ launched a blistering attack on Lord Hoffman's approach to construction. He argued that 'what appears to be the present law does no service to the international or domestic commercial community'. In particular, he stated that 'where the words used have an unambiguous and sensible meaning as a matter of ordinary language, I see serious objections in an approach which would permit the surrounding circumstances to alter that meaning'. He identified two principal objections in the following terms: Firstly, such an approach would seem to entail that even where the words that the parties have chosen to use have only one meaning; and that meaning (bearing in mind the aim or purpose of the agreement) is not self-evidently nonsensical, the court will not be allowed to adopt that meaning without an examination of the surrounding circumstances, which could involve discovery, interrogatories, cross-examination and the like; for a party seeking to challenge that meaning could assert with great force that until the circumstances are fully examined, it is impossible to decide whether or not they should override the plain words of the agreement. This would do nothing but add to the costs and delays of litigation and indeed of arbitration, much of which is concerned with interpreting agreements. Secondly, the position of third parties (which would include assignees of contractual rights) does not seem to have been considered at all. They are unlikely in the nature of things to be aware of the surrounding circumstances. Where the words of the agreement have only one meaning, and that meaning is not self evidently nonsensical, is the third party justified in taking that to be the agreement that was made, or unable to rely on the words used without examining (which it is likely to be difficult or impossible for third parties to do) all the surrounding circumstances? ... the law would have to treat the agreement as meaning one thing to the parties and another to third parties, hardly a satisfactory state of affairs. If the latter is the case, then unless third parties can discover all the surrounding

latitude for negotiating parties, that it affords contracting parties the freedom either to reach agreement or walk away, and that it keeps the court system free of potentially time-consuming and costly disputes. In the search for legal ideas within Europe's multi-level system of competing 'private law laboratories' this is of course an argument that must not pass by default. Indeed, evidential rules do provide certainty when they exclude the admissibility of specific evidence and in this sense the position under English from a purely procedural perspective is entirely efficient. If other European partners were to follow suit, economic actors would at least know prior to contracting that the precontractual phase of negotiations would not be examined in commercial trials. Though largely neglected to date in the literature, divergent drafting preferences are equally of great significance to the question of harmonisation. In practice English commercial drafters typically resort to 'entire agreement' and 'non-reliance' clauses in order to limit liability for any adverse precontractual representations. We can merely hint at how this technique fits when read against Article 1337 of the Italian civil code, which, as we observed previously, expressly provides that in the course of negotiations and in the formation of a contract parties must act at all times in good faith.[11] In the case of *Inntrepreneur Pub Co Ltd v. East Crown Ltd*, Lightman J left little to the imagination as to the central role of such clauses. As a 'pure contractual device', he saw the purpose of an entire agreement provision as a means:

> ... to preclude a party to a written agreement ... thrashing through the undergrowth and finding, in the course of negotiations, some (chance) remark or statement (often long forgotten or difficult to recall or explain) upon which to found a claim ... such a clause constitutes a binding agreement between the parties that the full contractual terms are to be found in the document containing the clause and not elsewhere". Consequently, there could be no threat of liability for precontractual representations of whatever shade. "Any promises or assurances made in the course of the negotiations (which, in the absence of such a clause may carry an effect as a collateral warranty) shall have no contractual force, save in so far as they are reflected and given effect in that document.[12]

circumstances and are satisfied that they make no difference, they cannot safely proceed to act on the basis of what the agreement actually says. This again would seem to be highly unsatisfactory'.

11 Three recent decisions have examined the effect of such clauses. See *Inntrepreneur Pub Co Ltd v. East Crown Ltd* [2000] 2 Lloyd's Rep 611 (ChD), *EA Grimstead & Son Ltd v. McGarrigan* [1999] WLR 852482 (CA), and again in the Chancery Division *Thomas Witter Ltd v. TBP Industries Ltd* [1996] 2 All ER 573 (ChD). For a cursory analysis of the cases, see S. Mills & L. Jacobson, 'Entire Agreement & Non-Reliance Clauses' (2001) 22(6) Company Lawyer 189.

12 At p. 614. As Mills & Jacobson argue, in the event of a written contract, the bare effect of such clauses is to effectively 'denude' the agreement of any collateral warranties, *ibid* at p. 16. Entire agreement and non-reliance clauses have been criticised for failing to properly control the potential for misrepresentation and bad faith bargaining. Yet in all three cases the fact that the parties were of equal bargaining power, had received legal advice and had ultimately signed the contract proved decisive for the courts. In construing such clauses in line with the Unfair Terms Act the courts have however left open the door

Nonetheless, though discounted by Lord Hoffman when handing down his recent restatement on the 'fundamental shift' in *Investors*, the courts increased emphasis on the 'matrix of facts' implies added judicial sensitivity to the precontractual formation of commercial contracts.[13] Indeed, post-*Investors* a number of cases have considered the issue, though merely fleetingly and largely to dismiss the notion. The general rule that negotiations will at no time be subject to a duty to bargain in good faith has also firmly taken root. This key tenet of English contract law has been copper fastened by the House of Lords' decision in *Walford v. Miles*,[14] and the judgment appears to leave little room for doubt that the English judiciary sees no reason for a civilian influence to alter the law's view of precontractual negotiations and bartering.

The facts in *Walford* have been well rehearsed in the literature. The case concerned a purported 'lock-out' agreement by which the claimants had endeavoured to ensure that the defendants would negotiate only with the claimants for the sale of the defendant's business. The agreement provided that the defendants would not deal with any other third party, would in any event terminate negotiations entered into with any third party and would 'continue to negotiate in good faith' with the claimants.[15] The reference to a requirement to negotiate in good faith provoked the ire of the court. In his judgment, Lord Ackner held that a duty to negotiate was 'inherently repugnant to the adversarial position of the parties involved in the negotiations'[16] and, just for good measure, added that

---

to a claim in misrepresentation under a non-reliance clause. A party wishing to rely on a non-reliance clause and estoppel will only succeed if he did not know that a previous representation was false (i.e. it was made negligently or innocently). Mills & Jacobson further suggest that even where a non-reliance clause is held to be unreasonable by a court, the 'clause is still likely to have an enormous evidential effect on the credibility of the party who is prepared to sign an agreement containing a non-reliance clause and subsequently seeks to avoid its clear meaning and effect', at 191.

13 As Berg observes: 'If pre-contract negotiations are treated as simply another background fact known to the parties, they will always have to be considered in the process of interpretation'. See A. Berg, 'Thrashing Through the undergrowth, 122 LQR 354, at 356.

14 [1992] AC 128. At first instance the trial judge held that an oral between the parties that required the defendants to terminate negotiations with any third party in return for the plaintiffs' promise to continue negotiations constituted a separate collateral agreement which was not 'subject to contract'. The defendants had repudiated that agreement and specific promises made by the first defendant constituted misrepresentations. The court awarded £700 special damages (as the wasted expenditure) with further damages in respect of the repudiation. The House of Lords found the seller's open-ended commitment to deal with only one potential purchaser void for uncertainty and therefore unenforceable. This considered view of lock-out agreements has been followed by the Court of Appeal in *Pitt v. PHH Asset Management Ltd* [1993] 4 All ER 961.

15 For Lord Ackner there were a number of 'vital' questions that appeared difficult to answer, including: 1. how is the vendor ever to know that he is entitled to withdraw from further negotiations? and 2. How is the court to police such an 'agreement?

16 The transcript of the judgment at p. 138F reads: 'A duty to negotiate in good faith is as unworkable in practice as it is inherently inconsistent with the position of a negotiating party; it is here that the uncer-

it was 'unworkable in practice'.[17] Lord Ackner reasoned that each party to a negotiation is entitled to pursue his own self interest 'so long as he avoids making misrepresentations'.[18]

An exception to the general rule in *Walford* is apparent from the decision in *Re Debtors*[19] in which it was held that Lloyd's was under an obligation to negotiate in good faith the terms of a 'hardship agreement' involving two Lloyd's names. By unilaterally breaking off negotiations, Carnworth LJ was of the view, albeit obiter, that Lloyd's may have been in breach of a duty to act in good faith which arose in this case because the position of Lloyd's in the negotiations was not the same as that of an ordinary party negotiating a private contract. Rather, it was performing functions in the public interest and as such Lloyd's freedom of action was restricted. This decision can, however, be distinguished on the grounds of the quasi-public role that Lloyd's was performing. *Walford v. Miles* thus remains leading binding authority for the view that either party is free to unilaterally terminate arms length negotiations at will, even at an advanced stage, and that no legal penalties will result. This freedom of contract model for precontractual negotiations and contract drafting has further been reinforced by subsequent case-law, and as McKendrick notes will require a House of Lords decision to unsettle the current rule.[20] Yet, their Lordships decision contrasts almost entirely with the US Court of Appeal (Third Circuit) decision in *Channel Home Centers Division of Grace Retail Corp. v. Grossman*,[21] which was considered and rejected as being of 'no assistance' by Lord Ackner in *Walford*.

tainty lies. In my judgment, while negotiations are in existence either party is entitled to withdraw from those negotiations, at any time and for any reason'.

17 Though the case has excited much comment, in many respects their Lordships were largely reiterating the view of Lord Denning M.R. in *Courtney v. Fairbairn Ltd v. Tolaini Brothers (Hotels) Ltd* [1975] 1 WLR 297 that 'if the law does not recognise a contract to enter into a contract (when there is a fundamental term to be agreed) it seems to me it cannot recognise a contract to negotiate', at 301-2. Lord Denning rejected as not well founded dictum in *Hillas & Co. Ltd v. Arcos Ltd* (1932) 147 L.T. 503, at 515 that such an agreement, provided it was supported by consideration could be recognised in law.

18 At 138. Lord Ackner took a different view to the Court of Appeal as to what was required in order to ensure 'business efficacy': there was a need to ensure that parties could negotiate freely and threaten to withdraw if necessary'. Lord Ackner advocated the benefits of an adversarial approach which allows parties the option to threaten melt down 'in the hope that the opposite party may seek to reopen the negotiations by offering him improved terms'.

19 Lloyd's Rep. I.R. 487. The case had been interpreted in some quarters as providing limited scope for developing a broader obligation to negotiate in good faith under all quasi-public contracts, if not in purely commercial contracts.

20 See, *inter alia*, *Pitt v. PHH Asset Management Ltd* [1994] 1 WLR 327, *SAM Business Systems Limited v. Hedley & Co.* [2002] EWHC 2733. See E. McKendrick, 'Contract Law – Updates 2005', at. Though the decision must now be considered in light of obiter comment in *Petromec Inc v. Petroleo Brasiliero SA Petrobas* [2005] EWCA Civ 891 (discussed further below).

21 795 F. 2d. 291 (3d Cir. 1986). The Supreme Court of Colorado has also held that an outright refusal to negotiate, where there is an agreement to do so, is in effect a breach of an agreement to negotiate in

In *Channel Home* the plaintiffs sent a letter of comfort to the defendant concerning the lease of certain business premises. From the letter of comfort language used it was entirely clear that the contract remained incomplete. A critical element of the case was the fact that in order to induce the would-be tenant (*Channel*) to proceed with the planned deal, Grossman agreed to 'withdraw the store from the rental market' and negotiate the lease deal 'to completion'. Later, Grossman abruptly withdrew from the ongoing negotiations and rather rashly granted the lease to a third party. In such circumstances, the US Court of Appeal determined that the parties had entered into a binding 'contract to negotiate'. Consideration for this 'agreement to negotiate' was found on the basis that the defendant agreed to withdraw the store from the rental market in return for a commitment to bargain with Channel. When the case was considered by the English Court of Appeal in *Walford*, Bingham L.J. was equally persuaded that the ceding of a comfort letter itself constituted good consideration, allied to a commitment not to withdraw from the negotiations immediately. The US Appeal court had further been motivated to find in favour of *Channel* as the comfort letter had been subsequently used by the defendant to secure additional financing aimed at advancing the proposed lease. The US Appeal Court thus decided that the parties would be obliged to use their best efforts to negotiate in good faith and with the aim of concluding an agreement. The decision remains equally significant as express reference was made to 'culpa in contrahendo' and, in handing down its ruling, the court stressed that the parties should negotiate in good faith – this despite the fact that there was merely an express commitment in the comfort letter itself that the parties would 'negotiate'.

2 Divergent interpretative and adjudicative styles and the impact on drafting

Importantly, despite the supposed 'fundamental change' that has overtaken contract law interpretation following Lord Hoffman's restatement in 1998, the traditionally literalist approach to contract interpretation endures and has resulted in a heavily detailed and verbose style of drafting among English commercial lawyers. The guiding principle for drafters appears to be 'when

good faith for a specified time period. Mere delay may also be tantamount to an outright refusal. *Vigoda v. Denver Urban Renewal Authority*, 646 P.2d 900 (Colo.1982); see also *American Broadcasting Cos. v. Wolf*, 52 N.Y. 2d 394, 420 N.E. 2d 363, 438 N.Y.S. 2d 482 (1981) which involved a sportscaster who entered into contract with CBS after undertaking to negotiate in good faith with ABC for 90 days. Dilatory tactics may similarly be construed as an attempt to frustrate a contract to bargain. See *Continental Ins. Co. v. NLRB*, 495 F.2d. 44 (2d Cir. 1974). It is noteworthy that the State of Massachusetts does not recognise an implied duty of good faith and fair dealing in negotiations absent a binding agreement committing the parties to such an arrangement, see *inter alia*, *Lafayette Place Assocs. v. Boston Redevelopment Authority*, 427 Mass 509, 517 (1998), *FDIC v. LeBlanc*, 85 F.3d 815 (1996), *Schwanbeck v. Federal-Mogul Corp.*, 412 Mass 703 (1992).

in doubt, write it out'. Leaving a matter unsaid on the grounds that it is self-explanatory to both contracting parties risks having an unwritten deal unpicked by the courts. The high cost of contract litigation in the UK similarly serves to concentrate minds. The principles applied by the courts when interpreting commercial contracts are, as a consequence, of enormous significance for contracting parties and their lawyers, perhaps more so than in any other European jurisdiction. This is so for a number of reasons. The first is that a significant number of the disputes that come before the courts raise issues of interpretation. The second is that many commercial parties make use of standard terms of business (or use industry-accepted standard form) and the precise meaning of these terms is a matter of considerable importance. UK based lawyers will spend a considerable amount of time and effort drafting such contract clauses against the backdrop of the canons of construction applied by the courts. Aware of these realities the courts are loathe to show much sympathy to a commercial party whose lawyer has not complied with the unwritten rules of technical drafting. This view was classically expressed by Hobhouse J in *EE Caledonia Ltd* v. *Orbit Valve Co Europe*[22] when he stated:

> ... it has to be borne in mind that commercial contracts are drafted by parties with access to legal advice and in the context of established legal principles as reflected in the decisions of the courts. Principles of certainty, and indeed justice, require that contracts be construed in accordance with the established principles. The parties are always able by the choice of appropriate language to draft their contract so as to produce a different legal effect. The choice is theirs.

Electricity Corporation v. Fletcher Challenge Energy Ltd[23], a New Zealand case, further reveals that the common law courts will determine the parties' intentions from the text of the contractual document rather than evidence of the negotiation phase, as:

> 'The question whether negotiating parties intended the product of their negotiation to be immediately binding upon them, either conditionally or unconditionally, cannot sensibly be divorced from a consideration of the terms expressed or implicit in that product. They may have embarked upon their negotiation with every intention on both sides that a contract will result; yet they have failed to attain that objective because of an inability to agree on particular terms and on the bargain as a whole. In other cases, which are much less common, the intention may remain but somehow the parties fail to reach an agreement on a term or terms without which there is insufficient structure to create a binding contract'.

Yet, the modern English approach to construction was rather neatly summed up by Sir Thomas Bingham MR in the 1995 case of *Arbuthnott v. Fagan*:

[22] [1993] 4 All ER 165, 173.

[23] [2002] 2 NZLR 433

> Courts will never construe words in a vacuum. To a greater or lesser extent, depending on the subject matter, they will wish to be informed of what may variously be described as the context, the background, the factual matrix or the mischief. To seek to construe any instrument in ignorance or disregard of the circumstances which give rise to it or the situation in which it is expected to take effect is in my view pedantic, sterile and productive of error. But that is not to say that an initial judgment of what an instrument was or should reasonably have been intended to achieve should be permitted to override the clear language of the instrument, since what an author says is usually the surest guide to what he means. To my mind construction is a composite exercise, neither uncompromisingly literal nor unswervingly purposive: the instrument must speak for itself, but it must do so in situ and not be transported to the laboratory for microscopic analysis.[24]

Contract drafting, the express terms of the parties' written contract and the appropriate wording of non-reliance and entire agreement clauses therefore have a much greater bearing on the thinking and energies of English commercial lawyers and the courts than the behaviour of the parties during the negotiation phase. Yet, doctrinally at least the position differs little from that adopted by lawyers and the courts in Spain and the US. The higher Spanish courts have consistently emphasised the need for a literal approach to contract interpretation.[25] Paragraph 1 of Article 1.281 of the Spanish civil code reveals the primacy

---

[24] [1995] 2 A.C. 145. Bingham MR was largely echoing the view of Lord Wilberforce in *Reardon Smith Line Ltd v. Yngvar Hansen-Tangen* [1976] 1 WLR 989 ("No contracts are made in a vacuum: there is always a setting in which they have to be placed. The nature of what is legitimate to have regard to is usually described as 'the surrounding circumstances' but this phrase is imprecise: it can be illustrated but hardly defined. In a commercial contract it is certainly right that the court should know the commercial purpose of the contract and this in turn presupposes knowledge of the genesis of the transaction, the background, the context, the market in which the parties are operating ...") at p. 995-997.

[25] "... las palabras usadas en el contrato pareciesen contrarias a aquélla intención, función interpretativa que no sólo ha de proyectarse sobre la literalidad y expresiones externas de los negocios o convenios, sino que debe abarcar, para determinar la real intención de los sujetos concernidos o contratantes, al conjunto de lo expresado, con atención a los hechos coetáneos y posteriores, ya que si las relaciones contractuales surgen por la expresión del consentimiento de los interesados, en el objetivo de traducir en actos y realidades de lo convenido, puede suceder que se aparte su puesta en práctica respecto de lo estipulado, de ahí que el Código Civil, de manera previsora, disponga en su artículo 1.285 que los contratos, desde su perfección, no sólo obligan al cumplimiento de lo expresamente pactado, sino también a todas sus consecuencias que según su naturaleza sean conformes a la buena fe, al uso y a la Ley". Desde esta perspectiva, y encaminada la labor interpretativa de los actos y negocios jurídicos a indagar el sentido de una declaración de voluntad expresiva del querer o intención real, la regla instrumental básica para efectuar la exégesis está contenida en Paragraph 1 of Article 1.281 of the Spanish Civil code, de la que, como se ha indicado, son subsidiarios o supletorios los criterios prevenidos en el párrafo 2.º y en los artículos siguientes del mismo Cuerpo legal sustantivo (S.S.T.S., Sala Primera, de 22 de marzo de 1950, 19 de febrero de 1981, 30 de marzo, 30 de abril, 17 de julio, 15 y 28 de diciembre de 1982, 16 de

of a literal interpretation of contracts, provided such an approach is 'intelligible'.[26] Literalism has further been a core feature of US contract law since the classical age of *Hotchkiss v. National City Bank*. Yet, Eisenberg describes how the current position in the US reinforces an objective interpretation that simultaneously allows subjectivity to play a much more significant role. As Eisenberg himself acknowledges, the approach to interpretation 'can be arranged along a spectrum that runs from objectivity to subjectivity'.[27] Crucially, in the context of incomplete agreements, Schwartz & Scott identify a relatively recent major shift in US doctrine, whereby the courts have increasingly 'relaxed the knife-edge character of the common law by which parties are bound or not bound at all'. He identifies a new 'default rule' that has emerged to govern cases where the parties fail to memorialise their commitments and 'contemplate further negotiations'. Building on the approach to interpretation of preliminary agreements outlined by Leval J in *Tribune*, Schwartz & Scott observe how litigated incomplete agreements are typically requiring the courts to impose on parties acceptance of a 'mutual commitment to negotiate together in good faith in an effort to reach an agreement'.[28] This new trend in interpretation is having a real baring on the regulation of incomplete contracts and has similarly been identified by Hunter.[29] It has been argued that the doctrine of good faith will not act to 'bootstrap' an agreement where none existed,[30] nor does the duty demand that the parties reach a definitive agreement; merely that they must not act unreasonably,

---

febrero de 1983, 4 de junio y 9 de octubre de 1985, 4 de marzo de 1986, 1 de julio, 26 de noviembre y 16 de diciembre de 1987, entre otras).

26 (S.S.T.S., Sala Primera, de 2 y 23 de febrero, 27 de marzo, 16 de noviembre y 12 de diciembre de 1981, 28 de diciembre de 1982, 16 de febrero y 14 de mayo de 1983, 20 de febrero de 1984, 5 de febrero, 14 y 29 de mayo, 17 y 24 de junio, 2 de julio, 18 de septiembre y 13 de noviembre de 1985, 4 de marzo de 1986 y 1 de abril de 1987, among others). Again, as in English law, words are similarly to be given their ordinary, everday or 'natural meaning' (see Supreme Court decisions dated December 4 1963, February 13 1964, May 3 and June 22 1984, among others), and the courts should aim to prevent the actual words used by the parties from 'twisting' the meaning of the contract. In the absence of doubt or ambiguity the court's need look no further. (See Supreme Court decisions dated February 20, May 3, June 22, December 16 1984, June 17, 1985 and July 7, 1986). The perfection of contracts operates in line with arts. 1261 y 1262 C.C. through the doctrines of offer and acceptance, and offers must be a 'firm and final offer'. Firm, in the sense of constituting a definitive proposal. See also, M. Martín Rodríguez, 'La interpretación del contrato civil y mercantil' in *La Unificación civil y mercantil en la contratación privada* (Ratio Legis, 2006) at 160-174.

27 See M.A. Eisenberg, 'Expression Rules in Contract Law and Problems of Offer and Acceptance' (1994) 82(5) Cal L Rev 1127.

28 A. Schwartz & R.E. Scott, *The Law and Economics of Preliminary Agreements*, 2006, available via www.law.bepress.com, at 15. Typical of this new trend is *Adjustrite Systems, Inc. v. Gab Business Service*, 145 F.3d 543, 547 (2d Cir. 1998) at 548.

29 H. Hunter, *Contextual Approach to Incomplete Agreements*, Lexis Database, May 2006.

30 See *In re Midway Airlines, Inc.*, 180 B.R. 851 (Bankr. N.D. III, 1995).

arbitrarily, capriciously, or inconsistently with reasonable expectations.[31] The US courts will further intervene, it is suggested, to sanction situations where one party takes 'opportunistic advantage' of another.[32]

3 The persistent reinforcement of bargaining freedom under English contract law

The current English position, whilst strong in sanctioning harmful conduct such as misrepresentation, has been slow to prevent opportunistic conduct in negotiations. Yet, despite a lack of sound systematisation and a heavy emphasis on bargaining freedom, as is apparent from case law exposition, the English law of contract is not entirely unprincipled. Rather, as Cardozo wrote in the 1920's, 'the common law does not work from pre-established truths of universal and inflexible validity to conclusions derived from them deductively. Its method is inductive, and it draws its generalisations from particulars.'[33] In this context the pure policy decision to exclude previous negotiations from the 'factual matrix' remains understandable, even if its operation proves problematic in practice. Importantly, Lord Hoffmann, in determining that only one exception to this general exclusionary rule (a claim for rectification of a poorly drafted contract), acknowledged that the boundaries of this exclusion are 'in some respects unclear' and in 2001, in *Bank of Credit and Commerce International* v. *Ali*,[34] Lord Nicholls sought to widen debate on the issue. In the judgment he stated (at paragraph 31) that he wished 'to keep the point open for careful consideration on a future occasion'.

The issue of the admissibility of precontractual negotiations has in fact arisen in a number of cases post-*Investors* and the courts have largely been content to reinforce the general exclusionary approach. The issue was consid-

---

31 *Ibid*, at 938.

32 *Ibid*, at 939.

33 B.N. Cardozo, *The Nature of the Judicial Process* (Yale University Press, 1921). Of course, Cardozo was always something of an early contextualist. In 1917 quoting from the decision in *McCall Co. v. Wright*, 117 N.Y. Supp 775 (1909) he observed that, 'The law has outgrown its primitive stage of formalism when the precise word was the sovereign talisman, and every slip was fatal. It takes a broader view today. A promise may be lacking and yet the whole writing may be 'instinct with an obligation', imperfectly expressed. (In *Lucy, Lady Duff Gordon* 222 N.Y. 91 (1917). Equally the words of Bingham L.J. in *Interfoto Picture Library Ltd v. Stiletto Visual Programmes Ltd* in 1989 continue to resonate: "English law has, characteristically, committed itself to no such overriding principle but has developed piecemeal solutions in response to demonstrated problems of unfairness ...This may yield a result not very different from the civil law principle of good faith, at any rate so far as the formation of the contract is concerned"., at [1989] Q.B. 433, at 445. A case which Brown sees as the English courts first meaningful, if admittedly tentative, step towards 'combining the technical approach to contract formation with notions of good faith'. *supra* at 367.

34 [2001] UKHL 8.

ered by the Privy Council, on appeal from the Court of Appeal of New Zealand in *Canterbury Golf International Ltd* v. *Yoshimoto*,[35] where the judgment of the Privy Council was delivered by Lord Hoffmann. Previously, Thomas J In the Court of Appeal of New Zealand had expressed the view that his construction of the contract was supported by two clauses in earlier drafts of the contract and argued that the rule that excluded evidence of precontractual negotiations should be departed from or relaxed. Whether he intended a relaxation of the rule uniquely in the case at hand or generally is not entirely clear from the ruling. In the Privy Council, however, Lord Hoffmann stated that the case did not provide a 'suitable occasion' for a re-examination of the law in relation to the admissibility of precontractual negotiations because, on the facts, the evidence concerning the precontractual negotiations was 'unhelpful'. At paragraph 28 of the judgment he declared that:

> Their Lordships do not think that it is helpful to try to construe the earlier version of clause 6.3 because it was dropped and the present clause ... substituted. It seems to them pointless to try to speculate upon why the change was made. No doubt each party had their reasons for proposing it ... All a court can do is decide what the final contract means.

The ruling of the Privy Council appears to have been proper on the facts as, despite the view of Thomas J, altering the final contract on the basis of two previously drafted provisions would have been tantamount to judicial re-writing. One would be minded of the comment made in the Massachussets case *Northern Heel Corp. v. Compo Industry Inc* that it would be 'unbefitting' for a court to 'accomplish by judicial fiat what the parties neglected to achieve contractually'.[36]

One further suggestion as to why evidence of precontractual negotiations is 'not helpful' is that since the parties' positions are in a state of flux pending the conclusion of the contract (as they clearly were in *Yoshimoto*) the court should not be asked to speculate upon the reasons that led the parties to change previous drafts before reaching a definitive agreement. There is certainly much validity in the argument that judicial construction should involve merely determining the meaning of the definitive contract; and not scrutinising the process that led to the formation of that contract. It was this argument that ultimately carried

35 [2002] UKPC 40.

36 851 F2d 456. See also *Kroutik v. Momentix Inc*, Mass (2003) (where it was noted that a court cannot 'through the vehicle of the implied covenant, add obligations to a contractual undertaking that the parties did not impose on themselves, unreported April 2, 2003). Or as Lord Mustill stated in *Charter Reinsurance Co Ltd* v. *Fagan* [1997] AC 313: [there] comes a point at which the court should remind itself that the task is to discover what the parties meant from what they have said, and that to force upon the words a meaning which they cannot fairly bear is to substitute for the bargain actually made one which the court believes could better have been made. This is an illegitimate role for a court (at 388). See D. Barker, 'A Return to Freedom of Contract' (2001) 151 New Law Journal 344. See also D.W. McLauchlan, 'The New Law of Contract Interpretation' (2000) 19 New Zealand Universities Law Review 147.

the Privy Council. Yet the universality of Hoffman's exclusionary rule appears suspect. Moving beyond an improper rewriting of the contract, as proposed by Thomas J, the question of generally admitting precontractual evidence retains its own validity. Where evidence of precontractual negotiations is allowed, other cases may reveal an entirely different complexion of the bargaining phase. Doubtless the admission of such evidence will, in very many instances, prove 'unhelpful'. More often than not admission may provide much more energy than light. Yet, should it necessarily prevent such evidence from being uniformly inadmissible? The point is made by Barton that there is little to be gained in terms of efficiency, cost or prompt dispute resolution via the courts by an effectively air-tight exclusionary rule. He argues that since lawyers are required to sift all evidence, including where relevant evidence of misrepresentation, duress or other forms of improper conduct during commercial negotiations, the courts could move to admit 'relevant' evidence arising from negotiations. In addition, he suggests that since the stated aim of the courts when interpreting contracts is to arrive at a commercially sensible understanding of the contract, the precontractual negotiations may provide very good evidence of the commercial aims of the parties, in the sense that they will provide evidence of what the parties were bargaining about and where the key points of conflict between them arose.

Indeed, as the current exclusion of precontractual negotiations is not absolute, there is scope for the controlled inclusion of additional material. Lord Hoffmann has acknowledged that such evidence will ordinarily be admissible in an action for rectification. In addition, where there is an ambiguity in the final written document, evidence of precontractual negotiations may be admissible to show that the parties had attached a particular meaning to a specific phrase.[37] As Barton notes the current approach is further confusing in that evidence of the background, the object and genesis of the transaction is ostensibly admissible but that evidence of the parties' previous negotiating positions and conduct

---

[37] *The Karen Oltman* [1976] 2 Lloyd's Rep 708 case is commonly cited in the literature. The case concerned a two year time charter that included an express clause affording the charterers the opportunity to 're-deliver the vessel after 12 months' trading subject to giving 3 months' notice'. The parties were at loggerheads as to meaning of the clause and in those circumstances the Court felt empowered to examine the extrinsic evidence to decide the actual meaning of the clause. See also the Court of Appeal decision in *The Pacific Colocotronis* [1981] 2 Lloyd's Rep. 40. The recent 2006 Court of Appeal decision in *Proforce Recruit Ltd v. The Rugby Group Ltd* [2006] EWCA Civ 69, which concerned the validity of an entire agreement clause that was rejected on summary judgment, appears equally significant. Berg has been critical of the decision in *ProForce* for questioning the power of entire agreement clauses in insulating parties from liability. The claimant argued that the entire agreement clause was not intended to exclude prior representations, agreements, negotiations or understandings if the evidence was produced to support one party's interpretation of a term contained in the contract. The Court of Appeal thought that the argument had a real prospect of success, but Berg suggests that 'with respect, the argument was wholly unrealistic', *supra* at 364.

in negotiations is not.[38] He suggests that in practice the current distinctions drawn by the courts are largely artificial and by no means easy to draw out. Berg takes a significantly opposing view. He stresses that in two of the more notable recent cases of rectification – and they tend to be few in number – where extrinsic evidence of the negotiation and drafting period was allowed, there was very little evidence for the court to scrutinise. In *The Karen Oltmann* case there were only six telexes and in *The Pacific Colocotronis* merely the ship-master's request for assistance. He appears to share the fears of Saville LJ that allowing such evidence would further inflate the cost of litigation, since 'in many transactions the pre-contract correspondence is voluminous'.[39] A similar concern was raised by Walker J in *NLA Group Ltd* v. *Bowers*.[40] However, in *The Tychy (No.2)* Lord Phillips MR appears to support the view of Barton. In a speech much closer to the thinking of Thomas J in *Yoshimoto* he stated that:

> It is . . . important, though not always easy, to identify what is extrinsic to the agreement and where the scope of Lord Hoffmann's principles forms an intrinsic part ... When a formal contract is drawn up and signed, care must be taken to distinguish between admissible background evidence relating to the nature and object of the contractual venture and inadmissible evidence of the terms for which each party was contending in the course of negotiations. Where, as in the present case, an agreement is alleged to have been reached in the course of dealings which do not culminate in the drawing up of a formal contract, the task

---

38 See A. Barton, GGLS conference on Legal Certainty, *supra* ch.1 fn 69, who notes that the position in Scottish law appears even more confused as a result of Hoffman's intervention. In *Proforce, supra*, it was observed that 'a lawyer must first obtain all the relevant background knowledge which was reasonably available to the parties in the situation in which they were at the time of the contract. This presents little difficulty if the transaction was a straightforward one, the lawyer was personally involved in the drafting and the transaction is fairly recent. However, in the writer's experience, it is extremely difficult for a lawyer to comply, even approximately, with *(Lord Hoffman's Restatement)* if the contract formed part of a deal in which he was not personally involved, particularly if the deal was done several years previously. In these situations, the lawyer has to say: "I've done my best to work out what clause 6.8 means. But what I've done falls materially short of 'interpretation' as defined by Lord Hoffmann." The artificial nature of the exclusionary rule and the potentially practical benefits of 'policing' precontractual negotiations appear to be gaining wider acceptance.

39 Berg, *supra*, at 362.

40 [1999] 1 Lloyd's Rep 109. The case similarly concerned Lloyd's and the trial of a preliminary issue. Walker J criticised counsel for the plaintiff for aiming to 'adduce the factual evidence of no fewer than five witnesses, with subpoenas served on two further witnesses (both of whom were defendants in the action) plus the expert's report to which I have already referred. At the 11th hour he reduced this volume of evidence to three factual witnesses plus one expert, with the principally inadmissible paragraphs of the statements of the factual witnesses blacked out in the witness statements which were put before me. Even on this basis, the sheer volume of the material he sought to deploy went well beyond the borderlines of what is permissible. Mr. Calver sensibly did not cross-examine the witnesses who were called, and as a result not too much time was wasted on the oral evidence. At p. 111.

> is to identify whether, and if so which, terms proposed in the course of negotiations have become the subject of a joint agreement. Judges have on a number of occasions noted the difficulty in distinguishing between admissible facts and inadmissible negotiations. Now that the courts give more weight to the adoption of an approach that seeks to give a commercially sensible construction to the clause in dispute, the justification for excluding precontractual negotiations from evidence appears suspect. They may in fact provide very good evidence of the issue that was at stake between the parties and, to that extent, should be admissible in evidence. The courts should continue to exclude from evidence 'self-serving utterances' but the reason for this exclusion is that it is for the court, not the parties, to decide what the contract means. Evidence of the subjective state of mind of the parties is irrelevant and this is so whether the evidence relates to their state of mind during the negotiations or at the time at which the contract was concluded. Evidence of precontractual negotiations should therefore be admissible in evidence unless that evidence relates to the subjective state of mind of the negotiating parties. This is not to say that a great deal of weight should necessarily be given to evidence of precontractual negotiations. The weight will very much depend upon the facts of the case. But in principle evidence of precontractual negotiations should be admitted, even if, in many cases, it ultimately proves to be 'unhelpful'.[41]

The Tychy (No.2) case suggests that the real issue at the heart of questions of precontractual liability in English law may be as much to do with procedural obstacles as it is to do with substantive fairness considerations. That said, the procedural rule is arguably merely a reinforcement of the substantive law position that commercial negotiations must lie beyond the radar of the courts. What is clear is that liability is inextricably linked to the question of how contracts are drafted and properly construed. Certainly, a change to the procedural rule may be a necessary first step in providing a gateway to greater European and transnational uniformity in this area but the trend away from literalism towards ever greater contextualism does appear inexorable, and may in time lead to subsequent changes to the procedural rule. Either way, it perhaps matters little in practice whether the English courts do ultimately move to entertain an ever more focused concentration on precontractual negotiations via procedural or substantive law adaptation. This exposition further reveals that in focusing so intensively to date on common principles and general clauses, the academic drafters of the Common Frame of Reference are arguably overlooking the significance of commercial drafting and narrow procedural rules as key causes of ongoing divergence in wider European contract law.

41 [2001] EWCA Civ 1198, at para 29. Obviously, as Lord Phillips himself observes, if evidence of precontractual negotiations were to be admitted the question would ultimately come down to a simple question of the weight to be attached to such evidence. If the case against such a rule was to be argued in reverse it would be difficult to argue convincingly that the English courts could not adequately distinguish in practice between 'self-seeking utterances' and relevant evidence.

Just to add a further layer of complexity to the problem of achieving coherence, it is clear that not all judges in England and Wales are entirely at ease with the new approach to commercial construction. Perhaps it is the great success of the literal approach to date, so neatly summed up long ago by Cozens-Hardy MR in *Lovell and Christmas Ltd* v. *Wall*,[42] and the uncertain limits of contextualism that is unnerving the judiciary. At that time, the Master of the Rolls noted:

> If there is one principle more clearly established than any other in English law it is surely this: It is for the court to construe a written document. It is irrelevant and improper to ask what the parties, prior to the execution of the instrument, intended or understood. What is the meaning of the language that they have used therein? That is the problem, and the only problem ...

Without doubt the literal approach is not without its merits and has further divided opinion in the US.[43] Evidently courts tasked with construing a contract literally are unburdened by evidence relating to the commercial purpose of the specific contract or the circumstances surrounding the agreement/conclusion of the contract, leading to arguably more efficient, if not necessarily more 'just' outcomes in litigation. If the task is merely to rule on the meaning of the words used by the parties on the basis of the documents alone, it is less awkward for those parties who invest much in prior drafting. Obtaining a quick and relatively inexpensive ruling on the meaning of a disputed term proves much less onerous. The difficulty is that increased reference to the factual matrix can only lead different judges in differing directions. If Hoffman's approach is to be neither 'uncompromisingly literal nor unswervingly purposive', then the scope for inconsistency of approach in arriving at 'commercially sensible' outcomes is clear. The most that can be said with any confidence is that the courts are generally unwilling to adopt a construction that leads to a very unreasonable result.[44]

Yet, only relatively recently has dissent been voiced, and much of it has been tempered. The apparent drawbacks in the literal approach have been well aired and the majority view holds, as in the US and Spain, that it would be unrealistic to interpret most modern commercial contracts divorced from the underlying business context in which the parties operate. As in other settings, such as in the interpretation of statutes, there has been a shift from a literal to a 'purposive

42 *Lovell and Christmas Ltd* v. *Wall* (1911) 104 LT 85, at p. 88. To put it familiarly, the current steer appears to be that the meaning of a contract is still to be found within its four corners but a little bit of Hoffman's 'factual matrix' will not harm unduly.

43 Whether 'good faith' interpretation should be applied expansively or as a mere gap filler has divided American scholars in courts in to 'two camps' of new formalists and contextualists, see Hunter, *supra*. Yet, the view of Scalia J in *Tymshare, Inc v. Covell*, 727 F.2d 1145, 1152 (Cir. 1984) that good faith in interpretation aims to honour 'the reasonable expectations created by the autonomous expressions of the contracting parties' rhymes with the modern English approach, despite the difficulty in defining 'reasonable expectations' (and discussed further in chapter 4).

44 The *Schuler AG* v. *L Wickman Machine Tool Sales* [1974] AC 235 serves as a suitable example.

approach'[45] to interpretation and it is perhaps unsurprising that this emphasis has gradually penetrated ever deeper into the interpretation of contractual documents. Despite the impact of Hoffman's restatement, the turning point can be seen to be the 1971 decision of the House of Lords in *Prenn* v. *Simmonds*[46]. Lord Wilberforce stressed (at p. 1383 and 1384) that:

> In order for the agreement ... to be understood, it must be placed in its context. The time has long passed when agreements, even those under seal, were isolated from the matrix of facts in which they were set and interpreted purely on internal linguistic considerations. There is no need to appeal here to any modern, anti-literalist tendencies ... We must ... inquire beyond the language and see what the circumstances were with reference to which the words were used, and the object, appearing from those circumstances, which the person using them had in view.

Importantly, however, this modern contextualism may still be trumped by the insistence in English commercial practice of drafting entire agreement clauses and non-reliance clauses. Such drafting technique looks set to continue to 'inspire' the courts to simply follow the lead of the business community and treat each clause on a rigidly case-by-case analysis, whilst upholding their general validity on the basis of commercial use and acceptability. In the overwhelming majority of cases this will effectively negate the possibility that the courts will even consider the precontractual stage. Certainly, ample precedents now exist on the appropriate means for drafting such clauses,[47] and in *EA Grimstead*, for instance, Chadwick LJ was of the 'clear view' that the entire agreement clause, as drafted, was entirely reasonable under the Unfair Terms Act 1977.[48]

[45] Yet see the dissenting speech of Lord Steyn in *Deutsche Genossenschaftsbank* v. *Burnhope* [1995] 1 WLR 1580, at 1589. *The Starsin* [2003] UKHL 12; [2004] 1 A.C. 715, further reveals that the meaning of a document is that conveyed to a reasonable person having all the background knowledge which would reasonably have been available to the parties *in the situation in which they were at the time of the contract'*. [Authors' emphasis] As has been pointed out in subsequent decisions, should the meaning of a contract become dependent on the time of formation, this implies added risk for third parties, who will be unable to know the situation the parties were in at the time of the contract. However, it could be argued that this type of muddled thinking is in part a by-product of the wider exclusionary rule.

[46] [1971] 1 WLR 1381.

[47] The appropriate form of 'entire agreement' words chosen in Chitty is as follows: This Agreement contains the entire and only agreement between the parties and supersedes all previous agreements between the parties respecting the subject-matter thereof. The non-reliance clause provides: each party acknowledges that in entering into this Agreement it has not relied on any representation or undertaking, whether oral or in writing, save such as are expressly incorporated herein', see Chitty on Contracts, 28th ed., para.12-102.

[48] At first instance it was argued that the entire agreement clause was an exclusion clause, and since it failed to distinguish between fraudulent, negligent and innocent misrepresentations it was too wide and offended against the reasonableness test laid down in s.11(1) of the UCTA 1977. That argument failed however to persuade the Court of Appeal. The court did open the door to an estoppel based attack on

The court further stressed the fact that the parties' prints were literally all over the contract. As such the court was satisfied that:

> [I]t is reasonable to assume that the parties desire commercial certainty. They want to order their affairs on the basis that the bargain between them can be found within the document which they have signed. They want to avoid the uncertainty of litigation based on allegations as to the content of oral discussions at pre-contractual meetings. Secondly, it is reasonable to assume that that the price to be paid reflects the commercial risk which each party – or more usually the purchaser – is willing to accept ... It is legitimate and commercially sensible, that both parties should be able to measure the risk and agree the price on the basis of the warranties that have been given and accepted.

Of course, as is evidenced by the 2001 case of *1406 Pub Co. Ltd v. Hoare* and subsequent caselaw, 'entire agreement' clauses are not entirely bullet proof; particularly from the 'threat' of a subsequent judicial finding of a collateral contract.[49] The case concerned a pub lease, an alleged tie-in arrangement and involved something of a repeat player, *Inntrepreneur* – a party that we encountered previously. Relying upon a pre-formulated Inntrepreneur lease, the lessor had given a precontractual assurance, supported by written evidence in the form of a series of brochures, that the lessees would not be locked in to specific tie-in agreements for the purchase of beer if they took on the lease as written. The lessees relied on this commitment and the Court had no difficulty in finding that this verbal commitment gave rise to a collateral contract notwithstanding the presence of an entire agreement clause. What was notable in the judgment is the court's contextualist vision. According to Popplewell J, as opposed to strict formal rule observance, the task of the court is to:

> ... consider the representation or assurance in the context of the totality of the facts, and the question to be addressed is whether reliance upon the inducement afforded by the representation or promise should be understood as intended to continue and extend to the contract subsequently concluded ... (at para 5).

exclusion clauses under the three step test in *Lowe v. Lombank* [1960] 1 WLR 196, yet due to the respondent's argument that specific precontractual representations had not in fact been made he was unable to rely on the possible remedy.

49 [2001] 23 E.G.C.S. 154 (Ch D). It is equally possible that inequality of bargaining power between the parties was what motivated the courts to find in favour of the lessees, even though the lessees had failed to notify their own solicitors of the assurance in order to have the lessor's verbal commitment written into the agreement. The court accepted that the lessees were satisfied with the assurance they received and the printed paperwork they were shown. There was also an acceptance by the learned judge that Mrs. Hoare, the wife and second lessee, was 'not a very well educated lady' and was not fully versed in tie-in undertakings. There was also evidence of repeated failures to properly disclose and Mrs Hoare it was suggested had 'naively believed the claimants' word was their bond. Sadly this is an outmoded concept,' observed Poppelwell J.

Continuing this analysis, in deciding the question of intention and inducement, Popplewell J stressed that an important consideration for the court would be 'whether or not the specific statement was followed by further negotiations and a written contract not containing any term corresponding to the statement' (at para 3). Obviously, such a state of affairs would make it harder to infer that such a term was intended. In addition, a lapse of time between the specific assurance and the making of the formal contract could further prove fatal, as 'the longer the interval, the greater the presumption must be that the parties did not intend the statement to have contractual effect (at para 4). The court decried the 'shabby' tie-in contract and articulated a commercially sensible decision that set aside the effect of a nefarious 'sales pitch'. Of course, a 'commercially sensible interpretation' was also paramount in the mind of Lord Steyn in the slide towards ever greater contexualism apparent in *Lord Napier and Ettrick* v. *R F Kershaw Ltd*:[50]

Loyalty to the text of a commercial contract, instrument, or document read in its contextual setting is the paramount principle of interpretation. But in the process of interpreting the meaning of the language of a commercial document the court ought generally to favour a commercially sensible construction. The reason for this approach is that a commercial construction is likely to give effect to the intention of the parties. Words ought therefore to be interpreted in the way in which a reasonable commercial person would construe them. And the reasonable commercial person can safely be assumed to be unimpressed with technical interpretations and undue emphasis on niceties of language. Yet what elevates the decision in *1406 Pub Co. Ltd v. Hoare* is its clarity of thought and exposition. Popplewell J applied a form of equitable estoppel argument. He was satisfied that promises and assurances were given, with the intent that they should be acted upon and form part and parcel of the contract. They were then acted upon and 'would not otherwise' have formed part of the contract. (at para 20). There was no need to 'thrash through the undergrowth' of previous negotiations as Lightman's five core legal principles on when a precontractual promise or representation may constitute a contractual warranty could be satisfied with reasonable effortlessness.[51] Besides the soundness of the decision, the case further reveals the intellectual vacuity of continuing to exclude evidence of precontractual negotiations on purely undeclared policy grounds as a general rule. For only via an analysis of the defendant's 'unfair sales pitch' and overall bargaining strategy was it possible to rescue the weaker party from a tie-in

50 [1999] 1 WLR 756, at p. 763.

51 In addition to the two legal principles discussed at paragraphs 3 and 4, a pre-contractual statement will 'only [have] contractual effect if the evidence shows that the parties intended this to be the case. Intention is a question of fact to be decided by looking at the totality of the evidence'; 'the test is the ordinary objective test for the formation of the contract; what is relevant is not the subjective thought of one party, but what a reasonable outside observer infer from all the circumstances'; and 'a representation of fact is much more likely to have been intended to have contractual effect than a statement of future fact or a future forecast'. (per Lightman J, *supra*, at p. 212).

arrangement that was never agreed and was indecently perpetuated by one party taking unfair advantage of the defendants' wider dependency on the lease.

Precontractual Disclosure and the Avoidance of a Positive Duty

An alternative Court of Appeal approach to both dependency and precontractual fairness considerations is provided by the recent 2004 decision in *Sykes v. Taylor-Rose*.[52] The facts concerned a precontractual failure to fully disclose that *The Guardian* newspaper labeled the House of Horrors case. It was similarly argued that the decision 'is likely to cause confusion among house-sellers and their legal advisers, and perhaps even encourage dishonesty'.[53] Having been labelled the 'house of horror' case, the decision received a degree of press attention but has thus far received little academic scrutiny.[54] The case concerned the murder of a 13 year old girl committed in the early 1980's. A biologist working at the University of Leeds and the father of the murdered girl was tried and convicted of the murder in 1985 after body parts belonging to the young girl were found in her father's laboratory. Regrettably, not every body part was discovered and there was strong suspicion that parts of the child's body may have been buried at the family home. The property was not purchased by the respondents, Mr. and Mrs Taylor-Rose, until September 1998. When the couple bought their new home they were entirely unaware of the previous events; and only learnt of the gruesome murder after their daughter received newspaper cuttings anonymously that outlined the evidence presented at the criminal trial. The couple moved out of the property immediately thereafter and decided to sell with the help of their solicitor. In subsequent discussions with their legal advisor they were informed that the seller was under no duty to inform the couple of the previous events, and 'they would be under no such obligation when they came to sell it'.

In 2000 the property went on the market and the couple were given specific legal advice as to how to respond to the 'Sellers Property Information Form', which is seen as a mechanism for better protecting new property buyers. The couple were sent an 'Important Note to Sellers' from their solicitor that set out a negative precontractual 'duty'. They were encouraged to be as deliberately evasive, or rather as non-committal as possible. One particular piece or written advice read: *If [the buyer] wants more information about it, he should get it from his own advisors, not from you.* Although, as was proved in court, the couple were entirely aware of the previous murder, the couple were asked, among other things, whether there was 'any other information which you think the buyer

[52] [2004] WL 62242; [2004] EWCA Civ 299; *Times*, March 2, 2004: *Independent*, March 2, 2004. See also M Pawlowski "Things that go bump in the night" (2000) 144 S.J. 1166. Cf. *Taylor v. Hamer* [2003] 1 E.G.L.R. 103, CA.

[53] *Guardian*, March 13 2004.

[54] See a lone yet first class academic comment from P. Giliker, 'Formation of Contract and Pre-contractual Information from an English Perspective', The Architecture of European Codes and Contract Law, SECOLA Conference, Vienna, 18-19 June 2004.

might have a right to know'[55] and opted to respond in the negative. Not unsurprisingly the Sykes later brought an action, following the airing of a television documentary in July 2001 that examined the nature of the past events in gruesome detail. Relying on the previous 2002 decision in *Taylor v. Hamer*, it was argued by counsel for the Sykes that 'the principle of caveat emptor, hallowed though it may have been in the past, is nearing the end of its useful life'.[56] The Court of Appeal rejected this submission and further refused to allow any appeal on this point. Importantly, absent a specific precontractual duty to disclose (that was tested at first instance), the Sykes' framed an appeal in negligent misstatement in tort, alleging that the vendors though not under a duty to disclose the background concerning the murder, were aware of the past events and answered wrongly or deceitfully when replying in the seller's information pack.

> This latter argument was rejected by the Court of Appeal which adopted a very narrow interpretation of the question asked. The court selected a well polished and 'finely tuned linguistic fork'[57] when considering whether the Sykes' had a *right*

---

[55] Question 13 of the standard Law Society form, which has since been withdrawn.

[56] At para.15. The *Taylor v. Hamer* case concerned in part the behaviour of sellers during precontractual negotiations for the sale of a stately home originally costing £3.25 million. The claimant sought to recover alternatively in the tort of deceit and breach of contract, after the property he was sold failed to meet the pre-sale description. Certain outdoor flagstones were removed from the property, and similarly to the facts in *Sykes* the defendant had been asked about the flagstones. As McNall notes, 'The language and moralistic tone of the majority judgments is strongly suggestive of the view that this was a case in which public policy should flex so as to permit the inclusion of precontract negotiations and the parties' declarations of subjective intent as part of the background knowledge aiding interpretation of the contract. If this is a defensible characterisation of the case, *Taylor* places the boundary of the exception postulated by Lord Hoffmann in *Investors* firmly within the realm of sales of land. Although the seller's behaviour fails to attract much sympathy, such a development must be treated with circumspection'. McNall argues that such a move 'would throw into considerable uncertainty the extent to which contracts for the sale of land can be said to represent the final agreement between the parties; this would generate a conflict with the recognition by high authority that "it is only the final document which records a consensus" (see Prenn v. Simmonds, at 1385). See C. McCall, *Let the Buyer Beware* (2003) Conveyancer and Property Lawyer, 432, at 442.

[57] Per Rogers CJ in the Supreme Court of New South Wales in *Banque Brussels Lambert SA* v. *Australian National Industries Ltd* (1989) 21 NSWLR 502, at p. 524. Rogers CJ argued that 'it is inimical to the effective administration of justice in commercial disputes that a court should use a finely tuned linguistic fork'. Cf. the approach of the English court of Appeal in *Kleinwort Benson Ltd v. Malaysia Mining Corporation Bernhad* [1989] 1 WLR 379 in a case involving a letter of comfort and the approach of the Supreme Court on similar facts. Further, after referring to the fact that the Court of Appeal in *Kleinwort Benson* had subjected the letter of comfort to minute textual analysis, stated that 'courts will become irrelevant in the resolution of commercial disputes if they allow this to dominate their consideration of commercial documents' (at p. 523). For a fuller discussion of the *Kleinwort Benson* case from a comparative

to the information,[58] and ultimately determined that the true aim of the questionnaire could be satisfied provided a party responded truthfully. Having considered the evidence and the manner in which the question was framed it decided that the respondents had indeed so responded.

It is clear that any answer, subjectively believed to be correct, would satisfy the court for as Aldous LJ noted 'The duty was to give a proper answer to the question. If all that was needed was an honest answer, then there could be no breach of duty'.[59]After taking legal advice, the respondents were informed that they were under no duty to disclose the history of the house. As such, having responded in the negative to the questionnaire, the respondents could not be held liable. There was some sympathy but much Pilate-like hand wringing for the appellants, particularly from Gibson L.J. who decided that the matter before the court was little more than 'a dry question of law' (at p. 48). Regardless, the traditional view ultimately prevailed:

> [I]t is for the buyer to decide what enquiries to raise and in what form. It cannot be doubted that a more specific and less subjective question going to the value of the property or to the ability of the purchaser to enjoy the property could have been asked.[60]

It is hard to see the advantages of such a ruling. Barring legal reform, it now seems inevitable that solicitors will be encouraged to engage in ever more thorough precontractual enquiries, with an adverse knock-on effect for buyers and sellers alike due to an increase in complexity and a likely rise in legal fees. The level of detail now required to satisfy precontractual inquiries legally remains an open question and the widely rejected Home Information Pack initiative of the Blair government is likely to increase cost for consumers with little in the way of

perspective, see P. Giliker, 'Taking Comfort in Uncertainty – To Enforce or Not the Letter of Comfort' (2003) 52(4) LMCLQ 219.

58 Applying the reasoning of the Court of Appeal in *Economides v. Commercial Assurance Co plc* [1998] Q.B. 587.

59 At para. 33. The pedantic treatment of the question of right was further illustrative of the court's obsessively linguistic approach. As Giliker observes, sellers of property do have a number of specific duties of disclosure in English law and cites the example of a duty to disclose defects relating to title. See also H. Beale (ed), *Chitty on Contracts* (29th edn, Sweet & Maxwell, 2004) at 6-152; Spencer et al, *Actionable Non-Disclosure* (2nd edn, Tottel, 1990), paras 7.06-7.16. There is also the routine practice of sending pre-contract enquiries in which vendors are expected to respond to specific questions relating to the property, see R. Abbey & M. Richards, *A Practical Approach to Conveyancing* (6th ed, Wildy & Sons, 2004) who also provide an analysis of the role of the 'Sellers Property Information Form'.

60 At para 50.

guaranteed protection.[61] Yet, as Giliker observes, the *Sykes* decision is helpful in identifying a number of important characteristics of English law:

1) a general duty of disclosure was not even raised before the Court of Appeal. It had been argued at first instance but was rejected, and the finding was not appealed;
2) the claimants had sold the property at a loss because they had taken the moral view that they could not in good conscience dispose of the property without disclosing its grisly past. The court refused to place this 'moral' standpoint within a legal framework, and
3) the case was argued both in the law of misrepresentation and under the tort of negligence.

In fairness to the couple it could be argued that as previous victims of the lack of a general disclosure duty in English law, and having sought and received legal advice, they acted in their own interest. As Posner noted in the US Court of Appeals decision in *Venture Associates Corp. v. Zenith Data Systems Corp.*, 'self-interest is not bad faith'.[62] The *Sykes* decision is, however, illustrative of a distinctly commercial, even classical approach to contract interpretation that continues to resonate. In contrast to Article 5.102 of the Principles of European Contract Law (discussed further below) for instance, in terms of interpretative method the courts in England and Wales will adopt the *caveat emptor* doctrine as a starting point before considering specific exceptions.

An identically rigid approach is apparent in US case-law but the courts have been reluctant to set aside contracts only where it is felt that one party could have avoided the bargain exercising reasonable prudence. In the Supreme Court of Virginia case of *Kuczmanski v. Gill*, for instance, rotten floors were insufficient to sustain recovery, as no statements regarding their condition were made to the aggrieved family and the defect was 'obvious to anyone who picked up a rug'. It is well established as a
principle of causation that there must be some nexus between the seller's failure to disclose a defect and the damage the purchaser suffers. Curnes has, however,

[61] See, however, the views of M. Pawlowski, (2004) 148 S.J. 497. Despite the *Sykes* case, and the press attention it received, much of the press reporting of the Home Information Pack proposal during Parliamentary reading of the Housing Bill in 2004/5 was diametrically opposed to the initiative. The Labour government's experience with the Home Information Pack (HIP) perhaps indicates a cultural divergence in British society that looks with a degree of scorn at the notion of legal information requirements. Certainly the popular press has been strongly opposed to the introduction of HIPs, and the initiative has been beset by delays and opposition. At present HIPs are compulsory for all residential properties with three or more bedrooms, however plans to extend the initiative to small one and two bed room homes has been postponed indefinitely until the current housing market has been assessed.

[62] 96 F.3d 275 (US Court of Appeals) September 18, 1996. (Hereinafter *Venture Associates*). A case concerning the enforceability of a letter of intent, which as Posner acknowledged, is alongside other preliminary agreements 'one of the most difficult areas of contract law' in union with the 'subset of such agreements that consists of agreements to negotiate toward a final contract', at 276.

highlighted the economic advantage of a pro-active disclosure duty in stressing that 'if the purchaser already knows the defective condition exists, the vendor's disclosure would not have placed him in a better position, so the vendor's non-disclosure cannot be termed a 'cause' of his injury'. Moreover, to prevent such a mistake, the would-be purchaser could always hire experts to inspect the home for defects. Yet, 'if the vendor already possesses this information, non-disclosure will mean that society spends more resources than necessary to avoid a misallocation of goods. As the party in the best position to prevent mistakes at minimal cost, the vendor should be required to share information he has acquired, so that the bargain reached reflects the real value of the property.[63] Of course, similar thinking has had a heavy bearing on modern Spanish consumer law which, as we noted previously, has consistently reinforced the economic benefit of a strong disclosure duty.

A notably contrasting approach to the *Sykes* approach is found in the 2002 Spanish Supreme court decision involving a failure to fully and properly disclose information regarding the dimensions of an apartment.[64] The case is particularly revealing of divergent adjudicative style and the extent to which precontractual information duties have taken hold in Spanish civil and consumer law. Baygur, SA, a construction company, appealed rather belatedly against an earlier decision of the Madrid Provincial court on the basis of a breach of Article 1225 of the Civil code. The court had found against Baygur for its failure to fully disclose the true dimensions of an apartment that was under construction. The apartment, once completed, was in reality significantly smaller – more than 20 square metres – than was initially agreed under contract. The judge at first instance had no difficulty in finding that as the contract could be set aside as the actual size of the apartment was not in accordance with what the parties had agreed. As such the claimant was entitled to full recovery, including taxes incurred on the property in the interim period. Baygur, SA was further obliged to make payment to the court in order to have the public register amended to include the actual size of the apartment.

Before the Supreme Court, the defendant sought to draw a distinction between the 'practical' area of the apartment and its construction site. Not surprisingly the Court was unpersuaded and held that the clause in the contract must be read literally. However, it added that "the literal rule of interpretation is not precisely that which has been followed by the court of First Instance ... as from its deliberations it is apparent that it has further weighed up, in accordance with article 1285 and considering the true intentions of the parties – the overall value of the various clauses; in such a manner that obscure clauses (las cláusu-

63 See E.J. Curnes, 'Protecting the Virginia Homebuyer: A Duty to Disclose Defects' (1987) 73 Va L Rev 459.

64 RJ 2002/2852, Sala Primera, March 20, 2002. On appeal from the Eighth Division of the Appeal Court of Madrid.

las oscuras) should not be allowed to favour those who have caused the obscurity (the contra proferentem rule under article 1288 Cc).[65]

As it was at no time made clear to the purchaser whether the stated size of the property (186.8 sq.m) referred to the construction size or the "practical area for use", which was a mere 96.6 sq.m. the court found against Baygur SA. The contract further fell to be considered under the Spanish unfair terms act. The mere reference to the superficial area, without further clarification, situated the term within Article 10(2) of the LGDCU.[66] As such, the finished property – with an area that was more than 20 square metres less than that originally agreed under contract – sufficed to frustrate the negotiations, it represented a qualitative change to the agreed terms and crucially it 'disrupted the balance in the contract'. The Supreme court was further motivated by the fact that as the property was under construction at the time of contracting it was therefore not possible for the respondent to fully inform himself of the actual size. In confusing the practical area with the overall apartment size the court was of the opinion that this error should be equated to an unfair term that disproportionately disadvantaged the consumer.[67]

4 A specific case cluster and shades of a rethink on reliance?

Leaving temporarily to one side the English courts uneasy reluctance to entertain evidence of precontractual negotiations and to impose broad disclosure duties, in the next two sections we will delve deeper into a body of US and Spanish contemporary commercial case-law which may cast doubt upon the accuracy of prevailing doctrinal views as to the real law in action in each jurisdiction in seeking to regulate incomplete contracts and manage

---

[65] The Supreme Court made reference to an earlier decision dated December 24, 1996 which provides that rulings of lower courts based on contractual interpretation should not be set aside unless the result is 'illogical, absurd, contrary to the law or weakens other provisions contained in the agreed contract'.

[66] Ley General para la Defensa de Consumidores y Usuarios 26/1984, July 19 (RCL 1984, 1906 y ApNDL 2943). Reference was also made to the Royal Decree 515/1989, April 21 [RCL 1989, 1091].

[67] A similar 2002 decision of the Supreme Court reveals that consumers should be furnished with 'all plans, basic projects ... advertising in regard to the quality of ... an apartment and all guarantees form part of the contract and can be relied upon even when they do not figure expressly in the final document'. Importantly, the Supreme court found that there was no general overriding duty under existing Spanish civil law requiring parties involved in the sale or leasing of apartments to provide information, although Article 7 of the LGDCU establishes that an advertised offer – including all specific terms, conditions and warranties – forms part of a contract and can be relied upon despite not being formally included in the agreed contract. Article 13.2 further makes specific reference to a duty of property developers to provide all relevant material used in its construction (see also Royal Decree, dated April 21 1989).

precontractual reliance.[68] The cases identified have been grouped under five broad headings: a refusal to negotiate; the use of improper tactics in negotiations, including presenting 'unreasonable' proposals; breach of an agreement to negotiate (in good faith) or to use reasonable endeavours; and the premature breaking off of negotiations (in bad faith).[69]

Reported cases do not necessarily provide a solid foundation for developing wider empirical or theoretical solutions, and arguably carry less weight in jurisdictions such as Spain, not dominated by rugged caselaw analysis and the binding force of precedent. Yet they do provide a much needed window to a complex arena, particularly in a broader climate of rule-fixation. Indeed, this study can claim to be the first comprehensive modern case law analysis of preliminary agreements and precontractual liability in the higher Spanish courts. It is hoped that a subsequent analysis of this case cluster will provide the basis for a deeper normative investigation that would aim to provide a more coherent framework for a European wide treatment of preliminary contracts and precontractual reliance.

4.1 US and Spanish commercial contracting and the realities of precontractual liability

The starting point for scholarly work on reliance investments and precontractual liability in the US has been the celebrated case of *Hoffman v. Red Owls Stores*.[70] The decision has been commonly viewed as cast iron authority

68 The specific case clusters across each jurisdiction were drawn from the electronic resources of Westlaw UK and Lexis Nexis UK, Westlaw Spain and Aranzadi Spain, Westlaw US and Westlaw International. The cases were isolated according to date and court (with an emphasis on the higher courts in each jurisdiction and decisions that fell within the time-frame of September 2002 – January 2007).

69 Eight cases were identified where the court found a preliminary agreement to negotiate further in good faith. These included *Fairbrook Leasing, Inc. v. Mesaba Aviation*, 295 F. Supp 2d 1063 (2003); *Lafayette Place Assoc. v. Boston Redevelopment Authority*, 694 N.E. 2d 820 (Mass 1998). *Liberty Environmental Environmental Systems, Inc. v. The County of Westchester*, 2000 U.S. Dist Lexis 17095 (S.D.N.Y. 2000). *R.G.C. International Investors, LDC v. Greeka Energy Corporation, et al.*, 2001 Del. Ch. Lexis 107. *In Re the Matterhorn Group*, 2002 Bktcy. Ct. N.Y. 2002. *Gillenardo et al v. Conner Broadcasting Delaware Co. et al*, 2002 Del. Super Lexis 402. *Horphag Research Ltd v. Henkel Corp.*, 115 F. Supp. 2d 455 (S.D.N.Y. 2000). *Glenview Partners v. Plexus*, U.S. Dist. Lexis 8880 (N.D. Iii. 2002). In an unreported case in Tennessee *Kandel v. Center for Urological Treatment and Research P.C.* the Court of Appeals declined to determine whether an agreement to negotiate in good faith would give rise to a cause of action, arguing that the facts of the case would not allow for such an interpretation, even if such a cause did exist.

70 *Hoffman v. Red Owl Stores*, 133 N.W. 2d 267 (1965). Although the UCC and the Restatement (Second) of Contracts both impose a duty of good faith and fair dealing on parties to a contract, there is no similar duty on parties to mere negotiations. Liability in *Hoffman* was founded on promissory estoppel. It was held that the defendants had induced the plaintiff, a prospective franchisee of a supermarket, to act to his detriment in the expectation that negotiations would lead to a completed franchise. Controversially, in reaching this decision the court determined that 'the promise necessary to sustain a cause of action

that bad faith in negotiations may result in a successful claim to recover reliance costs. Yet the case has only recently been re-examined from first premises by Scott who considers it the source of much confusion in contemporary US contract law and, in union with Schwartz, has criticised the decision for essentially standing contract theory on its head.[71] The facts of the case are oft repeated and concerned a failed franchising venture. The aim was to establish a new Red Owl franchise but the parties were mistakenly negotiating at cross purposes and the court found no *consensus ad idem* despite the detailed and prolonged negotiations that occurred over a period of years.[72] Despite Hoffman breaking off the negotiations, it was he that ultimately sued to recover his sunk negotiation costs and the Wisconsin Supreme Court duly obliged him. Johnston appears closest to the court's reasoning in considering that the Court reached its decision on the basis of promissory estoppel under §90 of the Restatement of Contracts.[73] However, the decision has also been justified on the grounds of misrepresentation by Kostritsky, bad faith by Farnsworth, a failure to properly disclose by Craswell and Johnston has recently argued that for generations of US contracts scholars and students the case has made the argument in favour of allowing recovery on the basis of promissory estoppel in situations displaying similar facts. Such divergences in the literature are clearly not the most comforting for those promoting the value of judicial interference in the bargaining process. Moreover, as

---

for promissory estoppel' need not 'embrace all essential details of a proposed transaction between promisor and promisee so as to be the equivalent of an offer that would result in a binding contract'. The court accepted that the defendants had led *Hoffman* to believe that $18,000 would be sufficient to obtain the franchise and, during the course of prolonged negotiations, Hoffman sold his bakery, purchased (in order to gain experience for his intended work with the franchise) and then sold a grocery store, secured an option to buy land for the planned supermarket and rented a property close to the planned site. The negotiations ended acrimoniously when the defendants demanded a larger contribution and Hoffman walked away. The fact that the plaintiff was awarded reliance damages despite the lack of a completed contract or even a clear offer has been queried and criticised, but perhaps no where as strongly and coherently as in the recent work of Scott (see fn 72 below).

[71] A. Schwartz & R.E. Scott, R.E., *supra* fn 28, at 8-9.

[72] For a heavily detailed analysis of the case, including the degree to which pleadings were incorrectly entered and the case was incorrectly fought, see R.E. Scott, *Hoffman and the Myth*, 2007, who argues that Hoffman would arguably have fared better had the case been fought on the grounds of negligent misstatement in tort. With a degree of relish no doubt, Scott also notes that those who present the *Hoffman* decision as reinforcing the notion of 'a new duty to bargain in good faith' will find the theory 'embarassed by the absence of any evidence of bad faith by Red Owl', at 21.

[73] Section 90(1) of the Restatement articulates the rule that 'a promise. which the promisor should reasonably expect to induce action or forbearance on the part of the promise or a third person and which does induce such action or forebearance is binding if injustice can be avoided only by enforcement of the promise. The remedy granted for breach may be limited as justice requires'. See J.S. Johnston, 'Investment, Information and Promissory Liability' (2004) 152 U Pa L Rev 1923. A key and obvious deficiency in the s.90 provision is the open-ended nature of the remedy, however chapter 4 considers ways in which the breadth of the provision may be appropriately restricted.

Schwartz and Scott observe the decision in Red Owl is an 'outlier', for it simply 'has not been followed in its own or other jurisdictions'.[74]

The Court took the view that under §90 there is no requirement that the promise giving rise to a cause of action must be so comprehensive in scope as to meet the requirements of an offer that would ripen into a contract if accepted by the promisee. In other words, 'applying the Court's analysis, the doctrine of promissory estoppel can properly be invoked to enforce a preliminary representation that does not qualify as a specific promise'.[75] With a degree of relish no doubt, Schwartz and Scott further note that those who present the *Hoffman* decision as reinforcing the notion of 'a new duty to bargain in good faith' will find the theory 'embarassed by the absence of any evidence of bad faith by Red Owl'.[76]

Yet, despite Scott's recent critique of the *Red Owl* decision, and the raft of conflicting interpretations in the literature, the judgment still offers broad scope for determining how best to protect the reliance interest in pre-contractual negotiations as does the earlier decision in *Heyer Products Co. v. United States*.[77] In *Heyer* it was alleged that the US Ministry of Defence had deliberately rejected a lower bid from the plaintiff out of spite and to punish the company for its earlier attendance at a Senate hearing, where it testified against the Ordnance Corps. The contract in question was awarded to a higher bidder and the court accepted that the Government was free to accept or reject any offer as it so pleased. Nonetheless, the plaintiff did recover expenses incurred in preparing the bid (but not lost profits) on the basis of an implied promise that the Government would give 'fair and impartial consideration' to its bid. The plaintiff successfully argued that the bids were 'not invited in good faith, but as a pretense to conceal the purpose to let the contract to some favored bidder'.[78] It is notable that Brown has also previously observed that although *Red Owl* and the previous decision in *Heyer*

74 Both authors argue that the Wisconsin Supreme Court decision was ultimately based on a flawed analysis and that the case would have been better fought on the grounds of negligent misstatement or alternatively, on weaker foundations for unjust enrichment (on the basis that Red Owl did receive valuable information as a result of the negotiation). At 10.

75 As Scott and Schwartz observe 'nothing in the law of contracts supports this legal analysis", *supra* at 10.

76 *Supra*. Curiously, unlike the Principles of European Contract Law, it is notable that the duty of good faith is not afforded general application under the Uniform Commercial Code. Section 1-203 is not formulated in such a way as to expressly cover contract negotiations. Similarly sections 161(b) and 176 are silent on duties applicable to contract negotiations. Section 161(b) does provide that non-disclosure may constitute misrepresentation should it 'amount to a failure to act in good faith and in accordance with reasonable standards of fair dealing', whilst section 176 simply states that a threat may be duress if it 'is a breach of the duty of good faith and fair dealing under a contract'. Only section 205 of the Second Restatement has been viewed as one possible route towards a generalised application of the 'fair dealing' requirement. Instead s.90 and s.208 have been promoted as the surest means of sanctioning general bad faith in negotiations.

77 140 F. Supp. 409 (Ct. Cl. 1956).

78 *Ibid.* at pp. 413-414.

have "failed to sire a long line of authority in the US, and that the decisions are typically treated as deviations from classical theory", he suggests that they could potentially serve as a platform for the development of the law in England. He notes that "both decisions require a promise with correlative reliance and it is easy for a court to be restrictive in its interpretation of such concepts; in the absence of a completed contract there may also be an ignorance regarding their applicability to lost opportunities. Moreover, it would be easy to distinguish the cases in those situations where there is a less obvious inequality of bargaining power".[79]

Moreover, Scott's view that precontractual reliance claims in the US have all but disappeared appears somewhat premature. Certainly, this author's case cluster reveals a notable decline in the number of reliance-based claims, yet also a high degree of judicial confusion that is further carried over into the literature. More recent State caselaw presents a traditional, if more carefully nuanced analysis of fair dealing in negotiations and recent decisions do still leave open the possibility of significant reliance damages arising out of failed business ventures. *Copeland v. Baskin Robbins USA* is one such case in point.[80]

The background to the *Copeland* dispute concerned the prolonged negotiation of a contingency agreement between the parties whereby the claimant sought to purchase an ice-cream manufacturing plant from the defendants that was under threat of closure. Copeland was content to purchase the plant from the ice-cream giant provided the company contracted to purchase a yearly quantity of ice-cream direct from the claimant. It was made clear to Baskin-Robbins from the outset that the 'co-packing' deal was critical to Copeland's interest in the plant. Baskin-Robbins prepared a letter of intent setting out the initial terms of the bargain which the claimant duly signed and returned with a non-refundable deposit. The plant would be purchased at a cost of $1.3 million in return for the supply of several million gallons of ice-cream over an initial three year period.

The parties continued to bargain however as to the ice-cream purchase price, product quality and control, the assumption of losses and other essentials. After several months without agreement, Baskin-Robbins broke off the negotiations

---

79 See I. Brown, 'The Contract to Negotiate: A Thing Writ in Water' (1992) 1 JBL 353, 364.

80 96 Cal. App.4th 1251 (2002). 117 Cal. Rptr. 2d 875. Whilst the case has provoked substantial comment in the US, it has thus far received no consideration from European scholars. The facts of the case are similar to those in *R.G. Group, Inc. v. Horn & Hardart Co.*, 751 F.2d 69, 72-74 (2d Cir. 1984), in which a deal fell apart because the parties could not agree on the territorial extent of the fast food franchise they were negotiating. Though he does not provide a battery of caselaw to support his assertion, Johnston's instinct appears correct from an analysis of Copeland. Most reliance cases do concern 'a failure by the parties to agree upon a key term [that] signals that there may have been no agreement on that term, and hence no deal, which would have made them both better off ...' and subsequent reliance based claims for recovery of out-of-pocket expenses, see Johnston, *supra*, at p. 1947. Importantly, Johnston also notes that on a general level, discovering 'an act of reliance and tying it to the promise may be just as formalistic an exercise as finding consideration', *supra*, at 1932.

unilaterally, stating that its parent company had 'recently . . . made strategic decisions around the Baskin-Robbins business' and that 'the proposed co-packing arrangement [is] out of alignment with our strategy . . . [As such] we will not be engaging in any further negotiations of a co-packing arrangement'. It thereafter returned a deposit previously forwarded by Copeland. As the appeal court later observed, regrettably for Copeland at this point 'many millions of dollars in anticipated profits melted away like so much banana ripple ice cream on a hot summer day'.

At first instance it was held that no contract existed between the parties. There was merely an 'agreement to agree' that was unenforceable. The appeal court upheld this finding, acknowledging that the letter of intent was not itself a binding expression of the entire transaction. In awarding summary judgment to Baskin-Robbins, the court availed of the opportunity to consider the distinction between an 'agreement to agree' which is unenforceable and an agreement to negotiate in good faith which 'can be formed and breached like any other contract'.[81] The Court stressed the need to protect parties whose investments of 'time, money and effort' should not be 'wiped out by another party's foot-dragging or change of heart' or by their 'taking advantage of a vulnerable position'.[82] Relying extensively upon the opinion of Professor Farnsworth, the Appellate court rejected the public policy arguments advanced by counsel for Baskin-Robbins.[83] Interpreting Farnsworth's analysis, the Court suggested that the academic's criticism of reliance-based claims were: 'directed at the theory propounded by some European courts and legal scholars that, even absent a contractual agreement to negotiate, a general obligation of fair dealing arises out of the negotiations themselves'.[84] The Court stressed that an implied covenant of good faith and fair dealing does not apply to all contract negotiations. Rather, in its view, such an implied covenant only applies if the parties have entered into an agreement to negotiate. To avoid an implied obligation of good faith and fair dealing, the letter of intent language used must be carefully drafted, perhaps in such a manner as to expressly rule out an agreement to negotiate.

Applying the court's thinking to the facts, Copeland would have been successful in his appeal had he not disavowed a reliance-based claim for damages. It is noteworthy that the Appellate Court asserted that the doctrines of

81 The court was moved to consider previous caselaw distinguishing an agreement to agree from an agreement to negotiate in good faith citing the *Channel Home Centers* case and the previous decision of the Court of Appeals in *Beck v. American Health Corp.*, 221 Cal. App. 3d 155 (1989).

82 Mirroring the analysis of Posner J in *Venture Associates*, at 278 and which finds further support in *Feldman v. Allegheny International Inc.*, 850 F.2d 1217, at 1221 (7th Cir. 1998) and *Runnemede Owners, Inc v. Crest Mortgage Corp.*, 861 F.2d 1053, at 1056 (7th Cir. 1998).

83 Counsel for Baskin-Robbins had sought to rely on E.A. Farnsworth, *Preliminary Agreements, 1987*.

84 As the court noted, such a general overriding duty of good faith and fair-dealing in negotiations had been previously rejected by the Appellate Court in *Los Angeles Equestrian Center, Inc. v. City of Los Angeles* (1993) 17 Cal. App. 432 following the earlier decision in *Racine & Laramie, Ltd v. Department of Parks & Recreation*, 11 Cal. App. 4th 1026 (1992).

unjustified enrichment and promissory estoppel fail to provide a party with 'an adequate vehicle for relief' when its negotiating partner breaks off negotiations or bargains in bad faith. In direct contrast to the complete absence of policy argument advanced by the English commercial courts, the Appellate court reasoned that due to the length, complexity and expense of business negotiations, public policy favours safeguarding parties to a business negotiation from bad faith practices.

The case thus provides significant authority under Californian contract law that where a contract to negotiate exists, pre-closing negotiations must be conducted in accordance with 'good faith and fair dealing' and that a failure to do so may result in a successful claim for reliance damages.[85] Despite the distinction drawn, the analysis of the Court of Appeal would appear to fit relatively neatly with the theories emanating from civil law jurisdictions in Europe, yet from what has preceded this discussion, is clearly unlikely to find favour at the commercial bar in England and Wales. The Appeals Court in *Copeland* observed the weakness of the existing law in protecting commercial parties and their legitimate expectations. An analysis of recent US decisions further reveals that absent conduct deemed 'illegal' or 'unlawful' during negotiations, a claim in unjustified enrichment appears hopeless.[86] Recourse to the doctrine of promissory estoppel in the alternative has also failed to convince most commentators.[87] Increasingly good faith and fair dealing and general notions premised upon the doctrine of unconscionability are dominating precontractual reliance debates. Of course, the Uniform Commercial Code provides that, 'every contract or duty within this Act imposes an obligation of good faith in its performance

[85] As the terms of the prospective contract were at no time fully agreed, lost expectation costs would be unquantifiable and therefore unrecoverable. The Appellate court was of the opinion, however, that a party's 'out-of-pocket' costs arising out of the negotiations, and possibly lost opportunity costs, should be recoverable. A position that appears to correspond neatly with the modern Dutch approach.

[86] See also *Fimon v. Kenroc Drywall Supplies, Inc 203* (Minn 2003), see also *First National Bank of St.Paul v. Ramier*, 311 N.W. 502 (1981).

[87] See *Beer Capitol Distributing, Inc v. Guinness Bass Import Co.*, 290 F.3d 877 (2002) where a claim in both unjust enrichment and promissory estoppel for reliance damages failed. The defendant admitted informing the plaintiff that he would be recommending the plaintiff as the exclusive distributor for Wisconsin. Schwartz and Scott further note that in 87% of preliminary negotiation cases analysed between 1999 and 2003, liability was denied in promissory estoppel or quantum meruit cases. Such findings confirm an identifiable reluctance in the US courts to reward such claims. See also S. De Long, 'The New Requirement of Enforcement Reliance in Commercial Promissory Estoppel' (1997) Wisc L Rev 943 (which analyses all reported promissory estoppel cases between 1995 and 1996 and reveals 'contemporary courts rigorously enforce s.90's requirement that the promise induce actual reliance by the promisee'). Cf. Hillman's analysis of 362 federal and state cases between 1994 and 1996 and who notes 'the crucial role' played by reliance in the courts to defeat or support a promissory estoppel claim 'either at a preliminary motion or final judgment stage of litigation') in R. Hillman, 'Questioning the "New Consensus" on Promissory Estoppel – An Empirical and Theoretical Enquiry' 98 Colum L Rev 580.

or enforcement',[88] and good faith has been described as 'honesty in fact in the conduct or transaction concerned'.[89] In the case of a merchant, good faith and fair dealing has been defined as 'honesty in fact and the observance of reasonable commercial standards of fair dealing in the trade'.[90]

Since the halcyon days of the 1980's, particularly following the controversial award in *Texaco Inc.* that built on the landmark *Hoffman* case, promissory estoppel had quietly emerged as a core theory upon which precontractual liability could be imposed in the US but has to date received little support, particularly in the courts. This argument is borne out by analysis of the case cluster. Instead, the need for 'good faith and fair dealing' during negotiations has emerged as a form of optional default. Kostritsky still sees promissory estoppel as a more coherent option. She suggests convincingly that the estoppel approach provides for more consistent outcomes and can be readily applied to negotiations, since where one party makes a promise during negotiations, and the other party relies upon that promise to his detriment, it can be argued that he was wrongly induced into prolonging negotiations.[91] US courts it is suggested will typically limit recovery to the reliance interest, though as Posner notes there remains a tension lurking just beneath the surface as to when, if ever, expectation interests under a failed contract may be recoverable. For the present, the judicial aim appears merely to be towards granting reliance damages, which puts the injured party back in the position it would have been had he not relied upon a promise.

Yet, the doctrine of good faith has further been shown to provide greater latitude – some argue undue latitude – to judges in striking out onerous terms and in refusing to enforce unconscionable bargains, and it has clearly not required much judicial creativity to expressly extend the good faith doctrine, most particularly under the latter definition that incorporates notions of 'fair' conduct, to the negotiation phase. That said, it appears undeniable that the duty of good faith and fair dealing in negotiations will only bite once the parties have entered into a binding preliminary agreement or given an express commitment. Moreover, as is apparent from the decision in *Detroit Tigers, Inc. & Ignite Sports Media, LLC*,[92] the duty is 'not intended to give a party to a negotiated bargain a second bite at the apple in the event it fails to prove breach of contract'.

Importantly, as noted in chapter 2, under New York law, following Judge Leval's approach in *Teachers Insurance & Annuity Association v. Tribune Co*, a framework has been established for dealing with preliminary agreements. The decision has been subsequently applied most notably in *Arcadian Phosphates,*

---

88 U.C.C. § 1-203.

89 *Ibid.* § 1-201(19).

90 Id. § 2-103(1)(b); see also id. § 3-103(a)(4). 'Good faith includes not only honesty but also observance of reasonable commercial standards of fair dealing'.

91 See M.E. Metzger & M.J. Phillips, 'The Emergence of Promissory Estoppel as an Independent Theory of Recovery' (1983) 35 Rutgers Law Review 472.

92 203 F. Supp. 2d 789 (2002).

Inc. v. Arcadian Corp.[93] Despite the concerns expressed by Judge Leval in *Tribune*, that 'it is fundamental to contract law that mere participation in negotiations and discussions does not create a binding obligation, even if agreement is reached on all disputed terms', alarmingly U.S. courts have increasingly recognised liability when the parties have not fully consummated a contract, but have drawn up a series of preliminary agreements in anticipation of reaching final agreement.

A US court will typically find that preliminary agreements are binding upon the parties when they have either reached complete agreement on all outstanding issues requiring negotiation, or have expressed mutual commitment to the primary terms of the agreement, even if other terms still remain to be fully agreed. The danger is clear – precontractual liability may be 'sneaking in by the back door' via preliminary agreements. The courts encounter most difficulty when the parties have partially agreed on a raft of terms, yet have failed to complete the contract with a number of crucial terms. There is an increasing judicial willingness to impose on parties a duty to negotiate in good faith towards a final contract. Yet, despite the criticism, arguably requiring the parties to work towards filling the gaps in incomplete contracts may be a much less contentious route than a simple 'finding' of a collateral contract or implied terms. Rather than stalking the literal terms and the context for an 'instinct of agreement', the encouragement of further negotiations in good faith may be a sensible option. Despite Lord Ackner's discontent with *Channel*, the decision does provide an arguably workable, if highly contextualised and unpredictable, platform or 'methodology' for regulating incomplete agreements. It is by no means a bright-line test, yet US courts typically focus upon five factors in determining the intent of the parties: the language of the preliminary agreement, the context of the negotiations, the existence of open terms, whether there is evidence of part performance under the preliminary agreement, and finally, whether there exists any express suggestion or demand to work towards a final contract.

In comparison to the US and England and Wales, preliminary agreements play a comparatively minor role in the formation of commercial agreements in Spanish legal practice. It has been suggested that the civil and commercial code (particularly Article 57 Commercial Code requiring parties to act in good faith) effectively act as a background safety net for contracting parties, providing in essence a bedrock of default rules, that in part explains why contracts are typically much less verbose than in Anglo-American practice.[94] Perhaps the diminished practical use of preliminary agreements in part explains why Spanish legal doctrine has traditionally relied so heavily on German legal science in promoting broad theories of precontractual liability. In practice, however, an

93 884 F. 2d 69, 71-72 (2d Cir 1989). See also Leval J in *Shann v. Dunk*, 84 F. 3d 73, 77-78 (2d Cir. 1996).

94 Though see F. Llodrà Grimalt, '*Letter of Intent*, Carta de Intenciones, Precontrato' (2002) 8 RdP 129 (discussing the increased use in Spanish business of 'common law' drafting techniques such as letters of intent and their potential binding force in Spain).

examination of recent caselaw reveals that the Spanish courts continue to take a firm approach in regulating precontractual bargaining. A general good faith obligation is imposed on parties to negotiations even in the absence of a specific precontractual commitment or agreement.[95] Importantly, Article 57 of the Commercial code and Article 7 of the Civil code impose an obligation on parties to act in good faith under contract. Article 1287 of the Commercial code further reveals that commercial fair dealing and trade practices are as important as in the US and may further act as background evidence of contractual intention. Whilst letters of intent have no contractual force, they may carry an obligation to negotiate in good faith and may give rise to liability to repay the sunk costs of one's opposite number in the event of an improper break-down in negotiations. Spanish legal theory has further questioned the autonomous nature of an option contract (contrato de opción) as a 'preparatory contract', given its dependence on the subsequent contract for its force and validity.[96] Yet, the option contract is arguably the most common form of precontractual agreement in Spanish practice. The classical doctrinal approach is to treat such contracts as mere contracts for the agreement of a future contract.[97] The emphasis rests on the need for co-operation between the parties in order to breathe live into the planned definitive contract. Legal theory has thus centred on this need for co-operation and the importance of the parties' consent in choosing whether or not to opt in or out of the final bargain. A party who 'concedes'[98] an option contract is obliged, during the agreed period, not to enter into any contract with a third party that would affect the rights of the other contracting party (e.g. by not selling the object of the contract). A breach of this obligation would result in a claim for damages

---

95 That said, the duty of good faith or 'buena fe' applies throughout the precontractual phase of negotiations. As a general rule, a breakdown in negotiations will not give rise to liability provided the parties have acted in good faith. Doctrinal opinion supports this view on the grounds that a more robust liability regime would cause parties to negotiate with such 'caution and circumspection' that it would irreversibly damage the overall bargaining process. An added practical problem for parties relying on lock-out agreements is the inability to mobilise the court system in time.

96 The courts have acknowledged an 'intimate connection' between preliminary contracts and the definitive contract. Moreover, if a party agrees to conclude a contract, but fails to carry through on that promise, the Court argued, albeit obiter, that the innocent party can demand performance, provided performancee remains possible. Chioveda, who was cited in the judgment, sees this as an appropriate fusion between the substantive and procedural goals of the law. See also, the Supreme Court's decision of February 26, 1994. In this case, as one party had not fully consented to the preliminary agreement (under art. 1261 CC) there could be no binding contract. There was ground for suggesting that there was a breach of an exclusivity agreeement but such an exclusivity arrangement endures only whilst negotiations are ongoing (mientras duren las negociaciones), and cannot bind a party indefinitely (sin que pueda trascender de este período ni perdurar aun después de extinguidas).

97 " ... between preliminary dealings and the definitive contract ... we encounter ... the pre-contract or promise to contract", L. Díez-Picazo & A. Gullón, *Sistema de Derecho civil – volume II* (Sixth Edition, Tecnos, 1989).

98 The 'promisario' or 'concedente'.

and, if the third party is aware of the pre-existing contract, he may also be required to make compensation.[99]

The interpretative role of the court in assessing precontractual claims for breach of 'a contract for a future contract' was discussed at length in a 1998 Supreme Court decision.[100] The parties *Servifilms, SL* and *Ivarte, SA* entered into an option contract relating to the planned development of four cinema complexes. The parties drafted a detailed preliminary contract containing a number of specific clauses on the 23 May 1980. At first instance *Ivarte SA* claimed damages for an alleged breach of this 'preliminary contract' back in November 1988. The court at first instance and the Provincial court of Madrid refused to find a 'precontract', arguing that the parties were still engaged in negotiations. The Supreme Court did however recognise that the agreement was more complex due to its long term nature but that the lower courts' decisions had been 'illogical, absurd and irrational'.[101] The Supreme Court held that the essence of such a pre-contract, or 'pactum de contrahendo',[102] is that of agreeing the basis of a future, 'definitive' contract, which the parties either cannot or choose not to conclude at a specific moment. As the parties had agreed upon all the necessary details for a future contract – i.e. consent, object, cause of the contract, etc – the parties were held "bound to be bound in the future".[103] Importantly, the Supreme Court reinforced the practical function of such preliminary contracts, which was deserving of legal protection, and promoted an instrumentalist view of the contract as guaranteeing a duty to subsequently act that has been relied on by the other side. The immediate and direct effect of such preliminary contracts is to allow for the progressive formation of commercial deals and such preliminary agreements should, in the Court's view, be welcomed and protected as they serve to clarify a situation of current uncertainty that would endure in the absence of such a preliminary contract.[104]

This post-modern view of contracting via 'progressive formation' arguably responds better to modern commercial deal-making and Canelutti, who was cited in the judgment, suggests that 'experts in negotiations know that something analogous occurs in the formation of most modern contracts'. Unlike the English courts which have typically considered incomplete agreements from

99 The Provincial court in Madrid in its judgment further highlighted the similarity between the Spanish position and Article 2932 of the Italian civil code which envisages the enforcement by the courts of an order to conclude a contract. If a party has agreed to conclude a contract but subsequently refuses, the aggrieved party may seek a court order to have the planned contract enforced.

100 See STS decision dated 24 July, 1998.

101 "un acuerdo de núcleo obligacional complejo al estar estructurado su contenido no con una técnica de reciprocidad simultánea, sino de tracto sucesivo".

102 The Supreme Court considers the terms 'pre-contract', 'preliminary contract' or 'preparatory contract' as entirely interchangeable.

103 *Supra.*

104 "Despejar jurídicamente una situación de incertidumbre que existe, en ausencia del contrato preliminar".

the 'ex post' perspective of litigation, Spanish courts have increasingly emphasised the reassuring role (su función aseguradora) of 'promises to contract' and non-binding preparatory agreements, which act as a motor for negotiations. A promise to contract signals a desire and willingness to be subsequently bound to a definitive contract (siendo coercible la celebración del contrato definitivo). This general view of preliminary agreeements further provides greater understanding of how civil courts approach awards for damages for breach – as an improper break on negotiations.[105] Such thinking mirrors Omri Ben-Shahar's recent law and economics research in the US that considers as a fundamental problem for contract law the question of how to achieve the right incentives for people to make reliance investments. Ben-Shahar fears that, if the law doesn't give people a right to recover their reliance investments in the event that the transaction fails to take shape (because the other party backs out) then parties will have an inadequate incentive to make such investments.[106]

Johnston argues, however, that whilst the courts had perhaps previously been somewhat unduly 'hospitable' in awarding precontractual liability claims on the basis of promissory estoppel, 'they have developed a body of doctrine that draws a line between the early "no agreement/no liability" stages and the late "agreement/liability" stages in transactional negotiations that tends to accord strikingly well with what is economically efficient'. On his 'view of the world', the simpler, more economically sound approach of analysing bargaining and promissory declaration is more advantageous in practice, than the 'admittedly creative, but ultimately disastrous, no-retraction regime suggested by Professor Ben Shahar. In Johnston's view, 'Under a no-retraction regime there would be no line between agreement and no agreement, and contractual liability could exist even in the absence of any communication'. Johnston warns that under

[105] El efecto ulterior, último o definitivo de la promesa del contrato preparatorio aparece cuando se observa que siendo coercible la celebración del contrato definitivo, quienes lo otorgan deben cumplir las obligaciones que de él nacen, y que la violación de ese deber compromete la responsabilidad pecuniaria de quien debe cumplirlo, de acuerdo con el principio general contenido en el artículo 1911 del Código Civil.

[106] As discussed previously, in *Contracts Without Consent: Exploring a New Basis for Contractual Liability*, *supra* Ch.1 fn. 84, Ben-Shahar presents his controversial and ostensibly impractical model, the 'no-retraction regime', whereby parties would be bound regardless of consent 'as a means of creating investments that will increase the value of transactions'. Regardless of the limitations of the model, the implication is clear that preliminary agreements are a matter of concern for US law and economics scholars and should likewise be of concern to European contract specialists. According to Johnston, Ben-Shahar's no-retraction regime errs in that "it mistakes the reliance problem, which clearly is part of the problem raised by precontractual liability cases, for the whole problem. The question of when contractual liability ought to attach to promissory statements is not only about how people invest (or don't) to increase the value of cooperation. It is also about the incentives people have in attempting to discern whether cooperation is mutually beneficial in the first place'. The question of precontractual liability clearly impacts on incentives in dealmaking, incentives 'not regarding reliance investments that increase the size of the pie, but incentives to invest in order to acquire and transmit information about the likelihood that there is any pie to split in the first place'. See Johnston, J.S., *supra* Ch.1 fn. 84.

such a regime transactions could be forced upon parties who want nothing to do with them – either because they've 'walked away from failed negotiations or because they were never in any negotiations to begin with'.[107]

As in the US, the higher courts in Spain and doctrinal opinion have considered the use of preliminary contracts as a tool for avoiding subsequent uncertainty, as a means of pre-arranging parties' investments and liabilities. Legal doctrine commonly refers to Article 2.932 of the Italian Civil code, and the role of preliminary agreements in teasing out the core issues of the definitive agreement. Rather than resisting these drafting techniques, it has been suggested that contracting partners should 'enhance legal certainty' and 'impose order' on the definitive contract through carefully drafted preliminary agreements. It is notable too, that the English and US courts have no significant problems enforcing option contracts. Their validity will typically stand or fall on pure construction alone. If drafted with sufficient certainty the English courts will certainly enforce them. As Parker J in *Von Hatzfeld-Wildenburg v. Alexander* [1912] 1 CH 284 observed:

> It appears to be well settled by the authorities that if the documents or letters relied on as constituting a contract contemplate the execution of a further contract between the parties, it is a question of construction whether the execution of the further contract is a condition or a term of the bargain or whether it is a mere expression of the desire of the parties as to the manner in which the transaction already agreed to will in fact go through. In the former case there is no enforceable contract either because the condition is unfulfilled or because the law does not recognise a contract to contract. In the latter case there is a binding contract and the reference to the more formal contract may be ignored.

An example of a legally binding agreement to contract would be the grant of an option to purchase. However, it has been suggested that where an option contract requires further negotiation or is linked to a requirement for a party to use 'best endeavours' to reach a definitive agreement then the option contract will fail for uncertainty. In *Little v. Courage Ltd*, Millet L.J argued controversially that:

> an undertaking to use one's best endeavours to obtain planning permission or an export licence is sufficiently certain and is capable of being enforced: an undertaking to use one's best endeavours to agree, however, is no different from an undertaking to agree, to try to agree or to negotiate with a view to reaching agreement; all are equally uncertain and incapable of giving rise to an enforceable obligation.[108]

---

[107] *Ibid.*

[108] See *Little v. Courage* (1994) 70 P & CR 469, per Millet J at p. 476. This viewpoint was subsequently by the Court of Appeal in *London and Regional Investments Ltd v. TBI Plc* [2002] EWCA Civ 355.

It is as incapable of enforcement by reference to objective criteria as an agreement to agree. As was stressed in *Malozzi v. Carapelli*[109] in an on-going contract, if the contract contains no indication of the objective criteria by reference to which the matter must be agreed, the provision cannot be enforced because it is insufficiently certain. The question for the English courts becomes essentially one of whether the parties effectively reserved to themselves an unfettered entitlement to refuse to agree, or whether the parties agreed to criteria which are sufficiently identifiable to give certainty and therefore legal enforceability to the provision. Yet, as in Spain and the US, such questions will more often than not require an individual judge to balance on the 'knife-edge' of assent/no assent, thus complicating the search for a definitive rule. Importantly, beyond implementing precontractual duties, particularly information duties, of mainly Community origin into domestic law, the legislator has not sought to lay down any general rule relating to precontractual liability in contracts, commercial or consumer, and as a consequence defining the nature of precontractual claims has been problematic for legal theorists. [110] This uncertainty has been further exacerbated both by the heavy categorisation of contracts and by the fact that, where no contract has been agreed it appears strictly speaking impossible to found a claim on the basis of contract. This contrasts with the position in Spanish Private International law where it is possible to recover damages in contract and 'reparation of harm' caused 'in the agreement of a contract'. Influenced by the position under German civil law, the rule is contractual and governed by contract law.[111]

General remedies further vary significantly depending on whether a case is brought on the basis of contract, extra-contractual liability, or on other grounds. The legal landscape is further cluttered by the fact that the Civil code does not specifically regulate the doctrine of unjust enrichment. The doctrine of *enriquicimiento sin causa* is an entirely jurisprudential and doctrinal construction in Spanish law, the poor relation of other sub-fields in the law of obligations.[112] The Supreme Court has further routinely discussed the 'nebulous' character

[109] [1976] 1 LJ Rep 407.

[110] See J.L. Lacruz, *Elementos de Derecho civil – Part I & II* (2nd edn, Dykinson Madrid, 1999) at 386-387.

[111] It has been argued that a claim may be based in contract relying upon the good faith principle under Article 1.258 C.c. or on the grounds of extra-contractual liability. The Spanish position has doubtless been influenced by French and Italian legal science, which traditionally have classified precontractual liability as tortious. See, *inter alia*, Cass.com. 28th June 1988, JCP 1988, éd G., IV, p. 319. The Italian vision of pre-contract as a tool for better stabilising negotiations in order to allow for subsequent performance of the main contract was first discussed in F. de Castro, 'La promesa de contrato' (1950) 3 ADC 1183. See also A. Roman García, *El Precontrato – Estudio Dogmático y Jurisprudencial* (Montecorvo, 1983).

[112] See A. Asín & M.A. Parra, 'Damages for occupation of an immovable: culpa in contrahendo and unjustified enrichment under French and Spanish law' (2005) 1 ERPL 67. See more extensively the highly complicated picture of damages in tort under Spanish law presented in *El Derecho Español de Daños en 2005: Características Diferenciales*, 6(1) Global Jurist Topics 1 (2005).

of preliminary dealings and highlighted the difficult choices facing the courts when deciding whether to impose liability. Whilst the freedom to negotiate, to exchange ideas and to ultimately reject proposals remains paramount in Spanish civil and commercial law previous judicial decision-making reveals deep, enduring uncertainties as to the breadth of the doctrine of precontractual liability and doctrinal approaches vary significantly.[113]

Indeed, writing in 1990 Álvarez González questioned the possibility of arriving at a satisfactory comprehensive precontractual liability system under Spanish law.[114] Commentators had also launched severe assaults on the both the notion of the 'precontract' itself and the absurd decisions arrived at in practice, particularly for threatening party autonomy.[115] Yet, recent Supreme Court jurisprudence has served to clarify the situation significantly by laying down guidance on when precontractual liability may attach. In its decision of December 16, 1999, the Supreme Court defined 'tratos preliminares'[116] as the 'series of acts and operations that parties undertake in discussing and preparing a contract'. In principle, such acts have no legal effect whatsoever, yet the court has laid down the circumstances in which preliminary dealings may give rise to claim under Article 1.902 of the Civil code. The test is ultimately based on a mixture of law and fact, thus complicating the pursuit of a general rule.[117]

The higher courts have not remained insensitive to wider calls for clarity in the field of precontractual liability, and the need to safeguard legal certainty. The Provincial court of Madrid[118] has previously discussed 'the greatness and the misery' of the doctrine of good faith under Article 7 of the Civil code. This

[113] See L. Díez-Picazo & A. Gullón, *Sistema de Derecho Civil – volume II* (6th edn, Tecnos, 1989).

[114] S. Álvarez-González, 'Ley aplicable a la responsabilidad precontractual en Derecho internacional privado español' (1990) XLII REDI 125. See also the criticisms levied by Cabanillas Sánchez in 'El ámbito de la Responsabilidad Precontractual o Culpa en Contrahendo' (1995) LXXI Revista Crítica de Derecho Inmobiliario 628.

[115] J. Alguer, 'Para la crítica del concepto de precontrato' (1935) 12 RDP 325. Those opposed to the imposition of precontractual obligations on the grounds that it upsets free negotiations have been.

[116] " ... dichas operaciones se desenvuelven en un área nebulosa y desde luego evanescente, pues las mismas hay que enfocarlas desde un punto de vista muy amplio – ideas, especulaciones, planteamientos- pero que siempre tendrán un denominador común, como es no suponer acto jurídico alguno, ya que de dichas referidas operaciones no se derivan, de manera inmediata, efectos jurídicos mensurables". See also STS, October 10th 1980, which further defines the essential non-binding nature of precontractual negotiations. In this specific case it was held that no contract of sale had been formed due to a lack of agreement on the sale price. As such the parties were still engaged in precontractual dealings.

[117] "... la aplicación judicial del Derecho es, como toda interpretación ... una elección entre varias valoraciones posibles hacia cuyos principios se orienta aquélla. Y en la medida en que la aplicación que de la norma se hace en la decisión judicial, considerada como realización de la referida elección, contiene elementos volitivos junto al acto de juicio lógico, cada decisión constituye un elemento de una nueva creación de Derecho (law in making) ... Presupone como dada una norma que, en realidad, debe ser primero elaborada, como hipótesis, para la situación conflictiva concreta.

[118] JUR 2004\89221. dated November 22, 2003.

contradiction was, in the view of the court, the result of 'inevitable antinomies' in the very concept itself. Balancing 'opportunity and rationality', or rather 'justice in a specific case with the overall validity of the law' was considered by the court to be the key challenge. There was a need to guarantee 'basic elements of law and justice, which are frequently in conflict'. In this conflict, recourse to general clauses implies the search for 'justice in the case at hand' and 'at the same time' an attempt to ensure 'overall coherence in the law'. The Provincial Court stressed that general clauses are positive norms aimed at the judge who, consequently by reference to 'good faith' and other 'meta-legal concepts', considers 'the views of the community and the individual'. Rarely does the necessary abstract configuration of the law allow for black and white decision-making, as judges are faced with an 'unending range of possible interpretations'. For the Provincial court, arriving at a decision implies a form of 'law in making' that under Article 7 requires consideration of 'previous experience', and 'ethical and social factors', in addition to the clauses of the contract.

Mercifully, the Spanish Supreme Court in a decision dated 16 December 1999 has put forward a more coherent framework on which to base precontractual liability claims, but has failed to provide much clarity as to the circumstances underlying liability.[119] The Spanish approach appears to combine loosely both aspects of contract and tort law, yet the overall clarity of the new test has been welcomed by doctrinal opinion.[120] The facts of the case concerned the purported breaking off of negotiations in bad faith. An appeal was brought by the *Banco Arabe Español, SA* (Aresbank) and *Arabe Española de Comercio, SA* (Arestrade) against *A&E, SA*. In an earlier Provincial court decision *A & E, SA* had argued successfully that both Aresbank and Arestrade were guilty of wrongfully breaking off negotiations.[121] Recovery was sought for 'out-of-pocket'

---

119 STS, dated December 16, 1999, RJ 1999\8978. The Court drew support from previous Supreme Court authority (see specifically decision of 16 May 1988 (RJ 1988\4308) and March 26 1993 (RJ 1993\2395).

120 The Supreme Court has stressed that absent a contractual link between the parties (al faltar relación contractual) precontractual liability emerges as an 'aquilian' right, since 'it cannot be denied that there has been a breach of the principle of neminem laedere (*'puesto que no puede negarse que exista una violación del principio 'neminem laedere'*). Certainly the Supreme Court has affirmed the traditional position advanced by leading theorists that a claim could be founded on the grounds of 'abuse of law' and/or 'extra-contractual liabilty' (*"... A lo que hay que añadir que dicha responsabilidad extracontractual se puede derivar directamente de dicha tesis jurisprudencial o a través de la teoría del abuso del derecho, como determina cierta doctrina española. Pero tanto en uno u otro caso lleva a desembocar ineludiblemente a la entrada en juego del artículo 1902 del Código Civil". Article 1.902 of the Code provides that "he who harms another, whether by act or omission, and as a consequence of fault or negligence, is required to repair the harm caused"*) yet regardless of procedural approach, modern caselaw analysis reveals consistent reference to the need to protect parties' legitimate expectations and guarantee that where parties' have placed 'trust and confidence' in the other side that that confidence should not be harmed. Though often poorly expressed in summing up, without doubt it is increasingly the protection of reasonable commercial expectation that is guiding the higher courts.

121 The Supreme Court ruling follows an appeal against the Provincial court decision of November 2, 1994.

expenses arising from the failed venture. The alleged sunk costs included research undertaken in 'advancing the initial steps of the project', travel expenses, other miscellaneous losses, and the loss of a chance to carry forward 'alternative projects in Tanzania'. The company also sought 'moral damages' (daño moral) for the Aresbank-Arestrade group's failure to carry forward the project after the prolonged negotiations.[122] Essentially, as in the Copeland case, *A & E, SA* were seeking to recover for the other side's footdragging and waste of their time, money and effort.

The First Division of the Supreme Court determined that a breach of preliminary dealings will be considered 'unlawful' or 'illegitimate' where there has been:

a) a reasonable expectation between the parties that a contract will ultimately materialise,
b) an unjustified breaking off of negotiations,
c) harm (or loss) occasioned by one of the parties, and
d) a causal link between the harm caused (or loss suffered) and the reasonable expectation created (in the mind of the innocent party).

A & E, SA had sought to rely entirely on Article 1.902 Cc and the Supreme Court had little difficulty in affirming the initial decision at first instance. In the view of the Supreme Court the two primary requirements for a successful claim were present. Firstly, there was evidence of a 'negligent' action during the preliminary dealings that amounted to a 'lack of loyalty'. Aresbank and Arestrade, it was decided, had unilaterally walked away from a well advanced project. Secondly, *A & E, SA*, as an innocent party to the negotiations, had suffered losses as a direct result of this 'negligent action'.[123]

The Court agreed that there was a causal link between the negligent action and the harm suffered but the reported decision fails to fully flesh out the nature of the 'negligent' action itself (beyond this reference to a 'lack of loyalty'). As far as recovery is concerned, for the Supreme Court the unilateral breaking off of negotiations 'in breach of the doctrine of good faith' gives rise to a claim for 'costs, effort and work carried out under the planned venture'.[124] No mention

---

[122] The trial judge had initially found in favour of *A & E, SA* and awarded 500,000 US dollars, see decision dated 14 July, 1992.

[123] no hay lugar a dudas de que se dan los dos *requisitos necesarios para que surja la responsabilidad extracontractual*, como son: *a) una acción negligente y* que *referida a dichos «tratos preliminares»*, que está constituida por una falta de lealtad cuyo núcleo fue una ruptura unilateral por parte de las entidades ahora recurrentes del proyecto inicial de los demandados en la instancia, *y b) unos perjuicios, que también dada la fenomenología de dichos «tratos preliminares», deben mensurarse desde un punto de vista del interés negativo*'. In this case all the elements necessary to give rise to a claim were present (todos los datos necesarios estan presentes para que surja con toda plenitud la presente responsabilidad extracontractual).

[124] The value of the claim totalled a mere 3,179,605 pesetas (19,109 Euros) plus legal costs. A claim of this monetary value would be treated under English procedural law as a fast track claim, with a one day trial

was made of recovery for 'moral' damages. Yet, the Supreme Court's decision does now provide a workable platform for parties framing a claim to recover damages for harm suffered through 'negligence' or bad faith in negotiations. That said, much like the decision in *Copeland* it fails to adequately identify the extent to which parties can freely negotiate. Would, for example, a simple promise to contract be actionable? The notion of an actionable bare promise to agree a contract was recently considered by the Spanish courts.[125] *Lacasa, SA* sought to recover against *Industrias del Turrón Sirvent Pla, S.A. & Others*, for the breach of a verbal promise to contract. It was further argued that the 'arbitrary' behaviour of the defendant's during contract negotiations had notably weakened the effect of an exclusivity agreement previously agreed between the parties. Importantly, following the initial series of meetings the parties decided not to draft a letter of intent. Lawyers acting for Lacasa did draft a memo on March 12, 1997 which outlined the initial positions of both parties. On April 1 1997, the claimant forwarded a fax setting out a number of additional parameters for agreement, but without making any formal offer. In response, it was accepted that this amounted to little more than a 'simple declaration of interest'. After a further two months of negotiations it was accepted that agreement would not be reached and the defendants telephoned Lacasa to wrap up the negotiations. Shortly thereafter the defendants entered into an alternative contract with a third party. The court had little difficulty rejecting the notion that a verbal contract had been agreed between the parties and held that there was insufficient evidence to impose precontractual liability.[126] It found that there was no real acceptance sufficent to bind the parties; there was merely a willingness to negotiate towards a future contract that ultimately failed to materialise. There had been acceptance only of the 'general framework for discussions presented by the offeree, as the starting point for a potential definitive purchase agreement in the future. Examining the negotiations the court was satisfied by the defendants argument that 'all of this, well understood, constitutes a mere statement of our intentions".[127]

---

and heavy emphasis on keeping down costs through careful case management.

[125] As was noted previously, a bare agreement to agree is not legally enforceable under English law and no obligations are imposed upon parties to negotiate, to use best endeavours or to reach agreement or to accept proposals even which in hindsight appear reasonable. This was first decided in the 1934 case *May & Butcher Ltd v. R* [1934] 2 KB 17 and the rationale for not enforcing such agreements was lucidly explained by Lord Denning in *Courtney*. See also more recently *Pagnan SpA v. Granaria B.V.* [1985] 1 Lloyd's Rep 547.

[126] The court did stress, however, that under Article 1451 of the civil code and Art. 708 LEC 1/2000 that, if a party refuses to sign the necessary documentation in order to give legal effect to an envisaged contract, the documentation can be notarised directly by the court. In the event that property subject to an envisaged contract has passed to a third party in good faith then only a claim for damages, as opposed to specific performance will be entertained. The court further stressed that any decision will be taken by the courts having considered trade practice and the opinions of the parties.

[127] The Court relied on a letter, which articulated a mere expression of interest in the proposal: «los planteamientos genéricos por Uds. ofertados..., como punto de partida mínimo que pueda servir de base

The non-committal language employed was to prove fatal to the claim. As no precontractual agreement had been hammered out, the most that the courts could find was an expressed willingness to continue negotiations, or what the court termed a mere 'agreement of intentions' (acuerdo de intenciones). Reinforcing bargaining freedom, the Court stressed that the preliminary dealings, by their very nature, in no way bind parties in and of themselves. The parties are free to bind themselves in whatever way they choose but are under "no obligation to perform that which as yet does not exist, and are [at all times] free to walk away from negotiations ... The parties found themselves in negotiations or 'preliminary dealings', nothing more, nothing less".[128]

The 1999 Supreme Court ruling has been further 'clarified' in 2001, in a case involving one of Spain's leading banks *La Caixa*.[129] The bank sought to challenge an earlier decision of the Provincial court of Barcelona before the Spanish Supreme court. *Aditu SA* were the owners of a factory purchased under a mortgage agreement agreed with *La Caixa*. The parties entered into negotiations to refinance. The aim was to enter into a new loan and mortgage arrangement with a third party but as these negotiations began to sour, the bank was accused by *Aditu SA* of breaking off negotiations in bad faith.[130] The case ultimately centred on the existence of a valid contract and the Supreme court seized the opportunity to affirm the requirements for a valid precontractual agreement.[131] At first instance and later on Appeal, analysing the same facts, the courts came to the same decision on the facts but entirely opposite legal conclusions[132] The Supreme Court ultimately rejected the notion that the

para un acuerdo definitivo de compraventa de la Sociedad. Todo ello, bien entendido, constituye una simple declaración de intenciones...», see also «difícilmente se puede incumplir lo que nunca se pactó. Don Silvio dejó claro desde el principio que se trataba nada más que de una simple declaración de intenciones, de unas conversaciones tendentes a llegar a una acuerdo que no llegó a producirse», judgment, at pt. 16.

[128] 'En tal ámbito, las partes son libres de llegar a acuerdos vinculantes para ellas, pero no para exigirse obviamente el cumplimiento de lo que todavía no existe, y pueden desistir de sus tratos ...'. The court relied on the Supreme Court's decision of December 16, 1999. The Court found that the notion of 'Vorverhandlungen Trattative' was a theory 'founded in German legal science and correctly assimilated into Spanish doctrine'. It similarly acknowledged the 'nebulous' and 'evanescente' character of such dealings, which of themselves at no point bind the parties, see RJ 1999\8978, Sentencia del Tribunal Supremo, no. 1091/1999 (Sala de lo Civil), de 16 diciembre. There was, however, insufficient evidence of acceptance of the Lacasa offer to satisfy article 1.261 of the Civil code and as a result there could be no binding contract. The documentation before the court was indicative merely of a negotiation process, with an exhange of ideas about price, installations, etc.

[129] *'La Caixa d'Estalvis i Pensions de Barcelona'*. STS decision dated April 20, 2001 (RJ 2001\5282).

[130] A commercial company, *Aditu, SA* brought a claim against the bank for recovery of 75.609.900 ptas.

[131] The Supreme Court was further tasked with deciding whether the parties had in practice entered into a loan contract, whether definitive or preparatory, or were merely involved in preliminary dealings.

[132] Ambas sentencias de instancia son coincidentes en la resultancia fáctica que declaran, pero totalmente disconformes en sus consecuencias jurídicas.

parties had entered into a precontractual deal but stressed that the improper/unlawful breaking off negotiations in bad faith is sufficient cause to ground a claim. Regrettably, again the court rather curiously failed to specifically state what that would imply. There was similarly a lack of clarity as to what would constitute reliance damages (or the 'negative interest' as it was referred to in the judgment). The Court did however make reference to 'costs, efforts and works performed'.[133] In this regard, greater clarity on the nature of recovery in damages is provided by the Supreme Court decision of June 14th 1999. The decision better illustrates the type of costs that may fall within a potential claim.[134] Again, the case concerned the breaking off of negotiations between *Doux Ibérica, SA*, a private enterprise, and the *Ayuntamiento de Alagón*, the local authority of Alagón.

Following various discussions, the parties agreed to enter into a form of collaboration that aimed at installing an industrial poultry abattoir in the municipal area of Alagón. The intention of the parties was that the Town hall would acquire an ideal plot of land that it would thereafter sell to *Doux Ibérica, SA*. The private company agreed to cover the purchase price of the land and any additional financial costs but sought official subsidies. The local authority had sought to recover 19,385,163 pstas (115,500 Euros) from Doux Ibérica SA after it purchased a suitable site for the abattoir. Yet, Doux contested the payment request on the grounds that the intention to establish an abattoir was at all times dependent upon the concession of financial assistance from the municipal authorities – financial assistance that had not been forthcoming. In correspondence with the authority it further added that 'giving the current situation in our sector, at this moment it is most probable that we would not commit to such an investment, even in the event that such concessions were advanced' – a similarly framed response to that presented to the unfortunate Mr. Copeland in the Baskin Robbins case.

On appeal before the Provincial court of Zaragoza, the local authorities of Alagón succeeded partially in their claim.[135] They had sought to recover a combined total of 85,123,088 ptas. (511,600 Euros) plus legal costs for the unjustified breaking off of negotiations by *Doux Ibérica, SA*. The claim comprised 36,316,606 ptas. (218,000 Euros) for 'financial, legal and professional costs', 43,806,482 ptas. (263,000 Euros) for 'lost revenue' resulting from an unjustified breach of negotiations, and 5,000,000 ptas (30,050 Euros) for 'moral costs' which the claimant sought for damage caused to the local authority's reputation. The Provincial court held that following preliminary contact, the parties had indeed embarked upon a collaboration that was of mutual interest and benefit – the installation of a major industrial poultry abattoir for an agreed sum – and that the local authorities initially appeared content to assist financially. In awarding damages of almost 9 million pesetas (54,000 Euros), the court acknowl-

[133] The court made reference to "gastos, esfuerzos y trabajos".

[134] STS RJ 1999\4105.

[135] SAP de Zaragoza (fourth section), decision dated 16 November 1994.

edged that Doux Ibérica, SA had not received promised concessions from the Ministry of Agriculture and that its position was further weakened by wider economic difficulties affecting the entire poultry sector but that the company had nonetheless been in breach of a precontractual duty.[136]

Again, in defining the unjustified breach of precontractual dealings, the Provincial court made reference to an 'act or omission contrary to the law' and 'unlawful conduct' and applied the Supreme Court's four-pronged test. The Court accepted that 1. a reasonable position of trust had developed between the parties regarding the progress of the contract; 2. there was an improper breaking off of negotiations; 3. the local authority had suffered harm as a result; and, 4. there was a definite causal link between the harm suffered and the trust developed between the parties. Relying directly upon the provisions of Article 1.902, Doux Ibérica, SA framed its appeal before the Supreme Court on the primary grounds that it had not acted unlawfully under the Code and there was no 'causal link' between its decision to break off the negotiations with Doux and the harm allegedly suffered by the local authority.

The Supreme Court did chastise Doux Ibérica for failing to inform the claimants sooner that it was experiencing economic difficulties, but found that the company had not acted negligently. Overturning the Provincial court of Zaragoza, the Supreme court stressed that when evaluating the conduct of the parties it was necessary to evaluate the degree of confidence fostered between both parties that a contract would ultimately result. The court stressed that, since the involvement of Doux Ibérica was at all times dependent upon the concession of external funding, no such confidence was created in the mind of the local authority that a contract would subsequently result after the purchase of the land. The involvement of Doux Ibérica was at all times dependent upon 'institutional economic support' which was not forthcoming. The apparent lack of diligence on the part of Doux Ibérica in failing to inform the claimants in respect of the economic hardship they were experiencing was not considered as sufficiently harmful to oblige the respondents to meet the appellants' costs. In the eyes of the Supreme Court the purchase of the land had been assumed at the local authority's own expense and risk, without any certainty that the project would proceed. As long as the respondents' conduct was premised upon the concession of financial assistance from the Ministry of Agriculture there was no legitimate expectation that a contract would result. As such, there could be no claim for precontractual liability in the absence of such financial concessions. In order to establish a successful claim it is necessary for a situation of trust to have been created that is thereafter broken by one of the parties' without justification. In its absence, the local authority had 'illogically pressured' the respondents.

Besides the degree of predictability and coherence provided by the Supreme Court's four part test, what is perhaps most significant is the extent to which evidence of 'improper' conduct can essentially be trumped by the notion of reasonable commercial expectiation. As will be developed further in chap-

[136] The judgment refers to an "Acción u omisión contraria a derecho" and to "conducta antijurídica".

ter 4, this does lend hope for a gradual convergence of common and civil law approaches given the numerous references in English academic and judicial opinion to the need to protect the legitimate expectations of commercial actors.

4.2 Comparing the legal effects of preliminary agreements

In section 4, we explore more concretely case-law related to specific preliminary agreements. Although there is no prescribed form for heads of agreement and letters of intent, etc they do typically set out the main terms agreed between the parties, may include a provisional timetable for the completion of negotiations, and/or set out the primary obligations of the parties during the negotiation process itself. The more complex, ambitious or speculative a project, the greater the likelihood that parties will resort to non-binding letters of commitment as a relatively inexpensive method of highlighting areas of both provisional agreement and ongoing contention but without incurring legal liability or major expenses. A sufficiently detailed document may in practice be legally binding and care must be taking to ensure that a legally binding commitment is not created unintentionally, or that parties do not enter into a non-legally binding commitment believing it to be binding.[137] In English law a simple *quantum meruit* claim will typically 'rescue' a party who commences work on a particular project or transaction on the basis of a (detailed) letter of intent, should the other side get 'cold feet'.

4.3 Heads of agreement, Letters of Intent and unenforceable Agreements to Agree

The 2002 English case of *AC Controls Ltd v. British Broadcasting Corporation*[138] revealed that an appropriately worded letter of intent will be

[137] This was the 'shocking' effect of the letter of intent language used in the high profile case of *Texaco Inc v. Pennzoil*, 729 S.W. 2d 768,. Though the case was ultimately settled between the parties for $3 billion dollars, a jury in Texas awarded Pennzoil over $10 billion in compensatory and punitive damages. The case arose after Getty Oil signed a a letter of intent for a merger deal with Pennzoil but subsequently backed out of the deal and merged with Texaco. As is further evidenced in *Newport Limited v. Sears, Roebuck & Co.*, 6 F. 3d 1058 (5th Cir. 1993) even use of the word 'preliminary' may not prevent liability. Applying Louisiana law it was held that the 'use of the word preliminary does not preclude the agreement from being final until later agreements are reached, or from being the only agreement in the event no other agreements are confected', at 1065. A court, it was argued, should look to the language of the letter of intent and the parties subsequent conduct.

[138] [2002] EWHC 3132, 89 Con L.R. 52. See also *British Steel Corporation v. Cleveland Bridge & Engineering Co. Ltd* [1984] 1 All ER 504, which has led to suggestions that if the courts can protect such 'reliance' investments via *quantum meruit* claims there is little need for precontractual liability to take greater root in the law. Evidently, however, the doctrine is intimately tied to notions of unjust enrichment and fails therefore to provide general protection to parties to negotiations from other bad faith practices or indeed to safeguard against other forms of early reliance investment.

binding even in the absence of a formally executed contract. The claimant AC Controls Ltd had submitted a tender and the defendants forwarded a letter of intent with a spending cap of £250,000 which was signed by AC. It was ultimately determined that, despite the use of letter of intent language, a contract had been formed from the clauses of the initial tender, the letter of intent itself and the defendant's signed letter which was construed as authorisation for A to commence work on the project. In this case there was a clear impression created in the mind of AC Controls management by the BBC that a final contract would materialise. As Poole observes, it is difficult to predict with absolute certainty which precontractual statements will be incorporated as terms and which will be regarded as mere representations. She argues that it is hard to resist the conclusion that the courts enjoy an element of discretion which the current vague guidelines provide, and 'would not like to see them replaced with anything more certain. The basic test of contractual intention allows the court to pick and choose those representations which are to have contractual status without reference to tight identifiable criteria. Predictability suffers as a consequence of this rule, but it may be a price we are willing to pay for the element of fairness it may import'.[139]

Yet, delving deeper into the case cluster, the majority of cases examined revealed that letters of intent and heads of agreement are commonly dismissed as mere unenforceable agreements to agree. Particularly illustrative in this regard is the US 2nd Court of Appeals decision in *Adjustrite Systems Inc v. Gab Business Service*.[140] The parties agreed to transfer $1 million in assets and signed an informal two-page document to memorialise their agreement. The District Court sympathised with Adjustrite but could not look beyond the four corners of the various documents.[141] This view found similar support in *Omnitech*

[139] See J. Poole, *Textbook on Contract Law* (8th Edition, Oxford University Press, 2006) at 2008. She adopts a surprisingly uber-formalist view that courts should reject legal intervention in incomplete contracts and instead limit their role to a rather literal enforcement of the express terms specifically agreed by the parties.

[140] 145 F.3d 543, 547 (2d Cir. 1998). A suitable example of a Heads of Agreement that failed to give rise to liability was that agreed, and subsequently repudiated by one of the parties in the Australian case of *Coal Cliff Colleries Pty Ltd v. Sijehama Pty Ltd* (1991) 24 N.S.W.L.R. 1. (discussed below). The HoA provided that: *The parties will forthwith proceed in good faith to consult together upon the formulation of a more comprehensive and detailed joint venture agreement ... which when approved and executed will take the place of these heads of agreement, but the action of the parties in so consulting and in negotiating on fresh or additional terms shall not in the meantime in any way prejudice the full and binding effect of what is now agreed.*

[141] "[T]here is no question in my mind that when Mr. Marks signed [the Agreement] he thought he had a deal, that he wrote to his principals and told them so, and later, for reasons of their own, they became disenchanted with the idea that they bought these assets and they wished to seek through their lawyers a way to exit from their responsibilities ... [But], regardless of what the [parties to the contract] think, if the contract is not adequate to satisfy the Statute of Frauds or if the contract is a mere agreement

International Inc. v. Clorox Co.,[142] but Buechler is correct in observing that, 'the decisions in this area, as a whole, continue to appear both confusing and inconsistent to the point where it is said to be virtually impossible to predict the outcome in any particular case'.[143] Previous judicial attempts to bring clarity, as in *Winston v. Mediafare Entertainment Corp.*[144] and *Mid-Continent Telephone Corp. v. Home Telephone Co.*[145] have also failed to bring necessary consistency, particularly as to when precontractual liability may ultimately attach.

4.4 Exclusivity arrangements and Lock-Out agreements

Exclusivity agreements, and most notably the 'lock-out' agreement, are frequently entered into by the parties at the outset of negotiations in order to give one party exclusive negotiating rights. The lock-out agreement has gained particularly favour in Britain as a means of negativing morally reprehensible behaviour in negotiations for the sale of property. Thompson cites the craze of 'gazumping' in the property market, where a seller would withdraw last minute from an agreement 'subject to contract' in order to secure a higher price for the property elsewhere. The lock-out device gradually emerged as one method of ensuring that the seller would 'stick around' at least for an agreed period.[146] As the English law does not imply exclusivity in negotiations, parties seeking such exclusivity will normally enter into a 'lock-out' agreement for

---

to agree, then it's not a contract no matter what the participant businessmen may have thought at the time".

142 11 F.3d 1316 (5th Cir 1994) 'where, as here, the contract can be interpreted from the four corners of the document, without recourse to extrinsic evidence, the interpretation is a matter of law'.

143 See G. Buechler, 'The Recognition of Preliminary Agreements in Negotiated Corporate Acquisitions: An Empirical Analysis of the Disagreement Process' (1989) 22 Creighton Law Review 573, at 574.

144 777 F.2d 1978. In *Winston* the 2nd Circuit put forward a four factor test for determining the parties' intent to be bound: 1. whether the parties had stated in writing an intention not to be bound; 2. whether there was part performance of the 'provisional' deal; 3. whether all of the terms of the alleged agreement had been appropriately settled and 4. whether the type of deal envisaged is normally formed in writing. The test itself is not particularly revealing, particularly point 3 (which would surely be evidence of a binding contract) and part 4.

145 319 F. Supp. 1176. (1970) This earlier test is equally problematic and mentions other superfluous incidentals such as the value of the proposed agreement, etc. More alarmingly, Buechler suggested back in 1989 that judicial activism was effectively unrestrained as good faith was a 'hidden consideration', with the court's resorting effectively to smell tests, sounding out the validity of the supposed contract on the basis of the parties' conduct. As a consequence, there was a direct link between 'the reason for the failure of the transaction and the result reached by the courts', *supra*, at 597.

146 The gazumping problem is currently adversely affecting property buyers throughout Ireland, following a boom in the market. With a relatively fixed property supply and a sharp rise in prices, developers have been able to take advantage in bad faith. The current rules on conveyancing effectively legitimise such sharp practice. The use of the lock out agreement has therefore been encouraged – see Irish/UK Property Bulletin, Issue 2 (2004) and M.P. Thompson, 'Compensation for Pre-Contractual Expenditure',

a specific period. Breach of a lock-out agreement or exclusivity arrangement should in theory entitle the non-breaching party to damages; at least to the extent that the non-breaching party is able to show loss caused by the breach. To avoid being unenforceable the lock-out must specify an agreed period for the negotiations and any liquidated damages must represent a real assessment of likely damages and not constitute a penalty.

Indeed, following *Walford v. Miles*, exclusivity undertakings in England are usually expressed in negative terms, i.e. an obligation not to negotiate with other parties for a given period (known as 'lock-out'). In general, there is also a requirement that the exclusivity period should be of a limited duration, in order to prevent it being unenforceable. Aligned to such exclusivity agreements, confidentiality agreements are typically employed in the absence of a general duty to act in good faith. It is seen as preferable for these to be entered into in the early stages of negotiations, prior to any confidential information actually being exchanged. In order to be binding, however, they must be executed by deed or supported by consideration (mutual exclusivity obligations) which reinforces the importance of careful drafting. The requirement of consideration is satisfied if one party gives information, whilst the other party is required to retain such information confidentially. The breach of a confidentiality agreement may entitle the injured party to claim damages for any loss suffered, though the parties may similarly stipulate in the contract the specific damages to be awarded in the event of a breach.

Importantly, lock-out type agreements will no doubt continue to be used in practice under English law, though clearly unenforceable where the parties fail to express a definitive timeframe for the negotiations. Even where unenforceable, it is suggested that they may well still impose a commercial or moral pressure on parties to continue negotiations with one other. As is apparent under Spanish contract law such agreements are generally viewed as unnecessary given the good faith obligation, which imposes a generalised duty of good faith and confidentiality on parties to negotiations.

It is further notable that a number of agencies advising business in the use of lock-out agreements have recently suggested that 'where appropriate, for example, in a cross-border situation, it may be worth considering expressly applying a law other than English law to a lock-out agreement. Most other European jurisdictions already recognise the validity and enforceability of lock-out agreements [regardless of whether they are definite or not] and, whilst it is advisable to have a written agreement, usually no specific formalities are required.[147] In *Walford*, Lord Ackner considered it helpful to make several positive observations about so-called 'lock-out' agreement and appeared much closer to Farnsworth's 'freedom of contract' approach when he suggested that:

Conveyancer and Property Lawyer, case comment, 1995 – and a number of developers are prepared to agree a 28 day lock-out in return for a non-refundable deposit of approximately £1,500.

[147] See for instance, 'Lock-Out Agreements, the Position After *Walford v. Miles*' (1992) 13(3) Comp Law 68.

> There is clearly no reason in the English contract law why A, for good consideration, should not achieve an enforceable agreement whereby B, agrees for a specified period of time, not to negotiate with anyone except A in relation to the sale of his property. There are often good commercial reasons why A should desire to obtain such an agreement from B. B's property, which A contemplates purchasing, may be such as to require the expenditure of not inconsiderable time and money before A is in a position to assess what he is prepared to offer for its purchase or whether he wishes to make any offer at all. A may well consider that he is not prepared to run the risk of expending such time and money unless there is a worthwhile prospect, should he desire to make an offer to purchase, of B, not only then still owning the property, but of being prepared to consider his offer. A may wish to guard against the risk that, while he is investigating the wisdom of offering to buy B's property, B may have already disposed of it or, alternatively, may be so advanced in negotiations with a third party as to be unwilling or for all practical purposes unable, to negotiate with A. But I stress that this is a negative agreement – B by agreeing not to negotiate for this fixed period with a third party, locks himself out of such negotiations. He has in no legal sense locked himself *into* negotiations with A. What A has achieved is an exclusive opportunity, for a fixed period, to try and come to terms with B, an opportunity for which he has, unless he makes his agreement under seal, to give good consideration. I therefore cannot accept [the] proposition ... that without a positive obligation on B to negotiate with A, the lock-out agreement would be futile. The agreement alleged in [this] claim contains the essential characteristics of a basic valid lock-out agreement, save one. It does not specify for how long it is to last.[148]

In the Court of Appeal, Bingham L.J. had sought to cure this legal deficiency by holding that the obligation upon Mr. Miles and his wife not to deal with other parties should continue to bind them 'for such time as is reasonable in all the circumstances'. In order to make such an arrangement workable, Bingham L.J. had little option but to resort to the notion of an implied duty of good faith. He stressed that:

---

[148] At p. 139. Lord Ackner was equally forthright in noting that the 'object of having a lock-out agreement is to diminish the risk of wasted expenditure. But one cannot be compensated for a loss of expectation. One can only be compensated for the breach of legal rights', at p. 132. Yet, elevating the damages aspect, which would most likely be nominal for the breach of a contract to negotiate in any event, may be missing a bigger picture. In *Hillas & Co. Ltd v. Arcos Ltd* it was long ago noted that "There is ... no bargain except to negotiate, and negotiations may be fruitless and end without any contract ensuing; yet even then, in strict theory, there is a contract (if there is good consideration) to negotiate, though in the event of repudiation by one party the damages may be nominal, unless a jury think that the opportunity to negotiate was of some appreciable value to the injured party" (at p. 505). However, perhaps the threat of a court order to re-negotiate a failed venture in good faith in a non-adversarial manner, would gradually inspire a new counter-ethic of co-operation in UK commercial settings.

> [t]he time would end once the parties acting in good faith had found themselves unable to come to mutually acceptable terms . . . the defendants could not . . . bring the reasonable time to an end by procuring a bogus impasse, since that would involve a breach of the duty of reasonable good faith which parties such as these must, I think, be taken to owe to each other.

The House of Lords, as we know, was unimpressed. This implied duty of good faith approach was the technique adopted in the *Midway Airlines* case in the US and it is not surprising that Brownsword has since called on the courts to mirror the US approach in future cases concerning the facts in *Walford v. Miles.*[149] As Bingham L.J. recognised, such an implied duty, if it were to exist, would have indirectly imposed upon Miles a duty to negotiate in good faith. Such a duty, for the reasons Ackner defended, cannot be imposed under English law. As Lord Ackner himself stressed:

> That it should have been thought necessary to assert such a duty helps to explain the reason behind the amendment to paragraph 5 and the insistence of Mr. Naughton that without the implied term, the agreement, as originally pleaded, was unworkable – unworkable because there was no way of determining for how long the Miles were locked out from negotiating with any third party.

In Spain, 'lock-out' agreements are prima facie enforceable but there is a distinct lack of caselaw decided before the higher courts. Lock-out agreements will also fully bind the parties if the language used is suitably committal. This is justified on the grounds that a contract may contain whatever terms the parties agree unless the subject matter is contrary to law, moral principles or public order.[150] The Supreme Court has not pronounced formally on the validity of 'lock-out agreements' but in a judgment of the 16 December 1995 the court held that letters of comfort, which merely affirm or support stated opinions or facts give rise merely to a 'moral' obligation.[151] Remedies for breach of a lock-out agreement are in theory the same as for breach of contract, but Diez Picazo suggests that in practice the courts would remedy such situations through an award of damages, as there would be no practical prospect of forcing a party back to the

[149] See R. Brownsword, who argues in favour of a 'principled jurisprudence' founded on 'key notions' such as the 'legitimate interest' and 'co-operative dealing' that better fits with 'defensible moral theory'. He notes that 'whilst the theoretical engagement now required is by no means easy, it is unavoidable if the rationality of the law is not simply to be made more transparent but to be put on a firm moral footing', see R. Brownsword, 'Two Concepts of Good Faith' (1994) 7 JCL 197, at 243-4.

[150] See Art.1 256 Código civil which states "los contratantes pueden establecer los pactos, cláusulas y condiciones que tengan por conveniente, siempre que no sean contrarios a las leyes, a la moral, ni al orden público".

[151] The Spanish legal position is much closer to the English judicial stance than that of the French courts, which have reinforced a Brownswordian 'moral' dimension to letters of comfort, See P. Giliker, *supra* (2003).

negotiating table nor would there be a suitable way to effectively prevent the other side from negotiating with a third party, etc. Importantly, it has recently been argued by the Spanish Supreme Court that this uncertainty problem, or 'true legal lacuna' (the absence of a fixed period for negotiation) was appropriately 'resolved' by the Court in a previous decision (dated October 5, 1996).[152] Despite the parties having failed to agree a fixed period for the negotiations, this gap can it is argued be filled with support from article 1.118 of the Civil code.[153] The aim of the court should be to determine the period of time that the parties would have likely agreed, having regard to the nature of the contract that was under negotiation. This pure gap filling approach was seen as being entirely in line with 'modern and uniform' trends in commercial contracting aimed at not defeating the parties' true intentions.[154]

Just as the previous decision in *Courtney and Fairbairn Ltd* failed to 'deter those several litigants in the long list of cases cited by Lord Ackner',[155] the decision in *Walford* may have been readily greeted in its immediate aftermath by Cumberbatch[156] for supposedly providing certainty and quelling debate on the issue, but a future House of Lords will most likely be required to cite an equally long list of cases sired by the uncertainty enshrined in law via *Walford*. The bullish and argumentative approach of Lord Ackner contrasts significantly with the thoughtful, well reasoned analysis of Bingham L.J. in the Court of Appeal. Clearly, the gap filling approach of introducing an implied term to negotiate in good faith advocated by Bingham LJ, and endorsed by the Spanish Supreme court, not only fits better with an emerging transnational consensus but on the facts in *Walford* alone, such an implied term would not have defeated the interests of the parties, who were agreed on all the material points relevant to

---

152 "El referido problema, sin embargo, ya fue resuelto por esta Sala, en su Sentencia de 5 octubre 1996 (RJ 1996\7041), en la que se declara lo siguiente: al constituir una verdadera laguna legal ... la condición (positiva, en este caso) debe considerarse o tenerse por no cumplida si transcurre el tiempo que verosímilmente se hubiese querido señalar, atendida la naturaleza de la obligación, sin que se produzca el acontecimiento futuro e incierto del que aquélla se hizo depender».

153 Despite the horrific drafting, the provision provides a most appropriate gap-filling option. The gist of Article 1.118, para.2, provides that where no time period is fixed [by the parties], a condition can still be satisfied provided a time period *that would most likely have been agreed* can be fixed having regard to the nature of the obligation. "Si no hubiere tiempo fijado, la condición deberá reputarse cumplida en el que verosímilmente se hubiese querido señalar, atendida la naturaleza de la obligación".

154 "... según el criterio de la más moderna y prácticamente uniforme doctrina científica, que es el que esta Sala aquí acepta y consagra, debe llenarse acudiendo al párrafo segundo del art. 1118 del Código Civil, que ha de considerarse aplicable a todo tipo de condiciones".

155 *Ibid.*

156 J. Cumberbatch, 'In Freedom's Cause: The Contract to Negotiate' (1992) 12(4) Oxford J Legal S 586. ('In that it purports to clarify this area of the law therefore, *Walford v. Miles* is to be welcomed', at 586). Yet, as is evidenced from the title of his paper, the decision failed in its primary goal to bring definitive certainty, see P. Gray, 'Promises to Negotiate in Good Faith: Are they Enforceable?' (1992) ICCLR 227.

the contract.[157] Two further weaknesses in the House of Lords' decision relate to a failure of counsel for the plaintiffs to lead evidence of other US decisions beyond that of *Channel homes*, or indeed, even more material to the legal question raised in *Walford*, the previous Australian decision in 1991 of *Coal Cliff Colleries Pty Ltd v. Sijehama Pty Ltd*, particularly the dissenting judgments[158]

In the Supreme Court of New South Wales, Kirby P suggested that a promise to negotiate could be enforceable where there is consideration for the promise and the promise is clear and part of a clear agreement between the parties. Unsettlingly, he suggested that each case would ultimately depend upon the construction of the particular contract but argued that the most obvious illustration that a promise to negotiate is intended to be a binding legal obligation will be where an identified third party has been given power to settle ambiguities and uncertainties (Such as a clause in the contract providing for arbitration or adjudication, etc to settle any remaining disputed terms). In other cases a court may be empowered to enforce an agreement by referring to a readily ascertainable external standard and adding, 'flesh to a provision which is otherwise unacceptably vague or uncertain or apparently illusory'.[159]

4.5 Agreements to use best endeavours to negotiate

The decision in *Courtney* that a bare agreement has no legal force in English law has been followed in a plethora of subsequent cases.[160] Moreover, between commercial parties an agreement to negotiate a contract

---

[157] As Lord Ackner accepted the essential terms of the planned purchase were agreed in principle at a meeting held just six days before the alleged to promise to negotiate the deal to its conclusion. (see p. 133 of the judgment). Of course, as Berg notes, 'the fallacy of Walford v. Miles is the assumption that adversarial, competitive negotiation is the only type of negotiation. Another well-recognised type is negotiation as a problem-solving, consensual process'. The courts have no difficulty in upholding an agreement to negotiate good faith in mediation (see *Cable & Wireless plc v. IBM United Kingdom Ltd* [2002] EWHC 2059, at [22] to [30]). Berg argues that an undertaking to negotiate in good faith ought to be treated as recognition by the parties that there are two types of negotiation – adversarial and problem-solving – and that use of the expression 'in good faith' signals an implied choice for the latter approach. He further suggests that if businessmen have given such an undertaking, 'in terms clearly showing an intention that it should be legally binding, for the court to deny effect to the undertaking is not commercially fair', *supra* (2003), at 362.

[158] *Supra*. The case concerned a proposed joint venture to mine coal. Though the court ultimately determined that agreements to negotiate in good faith are unenforceable, there was much more rounded debate, with two of the three judges discussing the circumstances in which such a promise may be enforceable.

[159] (1991) 24 NSWLR 1 at 27.

[160] *Albion Sugar Co. Ltd v. Williams Tankers Ltd* [1977] 2 Lloyd's Rep 457; *Scandinavian Trading Tanker Co AB v. Flota Petrolera Ecuatoriana* [1981] 2 Lloyd's Rep 425; *Star Steamship Society v. Beogradska Plovidna* [1998] 2 Lloyd's Rep 583; *Trees Ltd v. Cripps* (1983) 267 EG 596; *Voest Alpine Intertrading GmbH v. Chevron International Oil Co Ltd* [1987] 2 Lloyd's Rep 547.

does not impose any implied obligation to use best endeavours to reach agreement. Authority for this view is provided by *Scandinavian Trading Co A.B. v. Flota Petrolera Ecuatoriana (The Scaptrade)* [1981], a decision approved in *Walford v. Miles*. What had remained unclear was the extent to which an express commitment to use best endeavours to negotiate would be enforceable under English law, particularly in the light of the decision in *Phillips Petroleum Co UK v. Enron Europe Ltd.*[161] In *Walford v. Miles*, Lord Ackner observed a key distinction between agreements to negotiate and an agreement to use best endeavours:

> ... the Court of Appeal appears to have proceeded on the basis that an agreement to negotiate in good faith is synonymous with an agreement to use best endeavours and as the latter is enforceable so is the former. This appears to me, with respect, to be an unsustainable proposition, the reason why an agreement to negotiate, like an agreement to agree, is unenforceable, is simply because it lacks the necessary certainty. The same does not apply to an agreement to use best endeavours.

Lord Ackner was endeavouring to draw a distinction between an obligation to negotiate in good faith and a commitment to use best endeavours, however, it is by no means apparent what distinction he was endeavouring to make. Was he merely stating that an obligation to *negotiate* in good faith is unenforceable whereas an obligation to use best endeavours to *perform* an obligation is enforceable? Another possible interpretation is that, while an agreement to use best endeavours may refer to the mechanics of the negotiation process, an obligation to use best endeavours may oblige a party to make himself available for negotiations and not impede the closing of a deal. It is commonly argued that the difficulty of giving precise content to this obligation, while maintaining each party's freedom to pursue their own interests that makes such a promise too uncertain to be enforced. Farnsworth has argued that a commitment to use reasonable endeavours would require a firmer commitment from the parties to the deal than would a duty to negotiate in good faith. Burton and Anderson concur.[162] Lord Ackner's rather clouded thinking in relation to agreements to use best endeavours to negotiate has only recently been clarified by the lower courts.

The law in England and Wales now appears undeniably clear – a firm commitment to use reasonable endeavours gives rise to no duty in law. As recently as June 2006 the Technology and Construction court ruled such clauses void for uncertainty. In *Multiplex Constructions (UK) Ltd v. Cleveland Bridge UK Ltd*[163] the Queen's Bench division affirmed the position set out in

---

161 [1997] CLC 329.

162 S. Burton & E. Anderson, 'Contractual Good Faith: Formation, Performance, Breach, Enforcement' (Little Brown, 1995). See also the decision in *Thompson v. Liquichimica of America Inc.*, 481 F. Supp. 365 (S.D.N.Y., 1979), where the court accepted the logic of an agreement to use best endeavours which, unlike an agreement to agree, is sufficiently clear and discrete and therefore actionable.

163 [2006] EWHC 1341.

Philips Petroleum Co UK Ltd v. Enron Europe Ltd[164]and the earlier 1995 case of *Little v. Courage Ltd.*[165] In *Multiplex* a series of subcontracts were to be agreed concerning structural steelwork at the new, bedevilled Wembley Stadium. It had been argued that where parties commit to an obligation to use 'best endeavours' an implied reciprocal duty arises that requires the other party to act in such a manner as not 'unreasonably to frustrate the conclusion of an agreement'. Argument led on the fact that a term in an agreement which states that the parties will enter into a further agreement is not necessarily an unenforceable agreement to agree. For example, where the parties have entered into a provisional agreement which expressly requires or envisages the subsequent execution of a formal contract incorporating terms on which they have previously agreed, the courts would have little difficulty upholding an option contract.

5 Choice or imposition? Functional equivalence and the sustainability of the English position

Importantly, despite the 'new' symphony, Lord Hoffmann's *Restatement* has not, and is unlikely to orchestrate a revolutionary redirection of English commercial construction along the route proposed by Rogers CJ in *Banque Brussels.* Where the parties intended to use a 'finely tuned linguistic fork', then an English judge will likely continue to apply such a fork. However, whilst traditionally the English 'parol evidence' rule would operate to exclude extrinsic evidence seeking to vary, add or contradict the written terms, the rule has always been subject to exceptions. It is submitted that there will be a gradual recognition and acceptance of evidence of the precontractual negotiations in English commercial courts. Their Lordships have consistently dodged the issue but this non-debate does not appear to be premised upon any strong ideological opposition. Certainly, there is likely to be little disquiet among the business community that Lord Hoffmann's re-statement may tempt judges to engage in the re-writing of contracts under the guise of the adoption of a commercial construction. The courts have, however, been alive to this difficulty and have not, as yet, sought to engage in extensive re-writing of contracts. While such criticisms have their force, they have not won the day. Lord Hoffmann's re-statement has been cited on over 180 occasions and is now regularly applied by the courts. Both *National Bank of Sharjah* v. *Dellborg* and *Scottish Power plc* v. *Britoil (Exploration) Ltd* were decided in the early days of the life of Lord Hoffmann's restatement, before it had time to bed down in the case-law. Now that the principles are well-established criticisms are much more muted. There remains a concern about the amount of material that can be introduced in evidence under cover of the 'matrix of fact' but this does not require a wholesale re-evaluation. At most it

---

[164] [1997] C.L.C. 329 (CA)

[165] [1995] C.L.C. 164; (1995) 70 P. & C.R. 469.

requires additional judicial caution in relation to the scope of the actual 'matrix of fact'.

Importantly, as McKendrick observes, there are still essentially three principal choices open to the courts.[166] The first is to return to the old days and to resurrect the traditional, literal approach to the interpretation of contracts. This is unlikely to happen, although it is possible that the courts will try to curb the scope of Lord Hoffmann's restatement, particularly through a restrictive interpretation of the matrix of fact. The second is to keep the law as it is now. On this view evidence of precontractual negotiations and conduct subsequent to the making of the contract would continue to be generally inadmissible. The third view is that the law should continue to evolve and that the courts should expand the range of materials to which they have regard when interpreting contracts. One way in which the courts could evolve is through recognition of the contract to negotiate in good faith – an evolution that would be truly evolutionary rather than revolutionary and that would often allow the courts to better tally judicial outcomes with parties' reasonable expectations.

6 Enforcing Community-wide the contract to negotiate in good faith

Whilst expressly rejecting 'moral' standards in favour of certainty and the security of transactions, Brown suggests that one can 'perceive an underlying trend towards some concept based on a duty of fair dealing' premised upon what reasonable commercial expectation. Paradoxically, however, the English commercial courts have considered it appropriate at other times to chart a distinctly divergent course. Brown further acknowledges recent caselaw that reveals a 'marked tendency to revert to strict nineteenth century laissez-faire ideals of robust self-reliance and judicial non-interventionism'.[167] Brown cites the closing comments of Ralph Gibson L.J. in *Kleinwort Benson Ltd. v. Malaysia Mining Corp. Bhd* as particularly illustrative of this worrying trend.[168] He could also have relied on Slade LJ, whp recently observed in the Court of Appeal in *Banque Financière de la Cité S.A v. Westgate Insurance Co. Ltd* that: 'True it is that all contracts of insurance are ... based on the utmost good faith. However, in the case of commercial contracts, broad concepts of honesty and fair dealing, however laudable, are a somewhat uncertain guide when determining the exist-

[166] McKendrick, E. (2005) *supra*.

[167] *Supra*, at 367.

[168] Gibson L.J. arguing in the case that 'the consequences of the decision of the defendants to repudiate their moral responsibility are not matters for this court' at p. 394. See also A. Phang, 'Positivism in the English Law of Contract' (1992) 55(1) MLR 102 (criticising the 'extreme' black-letter positivism of the English courts generally and in particular that underlying Gibson's judicial philosophy).

ence or otherwise of an obligation which may arise even in the absense of any dishonest or unfair intent'.[169]

Brown sees the decision in *Walford* as paradigmatic of this wider non-interventionist philosophy and its foreclosure of good faith in negotiations. He notes that contemporary English decisions look increasingly anachronistic in their espousal of commercial certainty. Their Lordships decision in *Walford* ensures that 'unqualified certainty is engendered by unequivocally denying any efficacy to contracts to negotiate in good faith, but, on the facts of the case, this conclusion undoubtedly involves a condonation of bad faith in commercial negotiations rather than mere apprehension regarding the applicability of good faith".[170] Yet, despite the potential licensing of bad faith, as was noted previously, the *Walford* ruling has failed to provide the intended legal certainty, as evidenced by both doctrinal opinion – and the raft of criticisms levied -, and subsequent findings in both *Petromec Inc.*[171] and *AT&T v. Saudi Cable Co.*[172] Importantly, as Brown notes, 'whilst it cannot be said that a majority of legal systems have wholeheartedly adopted the contract to negotiate in good faith, many have an awareness of the problems engendered by such undertakings and do not consider good faith doctrines to be alien to commercial law'.[173] Although in *Walford*, Lord Ackner gave short shrift to the American approach, key lessons can be drawn from both the American and Spanish experience which would appear to be applicable in a future European contract law. The primary legal objection in English law relates to the fact that pure reliance on a promise would fail as a substitute for consideration. This argument is made most forcefully by Poole, Norisada and Furmston in rejecting the notion of a contract to bargain.[174] The spectre of reliance has also been seen as a threat to the liberal negotiation and formation of

[169] Bridge has also argued that a broad standard of good faith would be 'an imperfect translation of an ethical standard into legal ideology and rules. However much it might stimulate research or encourage inquiry into theories underlying contract law, its appropriate home is the university where it can perform these functions without wreaking practical mischief ... Good faith is an invitation to judges to abandon the duty of legally reasoned decisions and to produce an unanalytical incantation of personal values ...' in M. Bridge, 'Does Ango-Canadian Contract Law need a Doctrine of Good Faith?' (1984) 9 Can Bus LJ 385, at 412.

[170] At 368.

[171] *Petromec Inc v. Petroleo Brasiliero SA Petrobas, supra.*

[172] [2000] 2 All E.R. (Comm.) 625. (discussed further in chapter 4) The parties agreed to 'meet promptly and negotiate in good faith'. Lord Woolf M.R. engaged in a careful examination of US authorities and accepted that New York law does recognise a contract to negotiate in good faith as a binding contractual obligation.

[173] At 364-5.

[174] See M. Furmston, T. Norisada & J. Poole, *supra* Introduction fn. 35. Knapp, in advocating continued awards of reliance damages in the US notes however, that 'expressions of commitment, which under the bargain theory could usually be freely repudiated for lack of consideration, [at times] became binding obligations with the doctrinal Krazy Glue of promissory estoppel', see C. Knapp, 'Rescuing Reliance: The Perils of Promissory Estoppel' (1998) 49 Hastings LJ 1191, at 1223.

(commercial) contracts. Yet, a raft of United States' court decisions which have sought to protect pre-contractual bargaining are founded upon an 'implied offer' which is relied upon by the plaintiff. As Brown notes, 'extrapolating from this idea and using conventional contract terminology, it may be possible to evaluate the extent of the parties' resolution and commitment to securing a completed contract'.[175] As negotiations will vary dramatically from exploratory beginnings which remain inchoate to their culmination in a firm offer capable of immediate, unequivocal acceptance, an implied offer may lack sufficient precision to constitute an actual offer but it may induce substantial reliance in the other party that is worthy of protection.

Crucially, this shifts attention away from the representor and his promise, to the extent of reliance by the representee. By invoking the notion of estoppel, Brown argues that the offer or promise need not necessarily be definitive, provided that it provokes the reliance at the outset. As degrees of 'determination and earnestness' will vary in contracts to negotiate, the parties' negotiations may well have reached such an advanced stage that an implied offer exists as a clear manifestation of intent 'such that only minor technicalities or the formal execution of a document are envisaged as preceding the offeree's actual acceptance". A situation that was clearly reached in *Walford* as there was no longer any disputed terms left to agree. Both parties' reliance, it is argued by Brown, will be at its maximum immediately prior to the contract's completion. Perversely, as Buckley observes, it is typically at this point in negotiations when negotiating may be at its most adversarial and antagonistic as the parties endeavour to hammer out the best individual closing deal. If, on these facts, the offeror then fails to proceed there is a clear breach of the contract to negotiate which could rarely be justified on grounds of good faith. Brown submits that "this deployment of reliance achieves the objective mentioned earlier, that is to devise notions of good faith which function in adversarial bargaining and harmonise with the laissez-faire axioms of contract".

Brown correctly identifies that "within the principle of good faith negotiations it is consequently implicit that reasonable reliance has its counterpart in acceptable risk. A plaintiff must establish that he has crossed the threshold of risk to the extent that his reliance upon the defendant's acts or representations is justifiable. Such reasonable reliance is founded upon the defendant's actively encouraging or inciting the plaintiff to embark upon a course of conduct or, more controversially, acquiescing in that conduct. Good faith thus defined utilises the recognisable legal tools of promise, inducement, risk and reliance. Moreover, this analysis accords with a (modified) theory of freedom of contract in that it allows for a consideration of self-reliance. Brown argues that whereas tort law reconfigured could play a similar role, he suggests that good faith 'as an implied term' presents itself as a more appropriate tool that could be 'tied to the particular obligations created by the negotiations, its scope and content thus being more certain. This hypothesis 'shuns an ethereal moral principle prem-

[175] At 365.

ised upon fair dealing or honesty in commercial negotiations for it is the fear and suspicion of vacuous delineations of good faith or unconscionability which lead to their complete rejection. In estoppel, fiduciary obligations and economic duress, for example, English law has shown its ability to proscribe unfairness in commercial dealings. In establishing a duty of good faith in pre-contractual negotiations, its future task must be to take an objectively-defined middle-ground between the polar regimes of indefinable unconscionability and untenable deceit. A scheme for enforcing the subsidiary contract to negotiate may therefore be envisaged'.

First, it must be possible to identify the elements demanded for the formation of the contract, i.e. offer, acceptance, intent and consideration, the parties thereby agreeing to negotiate. Consideration might be an obstacle on certain facts but was clearly present in *Walford* and *Chanell*. Secondly, the parties must be under an obligation to negotiate in good faith, breach of this express or implied term being a breach of the subsidiary contract. For many it is this postulate which renders the proposed scheme impracticable if not impossible. Thirdly, the availability and extent of the damages would be dependent upon the degree to which the negotiations had progressed, i.e. from inception to consummation.[176] Using this analysis, it is arguable that expectation damages compensating the plaintiff for the lost bargain would have been available in *Walford*, but reliance damages would be more applicable in cases where negotiations are aborted at an earlier stage.[177]

7 Concluding remarks

This author shares the minority view of Brown that it is indeed regrettable that the House of Lords saw fit to confirm that a contract to negotiate is 'a thing writ in water' whilst also 'denouncing and censuring good faith in commercial law'.[178] Brown rightly observes that the common law possesses 'sufficient ingenuity to recognise novel claims and adapt settled rules in order to ascertain or imply contractual liability, some recent cases showing a judicial

[176] At 366-7. ('... as negotiation of deals does not fit into the mould of offer and acceptance, but that does not mean that basic contract principles are inadequate to protect the rights of parties if their negotiations fail. By applying those principles ... courts can reach fair resolutions of disputes that arise out of failed negotiations').

[177] Brown's approach would accord more fully with the current US approach, where 'reliance investments will not be recoverable in the absence of a sufficiently clear and definite assent', in Schwartz and Scott, *supra* at 12.

[178] Rather than being resisted, reliance and the fulfillment of reasonable commercial expectation 'play a unifying role in the obligation of good faith thereby aiding its definition'. Yet, see the critique of reasonable expectations and the 'slippery', 'elusive' nature of the concept in C. Mitchell, 'Leading a Life of its Own? The Roles of Reasonable Expectation in Contract Law' (2003) 23 Oxford J Legal Stud 639.

inclination to investigate new avenues of thought'.[179] Gordley has also recently queried whether subsequent English courts will 'consider the possibility that the rest of the world is right and that Lord Ackner was wrong'.[180] In support of that thesis, the clear absence of relevant US caselaw cited in *Walford*, such as the *Tribune* case, arguably gave a slanted view of the position under US – if not, the position under English law since *Hill v. Arcos*. To date, however, the courts have been required to follow *Walford*, merely tweaking the decision at the corners. It is further surprising how little impact the subsequent decision in *Allied Maples Group Limited v. Simmons & Simmons*,[181] has had on wider commercial contracting and interpretation in the courts and particularly in theory. Perhaps, the case has been undervalued as it related to a case in negligence against a solicitor, as opposed to a strictly commercial contract claim. *Allied* sued for the loss of a chance to negotiate a protective clause into a contract, following their solicitor's negligent advice during the drafting process (*Allied* were advised to delete a specific warranty that subsequently proved critical). It was argued and accepted on appeal that *Allied* would merely have to show that there was a substantial chance that it would have been successful in negotiating protection. Importantly, Hobhouse L.J. observed that:

> Where parties are engaged in negotiations on the detailed terms of a commercial deal upon which they are both agreed in principle and from which both are expecting to gain, it is in no way unrealistic to conclude that meaningful negotiations are possible within the framework of the deal when a difficulty of this kind arises ... Negotiations may depend upon the will of the parties and neither party was under any obligation at that stage to agree anything. But it is unrealistic to treat the outcome of further negotiation between commercial parties as arbitrary and wholly unpredictable. Those with experience of commercial negotiation are able, with a reasonable degree of accuracy, to form a view of what can be achieved by such negotiation.

Despite the traditional English insistence on a literal construction of contracts, what is striking within the period of the case cluster is the number of preliminary contract claims that are approached from the perspective of pure contract formation by the courts in all three jurisdictions. As a direct consequence, the overwhelming majority of cases alleging some form of precontractual reliance within the cluster, including both in the US and Spain ultimately failed.

[179] *Supra*, at 367.

[180] Gordley (2005), at 171. Ironically, Lord Ackner's view – though his Lordship was not addressed on the case by counsel – is fully endorsed in the previous US decision in *Feldman v. Allegheny International*, 850 F. 2d 1217 (7th Cir, 1988), at 1223. See also *Candid Products Inc. v. International Skating Union*, 530 F. Supp 1330 (1982), where it was held that 'an agreement to negotiate in good faith is amorphous and nebulous, since it implies so many factors that are themselves indefinite and uncertain that the intent of the parties can only be fathomed by conjecture and surmise', at p. 1336-7.

[181] [1995] 1 W.L.R. 1602.

Most were summarily dismissed on the basis that there had been mere 'tratos preliminaries' or preliminary dealings that failed to crystallise into a binding contract.[182] Recent US court decisions do, however, reveal high uncertainty and strong divergence in the treatment of these incomplete agreements across State lines, particularly as to when parties can safely retreat from negotiations. Yet, the modern willingness in the US to temper the severity of the rules of bargaining based upon offer, acceptance and consideration with ill-defined theories of reliance means that an evaluation of good faith is largely a prerequisite. Macaulay's article in 1991 on *The Reliance Interest and the World Outside the Law schools' Doors*[183] has not been as influential as many of his other contributions but would appear to mark the point of retreat from broad reliance claims in the US courts, particularly following the golden age of reliance from *Red Owl* through to the *Texaco Inc* judgment in the 1980s.

Moreover, the pioneering Californian case of *Copeland* in 2002, far from encouraging debate on the parameters of fair dealing, has resulted in the decision being flagged as a potential pitfall for businesses relying on Californian contract law.[184] Beyond *Copeland*, there is also particular ambiguity as to when a duty to negotiate in good faith may attach in the courts. The case cluster has further revealed a distinct confusion in the caselaw and literature in all three jurisdictions as to when claims should be raised in reliance, estoppel or for breach of good faith in negotiations and the Spanish courts continue to face an equally difficult task determining the doctrinal basis of precontractual claims. That said, the Supreme Court decision of the 16 December 1999 has brought a crucial element of clarity by introducing the four pronged test for determining liability.

---

182 See, *inter alia*, STS decision RJ 2003\8338. To borrow the observation of Kirby P in *Coal Cliff*, the courts will not enforce an agreement that is 'too illusory or too vague and uncertain to be enforceable', *supra*.

183 [1991] Wisc. L. Rev. 247. As Friedman observes the main thrust of modern US law has been in the very opposite direction. Notwithstanding the terminological impact of Fuller and Perdue's article *The Reliance Interest* there 'are no signs of weakening of the performance interest. On the contrary, one of the major trends in modern contract law is the strengthening of the protection accorded to the performance interest. Traditional limitations upon the availability of specific performance and upon the recovery of performance damages have either been removed or severely curtailed. There is a great discrepancy between *The Reliance Interest*'s intellectual appeal and its effect on substantive law. The article has made a deep impact on academic thinking, upon the language and discourse of contracts and led to the adoption of new terminology, which in the case of 'expectation' was an unhappy development. Its effect on substantive law is at best secondary. The attack upon the performance interest goes against the grain. This interest constitutes the very core of contract law. Its ample protection is likely to be maintained and possibly expanded as long as the essence of contract law as we know it remains', at 272.

184 I. Rivin, 'Californian court morphs Unenforceable 'Agreement to agree' into a 'Contract to Negotiate an Agreement' at http://library.findlaw.com/2002/Sep/26/126101.html. (arguing that the safest way to avoid potential liability is to 'set down your intent in an unambiguous written statement). Of course, such an approach is often 'easier said than done' particularly when negotiating with a foreign business partner, perhaps in an unfamiliar environment or via a conference call.

For those intent on fostering greater uniformity at European level in the field of precontractual liability, removing Lord Hoffman's procedural obstacle to evidence of negotiations is arguably a necessary first step. We have pinpointed the advantages of such a rule, yet there can be little doubt that the breadth of its exclusionary nature will on occasion prevent evidence from being heard in court that would illumine the meaning that parties sought to convey, and may further disguise real evidence of bad faith in negotiations. Lord Nicholls has suggested that the courts should now 'recognise that pre-contract negotiations are themselves part of the background of a contract and that, like other background material, they may be relevant when interpreting a contract'.[185] In 2006, the Court of Appeal in *Proforce Recruit Ltd* further lent support to the argument of Lord Nicholls that although the *Investors* principles have been applied or quoted in countless High Court and Court of Appeal cases, the principles are not always consistent with the reasonable expectations of the contractual parties.[186] Though unlikely, the Court of Appeal decision appears susceptible were it to be appealed before a less contextualist court, however, despite the use of the phrase 'subject to contract' and an entire agreement clause, it was decided that the heads of agreement and the parties subsequent conduct was sufficient to bind the parties. Arden LJ, whilst paying lip service to Lord Hoffman's principles, appeared equally supportive of greater flexibility to allow additional evidence of precontractual negotiations, premising her view on the wider international approach.[187]

Arguably, through the careful use of case management, particularly summary judgment as in the US and sanctions in costs, it ought to be possible to maintain sufficient order for the rule to be gradually relaxed.[188] Yet, the monetary sums involved in the cases analysed are equally important. Clearly, the high cost of commercial litigation in England remains a significant obstacle to any relaxation of the rule. That said, as was highlighted above, most successful Spanish claims concerned relatively minor sums that if replicated in the English courts would be disposed of procedurally in one day on the fast track. This study of the law in action reveals not only that the English, Spanish and US legal systems continue to accord parties the maximum freedom to negotiate, but that

[185] In *'My Kingdom for a Horse: The Meaning of Words'* (2005) 121 LQR 577, promoting their inclusion on the grounds of justice (at 586), certainty (at 587), best evidence (at 583), transparency (at 585) and the need to align the law with international practice under the CISG, the UNIDROIT Principles and PECL (at 586)

[186] The Court of Appeal further deciding that the parol evidence rule could be relaxed to allow evidence of precontractual negotiations to be heard in order to flesh out meaning desired by the parties, provided the court did not take into consideration the parties' subjective intent.

[187] At pt. 57. (citing the fact that the CISG and the UNIDROIT Principles (art. 4.3) both rely on pre-contractual negotiations when determining the intentions of the parties. It is perhaps significant that the Court of Appeal made no reference to the Principles of European Contract Law.

[188] A view that is unlikely to win over Berg, who notes that, 'with great respect, the position taken by Lord Nicholls would often make it considerably more difficult and time-consuming for a party to a commercial contract to ascertain his legal position. There are few transactions of substance in which the pre-contractual correspondence consists of just six items' (as in *The Karen Oltmann* case), *supra*, at 366.

the courts appear ill-equipped to deal satisfactorily with reliance based claims flowing from failed negotiations and incomplete agreements. The tools for accessing the merits of individual claims themselves appear heavily outmoded. On both sides of the Atlantic a similar orthodox approach to the question of preliminary agreements endures and under the classic rules of offer/acceptance (consideration), there is no contractual liability until a contract is made. The courts in practice further typically reinforce a classical view of the negotiation phase highlighting the need for 'bargaining freedom'. A reluctance to entertain precontractual reliance claims is not however a sole quirk of the English courts. In practice the courts appear universally unnerved by such claims, which can be seen as very much the exception in all three jurisdictions. Critically, however, as an area of contracting practice preliminary agreements have been hopelessly under-examined by both judges and scholars alike in all three jurisdictions. The lack of enforcement of existing rules on precontractual liability in the US and Spain further betrays a degree of judicial discontent and pinpoints a clear lack of synchronisation between decomposing academic law 'on the books' and the realities of the court room.

Yet, perhaps significantly, it is reasonable commercial expectation[189] that has emerged as the defining element in determining whether liability may attach in Spanish and US case law and doctrinal debate, lending much greater hope for a gradual coming together of civil and common law positions. Whilst good faith in negotiations has been described in Spanish literature as a need to show loyalty during the negotiation phase, in applying the test it has been inextricably linked to the doctrine of reasonable commercial expectation, so favoured by the English commercial court judge. Armed with the law in action in three jurisdictions, in chapter 4 we conclude by delving deeper into a possible reliance-based approach to precontractual liability in a future EC contract law.

---

[189] Or the interests of Lord Nicholls' 'notional reasonable person', *supra* at 583.

CHAPTER 4

A Methodology of Dispute Avoidance

I have no heroic suggestion for the introduction of a general duty of good faith in our contract law. As long as our courts always respect the reasonable expectations of parties our contract law can satisfactorily be left to develop in accordance with its own pragmatic traditions. And where in specific contexts duties of good faith are imposed on parties our legal system can readily accommodate such a well tried notion. After all, there is not a world of difference between the objetive requirement of good faith and the reasonable expectations of the parties.[1]

1 The need for a methodology of dispute avoidance for the Europeanisation of contract law

The preceding chapters have explored and critiqued the convergence thesis in EC contract law, querying the need for a comprehensive uniformity project. Divergence in relation to the treatment of preliminary agreements and precontractual reliance has been presented as one potential arena for increased litigation in the European context. Yet, what presents itself is the need for a new methodology for tackling divergence that looks beyond the delivery of the Common Frame of Reference. Arguably what is required going forward is a methodology of dispute avoidance, a broader strategy aimed at minimising the negative effects of the integration process. This method ought reasonably to prioritise not the law in books but the law in action. It must concentrate therefore on identifying and addressing actual problematic divergences. In chapter 3, we explored the degree of divergence/functional equivalence apparent in the judicial treatment of preliminary agreements and precontractual duties in the English, US and Spanish legal systems. The dominant theoretical approaches in each jurisdiction and their impact in practice were firstly explored, thereafter a specific cluster of recent cases was identified and analysed more concretely. An analysis of this case cluster confirms much of what has just recently been termed the 'myth' of precontractual reliance in US caselaw, a cautious 'intermediate' approach to precontractual liability in Spanish courts based increasingly on the primacy of protecting reasonable commercial expectation, and an entrenched business-oriented conservatism in the UK coming under challenge from a new pragmatism; a pragmatism that may provide a suitable foothold for the introduction of a broad duty of transactional care or of fair dealing in negotiations. In this chapter it is argued that such a move should be resisted.

Importantly, whilst there remains a heavy theorising of liability arising out of improper conduct in negotiations in US and Spanish literature, the court's deliberations and ultimate decision-making revealed strong reluctance to imposing liability, and a complete unwillingness absent a degree of consensus between the parties. Of the cases involving incomplete contracts and/or allega-

1 See Lord Steyn in 'Contract Law: Fulfilling the Reasonable Expectations of Honest Men' (1997) 113 LQR 433, at 439.

tions of foul play during negotiations, the majority failed. Where claims did succeed, the majority involved the very occasional claim for reliance damages. In this chapter we therefore reassess the concept of good faith and fair dealing in relation to commercial negotiations, explore the value of interfering in the bargaining process generally, and consider further the power of contract drafting solutions. Lastly – and as very much a last resort – aware that the power of the drafting pen may be significantly constrained in a multi-lingual market, a consideration is made of the need for a new detrimental reliance doctrine.

2 General commercial bargaining under the strain of precontractual fairness considerations

Contract law on both sides of the Atlantic has been criticised, albeit doctrinally by law and economics scholars rather than by business, for failing to adequately deal with the realities of commercial deal-making, the question of precontractual investment and, in particular, for failing to protect the rights of parties to failed negotiations, particularly those operating from a position of inferiority in terms of information gathering and/or bargaining generally. Yet, even less explored from a comparative perspective is the effect of competing legal regimes on parties' willingness to contract cross-border. As a socio-economic phenomenon, bargaining represents an attempt by competing individuals to achieve limited cooperation and prosper economic opportunities based on the coordination of their private, competing interests in the market. As Bigwood explains, as a legal phenomenon, the law of contract can therefore be seen as an 'imperfect institutional attempt to give jural effect to this instrumental phenomenon'. Bargaining is after all:

> the social and legal machinery appropriate to arranging affairs in any specialised economy ... The truth is that contract law's fundamental purpose is to enable people to achieve their private ends. In order to achieve our ends, our actions must have effects. Contract law gives legal effect to our actions. The enforcement of promises helps people to achieve their private ends by enabling them to rely upon each other and thus to coordinate their actions. An aspect of free society is the power of its citizens to enter into voluntary agreements to accomplish their private ends. Contract law provides a framework for private citizens to set the terms of voluntary association with each other.[2]

Unsurprisingly, therefore, contract law as a discipline has appeared much less concerned with situations where parties fail to 'set the terms of their voluntary association with each other'. Of course we could take issue with this 'voluntari-

[2] See R. Bigwood, *supra* Introduction fn. 23 (who highlights the 'private' aspect of bargaining, given that negotiation is a 'self-directed, free-form process', and notes that parties have little choice but to rely on the 'internal resources of the negotiation itself to assure fairness in dealing'), at 26.

ness' vision of modern contract law presented by Bigwood,[3] but more importantly for present purposes, it is only relatively recently that negotiation failure has impacted on the discipline, particularly in European literature. And, as Farnsworth and Bigwood observe, it is only relatively recently that scholars have turned their attention to the legal and ethical standards that apply to the negotiation process itself.[4] This despite the 'indispensable' position of contract negotiations in law and society.[5] For Bigwood, the bargaining process is itself too fluid and idiosyncractic to be entirely self-regulating. It is a process 'fuelled by the parties' desire for agreement with incentives inhering in the process for parties to capitalise selfishly on the resources (bargaining skills and other advantages) that each possesses relative to the other'. The difficulties that arise are further 'compounded by a lack of articulated limits on the use of such skills and advantages. Doubtless the inconsistencies and indeterminacies that lie between legitimate and illegitimate bargaining behaviour are augmented by factors unique to bargaining. We frequently assume in relation to bargaining that tactical practices, such as deception or pressure are 'all in the game' – that these are 'defining characteristics' of bargaining'. Indeed, Michelman laments the degree to which modern business negotiation is founded on lies and deceit.[6] Yet, as Tallon puts it, the negotiation of a contract is by no means a 'philanthropic exercise' and he stresses the impossibility of adequately defining 'pre-contractual bad faith'.[7] Of course, this diminished interest in bargaining is also partly attributable to the fact that Farnsworth's prediction that judicial willingness to impose reliance damages would gradually increase has not been borne out in practice. Moreover, the lack of helpful caselaw as to the meaning of precontractual bad faith continues to colour our perspective and has real normative implications.

It has been shown that the English legal system, in preference to affirming a general duty to negotiate in good faith is more comfortable sanctioning actual evidence of bad faith, yet in Spain and the US the 'nebulous' character of the pre-contractual bargaining stage greatly complicates the search for suitable default position to govern individual's conduct in commercial negotiations.

3 See, for example, A. Robertson, 'The Limits of Voluntariness in Contract' (2005) 29 Melbourne University Law Review 179 (relying heavily on the previous work of Slawson and Hillman in the US).

4 Farnsworth, *Preliminary Agreements.*

5 See R.P. Buckley, *supra* Ch.2 fn. 130 (noting further that as a means of facilitating private exchange, particularly in common business dealings, there are few practical alternatives to negotiation).

6 J.H. Michelman, 'Deception in Commercial Negotiation' (1983) 2(4) JBE 255. (who paints a particularly bleak image of commercial deal-making).

7 *La negotiation d'un contrat d'affaires n'est pas une enterprise philanthropique. Chacun cherche très normalement à retirer le plus d'avantages pour lui. Et la frontière de la mauvaise foi, de la déloyauté, de l'abus est bien incertaine et dépend de circonstances multiples. Il est impossible d'enfermer dans une définition la bonne foi précontractuelle.* Or as Fried adds, "Negotiation ... is conveniently perceived as a relatively norm-free process centred on the transmutation of underlying bargaining strength into agreement by the exercise of power, horsetrading, threat and bluff" in C. Fried, 'Right and Wrong' (Harvard University Press, 1978) at 107.

As modern business contracts are increasingly multi-party contracts of great complexity, actual negotiations will diverge significantly complicating further the search for appropriate legal rules for even one jurisdiction.[8] Agreements are typically teased out through a gradual refining process, involving perhaps several rounds of discussion and a raft of previous drafts. What is similarly apparent both in US and European market settings is the weakness of the traditional rules on contract formation to do justice to modern business negotiations. This should come as no surprise given their emergence in the discrete contracting age of yesteryear. Nonetheless, the judicial starting point in seeking to regulate incomplete agreements continues invariably to require a search for sufficient evidence of assent. Isolating the exact moment of formation appears increasingly fictitious and the pursuit of evidence that the parties were *ad idem* dominates much court time and resources, particularly in England and Wales. Schwartz and Scott simply attribute much of the current legal ambiguity to the courts lack of familiarity with handling contract incompleteness.

In comparison to European jurisdictions however, US courts have shown much greater awareness of the role of preliminary agreements and the realities behind their drafting. In *Feldman v. Allegheny International*, for instance, the Seventh Circuit acknowledged the degree of commitment, time and expense involved in hammering out complex mergers via preliminary agreements reinforced with duties to act and negotiate in good faith:

> A complex business transaction such as the purchase of five companies requires a significant expenditure of time, effort, research and finances simply to arrive at its terms. The books of the companies must be carefully reviewed, difficult judgments of valuation must be made, financing must be secured, new corporations may have to be formed, and various timing and risk allocation issues must be spelled out in detail in the purchase and sale contract, obviously incurring substantial legal fees. Depending upon the specifics of the deal, other professional services such as accounting and financing may have to be commissioned as well. Together, all these costs in executing a complex transaction may consume more than a trivial portion of the benefit the parties hope to realize. This cost may be too high if it need be borne without some assurance that it will culminate in a sale.[9]

Of course, judicial exploration for evidence of binding assent at times appears highly inefficient and it is not always guaranteed that a troublesome analysis of the parties' prior bargaining strategies will provide any greater clarity or guidance on how best to meet the parties 'legitimate' or 'reasonable' expecta-

[8] Gulliver emphasises the strategic nature of negotiation and interaction, and the range of different bargaining techniques aimed at working toward negotiated agreement (techniques, he argues, that are not easily captured by a single normative rule). See P.H. Gulliver, *Disputes and Negotiations* (Academic Press, 1979) at 5 (Reviewed by A. Paterson (1982) 45(3) MLR 360).

[9] *Supra* at 1221.

tions. As has been evidenced, the higher and lower courts in Spain commonly reach entirely different conclusions examining the very same facts. As such, the current English procedural rule excluding prior negotiations appears tempting on the grounds of both legal certainty (all parties to contracts under English law, domestic and foreign, are aware that their preliminary dealings will not be scrutinised should a dispute proceed to trial) and efficiency (again for the same reason). Under a future Optional Instrument or agreed European contract law, a procedural rule that excluded evidence of precontractual negotiations on policy grounds, whilst allowing specific exceptions (such as where the parties appear to have contractually agreed to negotiate in good faith, etc) should not therefore be readily dismissed. Evidently, to gain a satisfactory entrenchment for such a rule it would be necessary to go further in explaining the basis of such a policy decision, a step that the English commercial courts have thus far considered unnecessary to take.

That said, the majority US law and economics scholarship examined in this study suggests that the current English rule is helpless to prevent opportunistic and unconscionable conduct in the precontractual phase. The US-led theory is certainly strongly supported by English decisions in cases such as *Sykes v. Taylor Rose*. Whilst Norton[10] has argued that a functionalist approach to bargaining is satisfactory, as negotiation *inter partes* produces an internal 'process driven' ethic that is minimal but nevertheless satisfactory – a largely adversarial view that finds comfort in Buckley's contribution and the work of Scott[11] – Collins and Bigwood go further. Both appear to be on the same page in calling for a general duty of transactional or negotiating care. Bigwood accepts the fact that the law in this field is relatively modest as legal rules 'do not aspire to generate the sort of virtuous behaviour describable as "high quality compliance with norms". The law's ethic is more appropriately one of responsibility; an "ethic of obligation, not aspiration"; of "acceptable behaviour, not virtuous or supererogatory behaviour".[12]

---

[10] Judicial decisions have typically considered negotiation as a 'process of mutual discussion and bargaining, involving putting forward and debating proposal and counter-proposal, conceding, persuading, threatening, all with the objective of reaching what will probably be a compromise that the parties are able to accept and live with' per Hardie Boys J in *Capital Coast Health v. NZ Medical Laboratory Workers Union Inc* [1995] 2 ERNZ 305, at 320 and as 'a bargaining process, with give and take, and with stress upon and use of the strengths of one's own position and the weaknesses of the position of the other party ... it is pure bargaining ..." in *Renegotiation Board v. Bannercraft Clothing Co. Inc*, 415 US 1 [1974], 21-2.

[11] See in particular, R.E. Scott, 'A Theory of Self-Enforcing Indefinite Agreements' (2003) 102 Colum. L. Rev. Available via SSRN. (Scott highlighting the dangers of coercive external mechanisms or rules aimed at inducing compliance with contractual commitments and querying why individuals continue to write deliberately incomplete bargains 'in the shadow of a robust indefinitiveness doctrine [in the US courts]'.)

[12] *Supra* at 28.

It is also true that this traditional vision at times gives an unduly inflexible overview of the English law of contract in particular. Without doubt the courts in England and Wales have placed primary emphasis on the need for certainty and have felt much more comfortable approaching negotiations via specific remedial categories, such as *quantum meruit*, estoppel, the recognition of collateral warranties, and above all misrepresentation. The insistence on security of transactions has led the courts to presume that the parties can only intend to leave the risk period when they have expressed themselves with sufficient certainty so that their contract can be enforced by a court. As such, the courts look for a "concluded bargain ... which settles everything that is necessary and leaves nothing to be settled by the parties".[13] The use of entire agreement clauses and non-reliance clauses has further provided a typically English drafting solution to an otherwise problematic arena. Yet, the courts have also revealed an appreciation that 'business men often record the most important agreements in crude and summary fashion' and that 'it is accordingly the duty of the court to construe such documents fairly and broadly without being too astute or subtle in finding defects'.[14]

Such a high standard, if implemented strictly, would defeat the regulatory function of contract law in failing to provide a structure for agreements which the parties intended to be binding, but chose not to elaborate in detail due to time and expense constraints.[15] What is abundantly clear, however, is the fact that the stringent tests and rather cumbersome categorisations applied under English law to precontractual scenarios do grossly inflate the complexity of the law in this area, lending theoretical weight to the case for a more generalised duty, or more appropriately a coherent doctrine. Of course, English law is not alone as evidenced by the growing concerns expressed in US and Spanish legal opinion as to the prevailing theoretical disorder. The need to 'relocate' precontractual liability claims from somewhere between the shadowlands of contract and tort and to ensure that they occupy a satisfactory place in the wider law of obligations is a universal challenge. Echebarría Sáenz has discussed the need for a 'tertium genus' or third legal doctrine between contractual and extra-contractual liability to better explain and rationalise judicial interference in bargain-

13 Per Viscount Dunedin in *May & Butcher v. R* [1934] 2 KB 17, at p. 21.

14 The courts may therefore construe a contract to implement the parties' intentions, provided they do not go so far as to construct the agreement for them. See G.H. Fridman, 'Construing, without constructing, a contract' (1960) 76 LQR 521.

15 Cf. Collins (2003), who argues that by setting a high standard of certainty for finalised contracts, in such a way as to exclude most informal agreements, particularly during the negotiation stage, it may still be possible via a generalised duty to encourage and afford greater protection to legitimate expectation. Requiring parties to agree terms with sufficient clarity and precision that they may be enforced by courts need not be sacrificed by a sufficiently coherent duty. (at 329 et seq). Indeed, as noted previously, the case cluster did reveal an equally high concern in the US and Spain to ensure legal certainty, and the courts will not support an agreement expressed in vague terms.

ing;[16] and particularly illustrative of this concern is the recent doctrinal 'handbags' between Randy E. Barnett and Charles Knapp over the reliance interest in the US, and the use and abuse of promissory estoppel under section 90.

Knapp suggests that those of Barnett's persuasion are simply 'academic Felix Ungers', whose 'compulsive [doctrinal] tidiness' and desire for 'doctrinal purity' and 'neat ordering' effectively blinds their vision to the 'uses to which lawyering Oscar Madisons of the real world may put such doctrines (i.e. section 90) [in practice]'.[17] However, Barnett has since retaliated by warning that there is a danger for private litigants if the 'loaded gun' of section 90 is left 'lying casually around for some judicial Oscar Madison to pick up and misuse'.[18] Barnett is correct of course in highlighting the need for doctrinal clarity and consistency, particularly in removing the question of reliance from the necessary contract/ tort divide – a distinction that as Barnett observes remains critical. Whilst Grant Gilmore was a a lousy fortune-teller and the doctrinal wall that separates contract from tort law in the US has not collapsed, it has been dented nonetheless. Barnett is right not to be indifferent about the distinction (a distinction that seeks to preserve the doctrine of freedom of contract) for it is not merely a question energising doctrinal nutcases and that smacks of a 'first-year-law-school mentality'.[19] What is odd, however, is that Barnett has rather uncritically largely passed over Holmes observation that promissory estoppel is an equitable form of relief that 'sits on its own bottom'.

---

[16] *El contrato de franquicia* (McGraw-Hill, 1995) at 226 et seq (who is also critical of the dependence in Spanish legal theory on the 'breadth' and 'vagueness' of the good faith doctrine in trying to regulating precontractual 'information', 'loyalty' and 'protective' duties, at 224).

[17] C. Knapp, 'Rescuing Reliance', *supra* at 1244. (Knapp, in particular, is unenthused by the contract/tort debate in relation to promissory estoppel. He suggests that 'people make promises, people break promises, other people get hurt. Is this tort? Is this contract? As Karl Llewellyn once pungently remarked, 'what the hell'').

[18] R.E. Barnett, 'W(h)ither the Reliance Interest?' (2001) 38 San Diego Law Review 1. And see previously R.E. Barnett, 'The Death of Reliance' (1996) 46 J of Leg Ed 518. Importantly, the impact of reliance concerns on legal taxonomies has been more widely addressed in the US than in Europe. See, *inter alia*, R. Cooter, 'Unity in Tort, Contract, and Property: The Model of Precaution' (1985) 73 Cal L Rev 1, 11-16; R. Craswell, 'Offer, Acceptance, and Efficient Reliance' (1996) 48 Stan L Rev 481, 489-94. S. Shavell, 'Damage Measures for Breach of Contract' (1980) 11 Bell J of Econ 466. Of course, Friedmann rejects much of the terminology used in relation to reliance claims and is praiseworthy of the English approach ("In American legal literature the use of the unfortunate term 'expectation' interest persists. However, in other jurisdictions there are some signs that the more appropriate terminology, that speaks of the 'performance interest' is gaining ground"). See D. Friedmann, 'A Comment on Fuller and Perdue, the Reliance Interest in Contract Damages' (2001) 3 Issues in Legal Scholarship (available via bepress.com).

[19] C. Knapp, *supra*, at 1244. (perhaps because Barnett seeks to locate the promissory estoppel doctrine within both contract and tort, with contract absorbing much of the load. Indeed Barnett argues that 'while reliance remains a fundamental principle or end of contract law ... it is consent to be legally bound that provides the essential means to the end of protecting the right to rely on the commitments of others and to other vital ends as well', *supra* at 12.

As is discussed below, this author favours Holmes' analysis; an analysis that has gained most ground in the Australian courts and that appears to provide a more satisfactory and less problematic basis for justifying reliance claims in the wider law of obligations.[20] Whilst the Australian law of estoppel has undergone a wholesale – if still incomplete – transformation, this new direction has not been assimilated, let alone adequately analysed by English contract lawyers nor in the literature. In part, the complexity of the doctrine and its rather confused application in relation to contract bargains means that it is not easily covered within standard works on either contract, equity or property law. Instead fractures of the doctrine appear and are treated rather loosely and haphazardly.

What the Australian development exposes is that Knapp's entertaining, if rather lame academic cheap-shots are plainly wrong, and Barnett is right to worry about the correct location of reliance claims, simply because the terminology and taxonomy questions have proved just as problematic, if not more so, in practice than arriving at a satisfactory justification for the instrumentalist goal of protecting reliance. Johnston has argued that in the US, the common law rules regarding contract formation are 'so formalistic that parties will often reasonably rely on a promise and yet not receive any remedy at all because they relied before a contract had been legally created'. He suggests that this is 'the problem addressed by the doctrine of promissory estoppel and section 90 of the Restatement'.[21] Certainly this is the problem that the rule seeks to address – it just does so in a problematic manner, given the sheer breadth of section 90 and its poor drafting.[22] Yet Johnston's argument holds, the aim of the courts is essentially to protect detrimental reliance.

The use of estoppel to explain the basis of recovery for precontractual reliance has been considered previously,[23] but it would still face a number of obstacles in a European context, even under current English law. Whilst McFar-

[20] E. Holmes, 'The Four Phases of Promissory Estoppel' (1996) 20 Seattle University Law Review 45. What is notable in the last decade of debate in the US is that, bar the work of Farnsworth and Knapp, discussion of reliance and promissory estoppel has typically occurred outside of the leading journals. It is only relatively recently, and mainly via law and economics scholarship, that the arguments are returning to the contract mainstream.

[21] *Supra*, at 399.

[22] Linzer who was tasked with preparing much of the Commentary on Section 90 has recently revealed that he based his observations almost exclusively on the 'fact-specific' *Hoffman* case and realises today that the case had less to do with reliance on a promise than 'reliance on a relationship', a bargaining relationship that simply progressively unravelled over time, see P. Linzer, 'Rough Justice: A Theory of Restitution and Reliance, Contracts and Torts' (2001) 695 Wisc L Rev 702, at 719. Hindsight is a wonderful thing but as Gardner warns, 'analysing relationship breakdowns in terms of fault is at best a tasteless, and generally inept, undertaking', see S. Gardner, 'The Remedial Discretion in Proprietary Estoppel – Again' (2006) 122 LQR 492, at 496.

[23] See G. Jones, *Goff & Jones: The Law of Restitution* (5th edn, Sweet & Maxwell, 1998) (promoting equitable estoppel as the basis for a restitutionary claim and noting that 'The restitutionary claim conceals a claim for reliance loss, where no claim for damages for breach of contract can lie'), at 673.

lane, relying heavily on US and Australian doctrine, has recently advocated the protection of precontractual reliance under English law via a proprietary estoppel doctrine, such a welcome reforming attitude does still appear somewhat shortsighted in the context of European integration.[24] The promotion of a European-wide estoppel remedy, whether promissory as in the US or equitable as in Australia, would give rise to adjustment problems for all European jurisdictions. Moreover, as a newly emergent doctrine that remains 'in a state of flux',[25] the scope of the equitable estoppel doctrine in Australian law is itself unsettled and remains still very much contested. Yet, even the term 'estoppel' itself would not transplant easily beyond common law systems, and it would be unwise to inflict on non-common lawyers in the Union the same discomfort with the meaning and applicability of good faith and fair-dealing that arises in common law circles – even if an estoppel approach could win support on the grounds that it is transnational in spirit. Being rooted in equity, estoppel does have the added advantage that it conjures up similar equitable concerns to those raised in civil law systems via good faith. Indeed, Hesselink has encouraged the view that the 'content' of present day good faith 'could be regarded as a new *ius honorarium* or as civil law's equity'.[26]

By contrast, the primary advantage offered by a new European detrimental reliance doctrine would be that it would be terminology-neutral and could perhaps be better tailored (through competent drafting and application) in order to be much tighter in its scope than the open-ended notions of both good faith and fair dealing and estoppel, doctrines that have been further weakened both by complexity and over-usage.[27] In this chapter, the aim is therefore to look beyond the current resistance to precontractual reliance theories in England and Wales, and the empty policy arguments preventing scrutiny of evidence of precontractual negotiations, to sketch the parameters of a modern European detrimental reliance doctrine firmly rooted in broader notions of good faith and fair dealing. A doctrine that would aim to avoid in its application the 'doctrinal Krazy Glue' (of promissory estoppel) as operated previously in the US, and that would build on recent Australian experience with equitable estoppel. The aim here is not to supply a detrimental reliance theory for future European contract law, much less reveal its likely application. Rather, the aim is to discuss the

---

24 B. McFarlane, *The Problem of Pre-Contractual Reliance: Three Ways to a Third Way*, Global Fellows Forum, October 2006. Available via http://www.nyulawglobal.org/fellowsscholars/.

25 Per P. Kirby in *PS Chellaram & Co. Ltd v. China Ocean Shipping Co Ltd* (1991) 1 Lloyd's Rep 493, at p. 502.

26 See M.W. Hesselink, 'The Concept of Good Faith' in *Towards 2004*, at 493. Though a little dated, Hesselink cites Maitland on equity (1949) in suggesting that common lawyers: '... ought to think of equity as a supplementary law ... you ought to take the many equitable modifications of the law of contract, not as part of equity, but as a part, and a very important part, of our modern English law of contract', at 21.

27 As is discussed further below, the term 'estoppel' has always been the source of much confusion even in English law, and would arguably be a recipe for disaster if transplanted into such a contentious area of European private law.

need for such a doctrine, to explore its likely contours and discuss some of the primary challenges such a doctrine would face through an observance of recent international experience.[28]

Applying a similar world-view to Johnson, the aim of such a doctrine should be "merely" to validate limited incursion into private bargaining, principally in order to restore reliance expenditure to A in situations where A has acted to his detriment on a reasonably held belief or view, inspired by or attributable to B, that a contract would materialise. That detriment, as Pratt observes, consists 'in the costs incurred by the reliant party that are rendered ineffectual by the desertion of the assumption that led to the reliance'.[29] In support of McFarlane's view, in the absence of a contract, B would thus become liable to compensate A for the detriment he suffers in the absence of the contract. In late 2006, McFarlane argued that English law, '... in the doctrine of proprietary estoppel ... possesses a tool uniquely well-qualified to deal with the problem of pre-contractual reliance'.[30] He identifies the three primary problems caused by the current English law approach as 'coverage' (the law may fail to provide a claim to deserving parties), clarity (results lack transparency and predictability) and 'coherence'. We will discuss below the reasons why McFarlane plumps for a proprietary estoppel approach for English law as opposed to say, a detrimental reliance doctrine – an approach that is unconvincing and terminologically awkward in the context of emerging European contract law.

First, estoppel has traditionally been divided into a number of different forms, each with their own particular rules.[31] Proprietary estoppel for example applies only to the acquisition of an interest in land, estoppel by representation to statements of existing fact and estoppel by convention to a shared assumption of existing fact. In relation to negotiations, the most relevant form of estoppel is promissory estoppel, however, it does not provide a cause of action.[32] Building on the approach adopted by the Australian courts, Spence[33] has put forward a more

[28] Linzer appears to be gripped by the same dilemma. He notes that 'after fifteen or twenty years of looking at the borderlands of tort, contract and property, hope continues to spring eternal in my breast that I can make some sense out of the chaos of obligations at the margin', in P. Linzer, 'Rough Justice: A Theory of Restitution and Reliance, Contracts and Torts' (2001) Wisc L Rev 695, at 697.

[29] M.G. Pratt, 'Equitable Estoppel: Defining the Detriment – A Reply to Denis Ong' (2000) 12(1) Bond Law Review 48.

[30] *Supra*, at 2.

[31] There are divisions between common and equitable estoppel, between estoppel by conduct and estoppel by representation. Estoppel remedies are further subdivided into promissory, proprietary and estoppel by acquiescence. See A.K. Turner, *Spencer Bower & Turner: The Law Relating to Estoppel by Representation* (3rd edn, Butterworths, 2003) and S. Wilken & T. Villers, *Waiver, Variation and Estoppel* (Wiley, 1998).

[32] The term first emerged in the US and Williston's *The Law of Contracts* (1st ed, 1920) para 139.

[33] M. Spence, 'Protecting Reliance: The Emergent Doctrine of Equitable Estoppel' (Hart Publishing, 1999). Other Australian reliance theorists include, A. Robertson, 'Towards a Unifying Purpose for Estoppel' (1996) 22 Monash University Law Review 1; A. Beech, 'The Remedy for Estoppel: Identifying and Preventing Detriment' in R. Carrol (ed), *Civil Remedies: Issues and Developments* (Federation Press,

coherent conscience-based 'equitable' estoppel doctrine that is worthy of strong support and may offer the piece in the puzzle that European law requires in the area of precontractual liability. Spence's reliance doctrine is based on primary and secondary duties but can be reduced to the 'simple' premise that one is under an obligation to keep one's promises and a linked duty to prevent harm resulting from reliance on one's own words or conduct. This has largely sufficed as the intellectual foundation for promissory estoppel in the US and Spence suggests that modern contract law essentially ensures and protects promise-keeping.[34] What distinguishes equitable estoppel from other doctrines such as tort is the duty not to act in such an inconsistent manner as to cause harm. The primary advantage of Spence's equitable doctrine rests, however, with the fact that as a unified doctrine of common law and equity, equitable estoppel could act not just as a defence but as a cause of action.[35] In relation to contracts, Spence would limit recovery to strictly reliance based claims, the minimum necessary to do justice and recovery of expectation damages would only be possible as a very last resort. Limiting recovery to pure reliance damages should prevent a potentially blunt and imprecise instrument doing a lot of random damage to contract law. Indeed, Spence identifies four reasons why estoppel would not act as a rival, but rather a complement to contract. Firstly, whilst contract is founded on promise-keeping, estoppel is concerned with the protection of induced assumptions; secondly, the aim of contract law is to uphold bargains whereas the goal of estoppel is to protect reliance. Thirdly, contract remedies arise by virtue of the agreed contract whilst estoppel is a purely discretionary remedy. Fourthly, Spence argues that liability in estoppel can be circumvented by the parties by warning against reliance.[36]

1996). Critics of the reliance approach and advocates of a counterweight 'expectation' theory underlying new equitable estoppel, include D. Ong, 'Equitable Estoppel: Defining the Detriment' (1999) 11 Bond Law Review 136 and M.G. Pratt, 'Identifying the Harm Done: A Critique of the Reliance Theory of Estoppel' (1999) 21 Adelaide Law Review 209. Though the Australian doctrine of equitable estoppel remains in its infancy, the expectation theorists not surprisingly appear very much in the minority.

34 Gordley takes a similar view, however see the work of Smith on the weakness of pure promise theory and its inability to explain the entirety of contract law in S. Smith, *Contract Theory* (Oxford Clarendon Series, 2004).

35 It is important to bear in mind that the distinction between common law and equitable estoppel endures in Australia. Under Spence's proposal, however, the doctrine would act as a 'sword' aswell as a 'shield'. As such, there would not be a need to establish any kind of pre-existing relationship between the parties (clearly crucial for precontractual claims) and it would be sufficient for the party to prove detrimental reliance on an induced assumption. See however the decision in *Mobil Oil Australia Ltd v. Wellcome International Pty Ltd* (1989) 16 NSWLR 582, decided shortly after Spence's work was published that suggests that a 'particular legal relationship' or 'interest' between the parties is required in order to create potential estoppel relief.

36 At the heart of Spence's equitable estoppel doctrine is the notion of unconscionability, as it would only become relevant in situations where it would be unconscionable to allow a party inducing reliance to resile from that induced assumption without remedying the detriment caused, see Spence, *supra*, at 55

Spence further provides a loose type of checklist for regulating bargains via estoppel. He articulates eight different factors that a court would consider. He suggests that the more active and forthright a party is in inducing an assumption, whether by words or conduct, the more inclined a court should be to award relief. The parties' relationship, the content of the words or conduct used to induce an assumption, and the actual knowledge of the parties (i.e. awareness of the likelihood that there would be reliance) will also be critical. A court would also consider what the party inducing reliance had to gain from that reliance and whether the parties had any previous (business) relationship (i.e. again with the view to finding reliance more readily where the parties have been engaged in a long-term business relationship. In addition, Spence suggests that the parties bargaining strengths relative to one another would also be relevant (the implication being that parties of weaker bargaining power would be more likely to find themselves in a reliant position) as would evidence that a party inducing reliance had taken steps to avoid or dimininish reliance on his words or conduct.[37]

2.1 Fair dealing and the elusiveness of satisfactory meaning?

Of course, before getting to estoppel, the first obstacle with a detrimental reliance doctrine resting on broader European notions of good faith and fair dealing lies with what we mean by the 'broader notions of good faith and fair-dealing' itself. Most scholarly contributions discussing the meaning of the *"principio-norma"* in the context of arms length contract negotiations have been modest in their contributions.[38] Scholars appear to have been more concerned with the imposition of the duty than its actual content; with Cardozo's mere 'instinct' for an obligation left to stalk the bargaining stage.[39]

The dominant view in the US that a general duty of good faith and fair dealing applicable throughout negotiations is unnecessary does make sense. It further finds support in Spain in the recent work of Echebarría Sáenz, who similarly sees much greater value in an *ex-post* reliance doctrine.[40] Posner's reticence toward the 'chameleonic' character of the doctrine of good faith in

[37] In contrast to Robertson who adopts four basic elements to his own estoppel doctrine: assumption, inducement, detrimental reliance and reasonableness, Spence aims to put flesh on the notion of reasonableness. See further, A. Robertson, 'Knowledge and Unconscionability in a Unified Estoppel' (1998) 24 Monash University Law Review 115.

[38] Indeed, Hoch has further queried whether the concept of fair-dealing is not in reality redundant when tacked on to the doctrine of good faith, see M. Hoch, 'Is Fair Dealing a Workable Concept for European Contract Law' (2005) 5 Global Jurist Topics 1(2). She suggests that it may well have entered the contract mainstream at the time of the Unfair Terms Directive 1993 as a simple sop to English lawyers.

[39] 'A promise may be lacking, and yet the whole writing may be instinct with an obligation, imperfectly expressed', per Cardozo J in *Wood v. Lucy, Lady Duff-Gordon*, 222 NY 88, 118 N.E. 214 (1917).

[40] Though as is noted, in bringing forward a detrimental reliance doctrine, the key question is whether it should aim to sanction unjust conduct or merely protect reliance. As is noted the Spanish civil law has been more concerned with sanctioning injustice ('la injusticia del resultado generado por el ejercicio de

Empire Gas Corp v. Am. Bakeries Co.[41] has further weakened its reception into the 'nebulous' area of pre-contractual bargaining. Fisher and Ury observe that it is 'often hard to decide what it means to negotiate in good faith' and that 'people will draw the line in different places'.[42] In regulating negotiations generally it has been observed that 'probably in few other instances is the task of judging so difficult'.[43] Bigwood presents an equally cryptic sliding scale of fairness, that would have virtually no utility in practice. Mirroring an approach favoured by the English judiciary, Summers gives specific instances of bad faith, a number of which involve negotiations but does not go beyond a discussion of the established category of 'negotiating without serious intent to contract' and a commentary on the notion of 'abusing the privilege to break off negotiations' that is largely confined to a discussion of the *Red Owl* decision.[44] Burton, in discussing good faith performance, urges a general test whereby good faith would be limited to the exercise of discretion to recapture opportunities foregone at the formation of the contract, but he does not attempt to apply his analysis to contract negotiations.[45]

Knapp offers a more workable standard of fair dealing in negotiation, one under which 'neither can withdraw for an *unjustified* reason, and yet ... neither will be compelled to perform if – after good faith bargaining – actual agreement cannot be reached'.[46] Bad faith bargaining may consist of 'an insistence on terms so clearly unreasonable that they could not have been advanced' with any real expectation of acceptance, coupled with some 'demonstrable advantage to be

---

un derecho, la puesta en peligro de intereses o bienes jurídicos ajenos por la conducta ... en el iter formativo del contracto', at p. 240).

41 840 F. 2d. 1333 (1957).

42 Quoted by Bigwood in *Exploitative Contracts, supra,* at 27. Indeed, good faith and fair dealing are much like the doctrine of estoppel in one sense: in the words of Denning, there are 'few doctrines ... at once so potentially fruitful and so practically unsatisfying. It is more often cited than applied and more often applied than understood' in *Central London Property Trust Ltd v. High Trees House Ltd* (1947) 63 LQR 283, at p. 296.

43 *NLRB v. Herman Sausage Co.*, 275 F2d 229, 231 (5th Cir. 1960).

44 R. Summers, 'The General Duty of Good Faith – Its Recognition and Conceptualization' (1981/2) 67 Cornell LR 810.

45 S. Burton, 'Breach of Contract and the Common law Duty to Perform in Good Faith' (1980) 94 Harv. L. Rev 369.

46 C. Knapp, 'Enforcing the Contract to Bargain' (1969) 44 NYU L Rev 673. Knapp's theory has received previous judicial support. For in the context of ordinary contract negotiations, it has been held that imposing improper conditions can amount to a failure to negotiate fairly. The Seventh Circuit held it bad faith for a distributor of asphalt, negotiating a new contract with a producer, to condition its willingness to continue negotiating on the producer's assent to an illegal price-fixing provision. The breach of a duty to negotiate can also be made out if one party refuses to negotiate except on conditions that it cannot properly impose. Moreover, 'a statement of intention to perform except on conditions which go beyond the contract' amounts to a repudiation of the contract.

gained by avoiding the contemplated transaction'.[47] Determining the content of the duty of fair dealing under a particular agreement involves, as does determining the content of any contract duty, an inquiry into the expectations of the parties. In making this inquiry a court must look to the language of the agreement and to the surrounding circumstances.

The term most commonly used to describe the duty of fair dealing is 'good faith', but parties sometimes use the term 'best efforts' instead of or in addition to 'good faith'. Interestingly, Farnsworth suggests that the term 'best' or 'reasonable' efforts is generally understood in US contract law to describe a heavier burden than good faith, and prefers the terminology of fair dealing.[48] It is doubtful that the parties, where they do employ either term, use the terms in truly different senses. Although many agreements to negotiate in good faith say little about the content of the duty, by thoughtful drafting the parties can easily establish whether the negotiations are to be exclusive, can fix their time period, can determine what information must be disclosed, and what must be held in confidence. Intriguingly, despite Farnsworth's promotion of fair dealing in negotiations, he notes that, 'given the uncertain state of the law on such matters, no drafter should leave them to a court'.[49]

Evidently, as Poole, Furmston and Norisada observe, fair dealing has one meaning where negotiations have resulted in an agreement and an aggrieved party seeks to avoid that agreement for unfairness. Here the claim of unfairness goes to the means used to induce agreement, bringing in notions of fraud and duress. Fair dealing has an altogether different meaning where negotiations have failed to result in an agreement. The courts in England and Wales have paid scant attention to the meaning of fair-dealing in this context, but as in cases such as *AC Controls* have been more than adept at awarding damages under the *quantum meruit* doctrine for losses incurred under a deal that ultimately fails to materialise.[50] Even though, as McFarlane similarly notes, the basis and scope of such claims are far from clear-cut.[51] Again, Brown is the most helpful in isolat-

---

47 At 684-5.

48 Though the Uniform Commercial Code (UCC, section 2-103) and the Restatement (Second) on Contracts (section 205) now couple fair dealing and good faith, Farnsworth uses the term fair dealing in preference to good faith when considering contracting parties' duties during negotiations. He suggests that good faith denotes 'the sort of honesty that makes one a good faith purchaser, a reference quite different from the one intended in relation to the bargaining process', *Preliminary Agreements 1987*, at 1191.

49 *Supra* (2002), at 265.

50 In the wrongly decided US decision in *Itek Corporation v. Chicago Ariel Industry*, 248 A.2d 625 (Del 1986), for instance, the meaning of good faith in negotiations was simply avoided by the Supreme Court of Delaware.

51 The ambiguous nature of the *quantum meruit* doctrine has been discussed previously. McFarlane further cites the overly-complicated decision in *Brewer Street Investments Ltd v. Barclays Woolen Co. Ltd* [1954] 1 QB 428 in support, and notes how the doctrine has become intertwined with notions of unjust enrichment. Importantly, he further argues forcibly that such an approach should be abandoned in line

ing the parameters of fair dealing. He notes that among the most important of the surrounding circumstances [in any contract] are the 'behaviour of the parties up to the time of agreement and the state of the negotiations at that point. From these, reliable inferences may be drawn to supplement the language of the agreement ... Expectations generally build over time, so that the more advanced the negotiations, the more difficult it will be to justify a withdrawal. The previous relationship between the parties may also be important. If the parties have dealt with each other on other occasions, the pattern of those negotiations may help to establish an expectation'.[52]

2.2 Protecting the reliance interest and alternatives to general clauses – A contractual solution to precontractual investment?

Of course, Brown's reasonable expectation approach would still delegate enormous discretion to the courts, and those who retreat from fair dealing on the ground that 'generalised clauses' promising 'generalised cooperation' offer little by way of certainty either for commercial actors or the courts, have sought to promote alternative contract-based solutions. General clauses are seen as impractical because of a 'general tendency to disbelieve general pledges of cooperation'.[53] If the problem in precontractual settings cannot properly be resolved via the concept(s) of good faith of fair dealing, another alternative is for the parties to subdivide the various performance steps necessary to arrive at a final agreement into discrete sub-bargains. Again, there would be cost and time considerations that may weaken the creation of detailed express sub-bargains for each phase of performance. Such an approach may also threaten in a sense the parties' business relationship as founded upon trust and co-operation. Moreover, Macaulay has noted how businessmen tend only to reach for an agreed contract when a problem arises, rather than faithfully carrying out a venture according to the express terms of their deal.[54]

---

with the newly promoted US position under s.23 Restatement (Third) of Restitution and Unjust Enrichment (Tentative Draft) 2001. (see comment C: Anticipation of Contract: '.... Although such a claim may be framed in the language of unjust enrichment, the decisive issues in determining liability involve contract or tort, not restitution').

52 Brown, *supra*, at 376.

53 See J.P. Kostritsky, 'Bargaining with Uncertainty: Moral Hazard & Sunk Costs – A Default Rule for Precontractual Negotiations' (1993) 44 Hastings LJ 621 (Kostritsky observes in precontractual negotiations, 'the promisee faces the prospect that the promisor will act opportunistically by exploiting sunk costs that the promise invests on advice and perhaps at the request of the promisor), at 626. See also J.P. Kostritsky, 'A New Theory of Assent-Based Liability Emerging Under the Guise of Promissory Estoppel: An Explanation and Defence' (1987) 33 Wayne L Rev 895.

54 See S. Macaulay, 'Long-Term Continuing Relations: The American Experience Regulating Dealerships and Franchises' in C. Joerges (ed), Franchising and the Law: Theoretical and Comparative Approaches in Europe and the United States (Nomos Verlagsgesellschaft, 1991) at 179 *et seq*.

However, in a similar vein to the sub-bargain approach, Kostritsky sees mileage in a contractual vision that would minimise judicial involvement, though she further suggests that a law-supplied rule would likely prove the most efficacious and cost-effective solution to the opportunistic problem.[55] In Kostritsky's view, a default rule would be more efficient than private agreements and private sanctions as these would have to be individually negotiated, and such a rule would moreover provide greater universal legal certainty by extension. She further notes the role of section 45 of the Restatement (Second) of Contracts, by which the law in effect implies a term of irrevocability for part performance of a unilateral contract. In like manner, she seeks to justify judicial intervention in negotiations that allows the courts to supply terms (such as promises of irrevocability) or to impose liability for opportunistic behaviour in negotiations. Acknowledging that such interventionism would impose limits on the parties' freedom to contract, she suggests that it is possible to look at such 'incursions' as efforts by courts to increase parties' joint gains by serving the instrumental goal of controlling opportunism when other methods remain more costly.

Kostritsky argues that neo-formalists have taken an unduly restrictive approach in determining whether law-supplied terms or liability rules can be justified. She favours a new methodology that adopts an instrumentalist approach to legal intervention that centres on the ability of a default rule to maximise joint surplus, control one-party individualism/opportunism, provide incentives to continue a contractual bargain and that promotes continued investment in negotiations. A court would consider the following factors:

1) whether there are informational structures in place for disseminating information;
2) whether there are already sunk costs in place, which help to provide non-legal sanctions;
3) whether the context involves a homogeneous community that can effectively disseminate reputational information;
4) whether the parties have in fact opted out of legal sanctions by structuring their transaction to avoid a legal commitment.

[55] Kostritsky defines opportunism as allowing one party to part perform and 'having the other side change the complexion of the deal – either by revoking the original, by offering much less favourable terms or by seeking an alternative contracting partner'. Certainly, the English law has had no problem awarding *quantum meruit* claims, where one party part performs, as evidenced by the *AC Controls* case. Kostritsky argues that 'precontractual negotiation, unilateral contracts and subcontracting present a class of cases in which the recurring threat of opportunism is virtually the same threat' (at 629) Again, as with the contract to bargain, such a default rule, she suggests, would correspond with Coase's theory that 'where transaction costs are too high for parties to fashion their own rule, it is normatively correct to provide them with the rule that they probably would have chosen for themselves at the time of contracting had they been able to bargain" in R. Coase, 'The Problem of Social Cost' (1960) 3 J of Law and Econ 1, at 15-16.

The option contract (which Kostritsky sees as a 'finely crafted device to control opportunism in an imperfect world') is another method that lessens the negative side-effects of dealing with an uncertain partner. When a court is asked to add terms/impose liability rules beyond those expressly agreed by the parties it must decide whether legal intervention is justified. For Kostritsky, in specific situations legal intervention may be 'indispensable as a means of curbing opportunistic behaviour'. However, despite introducing a methodology to explore judicial intervention, Kostritsky does not consider the resultant impact on legal taxonomy and structure. This author shares Kostritsky's view that – all things being equal – private drafting, non-legal sanctions and option contracts aimed at controlling opportunistic and abusive activity are both more user-friendly and certain than reliance on general clauses, but may prove simply too costly and cumbersome in European market settings, where parties will be hampered by different substantive and procedural rules, aswell as perhaps vastly different views on the importance of contract drafting and of course linguistic barriers.[56] Importantly, a number of primary assumptions made in the US literature as to the potential power of the drafter's pen would be entirely utopian in the context of today's internal market.[57]

2.3 Balancing competing expectations and the limits of rigid commercial interpretation – the need for a new bridge

In order to protect reliance investments in European markets, there is clearly a need therefore to overcome both the current taxonomy and terminological difficulties, in addition to the hyper-formalism apparent in the application of classical formation rules. By creating a cause of action for a promisee who reasonably relied upon a belief that the promisor should have reasonably expected to induce such reliance, a detrimental reliance doctrine, used sparingly need not do violent damage to bargaining freedom, nor dispense with the traditional notion that contracts are created by assent. The 'expansive and uniquely Australian breed of equitable estoppel' does not appear to have damaged contractual freedom 'down-under', in large part because of the cautious approach adopted by the higher courts since Brennan J gave his influential judgment in the lead case of *Waltons Stores v. Maher*.[58] The learned judge was keen

56 For a more detailed analysis of such costs in US markets, see J.P. Kostritsky (1993), *supra*, at 641 *et seq*.

57 For a suitable example of the breadth of the gap between the current situation in the internal market and modern developments in the US (in relation to contract drafting freedom), see H.S. Noyes, 'If You Re(Build) It, They Will Come: Contracts to Remake the Rules of Litigation in Arbitration's Image' (2007) 30 Harv J Law & Pub Pol 579.

58 (1998) 164 CLR 387. Brennan J. further added that 'Estoppel yields a remedy in order to prevent unconscionable conduct on the part of the party who, having made a promise to another who acts on it to his detriment, seeks to resile from the promise ...'. And Pratt notes, relying on extensive Australian authority, that it has been the avoidance of detrimental reliance that has been the primary justication for intervention. Indeed Brennan J. is likewise clear that the court's ambitions are modest: '... the remedy

to emphasise that in moulding relief in estoppel 'the court, as a court of conscience, goes no further than is necessary to prevent unconscionable conduct'.[59] As such, the equitable estoppel doctrine as developed in the Australian courts is intimately connected to notions of unconscionability and can, it has been argued, be therefore carefully constrained. For as Pratt further notes, 'where the cost of reliance is slight, relative to the value of the promised benefit ... it may overshoot the bounds of good conscience to compel conferral of that benefit'.[60]

The facts surrounding the dispute in the *Waltons* case are rather straightforward, even though they were interpreted differently throughout the various stages of the trial right up until the High Court, mainly due to the various historical forms of estoppel that were pleaded (thus lending additional weight to McFarlane's coherence argument). The case concerned negotiations for the lease of retail premises. Waltons, an erstwhile retailer, aimed to build a new store in New South Wales and found a suitable site owned by Maher. The parties hammered out an agreement that committed Maher to demolish an old factory located on the site and to begin construction work on the new store according to Waltons specifications. In addition, it was agreed, that the property would be thereafter leased to Waltons, who made it clear that they required the new property to be delivered in a hurry. Acting on the assumption that an exchange of the contracts was a mere formality or pure paperwork that would take place 'as a matter of course', Maher began demolishing the old factory. In the meantime, however, Waltons began to have a change of heart and later sought to resile from their earlier agreement. They instructed their solicitor to go slow on the deal and Maher heard nothing further for a period of almost ten weeks (by which stage 40% of the new store had been completed). It was at this point that Waltons informed Maher that the deal was off, and that they no longer intended to continue with the lease.

Of course, on a technical reading of the parties' commitments at this point there was no contract. The deal could only become fully formalised with an exchange of written contracts via both parties solicitors. It could therefore be argued that Maher commenced work on the project at his own risk. As Linzer, notes, in such 'middle category' cases, 'when people haven't agreed to anything and haven't done anything wrong, why should they be held to a legal obligation?'[61] On a purely technical reading of Lord Hoffman's 'factual matrix' there was no contract, and as such no liability. Yet, as in *AC Controls v. BBC*, the High Court felt in this case that Maher deserved to be recompensed. Instead of

is to effect ... the minimum equity to do justice', even though at times 'the minimum equity will not be satisfied by anything short of enforcing the promise' (at p. 428-9). The facts of the case were similar to the earlier US case of *White v. Wheeler* 398 S.W. 2d 93 (1965) where a Texas court similarly awarded reliance damages.

59 *Supra*, at 419.

60 *Supra*, at 49.

61 *Supra* (2001), at 698. (noting further that any answering of the question raises issues not just of jurisprudence but of political freedom).

'finding' consent to be bound, the High Court relied on equitable estoppel. Of course, what makes the decision in *Waltons* so significant is that to 'do justice' and thereby sanction Walton's 'unconscionable' conduct, the High Court was required to stand three core tenets of traditional estoppel doctrine on their head. Firstly, there was clearly no existing contractual relationship between the parties,[62] secondly traditional estoppel typically only applied where one party had promised another that he/she need *not* do something, and thirdly traditional estoppel is intended to act only ever as a shield, and not a sword. It is intended solely as a defence, at least for the present under English law. In other words, 'to do justice' Maher would require a positive remedy, a cause in action even in the absence of a contract.

The High Court was clear. The essential ingredient of a 'new' approach to equitable estoppel was unconscionability that creates such a positive remedy. The upshot of the High Court's decision is that whereas the breach of a promise is not in and of itself unconscionable or actionable, breaking a promise will become unconscionable conduct when the promisee has sufficiently relied on the promise to his detriment. In other words, mere reliance is not enough, there is a need for detrimental reliance, encouraged or generated by the promisor.[63]

3 Estoppel, detrimental reliance and a challenge not just for English contract law

Curiously, McFarlane has suggested that "English law can in a stroke solve the problems of coverage, clarity and coherence with a 'proprietary estoppel' principle or model".[64] Such enthusiastic hyperbole aside, despite the careful analysis of the Australian High Court, one of the primary difficulties facing English law, in accepting, let alone applying reliance theories in contract, of whatever hue, is of course the enduring doctrine of consideration. As was emphasised in *Walton*, however, via the newly emergent equitable estoppel doctrine, reliance is not to be considered a mere substitute for consideration.[65] Mason CJ and Wilson J were both at pains to point out their concern that allowing estoppel to act as a positive remedy would undermine the doctrine of consideration, but after careful reflection ultimately determined that in practice,

62 Even though Deane and Gaudron JJ sought to convince themselves as much as the Court itself that there was an estoppel on an assumption of an existing fact (as Maher believed that a valid lease existed at the time he began demolition).

63 Evidence was further evinced at trial to suggest that an agent of Waltons based in New South Wales was fully aware of Maher's ongoing activity in demolishing and re-working the site.

64 *Supra* at 12. (though he does partly acknowledge that the proprietary estoppel doctrine should be 'accompanied by a change of name', on the grounds that 'the first half of the term' may be 'misleading' and that the word 'estoppel' is best avoided).

65 In short, 'reliance is not a simple stand-in for consideration in Australian law, at p. 402 (Mason CJ and Wilson J) and p. 426 (Brennan J).

it would not. Indeed in support of McFarlane's analysis, it was previous English proprietary estoppel cases such as *Crabb v. Arun District Council*[66] on which both judges ultimately relied in support of this proposition. Of course, preserving the doctrine of consideration under English law intact – and avoiding much of previous US experience – need not prove insuperable. In this regard, Pratt is masterful in highlighting the key distinction between consideration and reliance. He notes that:

Consideration functions to render promises legally binding. Reliance cannot render a promise legally binding unless it is requested as part of a bargain, in which case it *is* consideration. Reliance may operate to estop a promisor from abandoning an assumption induced by his or her promise. But this is conceptually distinct from rendering a promise binding in law. A binding promise results from the exercise of a legal power, one aspect of that exercise being the provision of consideration. Consideration perfects an obligation whose scope is defined by a promise, and which obtains independently of any influence of the promise on the actions of the promisee. In other words, the obligation of a contractual promise accrues independently of any harm that may befall the promisee if it is broken. Hence the irrelevance of the quantity of consideration. By contrast, reliance that is not bargained-for does not operate merely to perfect the obligation of a promise. Rather, it functions as evidence that a promise has so influenced the expectations of a promisee as to justify holding the promisor responsible for defeating them. It follows that the scope of the reliance will determine the scope of the inducing party's obligation.

Yet, the doctrines of both promissory and proprietary estoppel under English law have always had mixed blessings in commercial settings. In large part due to their origins, particularly the origins of promissory estoppel, which is particularly fuzzy. Denning J made an early name for himself with his peers on the bench by breathing new life into promissory estoppel in *Central London Property Trust Ltd v. High Trees House Ltd.*[67] In delivering his own vision of promissory estoppel, Denning J was required to dust off Lord Cairns' previous judgment in *Hughes v. Metropolitan Railway Co.*,[68] from which his appoach took much succour. In *Hughes*, Lord Cairns boldly stated the intellectual foundations of the general equitable principle on which Denning J would rely:

It is the first principle upon which all Courts of Equity proceed, that if parties who have entered into definite and distinct terms involving certain legal results – certain penalties or legal forfeiture – afterwards by their own act or with their own consent enter upon a course of negotiation which has the effect

[66] [1976] Ch 179. Indeed, McFarlane is equally supportive of 'proprietary estoppel' as there is no requirement for a previous relationship, contractual or otherwise, between the parties.

[67] [1947] 1 KB 130 [hereinafter *High Trees*]. Morgan views the *High Trees* case as 'one of the leading English decisions of its generation [which] has frequently been cited as the basis of the modern doctrine'. See S.M. Morgan, 'Comparative Analysis of the Doctrine of Promissory Estoppel in Australia, Great Britain and the US' (1985) 15 Melb ULR 134, at 136.

[68] (1877) 2 App Cas 439.

of leading one of the parties to suppose that the strict rights arising under the contract will not be enforced, or will be kept in suspense, or held in abeyance, the person who otherwise might have enforced those rights will not be allowed to enforce them where it would be inequitable having regard to the dealings which have thus taken place between the parties.[69]

On this basis, Denning J in *High Trees* relying on the general principle, argued, albeit obiter, that a landlord who had promised to accept a reduced rate for the period of the second world war could not subsequently reclaim the outstanding balance in the post-war period. Denning J was further supported in his reasoning by the intervening judgment of Bowen LJ in *Birmingham & District Land Company v. London & North Western Rail Co.*[70] which revealed that the equitable principle was of general application. As Giliker observes, however, the real question and problem for reliance theorists rests with the scope of the doctrine of estoppel generally under English law. Giliker observes that:

> the reason for such uncertainty lies in part in the uneasy relationship between promissory estoppel and the doctrines of estoppel by representation and waiver. The modern day doctrine is limited first by analogy to estoppel by representation, to a defensive role, and secondly by analogy to waiver, to the modification of pre-existing contractual relationships. Nevertheless, as will be seen, signs do exist that the English courts are prepared to re-examine the requirements of promissory estoppel and adopt a more flexible approach, which may permit a pre-contractual performer to bring a claim. As predicted by Lord Hailsham, 'the time may soon come when the whole sequence of cases based on promissory estoppel since the war, beginning with Central London Property Trust v. High Trees House Ltd, may need to be reviewed and reduced to a coherent body of doctrine by the courts'.[71]

McFarlane barely engages with the waiver/estoppel debate, perhaps wisely. The cases have attracted all due criticism,[72] though they have been regularly affirmed as good law. There are also strong arguments that they represent the posi-

---

69 *Supra*, at 488.

70 (1888) 40 ChD 268, CA.

71 See also *Woodhouse AC Israel Cocoa Ltd SA v. Nigerian Produce Marketing Co Ltd* [1972] AC 741, at 758. This case reveals that under the estoppel by representation doctrine, 'an estoppel, that is to say, the language used upon which the estoppel is founded, must be precise and unambiguous'. Giliker notes how the promissory estoppel doctrine declined during the nineteenth and twentieth centuries and cites the House of Lords decisions in *Jorden v. Money* and *Foakes v. Beer* 9 App. Cas. 605 (1854) as the source of much confusion. Following the Lords decision, the promissory estoppel doctrine does not apply to a case where a representation is not a representation of fact, but a statement of something which the party intends or does not intend to do. 'In the former case it is a contract, in the latter it is not'. She notes, however, that following the decision in *Waltons Stores*, 'the ground is prepared on a practical level at least'.

72 *Re Selectmove* [1995] 1 WLR 474.

tion both at common law and equity.[73] In order to circumvent these decisions, Denning J proposed a doctrine in *High Trees* that was a variant of estoppel by representation. His Lordship distinguished *Jorden v. Money* on the basis that the doctrine would only apply where the promisor intended to be legally bound, and by preventing the claimant from reneging on a 'promise intended to be binding, intended to be acted on and in fact acted on', Denning J evoked a clear analogy with the contractual doctrine of waiver and was willing to alter a contract even in the absence of consideration. Giliker argues correctly that, 'despite the influence of waiver, the foundations exist for promissory estoppel to become part of a wider concept of estoppel under the broad notion of unconscionability, as outlined by the High Court of Australia in *Waltons*'. She suggests that English law could achieve the same result by incremental development, based first on the flexible interpretation of the requirements of promissory estoppel, and then by analogy to the principles of proprietary estoppel where the courts have already adopted a broader approach:

The primary advantage of such a development in English law would be in relation to McFarlane's coherence and coverage problems. There is undoubtedly a need for a sounder explanation of those cases where recovery is already permitted following precontractual negotiations and busted deals under English law. If parties were provided with a clear cause of action and a modern doctrine, it would no longer be necessary to seek a 'benefit' or 'unjust ground' on which to found a claim. The courts would simply consider whether, in all the circumstances of the negotiations, the relationship between the parties, assurances given and the equity of the case justified the intervention. There is also no reason why this would lead to undue uncertainty. Indeed, the House of Lords in upholding the Court of Appeal's decision in *Woodhouse*, additionally found that the application of such a test prevented the doctrine outflanking the law of contract: 'it would really be an astonishing thing if, in the case of a genuine misunderstanding as to the meaning of an offer, the offeree could obtain by means of the doctrine of promissory estoppel something that he must fail to obtain under the conventional law of contract'.[74] Despite the tone and seriousness of their Lordships' ruling, the basis for granting relief was clearly one of equity.[75] The essence of the doctrine provides, much like in *Waltons Stores*, that some form of representation is required, whether words or conduct. As Giliker notes, 'although it imposes a level of certainty, few would argue that vague promises should form a basis for liability. Anyone relying on such discussions

[73] See, Treitel, *supra*, at 108, suggesting that *High Trees* is an exception to the general rule in *Foakes v. Beer* rather than an independent rule.

[74] Per Lord Hailsham, *supra*, at p. 757. Atiyah wonders on the basis of such reasoning why promissory estoppel is ever permitted to enforce such concessions, which contract refuses to enforce. In Atiyah, P.S., Consideration and Estoppel: the thawing of the ice (1975) 38 MLR 65.

[75] Such an objective test is found in The Post Chaser [1982] All ER 19, The Leonidas D (Allied Marine Transport v. Vale do Rio Doa Navegac) [1985] 2 All ER 796, 808 CA.

would thus be acting at their own risk. Such a requirement does not prevent limited intervention at the precontractual stage of negotiations'.[76]

Notions of reliance receive strong support in *Hughes, Birmingham* and act as a key condition of liability in *High Trees*. The analogy with estoppel suggests the need for reliance to one's detriment,[77] and this has been followed by the House of Lords[78] and the Privy Council.[79] Nevertheless, Lord Denning in a number of decisions has challenged this view: In none of these cases does the party who acts on the belief suffer any detriment ... he has conducted his affairs on the basis that he has that benefit and it would not be equitable now to deprive him of it. In *Brikom Investments v. Carr*, Lord Denning further weakened this requirement by holding that any representation calculated to influence the judgment of a reasonable man would suffice. Such a presumption of reliance was feared by many to threaten overly the boundaries of contract law and to undermine the need for consideration. It has since been emphasised that in *Brikom* and *El Nasr*, Lord Denning was in fact in the minority and the majority chose to adopt a more conservative approach which required the presence of detriment.[80] However, despite uncertainty as to the degree of reliance necessary for promissory estoppel, there is much to be said for the approach of the court in *The Post Chaser*.[81] Goff J suggested that the key concept was that of equity and that this principle was capable of reconciling the approaches of Lord Denning and the House of Lords in *Tool Metal* towards reliance. It would be open to the court, in any particular case, to infer from the circumstances of the case that the representee must have conducted his affairs in such a way that it would be inequitable for the representor to enforce his rights or to do so without reasonable notice.[82] The best view is therefore that the existence of detriment amounts to a *prima facie* example of circumstances where the court would intervene, but

76 *Supra*, at p. 376. See also M.P. Thompson, 'From Representation to Expectation: Estoppel as a Cause of Action' (1983) CLJ 257, at 260-263. (who also sees logic in integrating much of the courts reasoning into the negotiation process).

77 See *Carr v. London & North Western Railway Co* (1875) LR 10 CP 307, 317 where the defence failed due to an absence of a changed position.

78 *Ajayi v. Briscoe* [1964] 1 WLR 1326, where the defendants were unable to prove the requisite alteration of position.

79 In *High Trees* itself it has been argued that there was no detriment. Denning has denied extra-judicially the existence of detriment in the case: (1952) 15 MLR 1, 5.

80 In *Brikom*, both Cumming-Bruce and Roskill LJJ require detrimental reliance and oppose the idea of a presumption; both Roskill LJ at 671 warn that it 'would be wrong to extend the doctrine of promissory estoppel, whatever its precise limits at the present day, to the extent of abolishing in this backhanded way the doctrine of consideration'. Equally in *El Nasr*, where Megaw LJ found a contractual variation, whilst Stephenson LJ held detriment to be present and carefully reserved his judgment on Lord Denning's comments.

81 *Societe Italo Belge pour le Commerce et l'Industrie v. Palm & Vegetable Oils (Malaysia)* [1982 1 All ER 19.

82 *Ibid* at p. 27. See also Lord Cairns in *Hughes, supra* at p. 448, who refers to reliance in the sense that 'it would be inequitable having regard to the dealings which have thus taken place between the parties".

it is not a condition of liability. Indeed, the judgment of Goff J in *The Post Chaser* emphasises the equitable nature of the doctrine: the claimant must show an alteration of position to a degree that merits intervention. A further illustration can be found in the Court of Appeal decision of *D&C Builders & Rees*,[83] in which Lord Denning held that the doctrine would not apply where it would lead to an inequitable result. In that case, the promise was extracted from builders acting under economic duress. It was noted in *D&C Builders* that 'the principle may be applied, not only so as to suspend strict legal rights, but also so as to preclude the enforcement of them'.[84]

Yet, in pure commercial settings, particularly in the absence (complete or partial) of a contract, the doctrine of estoppel has acted merely as a stumbling block for overly-reliant, yet innocent parties. The recent 2001 decision in *Baird Textile Holdings Ltd v. Marks & Spencer plc*[85] revealed that even after a co-operative thirty year relationship of supplying the retail and food outlet, Baird were thwarted in bringing forward their claim in both contract and estoppel to have the contract renewed on the basis that there was never any written contract agreed between the parties. The Court of Appeal looked unsympathetically on the notion of an implied contract and took the view that both claims would fail as the manifest intention of M&S was not to create legal relations. The estoppel claim was seen as hopeless on the grounds that estoppel does not provide a cause of action. As Mitchell notes, a reasonable expectations approach produces two clear contradictory positions as an alternative interpretation is that the parties simply considered a written contract as surplus to requirements if not 'positively unhelpful to the development of the kind of relationship that would allow them to do business ... One can see how a 'reasonable expectations' argument can be used to support Baird or M&S, but each relies on a different basis for the reasonable expectation.[86] Predictably the court was less than forthcoming as to why the interpretation most favourable to Marks & Spencers should triumph over that most supportive of Baird. This result, in the eyes of Mitchell, does not support the attempt to make contract law more sensitive to the social dimension of agreement-making, but undermines it by privileging the legal framework in the resolution of the dispute'.[87] Particularly, when resort to the factual matrix revealed a statement presented in evidence from a former Chair-

83 [1966] 2 QB 617.

84 At 624.

85 [2001] EWCA Civ 274.

86 Mitchell, *supra*, at 649. (Her article is further replete with such contradictory decisions). Despite the absence of a contract there is a certain parallel with Knapp's view in *Enforcing the Contract to Bargain*, *supra*, at 728 that '... parties do often wish to register in an effective way their common commitment to an agreement ... If they have made such an agreement, the law has no business telling them their act of agreement was devoid of legal significance'. In like manner, relying on Baird's legitimate expectations alone they may well have considered that the law had no business telling them their absence of a contract was of critical legal significance.

87 *Supra*, at 650.

man and Chief Executive of Marks & Spencer that 'M&S was going to carry on doing business with the manufacturers season after season, year after year'. Of course such a statement itself can be interpreted in two ways – literally, or merely as pure every-day business-speak aimed at reassuring clients and shareholders. The question is whether a long term business relationship should count for more in practice, and before the courts, than the terms of a written contract to which neither side felt it necessary to commit in over thirty years. As Linzer would likely suggest, '... when we add to the defective dealings human interactions that give substance to what was said or done, the sum total of justice may be greater than the calculus of form'.[88] What hope then for a precontractual reliance claim before such a hyper-formalist court?

4 Beyond hyper-formalism and an over-theorising of precontractual reliance. Taxonomy considerations and a detrimental reliance doctrine for new European contract law

The cases identified and analysed in chapter 3 of this study appear at the borders of contract, tort and equity in each national system studied. In many respects they are all 'outliers', to a greater or lesser extent. Unwelcome misfit cases that fail to knit adequately within the modern rules on contract, that the laws of equity are not best adapted to handle, and about which a broad good faith doctrine has little to contribute. This is particularly clear in relation to letters of intent and heads of agreement. Since the styles of such comfort documentation are as varied as the parties who compile them, it is not surprising that they are a perennial source of unsatisfactory litigation. Put simply, the judicial hyper-formalism of the past and present is no longer adequate to handle incomplete bargains and long term contract relationships based on poorly prepared written agreements. The courts in their treatment of such imperfect expressions of the parties' deal via largely classical contract rules have resorted either to legal fiction (as in *AC Controls*) or, as in the US, gradually adopted a largely hidden spectrum or sliding scale to decide between non-binding and binding agreements. In this sense the cases are highly fact-specific, requiring ever more case-specific answers. Linzer is correct to argue that by ignoring the formal rules of contract law the courts in the US have generally been able to impose 'fairer' outcomes and by looking behind the contract to the parties' relationship have been able to sense the true nature of the bargain. Whilst such an approach has its many dissenters on the grounds that 'discretionary action can be arbitrary action',[89] Linzer's deference to the courts is tied

[88] *Supra*, at 652.

[89] See S. Macaulay, 'Comment – Resitution in Context' (1959) 107 U Pa L Rev 1133 (noting way back then that 'Restition presents many of the favourite problems of realistic jurisprudence insofar as that brand of legal thought centers upon the tension between decision based on rule and decision based on reaction

in with a demand for greater judicial openness as to how final decisions are determined. In his words: All things considered, I'd rather they [the courts] had to say outright that they were deciding the case viscerally.[90]

Resort to parties' legitimate expectations in relation to preliminary agreements will not wash. Despite the constant refrain that the courts seek to 'protect legitimate expectation', the 'doctrine' has been routinely exposed to criticism in English, Spanish and US opinion. Echebarría Sáenz sees the notion as a pure 'mask', as does Mitchell, for whom the doctrine is 'leading a life of its own' – untamed and unrestrained. Certainly under English contract law the notion has entered through the back door and would probably have gone by largely unnoticed but for the extra-judicial comments of Lord Steyn. Of course, strictly speaking the doctrine does not even belong to the private law sphere. In the UK, legitimate expectation is a public law doctrine. In addition to that, its own limits within public law are far from clear. Nolan is helpful in isolating the key distinction at play. He notes that while 'substantive legitimate expectations are aimed at improving public decision-making processes, reliance is aimed at remedying situations where one party has legitimately relied to his detriment on a failed promise or on the unconscionable conduct of another.[91]

Linzer seizes on the crux of the problem – the need to enhance judicial discretion and allow for legal sensitivity to the plight of those who have been 'victims' of bad faith bargaining and witnessed a potentially lucrative bargain unravel before their eyes after significant investment, but not too much discretion nor sensitivity. The aim is not simply to 'award everyone with an appealing story'.[92] Importantly, in addition, the cases of imperfect bargains and precontractual reliance do not affect repeat players alone. Big business, government

to individual cases', at 1137). See also H. Dagan, *The Law and Ethics of Restitution* (Cambridge University Press, 2004) at 287 et seq (discussing the best default rule for restitution in contractual contexts).

90 P. Linzer, *supra*, at 772.

91 D. Nolan, 'Review Article – The Classical Legacy and Modern English Contract Law' (1996) 59(4) MLR 603, at 608. Cf. J. Cartwright, 'Protecting Legitimate Expectations and Estoppel: English Law', Proceedings of the XVIIth Congress of the International Academy of Comparative Law, Utrecht, 2006, who is broadly supportive of a private law legitimate expectations doctrine. He notes that at times the protection of reasonable expectations occurs 'on a basis which is analogous to, or sometimes even explicity based on, doctrines of estoppel', at 19. For a recent analysis of the English public law doctrine, see P. Sales, 'Legitimate Expectations', via www.11kbw.com

92 *Supra*, at 773. See also, G.E. Maggs, 'Estoppel and Textualism' (2006) 54 Am J Comp L 167 (though discussing estoppel doctrine and textualism in the context of public statutory interpretation, Maggs highlights 'the unresolved tensions' caused by estoppel doctrine, and the desire to provide substantive and procedural justice, in textualist courts. A textualist judge, he opines, may look to six different categories to 'square accepted principles of estoppel with textualism'. Those categories include existing legislation, an implied term, the inherent equitable powers of the court, estoppel as a cause of action and/or binding precedent. We have seen the second category, the implied term relied upon to exhaustion in English contract law, but not surprisingly, as Maggs himself acknowledges, even in the public sphere it is awkward to those courts that adhere to textualism to justify reliance on estoppel doctrines.

and major corporations, from the BBC and the British Steel Corporation to La Caixa and major Texan Oil companies have all been dragged into litigation over preliminary agreements; but the operation of strict formal rules also threaten the investments of time and expense made by society's little people, the 'small fry'. From the Taylor-Rose family and their newly purchased crime-scene home, to the Hoffman's and the Copeland's of this world, to the other families and struggling couples in small businesses such as those developing photographs in *Walford*. With European markets dominated by small-to-medium sized businesses and small independent entrepreneurs, the complexion of reliance based claims changes. It may at times be a million miles from the multi-million dollar US claims of the 1980's but no less significant. A decision either way may well spell the end of a struggling business. As Linzer himself notes, what is required is a rule that can bend in individual cases without threatening the wider legal framework, for at present:

> Some of those real people are small fry like the people in ... Hoffman, etc. But others are giants like British Steel Corporation, Motorola, Resorts International, and American Airlines. The formal rules of contract are easy to apply, though they sometimes lead to bad results for good and well-meaning people who didn't know about them, or didn't believe that they needed to follow them for self-protection, or didn't even think of the eventuality that destroyed what they thought was a happy arrangement.[93]

A fact-specific approach is of course open to the charge that it will lead inevitably to 'soft' judicial outcomes based on 'sensitivity', and a raft of hopeless cases that serve only to reduce predictability and legal certainty; yet as this study has revealed, the courts do routinely provide justice in hard cases by relying on a range of doctrines and poorly justified reasoning that frequently provides individual relief but no greater universal legal certainty. Rather the law at its edges becomes ever more obscure as doctrines are bent and stretched to perform ill-suited roles, or valid claims are thwarted by obstructionist procedural rules that cannot be defended except on undisclosed policy grounds. What is missing in this untidy picture is fulsome judicial explanation aimed at clarifying the law whilst supporting and upholding those justice-based outcomes.

In this sense, the approach of the US courts in cases such as *Channel* provide a lead in dealing with incomplete agreements.[94] It will be recalled that the court in *Channel* stressed that the language of the preliminary agreement, the context

---

93 *Supra*, at 775.

94 As Farnsworth notes, 'the view taken in [the leading cases of] *Itek* and *Channel* has gained a substantial following, and the trend clearly favours enforceability. At least this is so where the parties have reached agreement on a significant number of the major terms of the ultimate agreement', see *Farnsworth on Contracts* (3rd Edition, Columbia University Press, 2004) at 363. We may not agree with the increasingly contextualist and 'dynamic' steer towards enforceability of preliminary agreements in the US but there is a need for a settled European approach that can provide certainty and predictability.

of the negotiations, the presence of any open terms, whether either party had part performed and/or any express suggestion or demand from either party to work towards a final contract could prove influential. The courts in Spain have been typically much less forthcoming when deciding between enforceability/ non enforceability, however, despite Temkins' reticence at an 'all or nothing' approach to enforcement of preliminary agreements, this is exactly what is required. In addition, the courts must be much more open and forthright in defending their decisions. In this regard, Lord Ackner's approach in *Walford* cannot be faulted.

On a more constructive front, however, the recent English decision in *Jennings v. Rice*,[95] a proprietary estoppel case that sought to provide clarity as to the application of judicial discretion, may serve as a helpful template. In this case Walker L.J sought to divide cases into strict 'bargain' and 'non-bargain' scenarios. Temkin in the US, like McFarlane, has promoted the view that courts should divide negotiations into three distinct phases – a similar approach to that adopted under Dutch civil law. The first and third categories are not controversial. Temkin's first phase implies no liability for parties at the outset of negotiations when the parties are merely testing the ground and considering early proposals. The third stage would be the agreement of a definitive contract. It is Temkin's second phase of negotiations that proves controversial. He suggests that the intermediate phase between no agreement and agreement may well see the deal harden and the parties enter into an agreement in principle. Temkin suggests that at this point the parties are aware that both have taken on commitments and only a good faith reason would justify either party walking away.

Admittedly, at this second stage Temkin only argues in favour of courts upholding agreement to negotiate in good faith towards a definitive agreement. Such an agreement would bind the parties to work constructively but without threat of legal sanction. More alarmingly, Temkins promotes the view that the subjective intent of the parties should be considered by the courts. However, even without worrying about largely artificial divisions in the negotiation phase and the parties' equally problematic subjective intent, the approach of the Court of Appeal in *Jennings v. Rice* provides an infinitely more appropriate starting point for justifying future judicial intervention in the case of incomplete contracts. This author is still unconvinced of the English proprietary estoppel doctrine for reasons set out above, but the forthrightness of the court in setting out the factors to be considered in exercising discretion is refreshing. Moreover, without squandering the crucial bargain/no bargain dichotomy that would lead contract law down a slippery slope, the case highlights the fact that an appropriately fashioned detrimental reliance doctrine could play a constructive role in regulating incomplete commercial agreements. That said, as in *Jennings*, the exercise of judicial discretion would have to be reasonably confined and adequately articulated. The facts of the case are not hugely relevant but the analysis of Walker LJ in *Jennings* illustrates what is achievable. Walker LJ was most

95 [2002] EWCA Civ 159.

forthcoming on the relevant grounds that will influence the court's discretion. The approach advocated by his Lordship does reveal a degree of overlap with Spence's earlier eight factor test for equitable estoppel but his Lordship's analysis is particularly helpful in relation to preliminary non-binding agreements for he notes that:

> ... assurances, and the claimant's reliance on them, [at times] have a consensual character falling not far short of an enforceable contract ... In a case of that sort both the claimant's expectations and the element of detriment to the claimant will have been defined with reasonable clarity ... In a case like that the consensual element of what has happened suggests that the claimant and the benefactor probably regarded the expected benefit and the accepted benefit as being ... equivalent, or at any rate not obviously disproportionate ... In such a case the court's natural response is to fulfil the claimant's expectations. But if the claimant's expectations are uncertain, or extravagant or out of all proportion to the detriment ... suffered, the court can and should recognise that the claimant's equity should be satisfied in another (generally more limited) way.[96]

Lord Justice Walker further suggested that only where the expectations of the claimant are unclear should the courts seek to exercise discretion. In so doing, proportionality would be key. Without any hierarchy or exhaustive list of factors, the courts in Lord Justice Walker's view should consider any misconduct on the part of the defendant or oppressive conduct on the part of the defendant (as in *Crabb v. Arun District*), but also whether there was a 'need for a clean break between the parties'.[97] It is to be welcomed that a list of other factors were also enumerated, but what makes proprietary estoppel an inappropriate doctrine to regulate incomplete agreements and the spectre of precontractual reliance is that previous authorities do not follow neatly into this bargain/no bargain divide. As Gardner also notes, 'in truth relatively few [proprietary] estoppel cases fall to one side or the other [of Walker LJ's dividing line] ... Very many cases sit somewhere between the two classes'. [98] Moreover, it is notable that such 'non-bargain' scenarios courts are to be approached by the courts employing 'wide judgmental discretion'. It is further unclear whether the various factors highlighted by Walker LJ would influence the quantum of any proprietary estoppel claim or

96 Importantly, though unconscionability is cited as a factor, unlike Spence's conscience-based, harm-led approach to estoppel, it is simply the principle of proportionality (between the degree of reliance and the detriment suffered) that Walker LJ considers determinitive of the proper measure in damages.

97 McFarlane focuses instead on the comments of Aldous LJ in *Jennings* who made no reference to the distinction drawn by Walker LJ between bargains/no bargains. Though he similarly points out the fact that Aldous LJ insisted on proportionality.

98 *Supra*, at 495-6. (Gardner noting further that 'given the context of so many estoppel cases ... a clear answer may only be possible if one takes an artificial, stylised view of the facts'. He further notes, at 511, that thus far the courts have not done enough to make the legitimacy of their discretionary power 'secure').

merely the type of remedy (e.g. damages or specific performance) available to the claimant.

A Simpler 'Solution'? – Preliminary Agreements and Limited Reliance Damages

The depth and clarity of Walker LJ's judgment aside, such a broad, unfettered judicial discretion in relation to 'bargain/non-bargain' reliance scenarios (such as those created by preliminary agreements) via proprietary estoppel is clearly inappropriate. Allowing such broad discretion in relation to precontractual liability via an ill-suited doctrine would result only in greater legal complexity and uncertainty. Instead, by maintaining the firm bargain/no bargain divide as a key point of departure, a European legal default rule should aim only to award limited, even nominal reliance damages in failed negotiation scenarios. In addition to encouraging parties to better allocate the risks of failure between them, limiting recovery to reliance damages would provide much needed clarity and coherence *ex ante*. Saunders, who has similarly explored the degree of deep US judicial confusion in relation to preliminary agreements, is of the same opinion.[99] He notes that there are sound reasons for limiting bad faith breach in negotiations to out-of-pocket expenses:

> First, limiting reliance to one party's expenditures provides the court with a concrete way to measure damages. Indeed, the information would be easily ascertainable in the company's tax records and books. Second, it avoids triggering the court's bias (against agreements to agree) as the party harmed is not pointing to any ultimate agreement. The party only wishes to recover the losses it suffered by negotiating with a party that conducted itself in bad faith. Moreover, it does not require the court to gaze into a crystal ball and predict what lost opportunities the company suffered. Third, and importantly, it encourages efficient breach of contract. A party will breach the agreement only when it is economically prudent to do so. For example, B Co. will only breach the good faith reliance contract with A Co. if the deal with C Co. will cover A Co.'s reliance expenditures and produce profit in excess of that amount. In doing so, A Co. will recoup its expenditures and search for another company with which to merge. In addition, B Co. will be better off by making more profits in the B–C deal.

Despite Farnsworth's argument to the contrary, in the context of ongoing negotiations involving agreements to negotiate, letters of intent or other preliminary

99 J. Sanders, 'Looking for Faith in All the Wrong Places – Rethinking Agreements to Negotiate in Good Faith' (2006) 7 UC Davis Bus LJ 5 (discussing the US court's fixation with agreements to agree and exposing the need to clarify the law in the interests of legal certainty and predictability. As opposed to Knapp's 'contract to bargain' or 'agreements to negotiate' which Sanders argues are too close in form and function to agreements to agree, he suggests parties should draft a specific 'good faith reliance contract' which would put courts on notice that parties seek a different type of bargaining commitment, that may fall short of an award in expectation damages but that signals the parties' are in a period of cooperative dependence).

signs of an agreement, out-of-pocket expenses are the only true detriment that will result from an induced assumption. It must be accepted that there is a risk of failure built in to every negotiation. Moreover, as was highlighted in chapter 3, in the US and Spain such out-of-pocket expenses are often the only recoverable loss in the event of bad faith breach, with other losses considered speculative. In this sense the legal rule would be faithful to the real law in practice. Therefore, rather than bending and stretching existing contract rules with gap filling and implied terms, or doing violence to ill-suited estoppel doctrines, a narrow detrimental reliance doctrine that allowed for limited recovery of 'out-of-pocket expenses' as reliance damages arising out of failed negotiations conducted in 'bad faith' appears infinitely superior. Whilst still a 'second-best' option to sound contract drafting, such an approach would certainly reduce complexity, and thereby prove much more efficient. It would also greatly reduce the breadth of judicial enquiry into parties' conduct during negotiations prompting less costly and time consuming trials. Saunders equally observes that in practice it is virtually impossible for a court to award anything other than reliance damages arising out of a failed venture.[100]

5 Concluding remarks

It could be argued on the basis of our findings in chapter 3 that judicial decisions on preliminary agreements and resultant reliance are so varied that they simply defy capture. Indeed, recent work by Saunders similarly highlights the often diametrically opposed positions adopted by courts across the United States. There is a clearly a broader lesson here for ongoing harmonisation initiatives at Community level and the need to look beyond general principles. In this concluding chapter, our focus has centred on the need for an alternative, workable solution to the reliance question. It is submitted that sound contract drafting remains the most appropriate manner for dealing with the spectre of reliance arising out of preliminary agreements, as opposed to general clauses. However, aware that such drafting solutions may prove costly and awkward in a linguistically diverse market, an examination was made of a sensible default rule. It was further accepted that any reliance doctrine would therefore imply an element of judicial discretion be it via a proprietary estoppel approach or the doctrine of good faith. The open and fluid judgment of Walker LJ was highlighted merely as a model for how such discretionary power can be best exposed, both for audit and critique. Yet the judgment also exposes a number of key weaknesses in relation to the proprietary estoppel doctrine when applied to bargaining. Proprietary estoppel is of only limited assistance and as such an alternative legal doctrine that would be terminology-neutral and more in line with the law in action has been discussed. It is submitted that a constrained detrimental reliance doctrine that would allow parties to potentially

[100] A view largely shared by Smith, *supra*, at 85 *et seq*.

recover out-of-pocket expenses only (and thereby prevent claims for speculative expectation losses arising out of failed ventures) is preferable. Arguably, under a single coherent and minimalist European doctrine, judicial decisions at both Community and national Member State level ought gradually to settle on what really constitutes bad faith in both drafting and negotiations. Ex-ante awareness among European businesses that only out-of-pocket expenses would be recoverable in the event of a failed cross-border deal would further eliminate one potential psychological impediment to intra-Community trade.

CHAPTER 5

Conclusions and Outlook

There is now a broad legal and political consensus that divergences between Member States' contract laws constitute a *de facto* impediment to trade and competitiveness in the internal market. Less clear cut, however, is the extent to which those existing divergences are necessarily problematic in practice. A lack of empirical enquiry has characterised the work of the European institutions to date in promoting the assumed need for modern principles of EC contract law and a Common Frame of Reference. Legal positivism and the quest for general principles has further blurred the need for such enquiry and distracted attention from the real law in action. In 2005, Gordley warned of the pernicious side of legal positivism that fails to consider 'what judges do'. In stepping outside, if not beyond, the narrower codification debate, it has been this primary pillar of the harmonisation initiative that has been central to this book. This study has sought to capture the real law in action and explore what courts actually do across three jurisdictions in relation to preliminary agreements and in regulating precontractual bargaining.

In exploring what judges actually do, this study has engaged with two holy grails of modern contract scholarship: the harmonisation of European commercial contract rules and the adequate treatment of incompleteness and precontractual reliance; phenomena largely overlooked thus far at Community level, and almost entirely by those promoting a comprehensive codification of European (consumer) contract rules. Indeed the Commission modernisation plans – most notably the Action Plan on coherence and the *Acquis* review – focus almost exclusively on problematic inconsistencies and failures in the implementation of Community consumer law. Since commercial contracting remains largely beyond the Commission's sphere of influence, it is perhaps unsurprising that the harmonisation initiative has taken on an unduly narrow consumer-oriented and Eurocentric focus. Yet, this study reveals that approach to be unsustainable in the long term. As the Commission increases its engagement in the field of general contract law, and as consumer law reforms ripple through the overall apparatus of general contract law, this will prompt either a re-conceptualisation of commercial contracting, calls for a uniform regime, or a further entrenched split between both sub-fields. In this context, as opposed to further systematisation and code-drafting, this book makes the case for a new methodology of dispute avoidance. By respecting that a workable degree of divergence between national systems is not necessarily problematic, and will on occasion provide legal and economic benefits via inter-jurisdictional competition, it is suggested that targeted harmonisation should aim to ameliorate suitability identified practical problems. It is further submitted that the declining role and influence of national courts in regulating commercial contracts remains a key factor militating against a comprehensive harmonisation of private law rules. What is required is greater cross-border doctrinal consistency in the use and implementation of general rules and principles. The adequate control of preliminary agreements and the spectre of precontractual reliance is clearly one specific area requiring greater doctrinal and practical coherence at Community level. The judicial colloquy regarding preliminary agreements even in domestic courts remains contradictory and unsettling for business. Moreover, uncertainty, opportunism, and sunk costs converge to make it difficult and costly to constrain the effects of behavioural opportunism in modern contract negotiations, a problem arguably greatly exacerbated in a multi-lingual market.

This book presents a cautious and confined strategy aimed at improved judicial control of preliminary agreements in particular and the bargaining phase more generally at Community level, and has exposed the need for greater judicial parallelism and openness in decision-making. Whilst ruling out a general duty to negotiate in good faith, the author promotes the validity of upholding an express[1] or suitably implied contract to bargain in good faith in a future European contract law, and calls, albeit more tentatively, for a new doctrine of detrimental reliance. Whilst a number of those academic lawyers most vociferous and active in promoting the cause of codification have tended to downplay the resistance of English commercial courts to the concept of good faith and fair dealing, without doubt, proposals in favour of such a general duty arising out of negotiations will continue to unsettle English courts. Support for the notion, both academic and judicial, will continue to wax and wane. That said, the contract to negotiate in good faith (as defined in this thesis as a consensual, problem-solving approach to negotiations) is not anathema to commercial actors, nor is it alien to English contract law – as evidenced by the straightforward approach of arbitrators in England and Wales in cases such as *AT & T v. Saudi Cable* in upholding and regulating non-adversarial forms of bargaining.

Despite Lord Ackner's now well-worn dicta in *Walford v. Miles*, the *Saudi Cable* case reveals that English lawyers have little practical difficulty policing an agreement to negotiate in good faith. The arbitration panel in London was able to determine that a party failed to negotiate properly and punish that failure with an award in damages. Moreover, with civil courts in England and Wales increasingly promoting the advantages of ADR and mediation, particularly post-*Dunnet v. Railtrack*[2], Lord Ackner's opposition to anything other than adversarial bargaining offers an indefensible, problematic, one-dimensional, mono-ethic template for commercial negotiations, whilst providing little by way of legal certainty. Indeed, not only has their Lordships' wider aim in *Walford* – to impose stability and certainty vis-à-vis commercial negotiations – rebounded, the decision offers a myopic vision that ignores alternative constructive styles of bargaining – a feature of modern business that at other times and in other settings, the courts of England and Wales have clearly had little difficulty upholding.[3] Express support for the contract to bargain in good faith, despite lending much needed

1 Preferably via the use of sound drafting and perhaps via Saunders 'good faith reliance clause'.

2 [2002] 2 All ER 850, where Railtrack Plc were heavily penalised in costs by the Court of Appeal for refusing to consider mediation, despite the parties being locked into 'without prejudice' negotiations). See also the Australian decision in *Aiton Australia Pty Ltd v. Transfield Pty Ltd* [1999] NSWSC 996, where parties were obliged to maintain an open-mind in negotiations, and to properly consider proposals.

3 See also dissenting opinion of Lord Hoffman in *BBCI v. Ali* [2001] UKHL 8, [2002].

certainty to the English law of contract post-*Walford*, can further be defended as a reinforcement of parties' bargaining freedom. Even where parties fail to express a definitive time-period for further negotiations to be conducted in 'good faith', the gap-filling approach promoted in the Spanish civil courts is justifiable where parties have indicated a preference for a less adversarial style of negotiations and should be followed by the courts in England and Wales, and in any new agreed EC contract law.

Of course, this argument in favour of enforcing the contract to bargain in good faith on the basis of international experience would appear to clash head-on with Michaels recent observations on the role of functional equivalence in comparative law, who suggests that empirical data and the analysis of similar solutions across legal systems may boost our general comparative knowledge and understanding of those legal systems analysed, but offers little guidance beyond that knowledge.[4] Michaels warns that 'equivalence functionalism provides surprisingly limited tools for [subsequent] evaluation'[5] and explains this discrepancy on the basis that functional equivalence theory implies "equal value" and thus "fails to decipher 'superiority'".[6] There is an element of truth in Michaels' warning and perhaps this author is 'guilty' of a form of applicative functional equivalence. Nonetheless, the logic for upholding an express or implied bargain to negotiate in good faith (and indeed the 'workability' of the notion in practice, even in English legal practice) flows both from comparative analysis and practical experience – analysis and experience that would appear to dent Michaels' argument. That said, few comparative law, or indeed law and economics, studies have been undertaken across the Union to test the validity and/or utility of differing approaches to precontractual liability across jurisdictions, much less the "superior" regime. Of the small number of economic studies that have addressed the optimal level of interference in contract bargaining, the majority have been US based.[7] In particular, a number of civil law jurisdictions have neglected thus far the economic analysis of law, though there are increasing signs of change.[8] A change of direction that will make future

4 R. Michaels, 'The Functional Method of Comparative Law' in M. Reinmann & R. Zimmermann, *Oxford Handbook of Comparative Law* (Oxford University Press, 2006). (who notes that functional equivalence has become a mantra and a *bête noire* of comparative law).

5 *Supra* at 374.

6 *Supra*. Michaels further notes that 'it is impossible to isolate the function of a legal institution [and by extension a legal rule] ... and to measure [it] ... against some ideal function, for no such ideal function exists ... In this strict sense, better-law theory is not compatible with functionalist comparative law', at 374.

7 Including most recently B. Medina & O. Grosskopf, *Why do we know what we know? Reevaluating the Economic case against Pre-contractual Disclosure Duties and for Break Up Fees*, 2006 Available via Bepress.

8 J. Alfaro Águila-Real, *Los Juristas Españoles y el Análisis Económico del Derecho*, and more concretely, Gómez Pomar, F., *European Contract Law and Economic Welfare: A View from Law and Economics* (who advocates a mimimum regulation of B2B contracts at Community level) Both articles have just appeared as this study concludes and are accessible via Indret.com.

comparative law analysis in European settings more complete and rewarding, if indeed more challenging. There are also glimmers of new thinking in relation to the critical importance of contract drafting.[9] Again, such analysis may prove modest but empirical enquiry and data must become the fuel of harmonisation.

Beyond the narrower contract to bargain in good faith, a modern, coherent doctrine to protect reliance investment appears equally necessary in an emerging European market where contracts continue to play a critical role as instruments of forward planning. What appears necessary is a doctrine that would seek to minimise the most unforgiving elements of raw adversarial bargaining through restricted awards of reliance damage. It is submitted that a more coherent detrimental reliance doctrine, geared towards a 'light' regulation of commercial bargaining, may provide a suitable alternative to the existing national patchwork of rules and confused doctrinal concepts. As evidenced by the work of the *Network for Uniform Terminology for European Private Law*, in addition to taxonomy, terminology remains critical. From the perspective of pure legal phraseology, a detrimental reliance doctrine is infinitely superior to the cumbersome and outdated common law 'estoppel' and 'quantum meruit' doctrines and the civil law's 'culpa en contrahendo', even if a constrained detrimental reliance doctrine may provide relief in many of the same ways that the current doctrines operate today. McFarlane has promoted a new 'proprietary estoppel' doctrine for the English law, however it seems preferable to work more universally towards an agreed European doctrine and in this regard 'detrimental reliance' presents itself as an attractive counter-proposal, again even if many of the doctrine's characteristics will overlap neatly with McFarlane's approach. This call for a new Community reliance doctrine may appear at odds with broader trends in the US, and an identifiable judicial retreat from the 'Krazy Glue' of promissory estoppel relief witnessed in previous decades in the States. Though virtually impossible to guage, however, it would certainly be worth exploring the extent to which familiarity in US business circles with the spectre of reliance and an awareness of the need for circumspection has gradually rendered the promissory estoppel doctrine both less contentious and much less necessary, if not largely redundant. Commercial actors in the US are also arguably confronted with significantly less obstacles when agreeing on negotiation positions and general drafting and, as such, sunk costs are likely to be proportionality higher in cross border negotiations in the internal market by comparison.

Though the tension between freedom of contract and detrimental reliance will endure – as if it could ever not –, provided a clear demarcation line remains between an enforceable bargain and a busted deal, the integrity of a future EC contract law will be guaranteed. In the UK, 'restitution lawyers have been meticulous in ensuring that the law of contract is not undermined by restitutionary

9 See F. Griffith Dawson & S. Styllis, 'Beyond the Pitfalls of Bad Contract Drafting Practices: A Selection of Cross Border Legal and Cultural Misunderstandings' (2007) 28(2) Bus. L. Rev. 26.

recovery'.[10] A similar care and circumspection will be necessary at Community level to avoid a Gilmorean 'death' of European contract law, before it even took shape. That said, as was noted in chapter 4, the cases covered in this book are marginal cases that arise at the extremes. These 'rompecabezas' or head-ache cases are not an easy fit within the classical rules of contract, nor easily resolved with satisfaction on the grounds of equity or good faith. For this reason, the introduction of a broad, generalised principle of good faith applicable to negotiations should be resisted. Introducing such a "principio-norma" as a further legal 'catch-all' would not remove the current confused array of rules and remedies applying to the existing precontractual regime, nor would it provide any greater consistency for dealing with hard cases. To those systems for whom the doctrine is supposedly 'repugnant', it would contribute little more than confusion and 'irritation'. The old piecemeal forms of protection would not easily give way to a new principle of good faith, leaving a deeply cluttered EC commercial contract law whilst weakening much of the consistency and rigidity that English contract law has prized so dearly.

What is required is less practical and doctrinal complexity and, by contrast with what we have at present, the operation of an *ex-post* detrimental reliance doctrine that is limited to recovery of parties' reliance interest. Arguably a single coherent doctrine applicable to both procedural and substantive expectations, and suitably fashioned on the basis of international experience, would gradually provide the necessary consistency. It will similarly require greater judicial forthrightness in the exercise of such a discretionary role. As Lord Goff noted long ago in his Maccabaean Lecture on Jurisprudence, jurists need not share the judges' 'intense view of the particular', as judicial reaction is aimed at resolving individual fact situations, rather than promoting the 'theoretical development of legal principles'. For Lord Goff, pragmatism is the watchword.[11] Yet, the majority of Europe's private lawyers, in thrall to codification, have lost sight of practical solutions and adopted an overly intense view of the general. It appears at times that contract law is now to be willed back to its former Enlightenment splendour, with the addition of a more finely attuned consumer conscience. Will alone cannot suffice however, and pragmatism will gradually yield increased private law differentiation, a European *ius divisione*. On a micro-level, the Commission's finalised Common Frame will further deliver outcomes grossly at odds with the solutions proposed by Europe's 'professorial-recht'. Of this we can be sure.

---

10 See D. Nolan, 'Review Article – The Classical Legacy and Modern English Contract Law' (1996) 59(4) MLR 603, 605. (who similarly notes the 'inadequacy' and 'haphazard' nature of current English approaches relying on N. Cohen, 'Two Freedoms and the Contract to Negotiate' in J. Beatson & D. Friedmann, *Good Faith and Fault in Contract Law* (Oxford University Press, 1995).

11 *The Search for Principle*, 76th Proceedings of the British Academy, 1983, at 182-5. See also A. Kramer, 'Common Sense Principles of Contract Interpretation' (2003) 23(2) Oxford J Leg Stud 173, who highlights the fact that the process of contractual interpretation (particularly in the case of incomplete deals) involves a search for pragmatic solutions, at 195.

The promotion of a civil code should be seen therefore as a retrogade step in that it fails to adequately account for cultural, social and economic diversity. It also avoids the 'elephant in the living room' for Europe's vocal body of systematisers and codifiers – harsh commercial reality that exposes the fact that the primary international sites for commercial business dispute resolution have little need for a potentially stillborn European civil code. Whilst arguably the Common Frame may serve as a template for future legislative drafting at Community level, it is much more likely to amount to little more than a tool for teaching and further academic research.[12] It is unlikely to be drafted with sufficient detail to be truly adequate in practice and whilst the compilation of additional non-binding common principles may assist future commercial actors, the strategy overlooks the not inconsiderable power of the drafter's pen to perform the task more efficiently at present. On a purely practical level it is submitted that the spectre of leading European businesses opting out of any (partially) agreed supranational code, allied to the overall decline of national court structures in regulating commercial contracts, constitute sufficient grounds to question the case for a costly, and potentially unworkable codification initiative. In developing EC contract rules the Community legislator has to date largely sacrificed coherence in an attempt to achieve greater substantive and procedural justice. It should receive due credit for prioritising the latter. Few European private lawyers will rejoice in Feinman's vision of legal indeterminancy, yet a desire to bring order and system to EC contract law responds to a distinctly outdated vision of the law.[13] Past and present experience further suggests that the prize of coherence and system will continue to remain just beyond the horizon.

12 See also J. Karsten & G. Petri, 'Towards a Handbook on European Contract Law and Beyond: The Commission's 2004 Communication 'European Contract Law and the Acquis Review: The Way Forward' (2005) 28(1) Journal of Consumer Policy 31.

13 'Deprived of certainty, some people adopt postures of abandonment, cynicism or nihilim. But we ought to rejoice in the law's indeterminancy, for it is that indeterminancy that gives us the freedom to choose. We are constrained in our choice by tradition, by logic, and by social circumstance only to the extent that we accept them as constraints', J.M. Feinman, 'The Meaning of Reliance: A Historical Perspectice' (1984) Wisc. L. Rev. 1373, 1385.

Bibliography

Academy of European Private Lawyers (ed.), *Code Européen des Contrats, Avant-projet*, Giuffrè, 2002.

Adams, J.N & Brownsword, R., *Understanding Contract Law*, Fifth Edition, Sweet & Maxwell, 2007.

Adler, R.S. & Silverstein, E.M., *When David Meets Goliath: Dealing with Power Differentials in Negotiations*, 5 Harvard Negotiation Law Review, 2000.

Agostini, E., *La Circulation des Módeles Juridiques*, 2 Revue Internationale de Droit Comparé 466, 1990.

Albaladejo, M., *Derecho Civil II – Derecho de obligaciones y contratos, volumes I-III*, Barcelona, 1994.

Alces, P.A., Frisch, D. & Mootz, F.L., *Commercial Contracting: An Integration of the Sales, Leases and Computer Information Transactions Law*, Lexis-Nexis, 2004.

Alces, P.A., *Commercial Codification as Negotiation*, 32 University of California Davis Law Review 17, 2001.

Alces, P.A. & Frisch, D., *On the UCC Revision Process: A Reply to Dean Scott*, 37 William & Mary Law Review, 1996.

Alfaro Águila-Real, J., *Imperialismo Económico y Dogmática Jurídica*, Revista de Derecho Mercantil, Julio-Septiembre, Número 233, 1999.

Alonso Pérez, M., *La responsabilidad precontractual*, Revista Crítica de Derecho Inmobiliario, 1971.

Alpa, G., *European Private Law: Statutory Bases and Action Plans*, paper delivered at conference on the theme of 'Codes and Constitutions – Processes and Cross-influences in the European Union and its Member States', European University Institute, Florence, October 8 –9, 2004.

Amissah, R., *Re-visiting the Autonomous Contract – Transnational contracting, trends and supportive structures*, at http://www.jus.uio.no/sisu/autonomous.contract.2000.amissah/toc

Amissah, R., *The Autonomous Contract – Reflecting the Borderless Electronic-Commercial Environment in Contracting*, available via www.cisg.law.pace.edu/cisg/biblio/amissah2.html

Anderson, M., *Drafting Confidentiality Agreements*, Law Society Publication, 2003.

Anderson, M., *Drafting and Negotiating Commercial Contracts*, Lexis-Nexis, 1998.

Anson, W.R., *Anson's Law of Contract*, Ninth Edition, Oxford University Press, 1998.

Appelbaum, R.P., Felstiner, W.L.F. & Gessner, V., *Rules and Networks – The Legal Culture of Global Business Transactions*, Hart Publishing, 2001.

Arroyo I Amayuelas, E. & Vaquer Aloy, A., *Un Nuevo Impulso Para El Derecho Privado Europeo*, La Ley, Número 5482, February, 2002.

Asín, A. & Parra, M-A., *Damages for occupation of an immovable: culpa in contrahendo and unjustified enrichment under French and Spanish law*, 1 European Review of Private Law 67, 2005.

Asúa González, C., *La culpa in contrahendo – Tratamiento en el Derecho alemán y en otros ordenamientos*, Universidad del País Vasco, Bilbao, 1989.

Atiyah, P.S., *Essays on Contract*, First Edition, Oxford Clarendon Press, 1996.

Atiyah, P.S., *An Introduction to the Law of Contract*, Fifth Edition, Oxford University Press, 1995.

Atiyah, P.S., *Pragmatism and Theory in English Law*, The Hamlyn Lecture Series, London, 1987.

Atiyah, P.S. & Summers, R.S., *Form and Substance in Anglo-American Law*, Oxford Clarendon Press, 1987.

Atiyah, P.S., *The Rise and Fall of Freedom of Contract*, Oxford Clarendon Press, 1979.

Badouin, J.L., 'Réflexion sur la Codification comme Mode d'Expression de le Règle du Droit', in *Unification, Liber Amicorum Jean Georges Sauveplanne*, Kluwer, 1984.

Bagheri, M., *International Contracts and National Economic Regulation – Dispute Resolution through International Commercial Arbitration*, Kluwer, 2000.

Barnard, C. & Scott, J. (eds), *The Law of the Single European Market. Unpacking the Premises*, Oxford Hart Publishing, 2002.

Barnes, D.W., *Remedies for Imperfect Transactions in Contracts and Torts*, 38 San Diego Law Review 193, 2001.

Barret, G. & Bernardeau, L. (ed.s), *Towards a European Civil Code – Reflections on the Codification of Civil Law in Europe*, ERA Forum Special Issue, Trier, 2002.

Barnett, R.E., *W(h)ither the Reliance Interest?*, San Diego Law Review, Winter, 2001.

Barnett, R.E., *The Death of Reliance*, 46 Journal of Legal Education 518, 1996.

Barnett, R.E., *Conflicting Visions: A Critique of Ian Macneil's Relational Theory of Contract*, 78(5) Virginia Law Review 1175, 1992.

Barnett, R.E., *A Consent Theory of Contract*, 86 Columbia Law Review 269, 1986.

Basedow, J., *Codification of Private Law in the European Union: The Making of a Hybrid*, 9(1) European Review of Private Law 35, 2001.

Basedow, J., *The Renascence of Uniform Law: European Law and its Components*, 18 Journal of Legal Studies, 1998.

Basedow, J., *A Common Contract Law for the Common Market*, 33 Common Market Law Review, Volume , 1996.

Beale, H., *English Law Reform and the Impact of European Private Law*, Clifford Chance & Institute of European and Comparative Law conference on the theme of Harmonisation of European Contract Law: Implications for European Private Laws, Business and Legal Practice, Keble College, Oxford, March 18-19, 2005.

Beale, H., Kötz, H., Hartkamp, A. & Tallon, D., *Contract Law: Cases, Material and Text*, Casebooks for a Common Law of Europe Series, 2002.

Beale, H., *Europeanisation of Private Law and English Law*, Position Paper presented at conference entitled on the theme of 'La Reforma dels Codis Civils en un Context d-Aproximació Europea', Jornades de Dret Català a Tossa, 2002.

Beale, H., *Continuing Contract Law Harmonisation Under The White Paper of 1985 – Partly with Modification*, Position Paper presented at The Society of European Contract Law (Secola) and The Centre for a Common Law of Europe, K.U., Conference entitled, *Communication from the Commission on European Contract Law (Harmonisation, Code, Optional Code)*, Leuven, November 30 – December 01, 2001.

Beale, H. (ed), *Chitty on Contracts*, Twenty-eighth Edition, Sweet & Maxwell, 1999.

Beale, H., *The Principles of European Contract Law and Harmonisation of the Laws of Contract*, in Festskrift til Ole Lando, GaJura A/S, 1997.

Beale, H., *The Europeanisation of Contract Law*, in Halston, R., Exploring the Boundaries of Contract, p.23 et seq., 1996.

Beale, H., Bishop, W.D. & Furmston, M.P, Cheshire, Fifoot & Furmston, *The Law of Contract*, Fourteenth Edition, London, 2001.

Beatson, J., *Anson's Law of Contract*, Twenty-eighth Edition, Oxford University Press, 2001.

Beatson, J. & Friedmann, D., *Good Faith and Fault in Contract Law*, Oxford Clarendon Press, 1995.

Bebchuk, L. & Ben-Shahar, O., *Pre-contractual reliance*, National Bureau of Economic Research Working Paper Series, April 2001.

Becker, M., *Promissory Estoppel Damages*, 16 Hofstra Law Review 131, 1987.

Beltrán Sánchez, E. & Nieto Carol, U., *Contratación Mercantil*, Cuadernos de Derecho y Comercio, 1998.

Benson, B.L., *To Arbitrate or to Litigate – That is the Question*, 8 European Journal of Law and Economics 151, 1999.

Benson, P., *The Theory of Contract Law – New Essays*, Cambridge University Press, 2001.

Ben-Shahar, O., *Formalism in Commercial Law: The Tentative Case Against Flexibility in Commercial Law*, 66 University of Chicago Law Review 781, 1999.

Bercovitz Rodríguez-Cano, A. (ed), *Contratos Mercantiles*, 2004.

Berg, A., *Thrashing Through the Undergrowth*, 112 Law Quarterly Review 354, 2006.

Berger, K.P., *The Practice of Transnational Law*, Second Edition, Kluwer, 2001.

Berger, K.P., *The New Law Merchant and the Global Market Place*, available via the *Transnational Law Database* at www.tldb.net

Berger, K.P., *The Creeping Codification of the Lex Mercatoria*, Kluwer, 2001.

Berger, K.P., *Harmonisation of European Contract Law: The Influence of Comparative Law*, 50(4) International & Comparative Law Quarterly 877, 2001.

Berger, K.P., *The Principles of European Contract Law and the Concept of the Creeping Codification of Transnational Law*, , available via the *Transnational Law Database* at www.tldb.net

Berger, K.P., *Transnational Law in the Age of Globalisation*, 42 Centro di Studi e Richerche di Diritto Comparato e Straniero, La Sapienza 2001.

Berger, K.P., *Renegotiation and Adaptation of International Investment Contracts; The Role of Contract Drafters and Arbitrators*, 36 Vanderbilt Journal of Transnational Law 1347, 2003/4.

Berger, K.P., *The Creeping Codification of the Law Mercatoria*, Kluwer, 2001.

Berkley, A. & Mimms, J., *International Commercial Arbitration – Practical Perspectives*, Centre of Construction Law & Management, 2001.

Bernstein, L., *Opting out of the Legal System: Extralegal Contractual Relations in the Diamond Industry*, 21 Journal of Legal Studies 115, 1992.

Bigwood, R., *Pre-contratual Misrepresentation and the Limits of the Principle in 'With v O'Flanagan'*, 64(1) Cambridge Law Journal 94, 2005.

Bigwood, R., *Exploitative Contracts*, Oxford University Press, 2003.

Birke, R. & Fox, C.R., *Psychological Principles in Negotiating Civil Settlements*, 4 Harvard Negotiation Law Review, Spring 1999.

Birks, P., *English Private Law – Volume I*, 2004.

Birks, P., *Unjust Enrichment*, Oxford Clarendon Law Series, 2003.

Birks, P., *The Classification of Obligations*, Oxford Clarendon Press, 1997.

Blair, W. & Brent, R., *A Single European Law of Contract*, 15 European Business Law Review 5, 2004.

Blanc-Jouvan, X., *Reflections on the "Common Core of European Private Law" Project*, Global Jurist Frontiers, Volume 1, Issue 1, Article 2, 2001.

Blase, F., *Leaving the Shadow for the Test of Practice – On the Future of the Principles of European Contract Law*, 3(1) Vindobona Journal of International Commercial Law and Arbitration, 1999.

Boodman, M., *The Myth of Harmonisation of Law*, 30 American Journal of Comparative Law 699, 1991.

Bonell, M.J., *The Unidroit Principles in Practice: Caselaw and Bibliography on the Unidroit Principles of International Commercial Contracts*, 2002.

Bonell, M.J., *The Unidroit Principles of International Commercial Contracts – Nature, Purpose and First Experience in Practice*, available via http://unidroit.org.

Bonell, M.J., *The Unidroit Principles in Practice: The Experience of the First Two Years*, 34 Uniform Law Review, 2001.

Bonell, M.J., *Do We Need a Global Commercial Code?* 106(1) Dickinson Law Review 87, 2001.

Bonell, M.J., *An International Restatement of Contract Law –The Unidroit Principles of International Commercial Law*, Second Edition, Kluwer, 1997.

Bonell, M.J., *The Need and Possibilities of a Codified European Contract Law*, 5(4) European Review of Private Law 505, 1997.

Bonell, M.J., *The Unidroit Principles of International Commercial Contracts and the Principles of European Contract Law: Similar Rules for the Same Purposes,* 2 Uniform Law Review 229, 1996.

Bonell, M.J., *Policing the International Commercial Contract Against Unfairness under the Unidroit Principles,* 3 Tulane Journal of International and Comparative Law, 1994.

Born, G.B., *International Commercial Arbitration – Commentary & Materials,* Second Edition, Kluwer, 2001.

Bradgate, R., *Commercial Law,* Third Edition, Butterworths, 2001.

Bridge, M.G., *Does Anglo-Canadian Law need a doctrine of Good Faith?,* 9 Canadian Business Law 385, 1984.

Bright, C. & Bright, S., *Beware the Letter of Comfort,* 138 New Law Journal 365, 1988.

Brouckaert, Boudewijn, Shäfer, H., 'Mistake of Law and the Economics of Legal Information' in Brouckaert, Boudewijn & De Geest, G., *Essays in Law and Economics II: Contract Law, Regulation and Reflections on Law and Economics,* Antwerp, 1995.

Brousseau, E. & Glachant, J-M, *Economics of Contracts,* Cambridge University Press, 2002.

Brown, I., *The Contract to Negotiate: A Thing Writ in Water?,* Journal of Business Law 353, 1992.

Brownsword, R., *Individualism, Cooperativism and an Ethic for European Contract Law,* 64(4) Modern Law Review 628, 2001.

Brownsword, R., *Contract Law – Themes for the Twenty-First Century,* 2000.

Brownsword, R., Hird, N.J. & Howells, G., *Good Faith in Contract: Concept and Context,* Ashgate, 1999.

Brownsword, R., Howells, G. & Wilhelmsson, T. (eds.), *Welfarism in Contract Law,* Ashgate, 1994.

Buckley, F.H., *The Fall and Rise of Freedom of Contract,* Duke University Press, 1999.

Buckley, R.P., *Adversarial Bargaining: The Neglected Aspect of Negotiation,* 75 Australian Law Journal 181, 2001.

Buckley, R.P., *Walford v Miles: False Certainty About Uncertainty – An Australian Perspective,* 6(58) Journal of Contract Law, 1993.

Burger, B., *Prinzipien eines Europäischen Vertragsrecht: Liberal, Marktfunktional, Solidarisch Oder?,* 2(1) Electronic Journal of Comparative Law, 1998.

Burnham, S.J., *Drafting Contracts,* Second Edition, 1993.

Bussani, M., *Integrative Comparative Law Enterprises and the Inner Stratification of Legal Systems,* 8 (1) European Review of Private Law, 2000.

Bussani, M. & Mattei, U. (eds), *Making European Law: Essays on the Common Core Project,* Trento, 2000.

Cabanillas Sánchez, A., *El ámbito de la responsabilidad precontractual o culpa en contrahendo,* 628 Revista Crítica de Derecho Inmobiliario, 1995.

Cafaggi, F. (ed), *The Institutional Framework of European Private Law*, Oxford University Press, 2006.

Cafaggi, F., *Revisiting the Relationship between Constitutional Law and Private Law in the Perspective of European Integration*, paper delivered at conference on the theme of "Codes and Constitutions – Processes and Cross-influences in the European Union and its Member States, European University Institute, Florence, October 8 –9, 2004.

Cafaggi, F. (ed), *Quale armonnizazzione per il diritto europeo dei contratti*, Cedam, Padua, 2003.

Cámara Lapuente, S., *Derecho Privado Europeo*, Colex, Madrid, 2003.

Cámara Lapuente, S., *The Hypothetical 'European Civil Code': Why, How, When?* Academy of European Law Conference on European Contract Law, Trier, March, 14-15, 2002.

Campbell, D., *Reflexivity and Welfarism in the Modern Law of Contract*, 20(3) Oxford Journal of Legal Studies 477, 2000.

Campbell, D. & Picciotto, S., *Exploring the Interaction Between Law and Economics: The Limits of Formalism*, 18(3) Journal of Legal Studies 249, 1998.

Cappelleti, M., *New Perspectives for a Common Law of Europe*, Reports from Symposium inaugurating the European University Institute, Florence, 1978.

Carbonneau, T.E., *Arbitration Symposium: The Ballad of Transborder Arbitration*, 56 University of Miami Law Review 773, 2002.

Carbonneau, T.E., *Lex Mercatoria and Arbitration – A Discussion of the New Law Merchant*, Transnational Juris Publication, 1992.

Caruso, D., *The Missing View of the Cathedral – The Private Law Paradigm of European Integration*, 3 European Law Journal, 1997.

Caruso, D., *La Culpa in Contrayendo – L'Esperienza Statunitense e Quella Italiana*, Milan, 1993.

Caruso, D., *Relazioni Precontrattuali e Teori dei Giochi*, Milan, 1991.

Cartwright, J., *Misrepresentation, Mistake and Non-Disclosure*, Sweet & Maxwell, 2007.

Cartwright, J., *Unequal Bargaining*, Oxford University Press, 1991.

Casanovas, P., *Las Formas Sociales del Derecho Contemporáneo: El Nuevo Ius Commune*, Universitat Autònoma de Barcelona, Working Paper Number 146, Barcelona, 1998.

Castrillón y Luna, V. *La Recodificación Sustantiva del Derecho Mercantil*, 7 Revista de Derecho Privado 3, 2004.

Castronovo, C., *Contract and the Idea of Codification in The Principles of European Contract Law*, in Festskrift til Ole Lando, Copenhagen, 1997.

Chamboredon, A., *Form and Substance? An Ideological Venture Beyond the Dichotomy in European Contract Law*, 8(1) European Review of Private Law, 2000.

Chapman, M.J., *Commercial and Consumer Arbitration – Statutes & Rules*, Blackstone, 1997.

Charny, D., *Formalism in Commercial Law: The New Formalism in Contract,* 66 University of Chicago Law Review 842, 1999.

Charny, D., *Non-Legal Sanctions in Commercial Relationships,* 104 Harvard Law Review 373, 1990.

Chen, J.C., *Code, Custom and Contract: The Uniform Commercial Code as Law Merchant,* 27 Texas International Law Journal 91, 1992.

Cohen, N. & McKendrick, E., *Comparative Remedies for Breach of Contract,* Hart Law, 2005.

Collins, H., *Utility and Rights in Common Law Reasoning: Rebalancing Private Law Through Constitutionalization,* Working Paper Series of the London School of Economics, number 6, 2007.

Collins, H. (ed.), *Social Justice in European Contract Law – A Manifesto,* 10(6) European Law Journal 653, 2004.

Collins, H., *The Law of Contract,* Fourth Edition, Lexis/Butterworths, 2003.

Collins, H., *Transaction Costs and Subsidiarity in European Contract Law,* Intervention at The Society of European Contract Law (Secola) and The Centre for a Common Law of Europe, K.U., Conference entitled, *Communication from the Commission on European Contract Law (Harmonisation, Code, Optional Code),* Leuven, November 30 – December 01, 2001.

Collins, H., *From Liberal Rights to Post-National Private Law Regulation,* Position Paper presented at The Society of European Contract Law (Secola) Conference entitled, *Sales and Trends in European Contract Law,* Rome, June 08-09, 2001.

Collins, H., *Formalism and Efficiency: Designing European Commercial Contract Law,* 8(1) European Review of Private Law 211, 2000.

Collins, H., *Regulating Contracts,* Oxford Clarendon Press, 1999.

Collins, H., *Legal Theory and Common Law,* Oxford Clarendon Press, 1996.

Collins, H., *European Private Law and the Cultural Identity of States,* 3 European Review of Private Law 353, 1995.

Collins, H., *Good Faith in European Contract Law,* 14(1) Oxford Journal of Legal Studies 229, 1994.

Cooter, R.D., *Decentralised Law for a Complex Economy,* Pennsylvania Law Review 1643, 1996.

Cornish, W.R. & Clark, G de N., *Law, Economy & Society in England,* 1750-1950, Sweet & Maxwell, 1989.

Corripio Gil-Delgado, M.R., *Los Contratos Informáticos – El Deber de Información Precontractual,* Comillas, 1999.

Cranford Smith, V., *Culture, Identity & European Intergration,* Oxford University Press, 2004.

Cranston, R., *Making Commercial Law,* Oxford University Press, 1997.

Craswell, R., *Offer, Acceptance and Efficient Reliance,* 48 Stanford Law Review 481, 1996.

Craswell, R., *Performance, Reliance and One-Sided Information,* 18(2) Journal of Legal Studies 365, 1989.

Craswell, R., *Contract Law, Default Rules and the Philosophy of Promising,* 88 Michigan Law Review 489, 1989.

Craswell, R., *Precontractual Investigation as an Optimal Precaution Problem,* 17 Journal of Legal Studies 401, 1988.

Craswell, R. & Schwartz, A., *Foundations of Contract Law,* Oxford University Press, 1994.

Dalton, A., *An Essay on the Deconstruction of Contract Doctrine,* 94 Yale Law Journal 997, 1985.

Danz, E., *La interpretación de los negocios jurídicos,* Revista de Derecho Privado, 1955.

Davison, P., *Evaluating Contract Claims,* Blackwell, 2003.

Deakin, S., *Two Types of Regulatory Competition: Competitive Versus Reflexive Harmonisation. A Law and Economics Perspective on 'Centros',* The Cambridge Yearbook of European Legal Studies – Volume II, 1999.

Deakin, S. & Michie, J. (eds.), *Contracts, Co-operation and Competition – Studies in Economics, Management and Law,* Oxford University Press, 1997.

Deflorian, L.A., *Consumer Protection, Fair Dealing in Marketing Contracts and European Contract Law – A Uniform Law?* 2(2) Global Jurist Frontiers, Article 4, 2002.

Dezalay, Y. & Garth, B.G., *Dealing in Virtue, International Commercial Arbitration and the Construction of a Transnational Legal Order,* University of Chicago Press, 1996.

De Castro y Bravo, F., *Derecho civil de España,* Editorial Civitas,1984.

De Castro y Bravo, F., *Limitaciones Intrínsecas de la Autonomía de la Voluntad,* Anuario de Derecho Civil, Madrid, 1982.

De Geest, G, *Towards an (Extremely Detailed) International Standard Code,* Intervention at The Society of European Contract Law (Secola) and The Centre for a Common Law of Europe, K.U., Conference entitled, *Communication from the Commission on European Contract Law (Harmonisation, Code, Optional Code*), Leuven, November 30 – December 01, 2001.

De la Fuente, M. y Echarri, A., *Modelos de Contratos Internacionales,* Seventh Edition, Madrid, 1999.

De la Sierra, S., *Una metodología para el Derecho Comparado europeo,* Cuadernos Civitas, Madrid, 2004.

De la Torre, A. & Moralejo Menéndez, I., *Lecciones de Derecho en los Contratos en el Comercio Internacional,* Ratio Legis, Salamanca, 2006.

De los Mozos, *La forma en los negocios jurídicos,* Anuario de Derecho Civil, 1968.

De Ly, F., *International Business Law and Lex Mercatoria,* Amsterdam, 1992.

De Witte, B., *The European Union's System of Competence and Private Law Harmonisation*, paper delivered at conference on the theme of "Codes and Constitutions – Processes and Cross-influences in the European Union and its Member States, European University Institute, Florence, October 8-9, 2004.

De Witte, B., *Soft Law in the European Union Legal Order*, Position paper presented at seminar on Soft Law, European University Institute, Florence, February 2003.

De Witte, B & Forder, C., (eds), *The Common Law of Europe and the Future of Legal Education / Le Droit Commun de l'Europe et l'Avenir de l'Enseignement Juridique*, Kluwer law International, 1992.

Dezalay, Y. & Garth, B.G., *Dealing in Virtue – International Commercial Arbitration and the Construction of a Transnational Legal Order*, University of Chicago Press, 1996.

De Zwann, J.W. (ed), *The European Union – An Ongoing Process of Integration*, Liber Amicorum Alfred E. Kellerman, Cambridge University Press, 2004.

Díaz-Ambrona Bardají, M.D., *Derecho Civil Comunitario*, Editorial Colex, Madrid, 2004.

Díaz Fraile, J.M. (ed.), *Estudios de Derecho Europeo Privado*, Civitas, Madrid, 1994.

Díez-Picazo, L. y Gullón, A., *Sistema de Derecho Civil*, Seventh Edition, Madrid, 1998.

Di Matteo, L. (ed), *International Sales Law – A Critical Analysis of CISG Jurisprudence*, Cambridge University Press, 2005.

Di Matteo, L., *Reviewing the Historical and Practical Significance of the Principles of European Contract Law*, 43 Harvard International Law Journal 569, 2002.

Di Matteo, L. & Sacasas, R., *Credit and Value Comfort Instruments: Crossing the Line from Assurance to Legally Significant Reliance and Toward a Theory of Enforceability*, 47 Baylor Law Review 357, 1995.

Di Matteo, L., *The CISG and the Presumption of Enforceability: Unintended Contractual Liability in International Business Dealings*, 22 Yale Journal of International Law 111, 1997.

Doris, M.J., *Harmonising By Numbers*, 32(6) European Law Review 877, December 2007.

Doris, M.J., *A European Insurance Market and EC Contract Law – Is there Life for One Without the Other?*, European Current Law, October 2007.

Doris, M.J., *Bargaining and Reliance in New European Contract Law*, accesible via Indret.com.

Doris, M.J., Review of '*European Contract Law – Scots and South African Perspectives*', 32(4) European Law Review 600, 2007.

Doris, M.J., *The Continued Resonance and Challenge of the Ius Commune in Modern European Contract Law*, 34(2) International Journal of Legal Information 391, 2006.

Doris, M.J., *Academic Misadventure or Model for Future European Governance? A Common Frame of Reference for a More Coherent EC Contract Law*, Society of Legal Scholars conference, September 2006.

Doris, M.J., *Did We Lose The Baby With the Bath Water? The Scholastic Contribution to the Common Law of Contracts*, 11(2) Texas Wesleyan Law Journal 361, 2004.

Doris, M.J., *Cross Border Contracting in the EU – Interoperability Problems and the Impact of a Community Wide Optional Instrument*, 12(1) Tilburg Foreign Law Review 36, 2004.

Doris, M.J., 'Seizing the Constitutional Moment? Governance, Interlegality and a Law of Lawmaking for the Europeanisation of Contract' in Astengo, F. & Neuwahl, N. (eds) *Governance and Policy Making in the European Union*, 2004

Doris M.J., *Beyond a Stillborn European Civil Code – The Commission's Action Plan on a More Coherent European Contract Law*, conference on 'European Contracting', Centre for the Study of Business and Commercial Law, Tromsø, Norway, March, 2003.

Doris, M.J., *The Dilemma of Choice – Harmonisation Which European Contract Laws?* Paper presented at the European University Institute, February, 2003.

Doris, M.J. & Marco, Colino, S., *Swings and Roundabouts in European Private Law*, PriME conference on 'Private Law and the Many Cultures of Europe', Helsinki, August, 2006.

Dougan, M., *Minimum Harmonization and the Internal Market*, 37 Common Market Law Review, Volume 853, 2000.

Drahozal, C.R., *Commercial Norms, Commercial Codes, and International Commercial Arbitration*, 33 Vanderbilt Journal of Transnational Law 79, 2000.

Drexl, J., *Community legislation continued: complete harmonisation, framework legislation or non-binding measures – Alternative approaches to European contract law, consumer protection and unfair trade practices?* 13(6) European Business Law Review 557, 2002.

Drobnig, U., *A Subsidiarity Plea: A European Contract Law for Intra-European Border-Crossing Contracts – The Case for a European Contract Act*, position paper presented at The Society of European Contract Law (Secola) and The Centre for a Common Law of Europe, K.U., Conference entitled, *Communication from the Commission on European Contract Law (Harmonisation, Code, Optional Code)*, Leuven, November 30 – December 01, 2001.

Echebarría Sáenz, J.A., *El contrato de franquicia*, McGraw-Hill, Madrid, 1995.

Eisenberg, M.A., *The Bargain Principle and Its Limits*, 95 Harvard Law Review 741, 1982.

Eisenberg, M.A., *Expression Rules in Contract Law and Problems of Offer and Acceptance*, 82(5) California Law Review, October 1994.

Elliot, C & Quinn, F., *Contract Law*, Third Edition, Longman, 2001.

Enonchong, N., *Duress, Undue Influence and Unconscionable Dealings*, Sweet & Maxwell, 2004.

Epstein, R.A. (ed.), *Contract – Freedom and Restraint*, Garland New York, 2000.

Epstein, R.A., *Unconscionability: A Critical Reappraisal*, 18 Journal of Law and Economics 293, 1975.

El Código civil española, edición preparada por Rodrigo Bercovitz, Rodríguez Cano y José Carlos Erdozain López, Editorial Tecnos, Madrid, 2005.

El Código civil española, edición preparada por Fernández Urzainqui, Madrid, 1997.

Esteban de la Rosa, F., *La protección de los consumidores en el Mercado interior europeo*, Estudios de Derecho privado europeo, Editorial Comares, Granada, 2003.

Fabra Valle, G., *Manual Práctico de Contratos Civiles*, Publicaciones Edisofer, Madrid, 1999.

Farnsworth, E.A., *Farnsworth on Contracts*, New York, 2004.

Farnsworth, E.A., *United States Contract Law*, Transnational Juris Publications, New York, 1991.

Farnsworth, E.A., *Precontractual Liability*, Transnational Juris Publications, New York, 1991.

Farnsworth, E.A., *Precontractual Liability and Preliminary Agreements: Fair Dealing and Failed Negotiations*, 87 Columbia Law Review 217, 1987.

Fauvarque-Cosson, B., *Comparative Law and Conflicts of Laws: Allies or Enemies? New Perspectives on an Old Couple*, Paper presented at conference on the Europeanisation of Contract, European University Institute, Florence, October 24-25, 2003.

Fawcett, J. (ed), *Reform and Development of Private International Law ~ Essays in Honour of Sir Peter North*, Oxford University Press, 2002.

Feiden, S. & Schmid, C.U. (eds), *Evolutionary Perspectives and Projects on Harmonisation of Private Law in the EU*, Working Papers Series of The European University Institute, Florence, Law No. 7, 1999.

Feiden, S. & Riedl, K. (eds), *Towards a Europeanised Judiciary? Practitioner's Experiences of National Judges with the Europeanisation of Private Law*, Working Papers Series of *The European University Institute*, Florence, Law No. 3, 2000

Felegmas, J., *Comparative Editorial Remarks on the Concept of Good Faith in the CISG and the Principles of European Contract Law*, 13 Pace International Law Review 399, 2001.

Ferrari, F., *Forum Shopping Despite International Uniform Contract Law Conventions*, 51(3) International and Comparative Law Quarterly 689, 2002.

Fletcher, I., Mestelis, L. & Cremona, M. (ed), *Foundations and Perspectives of International Trade Law*, Sweet & Maxwell Publishing, 2001.

Fox, W.F., *International Commercial Agreements – A Functional Primer on Drafting, Negotiating and Resolving Disputes*, Kluwer Law Publishing, 1988.

Fried, C., *Contract as Promise – A Theory of Contractual Obligations*, 1981.

Fuenzalida, V., Cuesta Saenz, C. & De la Madrid, J-M., *Código europeo de contratos*, Volumes I & II, Editorial Dykinson, 2004.

Furmston, M.P., Norisada, T. & Poole, J., *Contract Formation and Letters of Intent*, Wiley, 1998.

Fuller, L. & Perdue, W., *The Reliance Interest in Contract Damages*, 46 Yale Law Journal 373, 1937.

Galanter, M., *Symposium on Contracts: Contract in Court, or almost everything you may or may not want to know about contract litigation*, Wisconsin Law Review 577, 2001.

Galanter, M., *Worlds of Deals: Using Negotiation to Teach about Legal Process*, 34 Journal of Legal Education 268, 1984.

Gandolfi, G., *Communication sur le Droit Européen des Contrats*, position paper presented at The Society of European Contract Law (Secola) and The Centre for a Common Law of Europe, K.U., Conference entitled, *Communication from the Commission on European Contract Law (Harmonisation, Code, Optional Code)*, Leuven, November 30 – December 01, 2001.

García Amigo, M., *Lecciones de Derecho Civil II, Teoría General de las Obligaciones y* Contratos, McGraw-Hill, Madrid, 1995.

García Lorenzo, A., *The Role of Interest Groups in the European Union Decision-Making Process*, European Journal of Law and Economics, Kluwer Law Publishers, Volume 15, pp.251-261, 2003.

García Rubio, M.P., *Responsabilidad por ruptura injustificada de negociaciones*, La Ley, 1989.

Garcimartín Alférez, F.J., *Party Autonomy and its Limits in Cross Border Commercial Contracts*, Madrid, 2004.

Gardner, S., *The Remedial Discretion in Proprietary Estoppel – Again*, 122 Law Quarterly Review 142, 2006.

Garvin, L., *The Strange Death of Academic Commercial Law*, 68 Ohio State Law Journal, 2007.

Gessner, V. & Cem Budak, A., *Emerging Legal Certainty: Empirical Studies on the Globalisation of Law*, Ashgate, 1998.

Giliker, P., *Taking Comfort in Uncertainty To Enforce or Not the Letter of Comfort*, Lloyd's Maritime and Commercial Law Quarterly, 2004.

Giliker, P., *Formation of Contract and Pre-contractual Information from an English Perspective*, The Architecture of European Codes and Contract Law, Society of European Contract Law Conference, Vienna, 18-19 June 2004.

Giliker, P., *A Role for Tort in Pre-Contractual Negotiations? An Analysis of English, French and Canadian Law*, 52 International Comparative Law Quarterly 969, October 2003.

Giliker, P., *Precontractual Liability in English and French Law*, Kluwer, 2002.

Gilmore, G., *The Death of Contract*, Ohio State University Press, 1974.

Giménez Costa, A. & Bosch Capdevila, E., *Option and Pre-contract*, The Architecture of European Codes and Contract Law, Society of European Contract Law Conference, Vienna, 18-19 June 2004.

Glenn, H.P., *Legal Traditions of the World, Sustainable Diversity in Law*, Oxford University Press, 2000.

Glyn-Watkin, T., *An Historical Introduction to Modern Civil Law*, Laws of the Nations Series, Dartmouth Publishing Company Limited, Aldershot, 1999.

Glynn Watkin, T., *The Europeanisation of Law*, International Colloquium of the United Kingdom Committee of Comparative Law, Cardiff, 1998.

Goetz, C.J. & Scott, R.E., *Enforcing Promises: An Examination of the Basis of Contract*, 89(7) Yale Law Journal 1261, 1980.

Goldberg, V.P., *Readings in the Economics of Contract Law*, Cambridge University Press, 1989.

Goldberg, V.P., *Competitive Bidding and the Production of Pre-contract Information*, 8 Bell Journal of Economics 250, 1977.

Gómez Arboleya, E., 'El Racionalismo Jurídico y los Códigos Europeos' in *Estudios de Teoría de la Sociedad y del Estado*, Madrid, 1962.

Gómez Calle, E., *Los deberes precontractuales de información*, La Ley, Madrid, 1994.

Gómez Jene, M., *El Arbitraje Comercial Internacional en la Unión Europea: La Eficacia del Laudo Arbitral*, Madrid, 2002.

Goode, R., Kronke, H., McKendrick, E & Wool, J., *Transnational Commercial Law*, Oxford Clarendon Press, 2004.

Goode, R., *Contract and Commercial Law: The Logic and Limits of Harmonisation*, 7(4) Electronic Journal of Comparative Law, November 2003.

Goode, R., *Insularity or Leadership? The Role of the United Kingdom in the Harmonisation of Commercial Law*, 50(4) International Comparative Law Quarterly 751, 2001.

Goode, R., *Commercial Law in the Next Millennium*, The Hamlyn Lecture Series, Sweet & Maxwell, 1998.

Goode, R., *International Restatements of Contract and English Contract Law*, 2 Uniform Law Review 231, 1997.

Goode, R. & Cranston, R., *Making Commercial Law*, Essays in Honour of Roy Goode, Oxford University Press, 1997.

Goode, R, Kronke, H., McKendrick, E. & Wool, J., *Transnational Commercial Law – Primary Materials*, Oxford University Press, 2007.

Goode, R, Kronke, H., McKendrick, E. & Wool, J., *Transnational Commercial Law – Text, Cases and Materials*, Oxford University Press, 2007.

Gonzáles Aguilar, A., Ferreyros Soto, C. & Carrascosa López, V., *Los contratos en la sociedad de la información – formularios de contratos informáticos e Internet*, Colleción y Nuevas Technologías, Editorial Comares, Granada, 2004.

González Gozalo, A., *La formación del contrato tras la Ley de servicios de la sociedad de la información y de comercio electrónico*, Collección Estudios de Derecho Privado, Editorial Comares, Granada, 2004.

González Soler, M.D., Lima Torrado, J., Marín Castán, M.L., Prada García, A., Roldán Alvarez, C. & Rovetta Klyver, F., *Cuestiones y Textos de Historia de la Filosofía del Derecho, Moral y Política: Del Renacimiento a Kant*, Editorial Dynkinson, Madrid, 1997.

Gordley, J., *The Foundations of Private Law*, Oxford University Press, 2007.

Gordley, J., *The Future of European Contract Law on the Basis of Europe's Heritage, European Review of Contract Law*, 2 European Review of Contract Law 163, 2005.

Gordley, J., *The Enforceability of Promises*, Cambridge University Press, 2001.

Gordley, J., *The Common Law in the Twentieth Century – Some Unfinished Business*, 88 California Law Review 1817, 2000.

Gordley, J., *The Common Law in the 20th Century*, 81 California Law Review 1817, 2000.

Gordley, J., *Is Comparative Law a Distinct Discipline?* 46 American Journal of Comparative Law 701, 1998.

Gordley, J., *Codification and Legal Scholarship*, 31 Davis Law Journal 735, 1998.

Gordley, J., *Contract and Delict: Toward a Unified Law of Obligations*, 1 Edinburgh Law Review 345, 1997.

Gordley, J., *Comparative Legal Research: Its Function in the Development of Harmonised Law*, 43(4) American Journal of Comparative Law 555, 1995.

Gordley, J., *The Philosophical Origins of Modern Contract Doctrine*, Oxford Clarendon Press, 1991.

Gordley, J., *European Codes and American Restatements: Some Difficulties*, 81 Columbia Law Review 140, 1981.

Gordley, J. & Von Mehren, A., *The Civil Law System: An Introduction to the Comparative Study of Law*, Boston, 1977.

Gralf-Calliess, P., *Reflexive Transnational Law – The Privatisation of Law and the Civilisation of Private Law*, accessible at: http:www.uni-frankfurt.de/fb01/teubner/pdf-dateien/Reflexive.pdf.

Grundmann, S., *Actors in Codification Processes and the Horizontal Spread of Powers*, paper delivered at conference on the theme of 'Codes and Constitutions – Processes and Cross-influences in the European Union and its Member States', European University Institute, Florence, October 8 –9, 2004.

Grundmann, S., *The Role of Drafting and Discussion in the Process Leading to a Common Frame of Reference and a European Contract Law Code*, Paper presented at conference on the theme of the Europeanisation of contract, European University Institute, Florence, October 24-25, 2003.

Grundmann, S., *Consumer Law, Commercial Law, Private Law: How can the Sales Directive and the Sales Convention be so Similar*, 14 European Business Law Review 237, 2003.

Grundmann, S., *Information, Party Autonomy and Economic Agents in European Contract Law*, 39 Common Market Law Review 269, 2002.

Grundmann, S., *The Structure of European Contract Law*, 4 European Review of Private Law 505, 2001.

Grundmann, S. & Schauer, M. (eds), *The Architecture of European Codes and Contract Law*, Kluwer, 2006.

Grundmann, S. & Stuyck. J. (eds), *An Academic Green Paper on European Contract Law*, Kluwer, 2002.

Grundmann, S., Kerber, W. & Weatherill, S. (eds), *Party Autonomy and the Role of Information in the Internal Market*, de Gruyter, 2001.

Grundmann, S., 'General Principles of Private Law and Ius Commune Modernum as Applicable Law' in Baums, T., Hopt, K.J. & Horn, N., *Corporations, Capital Markets and Business in the Law – Liber Americorum Richard M. Buxbaum*, Kluwer, 2001.

Harding, C., *The Identity of European Law: Mapping out the European Legal Space*, 6(2) European Law Journal, June 2000.

Harris, J., *Contractual Freedom in the Conflict of Laws*, 20(2) Oxford Journal of Legal Studies 247, 2000.

Hartkamp, A., Hesselink, M.W., Hondius, E.H., Joustra, C, Du Perron, E. & Veldman, M. (eds), *Towards a European Civil Code*, Third Edition, Kluwer, 2004; Second Edition, Kluwer, 1998.

Hartkamp, A., *Perspectives for the Development of a European Civil Law*, Position paper presented at symposium entitled *The Process of Approximation of Domestic Law to the Law of the European Union – An Opportunity and a Challenge for the States of Central and Eastern Europe*, full text accessible at http://www.cbs.dk/departments/law/staff/ol/commission-on-ecl/

Hartkamp, A., *Judicial Discretion under the New Civil Code of Netherlands*, 40 American Journal of Comparative Law 551, 1992.

Hatzis, A., *The Absence of Theory: Common vs. Civil Law*, XIV Annual Conference of the European Association of Law and Economics, September 1997.

Hesselink, M.W., *The Politics of European Contract Law – Who has an interest in what kind of contract law for Europe?*, Intervention at The Society of European Contract Law (Secola) and The Centre for a Common Law of Europe, K.U., Conference entitled, *Communication from the Commission on European Contract Law (Harmonisation, Code, Optional Code)*, Leuven, November 30 – December 01, 2001.

Hesselink, M.W., *The New European Legal Culture*, Kluwer, 2001.

Hesselink, M.W., *The Principles of European Contract Law: Some Choices Made By The Lando Commission*, 1(1) Global Jurist Frontiers 4, 2001.

Hillman. R.A., *The Richness of Contract Law: An Analysis and Critique of Contemporary Theories of Contract Law*, Kluwer, 1997.

Hirsch, G., *European Contract Law – A Challenge for National and International Law, Economy and Society*, position paper presented at The Society of European Contract Law (Secola) and The Centre for a Common Law of Europe, K.U., Conference entitled, *Communication from the Commission on European Contract Law (Harmonisation, Code, Optional Code)*, Leuven, November 30 – December 01, 2001.

Hoch, M., *Is Fair Dealing a Workable Concept for European Contract Law*, Global Jurist Topics, Volume 5, Number 1, 2005.

Hondius, E., *Precontractual liability – Reports to the XIII Congress, International Academy of Comparative Law*, Montréal, Canada, August, 1990.

Horwitz, M.J., *The Historical Foundations of Modern Contract Law*, 87(5) Harvard Law Review, 1987.

Howells, G., Janssen, A. & Schulze, R., *Information Rights and Obligations: A Challenge for Party Autonomy and Transactional Fairness*, Ashgate, 2005.

Howells, G., *EC and USA – The Scope for Harmonised Legislative Activity Compared, European Review of Private Law*, 5 European Review of Private Law 601, 2002.

Howells, G., *European Consumer Law – The Minimal and Maximal Harmonisation Debate*, Position paper presented at The Society of European Contract Law (Secola) and The Centre for a Common Law of Europe, K.U., Conference entitled, *Communication from the Commission on European Contract Law (Harmonisation, Code, Optional Code)*, Leuven, November 30 – December 01, 2001.

Howells, G. & Wilhelmsson, T., *EC Consumer Law*, Ashgate, 1997.

Ibbetson, D.J., *An Historical Introduction to the Law of Obligations*, Oxford University Press, 1999.

Ioratti, E., A *Methodological Approach for a European Restatement of Contract Law*, 3(3) Global Jurist Topics, Article 4, 2003.

Institute for International Business Law and Practice, *Formation of Contracts and Precontractual Liability*, ICC Publication, Number 440/9, 1990.

Irti, N., *L'Età della Decodificazione*, Guiffrè, Milan, 1989.

Jamin, C. & Mazeaud, D., *L'Harmonisation du droit des contrats en Europe*, Études Juridiques, Economica, 2001.

Joerges, C., *The Challenges of Europeanization in the Realm of Private Law – A Plea for a New Legal Discipline*, 14 Duke Journal of Comparative and International Law 149, 2004.

Joerges, C., *The Coherence of Private Law, Codification and the Theory of the European Economic Constitution*, paper delivered at conference on the theme of "Codes and Constitutions – Processes and Cross-influences in the European Union and its Member States", European University Institute, Florence, October 8 –9, 2004.

Joerges, C., *Europeanisation as Process: Tensions between the Logic of Integration and the Logic of Codification*, Paper presented at conference on the theme of the Europeanisation of contract, European University Institute, Florence, October 24-25, 2003.

Joerges, C., *On the Legitimacy of Europeanising Europe's Private Law: Considerations on a Law of Justi(ce)-ficaction (justum facere) for the EU Multi-Level System*, The European University Institute Working Papers Series, Law 2003/3, 2003.

Joerges, C., *Interactive Adjudication in the Europeanisation Process? A Demanding Perspective and a Modest Example*, 1 European Review of Private Law 1, 2000.

Joerges, C., *The Science of Private Law And The Nation State*, The European University Institute Working Papers Series, Law 1998/4, 1998.

Joerges, C., *The Impact of European Integration on Private Law – Reductionist Perceptions, True Conflicts and a New Constitutional Perspective*, 3(4) European Law Journal 378, 1997.

Joerges, C., Sand, I.J., & Teubner, G., *Transnational Governance and Constitutionalism*, Hart Law Publishing, 2004.

Johnston, J.S. *Communication and Courtship: Cheap Talk Economics and the Law of Contract Formation*, 85 Virginia Law Review 385, 1999.

Jones, G. & Swadling, W., *The Search for Principle – Essays in Honour of Lord Goff or Chiveley*, Oxford University Press, 2000.

Kanning, A.J., *Domestic and Foreign Commerce as a Pathfinder for Unification of Commercial Laws of Nation-States in the 20th Century*, 14(3) European Business Law Review 351, 2003.

Karsten, J. & Petri, G., *Towards a Handbook on European Contract Law and Beyond: The Commission's 2004 Communication 'European Contract Law and the Acquis Review: The Way Forward*, 28(1) Journal of Consumer Policy 31, 2005.

Karsten, J. & Sinai, A.R., *The Action Plan on European Contract Law – Perspectives for the Future of European Contract Law and EC Consumer Law*, 26(2) Journal of Consumer Law and Policy, 2003.

Kennedy, D., *The Political Stakes in "Merely Technical" Issues of Contract Law*, 1 European Review of Private Law 7, 2001.

Kennedy, D., *Form and Substance in Private Law Adjudication*, 89 Harvard Law Review 1685, 1976.

Killian, M., *The CISG and the problem of common law jurisdictions*, 10 Journal of Transnational Law and Policy 217, 2001.

Komesar, N.K., *Law's Limits – The Rule of Law and the Supply and Demand of Rights*, Cambridge University Press, 2001.

Komesar, N.K., *Imperfect Alternatives – Choosing Institutions in Law, Economics and Public Policy*, University of Chicago Press, 1994.

Kostritsky, P., *Taxonomy for Justifying Legal Intervention in an Imperfect World : What to do when parties have not achieved bargains or have drafted incomplete contracts*, Wisconsin Law Review 323, 2004.

Kostritsky, P., *When Should Contract Law Supply a Liability Rule or Term?: Framing a Principle of Unification for Contracts*, 32 Arizona State Law Journal 1283, 2000.

Kötz, H. & Flessner, A., *European Contract Law – Formation, Validity and Content of Contracts*, Oxford Clarendon Press, 1997.

Knapp, C.L., Crystal, N.M. & Prince, H.G., *Problems in Contract Law – Cases & Materials*, Fourth Edition, Aspen Law, New York, 1999.

Kramer, A., *Common Sense Principles of Contract Interpretation*, 23(2) Oxford Journal of Legal Studies 173, 2003.

Kramer, M.H., *Dogmas and Distortions: Legal Positivism Defended*, 21(4) Oxford Journal of Legal Studies 673, 2001.

Kronman, A.T. & Posner, R.A., *The Economics of Contract Law*, Little Brown, 1979.

Kupfer Schneider, A., *Shattering Negotiation Myths: Empirical Evidence on the Effectiveness of Negotiation Style*, 7 Harvard Negotiation Law Review, Spring 2002.

Lando, O. & Beale, H., *The Principles of European Contract Law, Parts I – III*, Kluwer, 1998/2002.

Lando, O., *Why Does Europe Need a Civil Code?*, Intervention at The Society of European Contract Law (Secola) and The Centre for a Common Law of Europe, K.U., Conference entitled, *Communication from the Commission on European Contract Law (Harmonisation, Code, Optional Code)*, Leuven, November 30 – December 01, 2001.

Lando, O., *Optional or Mandatory Europeanisation of Contract Law*, 8(1) European Review of Private Law 59, 2000.

Lando, O., *Some Features of the Law of Contracts in the New Millennium*, 40 Scandinavian Studies in Law 343, 2000.

Lando, O., *The Common Core of European Private Law and the Principles of European Contract Law*, 21 Hastings International and Comparative Law Review, Summer 1998.

Lando, O., *Is Codification Needed in Europe? Principles of European Contract Law and the Relationship to Dutch Law*, 1 European Review of Private Law 157, 1993.

Lando, O., *Principles of European Contract Law: An Alternative to or a Precursor of European Legislation?*, 40 American Journal of Comparative Law 573, 1992.

Lando, O., *European Contract Law*, 31 American Journal of Comparative Law 653, 1983.

Lasarte Álvarez, C., *Contratos, En Particular,* Tomo Primero, Cuarta Edición, Revisada e Actualizada, 2001.

Lasarte Álvarez, C., *Contratos*, Tomo Primero, Tercera Edición, 1995.

Legrand, P., *Against a European Civil Code*, 60(1) Modern Law Review 44, 1997.
Legrand, P., *The Impossibility of Legal Transplants*, Maastricht Journal of European & Comparative Law 111, 1997.
Legrand, P., *Sens et Non-Sens d'un Code Civil Européen*, 4 Revue Internationale de Droit Comparé 779, 1996.
Legrand, P., *European Legal Systems are not Converging*, 45 International and Comparative Law Quarterly 52, 1996.
Legrand, P., *Comparative Legal Studies and Commitment to Theory*, 38 Modern Law Review 262, 1995.
Legrand, P., *Pre-Contractual Disclosure and Information: English and French Law Compared*, 6 Oxford Journal of Legal Studies 322, 1986.
Linzer, P., *Rough Justice: A Theory of Restitution and Reliance, Contracts and Torts*, Wisconsin Law Review 698, 2001.
Lipari, N., *Diritto Privato Europeo*, Cedam, Padua, 1997.
Loos, M., *Towards a European Law of Service Contracts*, 4 European Review of Private Law 565, 2001.
Lopez Rodríguez, A., *Lex Mercatoria and Harmonisation of Contract Law in the EU*, Djoef Publishing, 2003.
Macaulay, S., *The Real and the Paper Deal: Empirical Pictures of Relationships, Complexity and the Urge for Transparent Principles*, 66 Modern Law Review 44, 2003.
Macaulay, S., *Almost Everything That I Did Want To Know About Contract Litigation: A Comment on Galanter*, Wisconsin Law Rev 629, 2001.
Macaulay, S., *The Reliance Interest and the World Outside the Law Schools' Doors*, Wisconsin Law Review 247, 1991.
Macaulay, S., *Non-contractual Relations in Business: A Preliminary Study*, 28(1) American Sociological Review 55, 1963.
Macaulay, S., Kidwell, J., Whitford, W.C. & Galanter, M., *Contracts: Law in Action*, 2002.
Macneil, I.R. (ed.), *The Relational Theory of Contract: Selected Works*, Sweet and Maxwell, 2001.
Macneil, I.R., *The New Social Contract: An Inquiry Into Modern Contractual Relations*, Sweet and Maxwell Publishing, 1980
MacQueen, H.L. & Zimmermann, R. (eds), European Contract Law – Scots and South African Perspectives, Edinburgh University Press, 2006.
MacQueen, H.L., Vaquer, A. & Espiau Espiau, S., *Regional Private Laws and Codification in Europe*, European Comparative Law Series, Cambridge University Press, 2003.
Mangas Martín, A., *Tratado de la Unión Europea, Tratados Constitutivos de las Comunidades Europeos y otros actos básicos de Derecho Comunitario*, Tecnos, Madrid, 1999.

Mankowski, P., *Formation of Contract and Pre-contractual Information in Comparative Law*, The Architecture of European Codes and Contract Law, Society of European Contract Law Conference, Vienna, 18-19 June 2004.

Manzanares, J., *La responsabilidad precontractual en la hipótesis de ruptura injustificada de las negociaciones preliminaries*, Anuario de Derecho Civil, 1984.

Marciano, A. & Josselin, J.M. (eds.) *The Economics of Harmonizing European Law, New Horizons in Law and Economics Series*, Elgar Publishing, 2002.

Marín López, A., *La Doctrina del Derecho Natural en H. Groccio*, 2 Anales de la Cátedra Francisco Suárez, Granada, 1962.

Maris Van Sandelingenambacht, C.W., *Legal Postism and the End of European Private Law – Duncan Kennedy's Critique of Adjudication*, 1 European Review of Private Law 111, Kluwer, 2002.

Markesinis, B.S., *The Enduring (Double) Legacy of the Code Napoléon*, 121 Law Quarterly Review, January 2005.

Markesinis, B.S. (ed), *Always on the Same Path – Essays on Foreign Law and Comparative Methodology*, Oxford Hart Publishing, 2001.

Markesinis, B.S. (ed), *The Coming Together of the Common and the Civil Law*, Oxford Hart Publishing, 2000.

Markensinis, B.S., *Why a Code is not the best way to advance the cause of European Legal Unity*, 5(4) European Review of Private Law 519, 1997.

Markesinis, B.S. (ed), *The Gradual Convergence, Foreign Ideas, Foreign Influences and English Law on the Eve of the Twenty First Century*, Oxford Clarendon Press, 1994.

Markesinis, B.S., *A Comparative Introduction to the German Law of Torts*, Third Edition, Oxford Clarendon Press, 1994.

Markesinis, B.S., *An Expanding Tort Law – The Price of a Rigid Contract Law*, 103 Law Quarterly Review 354, 1987.

Marrella, F., *Choice of Law in Third Millenium Arbitrations: The Relevance of the Unidroit Principles of International Commercial Contracts*, 37 Vanderbilt Journal of Transnational Law 1137, 2003.

Martín Rodríguez, M.A., *La unificación civil y mercantil en la contratación privada*, Salamanca, 2006.

Martínez Gallego, E.M., *La Formación del Contrato a través de la Oferta y la Aceptación*, Marcial Pons, Madrid, 2000.

Mather, H., *Contract Law and Morality*, Contributions in Legal Studies, London, 1999.

Mattei, U., *Hard Code Now! A Critique of "Softness" and a Plea for Responsibility in the European Debate over Codification*, Position paper presented at The Society of European Contract Law (Secola) and The Centre for a Common Law of Europe, K.U., Conference entitled, *Communication from the Commission on European Contract Law (Harmonisation, Code, Optional Code)*, Leuven, November 30 – December 01, 2001.

Mattei, U. & Monti, A., *Comparative Law and Economics: Borrowing and Resistance*, 1(2) Global Jurist Frontiers, Article 5, 2001.

Mattei, U., *Efficiency and Equal Protection in the New European Contract Law: Mandatory, Default and Enforcement Rules*, Position Paper presented at The Fifteenth SOKOL Colloquium on Private International Law entitled, *Unity and Harmonisation in International Commercial Law*, in Virginia Journal of International Law Association, 1999.

Mattei, U., *The Issue of European Civil Codification and Legal Scholarship*, 21 Hastings International and Comparative Law Review 883, 1998.

Mattei, U., *Efficiency in Legal Transplants – An Essay in Comparative Law and Economics*, 14 International Review of Law and Economics 3, 1994.

Mayorga Toledano, M.C., *El contrato mercantil de franquicia*, Colección Estudios de Derecho Mercantil, Editorial Comares S.L., 2003.

McFarlane, B., *The Problem of Pre-Contractual Reliance: Three Ways to a Third Way*, NYU Global Fellows Forum Paper, October, 2006.

McGregor, H., *Contract Code: Drawn Up on Behalf of the English Law Commission*, Guiffrè, Milan, 1993.

McKendrick, E., *Harmonisation of European Contract Law: The State We're In*, Clifford Chance & Institute of European and Comparative Law conference on the theme of Harmonisation of European Contract Law: Implications for European Private Laws, Business and Legal Practice, Keble College, Oxford, March 18-19, 2005.

McKendrick, E., *The Frontiers of Contract Law – Interpretation of Contracts and the Admissibility of Precontractual Negotiations*, 7 Singapore Academy of Law Journal 248, 2005.

McKendrick, E., *Contract Law: Text, Cases and Materials*, Oxford University Press, 2003.

McKendrick, E., *Contract Law*, Fifth Edition, Oxford University Press, 2003.

Median Alcoz, M., *La Ruptura Injustificada de los Tratos Preliminares*, Revista de Derecho Privado, 2005.

Merryman, J.H., *The Loneliness of the Comparative Lawyer – And other Essays in Foreign and Comparative Law*, Kluwer, 1999.

Merryman, J.H., *The Civil Law Tradition*, Stanford University Press, 1969.

Mitchell, C., *Leading a Life of its Own? The Roles of Reasonable Expectation in Contract Law*, Oxford Journal of Legal Studies, Volume 23, Number 4, 2003.

Möllers, T., *European Directives on Civil Law, The German Approach: Towards the Re-Codification and New Foundation of Civil Law Principles*, 6 European Review of Private Law 777, 2002.

Moral Soriano, L., 'Theoretical Approach to the Tension between Form and Substance in English Judicial Reasoning' in Ladeur, K-H (ed.), *The Europeanisation of Administrative Law – Transforming National Decision-making Procedures*, Ashgate Publishing, 2002.

Morskin, M. (ed), *Commercial Contracts – Strategies for Negotiating and Drafting*, Aspen Publishing, 2005.

Muir Watt, H., *European Integration, Legal Diversity and the Conflict of Laws*, 9(1) Edinburgh Law Review, 2005.

Muir Watt, H., *Choice of Law in Integrated and Interconnected Markets*, 7(3) Electronic Journal of Comparative Law, 2003.

Muir Watt, M., *Legal Diversity and the Internal Market* (on file with author).

Murillo, M., *Forma y Nulidad del Precontrato*, Navarra, 1993.

Musy, A., *The Good Faith Principle in Contract Law and the Precontractual Duty to Disclose: Comparative Analysis of New Differences in Legal Cultures*, December, 2000. http://www.icer.it/menu/f_papers.html

Nicholas, B., *The Pre-Contractual Obligation to Disclose Information: English Report* in Harris, D. & Tallon, D. (eds), 'Contract Law Today: Anglo-French Comparisons', 1989.

Nickel, R., *Private Law Codes and Judges in a Constitutional Setting – The Emergence of private constitutional law through constitutional private law*, paper delivered at conference on the theme of "Codes and Constitutions – Processes and Cross-influences in the European Union and its Member States, European University Institute, Florence, October 8 –9, 2004.

Niglia, L., *The Death of Formalism in English Contract Law*, Journal of Contract Law, 2004.

Niglia, L., *The Transformation of European Contract Law*, Aspen/Kluwer Law Publishing, 2002.

Niglia, L., *The Non-Europeanisation of Private Law*, European Review of Private Law, Volume 9, Number 4, pp.575-599, Kluwer Law International, 2001.

Nottage, L., *Convergence, Divergence and the Middle Way in Unifying or Harmonising Private Law*, The European University Institute Working Paper Series, 2001.

O'Callaghan, X., *Compendio de Derecho Civil – Volumes I-II*, Madrid, 1993.

Ogus, A., *Competition Between National Legal Systems: A Contribution of Economic Analysis to Comparative Law*, 48(2) International Comparative Law Quarterly 405, 1999.

Oppenheimer, A., *The Relationship Between European Community Law and National Law*, Volumes I & II, 1994 & 2003.

Oliver, D., *Constitutional Concepts, Sources and Cultures and their Influence upon Private Law Systems – Codified or Uncodified*, paper delivered at conference on the theme of "Codes and Constitutions – Processes and Cross-influences in the European Union and its Member States, European University Institute, Florence, October 8 –9, 2004.

O'Malley, P., *Uncertain Subjects: Risks, Liberalism and Contract*, 29(4) Journal of Economy and Society 460, 2000.

Orduña Moreno, F.J. y Campuzano Laquillo, A.B., *Contratación y Consumo*, Tirant lo Blanch, Valencia, 1998.

Örücü, E., *Critical Comparative Law: Considering Paradoxes for Legal Systems in Tradition*, 4(1) Electronic Journal of Comparative Law, July 2000.

Pálsson, M.G., *Unfairness in European Contract Law and International Trade Contracts*, PhD thesis of the European University Institute, 2001.

Pagador López, J., *La Directiva Comunitaria Sobre Cláusulas Contractuales Abusivas*, Marcial Pons, Madrid, 1998.

Parra Rodríguez, C., *El Nuevo Derecho Internacional de los Contratos*, Bosch Editorial, 2001.

Paterson, J.M., *The Contract to Negotiate in Good Faith – Recognition and Enforcement*, 10 Journal of Contract Law 120, 1996.

Peppet, S.R., *Can Saints Negotiate? A Brief Introduction to the Problems of Perfect Ethics in Bargaining*, 7 Harvard Negotiation Law Review, Spring 2002.

Petsche, M., *The Growing Autonomy of International Commercial Arbitration*, PhD Thesis of the European University Institute, 2004.

Pollack, M.A., *The Engines of European Integration – Delegation, Agency and Agenda Setting in the EU*, Oxford University Press, 2003.

Pfersmann, O., *Le droit comparé comme interpretation et comme théorie du droit*, Revue internationale du droit comparé 275, 2001.

Poole, J., *Textbook on Contract*, Eighth edition, Oxford University Press, 2006.

Poole, J., *Casebook on Contract*, Eighth edition, Oxford University Press, 2006.

Posner, A., Eggleston, K. & Zeckhauser, R.., *The Design & Interpretation of Contracts: Why Complexity Matters*, 95(1) Northwestern University Law Review, 2000.

Posner, R., *Economic Analysis of Law*, Fifth Edition, 1998.

Pound, R., *Liberty of Contract*, 18 Yale Law Journal, 1909.

The Private Law Systems in the European Union: Discrimination on the Grounds of Nationality and the Need for a European Civil Code, European Parliament Legal Affairs Series, JURI-103EN, 2000.

Puig-Brutau, J., *Fundamentos de Derecho Civil*, Bosch S.A., Barcelona, 1976.

Quigley, C., *European Community Contract Law – Parts I & II*, Kluwer Law Press, London, 1997.

Radeideh, M., *Fair Trading in EC Law – Information and Consumer Choice in the Internal Market*, Europa Law Publishing, 2005.

Radley-Gardner, O., Beale, H., Zimmermann, R. & Schulze, R., *Fundamental Texts on European Private Law*, Hart Law Publishing, 2003.

Reich, N., *The Tripartite Function of Modern Contract Law in Europe: Enablement, Regulation, Information*, (on file with author).

Reich, N., *The Consumer as Citizen – the Citizen as Consumer – Reflections on the Present State of the Theory of Consumer Law in the EU*, available via IACL.ca.

Reich, N., *Some Critical Comments on the Commission Communication on 'European Contract Law'*, Intervention at The Society of European Contract Law (Secola) and The Centre for a Common Law of Europe, K.U., Conference entitled, *Communication from the Commission on European Contract Law (Harmonisation, Code, Optional Code)*, Leuven, November 30 – December 01, 2001.

Reimann, M. & Zimmermann, R., *The Oxford Handbook of Comparative Law*, Oxford University Press, 2006.

Reinmann, M. (ed.), *The Reception of Continental Ideas in the Common Law World 1820-1920*, Comparative Studies in Continental and Anglo-American Legal History Series, Berlin, 1993.

Rickett, C. & Telfer, T., *International Perspectives on Consumer's Access to Justice*, Cambridge University Press, 2003.

Riedl, K., *The Work of the Lando Commission from an Alternative Viewpoint*, 2(1) European Review of Private Law, 2000.

Riles, A. (ed.), *Rethinking the Masters of Comparative Law*, Hart Law, 2001.

Riley, C.A., *Designing Default Rules in Contract Law: Consent, Conventionalism and Efficiency*, 20(3) Oxford Journal of Legal Studies 367, 2000.

Rodota, S., *Forms and Styles of Codification and their Constitutional Value*, paper delivered at conference on the theme of "Codes and Constitutions – Processes and Cross-influences in the European Union and its Member States, European University Institute, Florence, October 8 –9, 2004.

Roman García, A., *El Precontrato – Estudio Dogmático y Jurisprudencial*, Madrid, 1980.

Roos, N., *NICE Dreams and the Realities of European Private Law*, Maastricht University Publication, 2002.

Roppo, V., *Formation of Contract and Pre-contractual information from an Italian and Romance Perspective*, The Architecture of European Codes and Contract Law, Society of European Contract Law Conference, Vienna, June 2004.

Rossett, A., 'The Unification of American Commercial Law: Restatements and Codification' in *Diritto Privato Europeo: Problemi e prospettive*, Guiffrè, Milan, 1989.

Rose, F., *Statutes on Contract, Tort and Restitution 2004-2005*, 2004.

Roth, W-H., *Transposing "Pointillist" EC Guidelines into Systematic National Codes – Problems and Consequences*, Position Paper presented at The Society of European Contract Law (Secola) Conference entitled, *Sales and Trends in European Contract Law*, Rome, June 2001.

Rubin, G.R., *Law, Economy and Society, 1750-1914: Essays in the History of English Law*, Professional Books, London, 1984.

Ruiz Muñoz & Miguel Botana García, G.A., *Curso sobre protección jurídica de los consumidores*, McGraw-Hill, 1999.

Sacco, R., *Legal Formants: A Dynamic Approach to Comparative Law*, 39 American Journal of Comparative Law 1, 1991.

Salvador Coderch, P., Fernandez Crede, A., *Autonomía Privada, Fraude de Ley e Interpretación de los Negocios Jurídicos*, accesible via Indret.com.
Samuel, G., *An Introduction to Contractual and Tortious Obligations*, Cavendish Publishing, 2004.
Sarkar, R., *Transnational Business Law – A Development Law Perspective*, Kluwer, 2003.
Schlesinger, R.B., *Formation of Contracts: A Study on the Common Core of Legal Systems*, Ocean Publications, 1968.
Schmid, C.U. & Doris, M., *European Tenancy Law and Procedure*, EUI Electronic Publication of the European Private Law Forum, Florence, 2005.
Schmid, C.U., *Legitimacy Conditions for a European Civil Code*, The European University Institute Working Papers Series, Law 2001/2, 2001.
Schmid, C.U., *The Emergence of a Transnational Legal Science in European Private Law*, 19 Oxford Journal of Legal Studies, 1999.
Schmid, C.U., *'Bottom Up' Harmonisation of European Private Law: Ius Commune and Restatement*, EUI Working Paper Series, Number 99/7, 1999.
Schmidt-Szalewski, J., *La période précontractuelle en droit français*, Revue Internationale du Droit Comparé 545, 1990.
Schmidt, V.A., *Democracy and Discourse in an Integrating Europe and a Globalising World*, 6(3) European Law Journal 277, 2000.
Schulte-Nölke, Schulze, R. & Bernardeau, L., *European Community Contract Law*, Schriftenreihe der Europäischen Rechtsakademie Trier, 2002.
Schulze, R., Ebers, M. & Grigoleit, H.C., *Informationspflichten und Vertragsshluss im Acquis communautaire*, Tübingen, 2003.
Schulze, R., *A Century of the Bürgerliches Gesetzbuch: German Legal Uniformity and European Private Law*, Columbia Journal of European Law, 1999.
Schwartz, A. & Scott, R.E., *Contract Theory and the Limits of Contract Law*, Center for Law, Economics and Public Policy Research Paper, 113 Yale Law Journal 2003.
Schwartz, A. & Scott, R.E., *The Political Economy of Private Legislatures*, 143 University of Pennsylvania Law Review 595, 1995.
Schwartz, A., *Relational Contracts in the Courts: An Analysis of Incomplete Agreements and Judicial Strategies*, 12 Journal of Legal Studies 271, 1992.
Schwarze, A., *Design for an Empirical Data Investigation into the Impact of Contract Law Harmonisation under the White Paper of 1985*, Intervention at The Society of European Contract Law (Secola) and The Centre for a Common Law of Europe, K.U., Conference entitled, *Communication from the Commission on European Contract Law (Harmonisation, Code, Optional Code)*, Leuven, November 30 – December 01, 2001.
Schwarze, A., *Enforcement of Private Law: The Missing Link in the Process of European Harmonisation*, 8(1) European Review of Private Law, 2000.

Schwintowski, H.P., *The European Civil Code*, Intervention at The Society of European Contract Law (Secola) and The Centre for a Common Law of Europe, K.U., Conference entitled, *Communication from the Commission on European Contract Law (Harmonisation, Code, Optional Code)*, Leuven, November 30 – December 01, 2001.

Sciara, S., *Market Freedom and Fundamental Social Rights*, The European University Institute Working Papers Series, Law 2002/3, 2002.

Scott, R.E., *Hoffman v Red Owls and The Myth of Precontractual Reliance*, Columbia Law School Working Paper Series, 2006.

Scott, R.E., *A Self-Enforcing Theory of Indefinite Agreements*, 103(7) Columbia Law Review 1641, 2003.

Scott, R.E., 'The Uniformity Norm in Commercial Law: A Comparative Analysis of Common Law and Code Methodologies' in *The Theory of Contract Law – New Essays*, Cambridge Studies in the Philosophy of Law, Cambridge University Press, 2001.

Sefton-Green, R. (ed), *Mistake, Fraud and Duties to Inform in European Contract Law*, The Common Core of European Private Law Series, Cambridge University Press, 2005.

Senden, L., *Soft Law in European Community Law*, Hart Publishing, 2004.

Shell, G.R., *Opportunism and Trust in the Negotiation of Commercial Contracts – Towards a New Cause of Action*, 44 Vanderbilt Law Review 221, 1991.

Simpson, AWB., *Innovation in Nineteenth Century Contract Law*, 58 Law Quarterly Review 247, 1975.

Slawson, W. D., *Binding Promises: The Late Twentieth Century Reformulation of Contract Law*, Princeton University Press, 1996.

Smith, S.A., *Contract Theory*, Oxford Clarendon Law Series, 2004.

Smith, J.K. & Smith, R.L., *Contract Law, Mutual Mistake and Incentives to Produce and Disclose Information*, 19 Journal of Legal Studies 401, 1990.

Smits, J., *The Need for a European Contract Law – Empirical and Legal Perspectives*, Europa Law Publishing, 2004.

Smits, J., *Toward a Multi-Layered Contract Law for Europe*, Position paper presented at The Society of European Contract Law (Secola) and The Centre for a Common Law of Europe, K.U., Conference entitled, *Communication from the Commission on European Contract Law (Harmonisation, Code, Optional Code)*, Leuven, November 30 – December 01, 2001.

Smits, J., *The Future of European Contract Law: On Diversity and the Temptation of Elegance*, position paper presented at conference entitled, *Towards a European Ius Commune in Legal Education and Research*, Maastricht, October 25-26, 2001.

Smits, J., *A Principled Approach to European Contract Law*, 7 Maastricht Journal of European and Comparative Law 221, 2000.

Smits, J., *The Europeanisation of national legal systems: some consequences for legal thinking in civil law countries*, available via unimass.nl.

Snyder, *Economic Globalisation and the Law in the 21st Century*, in Sarat, A. (ed) The Blackwell Companion to Law and Society, Blackwell Publishing, 2003.

Snyder, F., *The Europeanisation of Law: The Legal Effects of Integration*, Hart Law, 2000.

Soler Matutes, P., *El Contrato para la Elaboración de Programas de Ordenador – Contrato de desarrollo de software*, Editorial Aranzadi, 2004.

Spamann, H., *Choice of Law in a Federal System and an Internal Market*, Jean Monnet Working Paper, 8/01, 2001.

Spence, M., *Protecting Reliance – The Emergent Doctrine of Equitable Estoppel*, Hart Law Publishing, 1999.

Stark, T.L., *Negotiating and Drafting Contract Boilerplate*, ALM Publishing, New York, 2003.

Steiner, J. & Woods, L., *EC Law – A Textbook*, Eighth Edition, 2003.

Staudenmayer, D., *The Way Forward in European Contract Law*, 2 European Review of Private Law 95, 2005.

Staudenmayer, D., *Future Perspectives on European Contract Law*, Clifford Chance & Institute of European and Comparative Law conference on the theme of 'Harmonisation of European Contract Law: Implications for European Private Laws, Business and Legal Practice', Keble College, Oxford, March 18-19, 2005.

Staudenmayer, D., *The Commission Action Plan on European Contract Law*, 2 European Review of Private Law 113, 2003.

Staudenmayer, D., *The Commission Communication on European Contract Law and the Future Prospects*, 51 International and Comparative Law Quarterly 673, July 2001.

Staughton, C., *How Do The Courts Interpret Commercial Contracts?* 58 Cambridge Law Journal 303, July 1999.

Stephan, P.B., *The Futility of Unification and Harmonisation in International Commercial Law*, 39 Vanderbilt Journal of International Law 303, 1999.

Stuyck, J., *EC competition law after modernisation: more than ever in the interest of consumers*, 28 Journal of Consumer Policy 1, 2005.

Symposium on the *Uniform Commercial Code, Is the UCC dead, or alive and well? International Perspectives*, 29 Loyola of Los Angeles Law Review 969, April 1996.

Symposium on the *Uniform Commercial Code: Does One Size Fit All?* 28 Loyola of Los Angeles Law Review 219, 1994.

Temkin, L., *When Does The Fat Lady Sing? An Analysis of Agreements in Principle in Corporate Acquisitions*, 55 Fordham Law Review 125, 1986.

Tetley, W., *Good Faith in Contract, particularly in the Contracts of Arbitration and Chartering*, 35(4) Journal of Maritime Law and Commerce, October 2004.

Teubner, G., *Legal Irritants: Good Faith in British Law or How Unifying Law Ends Up in New Divergences*, 61(1) Modern Law Review 11, January 1998.

Thorpe, C. & Bailey, J., *Commercial Contracts – A Practical Guide to Deals, Contracts, Agreements and Promises*, Revised Edition, 1999.

Tilmann, W., *The Legal Basis For A European Civil Code*, European Review of Private Law 471, 1997.

Treitel, G.H., *Some Landmarks of Twentieth Century Contract Law*, Oxford Clarendon Law, 2002.

Treitel, G.H., *The Law of Contract*, Sweet and Maxwell, 1995.

Tridimas, T. & Nebbia, P. (ed.), *European Union law for the Twenty First Century – Rethinking the New Legal Order*, Volume 2, 2004.

Truilhe-Marengo, E., *Towards a European Law of Contracts*, 10(4) European Law Journal 463, July 2004.

Tuori, K., *EC Law: An Independent Legal Order or a Post-Modern Jack-in-the-Box*, in Eriksson & Hurri (eds), Dialectic of Law and Reality, pp.397-415, Helsinki, 1999.

Valentine Palmer, V., *Mixed Jurisdictions Worldwide – The Third Legal Family*, Cambridge University Press, 2001.

Van Boom, W. & Loos, M. (eds), *Collective Enforcement of Consumer Law – Securing Compliance in Europe Through Private Group Action and Public Authority Intervention*, Europa Law Publishing, 2007.

Van Caenegen, R.C., *An Historical Introduction to Private Law*, Cambridge University Press, 1994.

Van den Berg, R., *Forced Harmonisation of Contract Law in Europe – Not to be Contined*, position paper presented at The Society of European Contract Law (Secola) and The Centre for a Common Law of Europe, K.U., Conference entitled, *Communication from the Commission on European Contract Law (Harmonisation, Code, Optional Code)*, Leuven, November 30 – December 01, 2001.

Van den Berg, R., *The Subsidiarity Principle in European Community Law: Some Insights From Law and Economics*, 1(4) Maastricht Journal of European and Comparative Law 337, 1994.

Van Erp, J.H.M., *European Private Law: Postmodern Dilemmas and Choices – Towards a Method of Adequate Comparative Legal Analysis*, 3(1) Electronic Journal of Comparative Law, August 1999.

Van Gerven, *Codifying European Private Law? Yes, if ...!*, European Law Review 156, 2002.

Van Gerven, *Codifying European Private Law*, Position paper presented at The Society of European Contract Law (Secola) and The Centre for a Common Law of Europe, K.U., Conference entitled, *Communication from the Commission on European Contract Law (Harmonisation, Code, Optional Code)*, Leuven, November 30 – December 01, 2001.

Van Gerven, *Coherence of Community and national laws: Is there a legal basis for a European Civil Code*, 5(4) European Review of Private Law, 1997.

Van Gerven, *ECJ case-law as a means of unification of private law*, 2 European Review of Private Law 293, 1997.

Van Gerven, *The Case-law of the European Court of Justice and National Courts as a contribution to the Europeanisation of Private Law*, European Law Review 367, 1995.

Van Hoecke, M., *Epistemology and Methodology of Comparative Law*, Hart Law Publishing, 2004.

Van Hoecke, M. & Ost, F., *The Harmonisation of European Private Law*, Hart Law Publishing, 2000.

Van Hoecke, M. & Warrington, M., *Legal Cultures, Legal Paradigms and Legal Doctrine: Towards a New Model for Comparative Law*, 47 International and Comparative Law Quarterly 495, 1998.

Van Laer, C.J.P., *The Applicability of Comparative Concepts*, 2(2) Electronic Journal of Comparative Law, August 1998.

Vickers, J., *Contracts and European Consumer Law: An OFT Perspective*, Clifford Chance & Institute of European and Comparative Law conference on the theme of 'Harmonisation of European Contract Law: Implications for European Private Laws, Business and Legal Practice', Keble College, Oxford, March 18-19, 2005.

Viguri Perea, A., *Los Tratos Preliminaries: las cartas de intenciones y otros documentos legales precontractuales*, PPU, Barcelona, 1994.

Vincent-Jones, P., *Contractual Governance: Institutional and Organisational Analysis*, 20(3) Oxford Journal of Legal Studies 317, 2000.

Vogenauer, S. & Weatherill, S., *The Harmonisation of European Contract Law – Implications for European Private Laws, Business and Legal Practice*, Hart Law Publishing, 2006.

Von Bar, C., *Paving the Way Forward with Principles of European Private Law*, Position paper presented at The Society of European Contract Law (Secola) and The Centre for a Common Law of Europe, K.U., Conference entitled, *Communication from the Commission on European Contract Law (Harmonisation, Code, Optional Code)*, Leuven, November 30 – December 01, 2001.

Von Mehren, A.T., *The Rise of Transnational Legal Practice and the Task of Comparative Law*, 75 Tulane Law Review 1215, 2001.

Von Mehren, A.T. & Gordley, J., *The Civil Law System – An Introduction to the Comparative Study of Law*, Second Edition, Boston, 1977.

Waddams, S., *Dimensions of Private Law – Categories and Concepts in Anglo-American Legal Reasoning*, Cambridge University Press, 2003.

Wagner, G., *The Economics of Harmonization: The Case of Contract*, 39 Common Market Law Review 995, 2002.

Watson, A., *Legal Transplants and European Private Law*, 4(4) Electronic Journal of Comparative Law, 2000.

Watson, A., *Legal Transplants*, Harvard University Press, Boston, 1987.

Watson, A., *The Making of the Civil Law*, Harvard University Press, Boston, 1981.

Watson, A., *Legal Transplants: An Approach to Comparative Law*, Virginia University Press, 1974.

Weatherill, S., *Constitutional Issues – How Much is Better Left Unsaid?*, Clifford Chance & Institute of European and Comparative Law conference on the theme of 'Harmonisation of European Contract Law: Implications for European Private Laws, Business and Legal Practice', Keble College, Oxford, March 18-19, 2005.

Weatherill, S., *The European Commission's Green Paper on European Contract Law: Context, Content and Constitutionality*, 24 Journal of Consumer Policy 339, 2001.

Weatherill, S., *EC Consumer Law and Policy*, Longman, 1997.

Weiacker, F., *A History of Private Law in Europe – With Particular Reference to Germany*, Oxford Clarendon Press, 1995.

Weiacker, F., *Storia del Diritto Privato Moderno*, Milan, 1967.

Weiler, J, *The Transformation of Europe*, 100 Yale Law Journal 2403, 1991.

Werro, F., *L'Européanisation du droit privé: vers un Code Civil Européen?* Fribourg, 1998.

Whincup, M.H., *Contract Law and Practice: The English System and Continental Comparisons*, Fourth Edition, Kluwer, 2001.

Whittaker, S., *Unfair Contract Terms, Public Services and The Construction of a European Conception of Contract*, 116 Law Quarterly Review 95, 2000.

Wightman, J., *Contract – A Critical Commentary*, Law and Social Theory Series, London, 1996.

Wilhelmsson, T., *The Legal, the Cultural and the Political – Conclusions from different perspectives on Harmonisation of European Contract Law*, 13(6) European Business Law Review 541, 2002.

Wilhelmsson, T., *Real Life Instead of Dead Concepts, The Design of an Optional Restatement of European Contract Law*, Position Paper presented at The Society of European Contract Law (Secola) and The Centre for a Common Law of Europe, K.U., Conference entitled, *Communication from the Commission on European Contract Law* (*Harmonisation, Code, Optional Code*), Leuven, November 30 – December 01, 2001.

Wilhelmsson, T., *European Contract Law Harmonisation: Aims and Tools*, 1 Tulane Journal of International and Comparative Law 23, 1993.

Ziller, J., *La répartition constitutionnelle des competences et la codification du droit privé dans une perspective comparée*, paper delivered at conference on the theme of "Codes and Constitutions – Processes and Cross-influences in the European Union and its Member States, European University Institute, Florence, October 8 –9, 2004.

Ziller, J., *The Constitutional Dimension of the Europeanisation of Private Law in light of the New Constitution for Europe*, Position paper presented at conference entitled *The Europeanisation of Contract*, The European University Institute, October 24-25, 2003.

Zimmermann, R. & Whittaker, S., *Good Faith in European Contract*, Cambridge University Press, 2000.

Zimmermann, R., *The Law of Obligations – Roman Foundations of the Civilian Tradition*, Oxford Clarendon Press, 1996.

Zimmermann, R., *Civil Code and Civil Law: The Europeanization of Private Law within the European Community and the Re-emergence of a European Legal Science*, 1 Columbia Journal of European Law 63, 1994.

Zumbansen, P., *Piercing the Legal Veil: Commercial Arbitration and Transnational Law*, 8(3) European Law Journal 400, 2002.

Zumbansen, P., *Utopia or Revolution? A Short Essay on the Dislocated Nature of the Lex Mercatoria Debate*, (on file with author).

Zweigert, K. & Kötz, H., *An Introduction to Comparative Law*, Third Edition, Oxford Clarendon Press, 1998.

Table of Cases

European Court Decisions

Case C-237/02 *Freiburger Kommunalbauten gmbh Baugessellschaft & Co. KG v. Hofstetter* [2004] ECR I-3403; [2004] CMLR 13.

Case C-334/00 *Fonderie Officine Meccaniche Tacconi SpA v. Heinrich Wagner Sinto Machinenfabrik GmbH* [2002] ECR I-7357

Case C-376/98 *Germany v. Parliament and Council ('Tobacco Advertising')* [2000] ECR I-8419

Joined cases C-240/98 to C-244/98 *Océano Grupo Editorial SA v. Rocío Murciano et al* [2000] ECR I-4941

Case C-381 *Ingmar v. Leonard Eaton Technologies* [2000] ECR I-9305

Case C-212/97 *Centros Ltd v. Ervervs-og Selskabsstrlysen* [1999] ECR I-459

Case C-45/96 *Bayerische Hypotheken und Wechselbank AG v. Edgar Dietzinger* [1998] ECR I-1199.

Case C-91/92 *Paolo Faccini Dori v. Recreb Srl* [1994] ECR I-3325

Case C-89/91 *Shearson Lehman Hutton v. TVB Trenhandgesellscahft für Vermögensverwaltung und Beteiligungen mbH* [1993] ECR 1-139.

Case C-339/89 Ålsthom *Atlantique v. Sulzer* [1991] ECR I-107

Case C-2/88 *GB-INNO-BM v. Confédération du commerce luxembourgeois,* [1990] ECR I-667

Case C-120/78 *Rewe-Zentral AG v. Bundesmonopolverwaltung für Branntwein ('Cassis di Dijon')* [1979] ECR 649

UK and Commonwealth Court Decisions

AC Controls Ltd v. British Broadcasting Corporation [2002] EWHC 3132

AT & T v. Saudi Cable [2000] 2 All E.R. (Comm) 625

Agnew & Others v. Länsforakringsbolagens A.B., HL decision, 17 Feb 2000

Aiton Australia Pty Ltd v. Transfield Pty Ltd [1999] NSWSC 996

Albion Sugar Co. Ltd v. Williams Tankers Ltd [1977] 2 Lloyd's Rep 457

Al-Kandari v. JR Brown & Co. [1988] Q.B. 665

Alstom Facilities Ltd v. Jarvis Facilities Ltd [2004] EWCH 1232

Anglo Group Plc v. Winther Brown & Co. Ltd. [1997] TCC 413

Ansys Incorporated v. Lim Thuan Khee and Another, Chancery Division, unreported 19 May 1999

Antaios Cia Naviera SA v. Salen Rederierna AB, the Antaios [1985] AC 191

Arbuthnott v. Fagan [1995] CLC 1396

Baird Textiles v. Marks & Spencer [2002] 1 All ER 737

Bank of Credit and Commerce International v. Ali [2001] UK 8 (HL)

Bank of New Zealand [1991] NZLR 178

Bannerman v. White (1861) 10 CBNS 844

Banque Brussels Lambert SA v. Australian National Industries Ltd (1989) 21 NSWLR 502

Banque Financière de la Cité v. Westgate Insurance Co Ltd [1991] 2 A.C. 249

Banque Keyser Ullmann SA v. Skandia (UK) Insurance Co Ltd [1990] 1 Q.B. 665

Bell v. Lever Bros [1932] A.C. 161
Beta Investment SA v. Transmedia Europe Inc. [2003] EWHC 3066
Bisset v. Wilkinson [1927] A.C. 177
Box v. Midland Bank [1979] 2 Lloyd's Report 391
Bradford Third Equitable Benefit Building Society v. Borders [1941] 2 All E.R. 205
British Fermentation Products Ltd v. Compair Reavell Ltd. [1999] 2 All E.R. 389
British Steel Corporation v. Cleveland Bridge and Engineering Ltd. (1981) 24 BLR 94
Butler Machine Tool v. Ex-Cell-O Corporation [1979] 1 WLR 401
Canada Steamship Lines Ltd v. The King [1952] AC 192
Candler v. Crane, Christmas & Co [1951] K.B. 164
Canterbury Golf International Ltd v. Yoshimoto [2002] UK PC 40
Capital Landfill (Restoration) Ltd v. William Stockler & Co., unreported 5 September 1991
Chevron International Oil Co Ltd [1987] 2 Lloyd's Rep 547
Commonwealth v. Verwayen (1990) 170 CLR 394
Confetti Records and Others v. Warner Music UK Ltd [2003] EWHC 1274
Courtney & Fairbarn v. Tolaini Brothers (Hotels) Ltd [1975] 1 WLR 297
Crabb v. Arun District Council [1976] Ch 179, CA
Curtis v. Chemical Cleaning & Dyeing Co Ltd [1951] 1 K.B. 805
Davies v. London & Provincial Marine Insurance Co (1878) 8 Ch D 469
Derry v. Peek (1889) 14 App Cas 337
Dick Bentley Productions Ltd v. Harold Smith (Motors) Ltd [1965] 1 W.L.R. 623
Deutsche Genossenschaftsbank v. Burnhope [1995] 1 WLR 1580, 1589
Dunnett v. Railtrack [2002] 2 All ER 850
EA Grimstead & Son Ltd v. McGarrigan [1999] WLR 852482 (CA)
EE Caledonia Ltd. v. Orbit Valve Co. Europe [1993] All ER 165
Economides v. Commercial Assurance Co plc [1998] Q.B. 587
Electricity Corporation of New Zealand Ltd v. Fletcher Challenge Energy Ltd [2002] 2 NZLR 433
Esso Petroleum Co Ltd v. Mardon [1976] QB 801
First Energy v. HIB [1993] 2 Lloyd's Rep 194
Fletcher v. Krell (1872) 42 L.J. Q.B. 551
George Mitchell (Chesterhall) Ltd v. Finney Lock Seeds Ltd [1983] QB 284
Gretton v. British Millerain Co. Ltd. unreported, 2 November 1998
Harmon CFEM Facades v. Corporate Officer of House of Commons (2000) 72 Con LR 21
Hedley Byrne v. Heller and Partners [1964] A.C. 465
Hillas & Co. Ltd. v. Arcos Ltd (1932) 147 L.T. 503
Heilbut, Symons & Co v. Buckleton [1913] A.C. 30
Henderson v. Merrett Syndicates Ltd [1995] 2 A.C. 145

Hong Kong Fir Shipping Co. Ltd. v. Kawaskai Kishen Kaisha Ltd [1962] 2 QB 26
Howard Marine and Dredging Co Ltd v. Ogden & Sons (Excavations) Ltd [1978] Q.B. 574
Hughes Aircraft Systems International v. Air Services Australia (1997) 146 ALR 1
Interfoto Picture Library Ltd v. Stiletto Visual Programmes Ltd [1989] Q.B. 433
Inntrepreneur Pub Co Ltd v. East Crown Ltd [2000] 2 Lloyd's Rep 611 (ChD)
Investors Compensation Scheme v. West Bromwich Building Society [1998] 1 WLR 896
JEB Fasteners Ltd v. Marks Bloom & Co. (a firm) [1983] 1 All ER 583
Karen Oltman [1976] 2 Lloyd's Rep 708
Kleinwort Benson Ltd v. Malaysia Mining Corporation Bernhad [1989] 1 WLR 379
Little v. Courage Ltd (1995) 70 P & CR 49
Lovell and Christmas Ltd v. Wall (1911) 104 LT 85
Maddison v. Addison (1883) 8 App Cas 467
Mannai Investment Co. Ltd. v. Eagle Star Life Assurance Co. Ltd. [1997] 2 WLR 945
Martel Building Ltd. v. Canada (2000) 193 DLR (4th) 1, SCC
May & Butcher Ltd v. R. [1934] 2 KB 17
Midland Bank plc v. Cox McQueen [1999] 1 FLR 1002
Mobil Oil Australia Ltd v. Wellcome International Pty Ltd (1989) 16 NSWLR 582
Molyneux v. Harvey [1903] 2 K.B
Mowlem Plc v. Stena Line Ports [2004] EWHC 2206
National Bank of Sharjah v. Dellborg, unreported, 9 July 1997
National Provincial Bank of England Ltd v. Glanusk [1913] 3 K.B. 335
NLA Group Ltd v. Bowers [1999] 1 Lloyd's Rep 109
Pagnan SpA v. Granaria B.V. [1985] 1 Lloyd's Rep 547
Petromec Inc v. Petroleo Brasiliero SA Petrobas (No.3) [2005] EWCA Civ 891, [2006] 1 Lloyd's Rep. 121
Phillips Petroleum Co. UK Ltd v. Ors & Enron Europe Ltd. [1997] C.L.C. 329
Pitt v. PHH Asset Management Ltd [1993] 4 All ER 961
Prenn v. Simmonds [1971] 1 WLR 1381
Proforce Recruit Ltd v. The Rugby Group Ltd [2006] EWCA Civ 69
Rayner v. Davies [2002] EWCA Civ 1090
Reardon Smith Line Ltd. v. Yngvar Hansen-Tangen [1976] 1 WLR 989
Re Spectrum (in Liquidation) [2005] UKHL 41
Ross v. Caunters [1980] Ch 297
Rose & Frank Co. v. Grompton Bros. [1923] 2 K.B. 261
Routledge v. McKay [1954] 1 W.L.R. 615
SAM Business Systems Limited v. Hedley & Co. [2002] EWHC 2733
Scandinavian Trading Tanker Co AB v. Flota Petrolera Ecuatoriana [1981] 2 Lloyd's Rep 425

Schuler AG v. Wickman Machine Tool Sales [1974] AC 235
Scottish Power plc v. Britoil (Exploration) Ltd, The Times, 2 December 1997
Shamil Bank of Bahrain v. Beximco Pharmaceuticals [2004] 2 Lloyd's Rep 1
Shanklin Pier v. Detel Products Ltd [1951] 2 K.B. 854
Shell Tankers (UK) Ltd v. Astro Comino Armadora SA (The Pacific Colocotronis) [1981] 2 Lloyd's Rep. 40
Sidaway v. Board of Governors of the Bethlem Royal Hospital [1985] A.C. 871
Scottish Power plc v. Britoil (Exploration) Ltd, The Times Law Reports, 2 December 1997
Smith v. Hughes (1871) LR 6 Q.B. 597
Spring v. Guardian Assurance plc [1994] 2 A.C. 296
Star Steamship Society v. Beogradska Plovidna [1998] 2 Lloyd's Rep 583
Stent Foundations v. Carillion Contracts Ltd [2000] BLR 188
Sykes v. Pannell Kerr Forster unreported QBD, 30 March 2001
Sykes v. Taylor-Rose [2004] EWCA Civ 299; *The Times*, 2 March 2004: *The Independent*, 2 March 2004
Suisse Atlantique Société d'Armement Maritime SA v. NV Rotterdamsche Kolen Centrale [1967] 1 AC 361
Taylor v. Hamer [2003] 1 EGLR 103
Tesco Stores Ltd v. Costain Construction Ltd & Others [2003] EWHC 1487
The Starsin [2003] UKHL 12; [2004] 1 A.C. 715
The 'Tychy' (No.2) [2001] EWCA Civ 1198; [2001] 2 Lloyd's Rep 403
Thomas Witter Ltd v. TBP Industries Ltd [1996] 2 All ER 573
Thomson v. Christie's [2004] EWHC 1101 (QB)
Voest Alpine Intertrading GmbH v. Chevron International Oil Co Ltd [1987] 2 Lloyd's Rep 547
Von Hatzfeld-Wildenberg v. Alexander [1912] 1 Ch 284
Walford v. Miles [1992] AC 128
Walton Stores (Interstate) Ltd v. Maher (1988) 164 CLR 387
Williams v. Natural Life Health Foods Ltd [1998] 1 WLR 830
With v. O'Flanagan [1936] Ch 575

Spanish Court Decisions

Sentencia del Tribunal Supremo, RJ 2005\0191, Sala de lo Civil, March 09, 2005
Sentencia del Tribunal Supremo, RJ 2003\3528, Sala de lo Civil, April 23, 2003
Sentencia del Tribunal Supremo, RJ 2002\3115, Sala de lo Civil, April 17, 2002
Sentencia del Tribunal Supremo, RJ 2002\2664, Sala de lo Civil, March 23, 2002
Sentencia del Tribunal Supremo, RJ 2002\2848, Sala de lo Civil, March 18, 2002
Sentencia del Tribunal Supremo, RJ 2001\8655, Sala de lo Civil, October 22, 2001

Sentencia del Tribunal Supremo, RJ 2001\6015, Sala de lo Civil, February 19, 2001
Sentencia del Tribunal Supremo, RJ 1999\8978, Sala de lo Civil, December 16, 1999
Sentencia del Tribunal Supremo, RJ 1999\4105, Sala de lo Civil, June 14, 1999
Sentencia del Tribunal Supremo, RJ 1999\1873, Sala de lo Civil, April 05, 1999
Sentencia del Tribunal Supremo, RJ 1998\6393, Sala de lo Civil, July 24, 1998
Sentencia del Tribunal Supremo, RJ 1998\3715, Sala de lo Civil, June 03, 1998
Sentencia del Tribunal Supremo, RJ 1998\4308, Sala de lo Civil, May 16, 1998
Sentencia del Tribunal Supremo, RJ 1998\2385, Sala de lo Civil, April 03, 1998
Sentencia del Tribunal Supremo, RJ 1996\2143, Sala de lo Civil, December 10, 1996
Sentencia del Tribunal Supremo, RJ 1996\1343, Sala de lo Civil, December 5, 1996
Sentencia del Tribunal Supremo, RJ 1996\2267, Sala de lo Civil, June 25, 1996
Sentencia del Tribunal Supremo, RJ 1996\3864, Sala de lo Civil, May 30, 1996
Sentencia del Tribunal Supremo, RJ 1996\1163, Sala de lo Civil, January 25, 1996
Sentencia del Tribunal Supremo, RJ 1995\7229, Sala de lo Civil, December 28, 1995
Sentencia del Tribunal Supremo, RJ 1995\8081, Sala de lo Civil, November 08, 1995
Sentencia del Tribunal Supremo, RJ 1995\5714, Sala de lo Civil, July 19, 1995
Sentencia del Tribunal Supremo, RJ 1995\2333, Sala de lo Civil, March 29, 1995
Sentencia del Tribunal Supremo, RJ 1994\4923, Sala de lo Civil, June 15, 1994
Sentencia del Tribunal Supremo, RJ 1994\3717, Sala de lo Civil, May 06, 1994
Sentencia del Tribunal Supremo, RJ 1994\1198, Sala de lo Civil, February 26, 1994
Sentencia del Tribunal Supremo, RJ 1993\9834, Sala de lo Civil, December 04, 1993
Sentencia del Tribunal Supremo, RJ 1993\9876, Sala de lo Civil, October 8, 1993

Sentencia del Tribunal Supremo, RJ 1993\2395, Sala de lo Civil, March 26, 1993
Sentencia del Tribunal Supremo, RJ 1992\1334, Sala de lo Civil, December 30, 1992
Sentencia del Tribunal Supremo, RJ 1992\9409, Sala de lo Civil, November 16, 1992
Sentencia del Tribunal Supremo, RJ 1992\5467, Sala de lo Civil, June 23, 1992
Sentencia del Tribunal Supremo, RJ 1992\832, Sala de lo Civil, February 06, 1992
Sentencia del Tribunal Supremo, RJ 1988\9476, Sala de lo Civil, December 23, 1991
Sentencia del Tribunal Supremo, RJ 2001\8737, Sala de lo Civil, October 16, 1991
Sentencia del Tribunal Supremo, RJ 1991\6914, Sala de lo Civil, October 11, 1991
Sentencia del Tribunal Supremo, RJ 1991\2304, Sala de lo Civil, May 10, 1991
Sentencia del Tribunal Supremo, RJ 1990\9043, Sala de lo Civil, November 23, 1990
Sentencia del Tribunal Supremo, RJ 1990\2434, Sala de lo Civil, October 16, 1990
Sentencia del Tribunal Supremo, RJ 1990\6412, Sala de lo Civil, October 6, 1990
Sentencia del Tribunal Supremo, RJ 1989\6970, Sala de lo Civil, October 28, 1989
Sentencia del Tribunal Supremo, RJ 1989\3243, Sala de lo Civil, April 20, 1989
Sentencia del Tribunal Supremo, RJ 1988\9736, Sala de lo Civil, December 20, 1988
Sentencia del Tribunal Supremo, RJ 1988\9430, Sala de lo Civil, December 12, 1988
Sentencia del Tribunal Supremo, RJ 1988\7595, Sala de lo Civil, November 21, 1988
Sentencia del Tribunal Supremo, RJ 1988\1278, Sala de lo Civil, February 23, 1988
Sentencia del Tribunal Supremo, RJ 1987\2482, Sala de lo Civil, April 01, 1987
Sentencia del Tribunal Supremo, RJ 1987\3849, Sala de lo Civil, March 11, 1987
Sentencia del Tribunal Supremo, RJ 1987\359, Sala de lo Civil, January 27, 1987
Sentencia del Tribunal Supremo, RJ 1986\1212, Sala de lo Civil, February 22, 1986

Sentencia del Tribunal Supremo, RJ 1985\4569, Sala de lo Civil, October 02, 1985
Sentencia del Tribunal Supremo, RJ 1985\4474, Sala de lo Civil, September 26, 1985
Sentencia del Tribunal Supremo, RJ 1985\555, Sala de lo Civil, February 15, 1985
Sentencia del Tribunal Supremo, RJ 1984\2397, Sala de lo Civil, May 04, 1984
Sentencia del Tribunal Supremo, RJ 1984\694, Sala de lo Civil, February 20, 1984
Sentencia del Tribunal Supremo, RJ 1983\3676, Sala de lo Civil, October 24, 1983
Sentencia del Tribunal Supremo, RJ 1982\6555, Sala de lo Civil, November 22, 1982
Sentencia del Tribunal Supremo, RJ 1982\6536, Sala de lo Civil, November 10, 1982
Sentencia del Tribunal Supremo, RJ 1982\5580, Sala de lo Civil, October 30, 1982
Sentencia del Tribunal Supremo, RJ 1982\4247, Sala de lo Civil, July 16, 1982
Sentencia del Tribunal Supremo, RJ 1981\2615, Sala de lo Civil, June 27, 1981
Sentencia del Tribunal Supremo, RJ 1980\3623, Sala de lo Civil, October 10, 1980
Sentencia del Tribunal Supremo, RJ 1973\2938, Sala de lo Civil, July 13, 1973
Sentencia del Tribunal Supremo, RJ 1970\2049, Sala de lo Civil, April 28, 1970
Sentencia del Tribunal Supremo, RJ 1966\5706, Sala de lo Civil, December 7, 1966
Sentencia del Tribunal Supremo, RJ 1965\0262), Sala de lo Civil, January 29, 1965
Sentencia del Tribunal Supremo, RJ 1964\3097, Sala de lo Civil, June 04, 1964
Sentencia del Tribunal Supremo, RJ 1964\0204), Sala de lo Civil, January 18, 1964
Sentencia del Tribunal Supremo, RJ 1956\1163, Sala de lo Civil, March 16, 1956
Sentencia del Tribunal Supremo, RJ 1954\1998, Sala de lo Civil, June 30, 1954
Sentencia del Tribunal Supremo, RJ 1952\0185, Sala de lo Civil, May 21, 1952
Sentencia del Tribunal Supremo, RJ 1952\475, Sala de lo Civil, February 2, 1952

Sentencia del Tribunal Supremo, RJ 1950\1694, Sala de lo Civil, November 29, 1950
Sentencia del Tribunal Supremo, Sala de lo Civil, March 9, 1929
Sentencia de la Audiencia Provincial, SAP de Baleares, March 11, 2005
Sentencia de la Audiencia Provincial, SAP de Salamanca, January 31, 2005
Sentencia de la Audiencia Provincial, SAP de Almeria, October 27, 2003
Sentencia de la Audiencia Provincial, SAP de Valencia, October 28, 2002
Sentencia de la Audiencia Provincial, SAP de Barcelona, June 19, 2002
Sentencia de la Audiencia Provincial, SAP de Barcelona, January 14, 2002
Sentencia de la Audiencia Provincial, SAP de Barcelona, December 16, 2001
Sentencia de la Audiencia Provincial SAP de Tarragona, October 26, 2001
Sentencia de la Audiencia Provincial (SAP) de Baleares, June 15, 2001
Sentencia de la Audiencia Provincial (SAP) de Almeria, June 19, 1997
Sentencia de la Audiencia Provincial (SAP) de Sevilla, January 8, 1996
Sentencia de la Audiencia Provincial (SAP) de Zaragoza, November 16, 1994
Sentencia de la Audiencia Provincial (SAP) de Navarra, January 20, 1994
Sentencia de la Audiencia Provincial (SAP) de Guadalajara, May 13, 1993

US Court Decisions

Adjustrite Systems, Inc. v. Gab Business Service, 145 F.3d 543, 547 (2d Cir. 1998)
American Broadcasting Cos. v. Wolf, 52 N.Y. 2d 394, 420 N.E. 2d 363, 438 N.Y.S. 2d 482 (1981)
American Cyanamid Co. v. Elizabeth Arden Sales Corp., 331 F. Supp. 597 (S.D.N.Y. 1971)
Arcadian Phosphates, Inc. v. Arcadian Corp., 884 F.2d 69 (2d Cir. 1989)
Banco Espirito Santo de Investimento v. Citibank, 2003 U.S. Dist. Lexis 23062 (S.D.N.Y. 2003)
Banque de Paris et des Pays-Bas v. Amoco Oil Co.,573 F Supp. 1464 (S.D.N.Y. 1983)
Beck v. American Health Corp., 221 Cal. App. 3d 155 (1989)
Beer Capitol Distributing Inc. v. Guiness Bass Import Co., 290 F.3d 877 (7th Cir. 2002)
Brause v. Goldman, 199 N.Y.S.2d 606, 611 (1st Dep't 1960), aff'd , 210 N.Y.S.2d 225 (1961)
Budget Mktg. v. Centronics Corp., 927 F.2d 421 (8th Cir. 1991)
Burbach Broad Co. of Deval v. Elkins Radio Corp., 278 F. 3d 401 (4th Cir 2002)
Candid Products Inc. v. International Skating Union, 530 F. Supp 1330 (1982)
Channel Home Centers Division of Grace Retail Corp. v. Grossman 795 F. 2d. 291 (3d Cir. 1986)
Chevron U.S.A., Inc. v. Martin Exploration Co., 447 So. 2d 469, 472 (La. 1984)
Chromalloy Am. Corp. v. Universal Hous. Sys. of Am., 495 F Supp. 544 (S.D.N.Y. 1980)

Continental Ins. Co. v. NLRB, 495 F.2d. 44 (2d Cir. 1974)
Copeland v. Baskin Robbins U.S.A., 117 Cal. Rptr. 2d 875, (Cal. Ct. App. 2002)
De Laurentiis v. Cinematografica De Las Americas, S.A., 174 N.E.2d 736 (N.Y. 1961)
Detroit Tigers, Inc. & Ignite Sports Media, LLC, 203 F. Supp. 2d 789 (2002)
Fairbrook Leasing, Inc. v. Mesaba Aviation, 295 F. Supp 2d 1063 (2003)
Feldman v. Allegheny International, 850 F. 2d 1217 (7th Cir, 1988)
FDIC v. LeBlanc, 85 F.3d 815 (1996)
Fimon v. Kenroc Drywall Supplies Inc., (unreported Minn. 2003)
First National Bank of St.Paul v. Ramier, 311 N.W. 502 (1981)
Garner v. Boyd, 330 F. Supp. 22 (N.D. Tex. 1970)
Glenview Partners v. Plexus, U.S. Dist. Lexis 8880 (N.D. Iii. 2002)
HDA Parking Dev., Inc. v. Mount Vernon Hosp. Inc., 687 (NYS 2d 663)
Heyer Products Co. v. United States, 140 F. Supp. 409 (Ct. Cl. 1956)
Hoffman v. Red Owl Stores, 133 N.W. 2d 265 (Wis. 1965)
Horphag Research Ltd v. Henkel Corp., 115 F. Supp. 2d 455 (S.D.N.Y. 2000)
Hotchkiss v. National City Bank, 200F. 287, 293 (S.D.N.Y.) 1911
Itek Corp. v. Chicago Aerial Industry Corp., 248 A.2d 625 (1968)
Lafayette Place Assocs. v. Boston Redevelopment Authority, 427 Mass 509 (1998)
Liberty Environmental Environmental Systems, Inc. v. The County of Westchester, 2000 U.S. Dist Lexis 17095 (S.D.N.Y. 2000)
Markov v. ABC Transfer & Storage Co. 457 P.2d 535 (Wash.1969)
May Metropolitan Corp. v. May Oil Burner Corp., 49 N.E.2d 13 (N.Y. 1943)
Mid-Continent Tel. Corp v. Home Tel. Co., 319 F. Supp 1176 (N.D. Miss 1970)
Mutual Export Corp. v. Westpac Banking Corp. 789 F. Supp. 1279 (S.D.N.Y. 1992)
New Line Productions, Inc. v. Little Caesar Enterprises, Inc., No. CV-97-7073-DT, 1999 WL 420185, (C.D. Cal. May 9, 1999)
Newport Limited v. Sears, Roebuck & Co., 6 F.3d 1058 (5th Cir. 1993)
New State Ice Corporation v. Liebmann, 285 U.S. 262, 311 (1932)
Omnitech International, Inc. v. Clorox Co., 11 F.3d 1316 (5th Cir. 1994)
Pancratz Co. v. Kloefkorn-Ballard Construction and Development, 720 P.2d 906 (Wyo.1986)
Pennzoil Company v. Texaco, Inc., 107 S. Ct. 1519 (1987)
Phoenix Mutual Life Ins. Co. v. Shady Grove Plaza, L.P., 734 F. Supp. 1181 (D. Md. 1990)
Radford v. McNehy, 104 S.W. 2d 472 (1934)
R.G. Group, Inc. v. Horn & Hardart Co., 751 F.2d 69, 74 (2d Cir. 1984)
Rutgers v. Martin Woodlands Gas Co., 974 F.2d 659, 661 (5th Cir. 1992)
Shann v. Dunk, 84 F.3d 73 (2d Cir. 1996)
Schwanbeck v. Federal-Mogul Corp., 412 Mass 703 (1992)
Space Imaging Europe, Ltd. v. Space Imaging, L.P., 38 F. Supp. 2d 326, 333 (S.D.N.Y. 1999)

Teachers Ins. and Annuity Ass'n v. Tribune Co., 670 F. Supp. 491, 497 (S.D.N.Y. 1987)

Texaco, Inc. v. Pennzoil, Inc, 729 S.W.2d 768 (Tex. App. 1987), 485 U.S. 994 (1988)

Thompson v. Liquichimica of America Inc., 481 F. Supp 365 (S.D.N.Y., 1979)

Tymshare, Inc v. Covell, 727 F.2d 1145, 1152 (Cir. 1984)

United Magazine Co. v. Prudential Insurance Co.,877 F. Supp. 1076 (S.D. Ohio 1995)

Vigoda v. Denver Urban Renewal Authority, 646 P.2d 900 (Colo.1982)

Wheeler v. White, 398 S.W. 2d. 93 (Tex. 1965)

Winston v. Mediafare Entertainment Corp., 777 F.2d 78, 80 (2d Cir. 1986)

Wood v. Lucy, Lady Duff-Gordon., 222 N.Y. 88, 118 N.E. 214 (1917)